CAMBRIDGE LIBRARY COLLECTION

Books of enduring scholarly value

History

The books reissued in this series include accounts of historical events and
movements by eye-witnesses and contemporaries, as well as landmark studies that
assembled significant source materials or developed new historiographical methods.
The series includes work in social, political and military history on a wide range of
periods and regions, giving modern scholars ready access to influential publications
of the past.

The Economic Development of a Norfolk Manor 1086-1565

This highly detailed analysis of the medieval records of Forncett Manor, first
published in 1906, is a case study of the development of an agricultural estate from
early medieval to Tudor times. The economic system of the manor and the people
who depended on it, aristocrats, tenants and serfs, is described and statistics are
given where they can be extrapolated from the surviving records. Appendices list
and transcribe important sections of the archive, including lists of tenants and
financial records, as well as relevant passages of the Domesday Book. Starting from
the documentary evidence, Harvard-trained Davenport does not speculate beyond
the facts and offers little interpretation. However, she creates a highly instructive
case study for medieval economic history that remains a rich source of valuable
information for historians of later generations.

T0382626

Cambridge University Press has long been a pioneer in the reissuing of out-of-print titles from its own backlist, producing digital reprints of books that are still sought after by scholars and students but could not be reprinted economically using traditional technology. The Cambridge Library Collection extends this activity to a wider range of books which are still of importance to researchers and professionals, either for the source material they contain, or as landmarks in the history of their academic discipline.

Drawing from the world-renowned collections in the Cambridge University Library, and guided by the advice of experts in each subject area, Cambridge University Press is using state-of-the-art scanning machines in its own Printing House to capture the content of each book selected for inclusion. The files are processed to give a consistently clear, crisp image, and the books finished to the high quality standard for which the Press is recognised around the world. The latest print-on-demand technology ensures that the books will remain available indefinitely, and that orders for single or multiple copies can quickly be supplied.

The Cambridge Library Collection will bring back to life books of enduring scholarly value (including out-of-copyright works originally issued by other publishers) across a wide range of disciplines in the humanities and social sciences and in science and technology.

The Economic
Development of
a Norfolk Manor
1086-1565

Frances Gardiner Davenport

CAMBRIDGE UNIVERSITY PRESS

Cambridge, New York, Melbourne, Madrid, Cape Town, Singapore,
São Paolo, Delhi, Dubai, Tokyo, Mexico City

Published in the United States of America by Cambridge University Press, New York

www.cambridge.org
Information on this title: www.cambridge.org/9781108016056

© in this compilation Cambridge University Press 2010

This edition first published 1906
This digitally printed version 2010

ISBN 978-1-108-01605-6 Paperback

THE ECONOMIC DEVELOPMENT
OF A NORFOLK MANOR,

1086—1565

CAMBRIDGE UNIVERSITY PRESS WAREHOUSE,

C. F. CLAY, Manager.

London: FETTER LANE, E.C.

Glasgow: 50, WELLINGTON STREET.

Leipzig: F. A. BROCKHAUS.

New York: THE MACMILLAN COMPANY.

Bombay and Calcutta: MACMILLAN AND CO., Ltd.

St Mary's Church and Dam Meadow, Forncett.

THE ECONOMIC DEVELOPMENT

OF A

NORFOLK MANOR

1086—1565

BY

FRANCES GARDINER DAVENPORT, Ph.D.

OF THE DEPARTMENT OF HISTORICAL RESEARCH IN THE
CARNEGIE INSTITUTION OF WASHINGTON

CAMBRIDGE :
at the University Press
1906

Cambridge:

PRINTED BY JOHN CLAY, M.A.
AT THE UNIVERSITY PRESS.

TO

LUCY MAYNARD SALMON

PREFACE.

SOME explanation of the circumstances which led to the writing of this book may serve to make clear the point of view from which the subject is considered.

During the year 1895–6, in connection with a course in Economic History in Radcliffe College, I transcribed a number of Court Rolls of the manor of Moulton, Norfolk, belonging to the Library of Harvard University. In the summer of 1896 a search in England for other material relating to Moulton failed to bring to light further important documents concerning that manor; but a comparatively rich series of manorial documents was found to be in the possession of the steward of the adjoining manor of Forncett. The owner of Forncett Manor, Mr A. C. Cole, most kindly allowed an examination of these, and to facilitate the work consented to deposit them in the Public Record Office. Through the courtesy of the officials of the Public Record Office, permission was obtained to consult the rolls there. Mr Cole has since presented these rolls to the Cambridge University Library, where they now are.

Some of the results of this study of the Forncett records were printed in a paper on the "Decay of Villeinage in East Anglia" (*Transactions of the Royal Historical Society*, N. S. XIV., 1900), part of which is reprinted with some additions and alterations on pages 88–97 of this book.

A fellowship held from the Association of Collegiate Alumnæ during the year 1902–3 made possible a further examination of the Forncett MSS. and the completion of this volume.

No attempt has been made in this work to consider the history of Forncett Honor, or to treat of other than economic conditions in Forncett Manor.

It is a pleasure to acknowledge the many kindnesses that have lightened a laborious task. My best thanks are due to Mr A. C. Cole, Mr Hubert Hall, and especially to Professor W. J. Ashley, under whose direction the work was begun. I am also much indebted for advice and assistance to Professor J. F. Jameson, Professor F. W. Maitland, and Mr W. J. Corbett. Miss E. M. Leonard has kindly supplied the photograph of St Mary's Church, which serves as the frontispiece of the book.

F. G. D.

May, 1906.

CONTENTS.

PLATES.

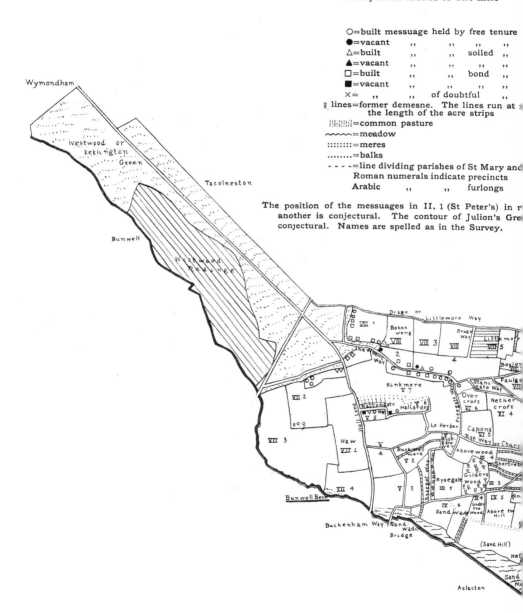

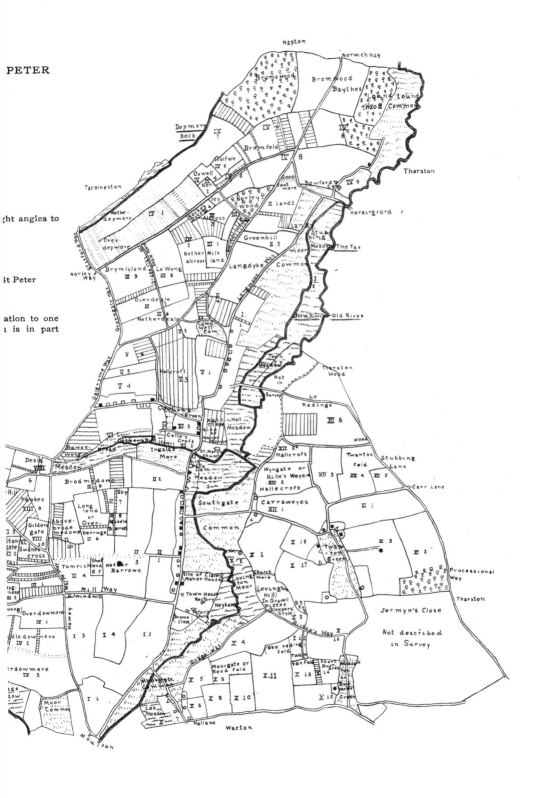

THE ECONOMIC DEVELOPMENT OF A NORFOLK MANOR, 1086–1565.

CHAPTER I.

AN ELIZABETHAN SURVEY AND DOMESDAY BOOK.

THE parishes of Forncett St Mary and Forncett St Peter lie in the county of Norfolk, hundred of Depwade, some twelve miles south-west of Norwich.

It is the purpose of this book to give such information regarding economic conditions in the vill and manor of Forncett to about 1565 as can be gathered from the extant records relating to the manor[1].

The first chapter is based on an examination of two records— a Survey of Forncett[2], drawn up in 1565, and Domesday Book, in so far as it directly relates to Forncett. Five subjects are considered:

1. The topography of Forncett vill (p. 2).

2. The territorial development of Forncett manor (p. 8).

3. The distribution of homesteads considered in relation to the tenures by which they were held (p. 13).

4. The extent of land in Forncett vill held of Forncett manor by each kind of tenure (p. 15).

5. The bond tenements (p. 17).

---

[1] A list of the more important of these documents, up to 1565, is given in Appendix I.

[2] For purposes of description, the Surveyor divided each of the Forncett parishes into a number of precincts; that is, tracts of land generally clearly defined by natural boundaries or roads. He first described the bounds of a precinct, next the bounds of a furlong within that precinct, and then each strip within the furlong, giving the name of the holder, the tenure, and acreage of the strip. Besides the survey of the vill of Forncett, the book contains a partial survey of the vill of Aslacton, much of which was included in Forncett manor. These surveys proper are followed by a list of the tenants of Forncett manor and by a full description of the lands held of that manor by each tenant; last comes a list of the 'tenements' of the manor. In the case of some of these the Surveyor named the tenants who, in 1565, held the strips of which the tenement was composed; other tenements he was unable to identify.

From the Survey, the map of Forncett vill has been constructed. Precincts are indicated on the map by Roman numerals, furlongs by Arabic numerals. The separate strips are

1. *The topography of Forncett vill.*

The boundaries of Forncett in 1565 were, for the most part, watercourses, roads, or lines dividing ancient waste. The northern boundary of St Mary's parish was a line dividing the mark in which probably at an early period the vills of Hapton and of Forncett St Mary intercommoned. To the north lay Hapton common, and to the south, in Forncett, were Broomwood, the lord's pasture, known as Broomwood Bayes[1], Lound wood, and Lound common. On the east, the stream or 'beck,' known as the Tas, separated St Mary's from Tharston, while a road divided St Mary's from the 'ridding' or clearing in St Peter's, east. North of the ridding, in St Peter's, lay Tharston wood ; so that here, too, the boundary divided the waste. The western and north-western limits of St Mary's as far as Broomwood were marked partly by roads and partly by Deepmore Beck.

Littlemore or Drage Way was the northern boundary of St Peter's as far as Westwood Green. That part of Forncett that comprised Westwood (alias Keklington) Green and Westwood (alias Bunwell) Ridding is a strip a mile and a half in length thrust out like an arm toward the north-west and reaching as far as Wymondham. Next it was Tacolneston common. A strip somewhat similar in shape though very much smaller lies east of Moor common where Moulton common protrudes into Forncett. In both cases, doubtless, the projecting parts were sections of the waste—a fact which accounts for the artificial character of the greater part of their boundary lines[2].

shown only in IV. 1 and IV. 7 of St Mary's parish (now in Tacolneston) where the fields are still uninclosed. Some of the balks have been ploughed up; but many of the strips have to-day the same breadth and length that they had when described by the Surveyor three hundred and forty years ago. In marking the position of the balks the Ordnance Map has been followed, on which they are indicated by broken lines.

An abstract of the survey of IV. 1, St Mary's parish, is given in Appendix II. For an account of some similar surveys, see the paper by W. J. Corbett, 'Elizabethan Village Surveys' (*Transactions of Royal Historical Society*, N.S. Vol. XI. 1897).

[1] Spelled 'Baythes' in the Survey, but 'Bayes' is the usual form in the other records.

[2] That the strip in Forncett called Westwood was part of a larger waste also known as Westwood may be inferred from the following passages from the Hundred Rolls (1275).

1. (i. 529.) '*Hundredum de Depwade*. *De feodis*, etc. Dicunt quod Rogerus Hardi defunctus appropriavit sibi injuste ii. acras de pastura Regis quae vocatur Westwod. Et Robertus de Tateshale appropriat sibi emendas de animalibus extraneorum inventis in eadem pastura.'

2. (i. 530.) '[*Hundredum de Depwade.*] *De purpresturis*, etc. Item ballivus domini Regis voluit tenuisse hundredum suum in pastura domini Regis quae vocatur Westwod et

South-west of St Peter's ran Bunwell Beck as far as Moor common. Further east, the Tas for a short distance forms the boundary, which, crossing a meadow, follows an ancient road known locally as 'the British Road.' In 1565, as now, it was called Hollane, *i.e.* Ditch Lane. This road is sunk so deep below the level of the fields that it has been abandoned in part for a parallel road running next it, but on higher ground.

The Survey mentions the Processional Way and Stubbing Lane as eastern limits of St Peter's. The former name is a common one, signifying, of course, the way along which the procession moved when the parish was perambulated; the latter name indicates a clearing.

At least as early as the thirteenth century the name Forncett was applied to the entire area included within these boundaries, and the term 'Forncett vill' will be used in this book to denote that area.

As early as 1066 several settlements, or túns, were situated either wholly or in part within these limits. Thus, in Domesday Book, we read of Fornesseta, of Kekelingtuna, of Tuanatuna, and of Middletuna. The returns made by sheriffs in 1316 as to what townships were in each hundred name Fornesete, Galegrym, Thwantone, Sugate, and Kitelyngton[1]. In later manorial records Moorgate and Lovington

Ricardus de Purle tunc ballivus Roberti de Tateshal inde fugavit ballivum praedictum dicens quod non debuit tenere hundredum infra libertatem domini sui.'

3. (i. 473.) '[*Inquisicio facta...in hundredo de...Depwade.*] *De omnibus purpresturis quibuscumque factis super Regem vel regalem dignitatem,* etc. Item dominus Robertus de Tateshale facit annuatim quandam cerchiam in pastura de Bonewelle et Carleton quae tenetur de Rege in capite et accipit emendas de bestiis extraneorum. Item Rogerus Hardi appropriavit sibi ii. acras de dicta pastura et habet xxx. annos elapsos.'

4. (i. 467.) '*Inquisicio facta...in...Depwade. Quae etiam maneria solent esse in manibus Regum praedecessorum Regis et qui ea tenent et quo waranto et a quo tempore et per quem et quomodo fuerunt alienata.* Item homines de Cariltun [Carleton] et Bunewelle tenent unam pasturam communem in villis supradictis quam tenent de domino Rege in capite per servicium xis. per annum reddend' ballivo hundredi.'

From these passages it seems evident that the common pasture held by the men of Bunwell and Carleton directly from the King (extracts 3 and 4) was identical with the pasture known as Westwood (extracts 1 and 2) and was part of the same waste as the strip in Forncett which adjoined Bunwell and was also known as Westwood.

As the map shows, one-third of the Forncett section of Westwood became lord's demesne, and two-thirds common pasture. In 1272–1275, some of the wood was still standing, while some had already been converted into arable demesne. Cf. Appendix VIII., xxxi., xl., and *Rot. Hund.* I. 529. 'Item comes Norfolciae habet warennam in dominicis suis in Forneset, Westwod, et in assarto juxta Westwod injuste.' i. 472. 'Item comes Marescallus appropriavit sibi warennam in quodam bosco qui vocatur Westwde et in quodam asserto (sic) juxta dictum boscum et in bosco qui vocatur Gilderis in Fornesete et Tacolffistun (sic) set quo warento nesciunt.'

[1] Nomina Villarum: Palgrave's *Parliamentary Writs*, II. pt 3, p. 312, or *Feudal Aids*, III. 476 (Public Record Office Publications).

are mentioned[1]. The Fornesseta of Domesday is clearly Forncett St Mary. Galgrym was in the south-west of that parish[2]. Twanton lay in St Peter's, east of the main Norwich road, and seems also to have included precincts I. and II. West of Twanton lay Keklington. Southgate must have been the row of houses opposite Southgate common. Middleton lay midway between the east and west boundaries of southern Twanton[3]. Moorgate was west of Middleton and south of Lovington. Deducting Southgate, Moorgate, Lovington, and Middleton from the greater Twanton there is left the lesser Twanton, near Twanton Green.

The presence of so many clusters of houses within the vill suggests, though it does not prove, that the vill, considered as a territorial unit, may not have existed from the time of earliest settlement in the same form in which we find it in 1565[4]. In the absence of clearer evidence, however, it is impossible to trace the course of the territorial development of the vill, if indeed such a development occurred.

The existence of two churches within the vill at so early a period as 1086 strengthens the impression of an original lack of unity[5].

---

[1] The earliest appearances of these names that I have noted are, Moorgate, Account Roll of 1376 (Appendix IX., xlvii.); Lovington, Court Roll of 1455. We read of 'Lovington Moor,' 'Lovington Heads,' and 'Lovington Hill,' but it is not clear that in the fifteenth century there was any house in Lovington, though possibly the houses in X. 1 or X. 2 were included in this district.

[2] Whether there were two distinct settlements within the parish of Forncett St Mary corresponding to the two groups of houses, is doubtful. In Domesday Book the name Fornesseta appears to include both hamlets; while later the hamlet of Galgrym is sometimes distinguished. But if Blomefield, *Hist. of Norfolk*, v. 224, n. 7, is right in deriving Galgrym from Galley (Gallows) Green, the name is certainly of late origin. The proximity of the hamlets points to the conclusion that they were originally a single settlement. The situation of this settlement was peculiarly favourable, for it was close to broad, rich meadows and to fertile arable.

[3] Blomefield asserts (*Hist. of Norfolk*, v. 224) that Middleton was another name for Forncett St Mary, but there can be no doubt that he was mistaken in this, and that Middleton was in the south-east part of St Peter's parish. For (1) Middleton Green lay here; (2) in Domesday, Middleton is mentioned only in connection with a tenement held by Earl Alan of Richmond. Now, from a 'Rental of Richmond Rents pertaining to the manor of Forncett, 2 and 3 Philip and Mary,' we learn that the land held of Richmond and situated in Middleton was west of Middleton Green. (3) The Survey shows that there were no Richmond lands in St Mary's parish; nor in any of the records is there anything to suggest the identity of Middleton and St Mary's.

[4] In this connection it may be worth noting that the northern boundary of Forncett St Peter, between St Mary's and Westwood, seems somewhat more like a late boundary—perhaps a parish boundary—than like a boundary fixed at the time of settlement. It is not determined by any natural feature but followed a road across the open fields. It apparently cut through the hamlet of Keklington, since, in 1565, there was no break in the closely built row of houses that stretched north and south of this line, along the border of the waste.

[5] See Appendix III., v., vi. The church in 'Fornesseta,' known in later records as

The present area of the parish of Forncett St Mary is 760 acres. In the section of the Survey relating to that parish 751 a. 1 r. are described, exclusive of the commons, whose area is not given. The parish of the Survey had somewhat different limits from the parish of to-day, and its acres were medieval acres, averaging in this parish less than the statute acre, although the average arable acre was very nearly statute size[1].

The Surveyor divided the parish as follows:

Messuages, crofts and gardens	52 a., 3 r.
Arable	479 a., ½ r.
Meadow (106 a., ½ r.), marsh and low pasture ...	114 a., 1½ r.
Wood (75 a.) and hill pasture (30 a.)	105 a.
	751 a., 1 r.

But using the map as a basis of measurement and computing in statute acres we reach more complete and somewhat different results:

Messuages, crofts and gardens	28 a.
Arable	473 a.
Meadow, marsh and low pasture	84 a.
Wood and hill pasture (114 a.), and land east of Tas, probably wood or waste (25 a.)	139 a.
Commons	102 a.
	826 a.

St Mary's, stood next to the manor house; the church in Twanton, known later as St Peter's, had been endowed by the villagers with 60 acres of glebe. At least as early as the thirteenth century and until 1845, the two rectories were held together under one rector, whose residence, in 1565, was close to St Peter's Church in Twanton.

[1] The area of the commons was about 102 acres. The Survey omits the tract—25 acres—lying east of the Tas and in the parish of St Mary, and also some six acres south of the church. On the other hand it includes the so-called 'lost-lands'—66 acres (IV. 1, and part of IV. 2, and IV. 7) which were later transferred to Tacolneston parish.

As is well-known, medieval acres were of four variable rods in width, and of varying length, with only a general tendency to conform to the normal length of 40 rods. Many of the meadow 'acres' in Forncett were not half that length; the length of some of the arable strips in IV. 1 near Stixford Way was, and is, nearly twice that of other strips further east in the same furlong. The Forncett rod was doubtless 16½ feet; for about 1308 this was the length of the rod of Clavers manor, which was originally part of Forncett manor and much of which lay within Forncett vill. (Blomefield, v. 259.) As the area of St Mary's in 1565 was about 826 acres, as 751¼ acres are described and more than 130 acres are omitted from the description, it follows that the 'acres' of the Survey average less than the statute acre. The object of the Survey was to register tenures, rather than exact areas. Hence the Surveyor, as a rule, gave the acreage of the strip as it was given in the copy of court roll or other title deed. But sometimes an obvious discrepancy between the actual and the recorded size of the strip occasioned some such comment as: 'T. B. tenet per nomen iii. ac. tamen patet esse iiii. ac.' In describing Sandwade meadow (St Peter's) the Surveyor departed from his usual custom and gave the dimensions of the holdings in perches instead of in rods and acres, thus: 'R. B. tenet 24 perticas prati.' 'E. A. tenet 3 perticas prati.' 'W. B. tenet...unam peciam prati in fine aquilonari continentem 7 perticas et in australi fine 10 perticas.' The perches evidently measured the width of the pieces, and were less than half the length of the normal arable rod. The length of the pieces was also far below the normal.

The present area of the parish of Forncett St Peter is 1901 acres. But the Survey contains an account of only 1281 acres, and some 550 'perches' of meadow[1].

Messuages, crofts and gardens			118 a., 2 r.		
Arable ...	...	...	... 1063 a., 1 r.		
Meadow	...	...	... 55 a., 1 r., 550 'perches'		
Marsh ...	...	...	... 10 a., 1 r.		76 a., 2 r., 550 'perches'
Pasture	...	...	... 11 a.		
Wood ...	...	...	... 22 a., 3 r.		
			1281 a., 550 'perches'		

But measuring upon the map we get the following figures in statute acres:

Messuages, crofts and gardens			...	...	...	...	101 a.	
Arable	...	...	...	...	...	...	...	1364 a.
Meadow, marsh and low pasture			...	...	...	...	78 a.	
Wood	...	...	...	...	...	...	...	47 a.[2]
Commons	...	...	...	...	...	...	...	311 a.
								1901 a.

The Domesday dimensions of Fornesseta (St Mary's) are one and a half miles by three-fourths of a mile. Measuring on the meridian and parallel of St Mary's Church, these are very nearly the dimensions of the present parish. The waste, in 1565, was not intersected by these lines, so that no light is thrown on the question whether the measurements of Domesday Book included the waste land of the vill.

The Domesday dimensions of Twanton are eleven by six furlongs. Measuring as before on lines passing through the church, the distance from the eastern limit of St Peter's to the western boundary of precinct I. is between eleven and twelve statute furlongs; the width of the parish north and south is between seven and eight statute furlongs.

The dimensions of Keklington are not given in Domesday, so that the large district between precincts I. and II. and Westwood— some 600 acres—is apparently not included in the measured area of the Record.

[1] The section of the Survey relating to this parish is imperfect. Seven folios, describing the first precinct and part of the second, are missing. But the lost portion can be partly reconstructed from the section of the Survey in which the holdings of the tenants are described, as well as from the Court Rolls of Forncett and of Moulton manors. The reconstruction is necessarily incomplete since some land in these precincts was held of Clavers manor, of which we have no rolls. Moreover, as the map shows, the south-east corner of Forncett St Peter (about 130 acres) was not surveyed, nor some 24 acres of the 'ridding' in the north-east of this parish. The 'ridding' south of Westwood Green is also omitted, and the acreage of the commons is not stated. Thus the Survey proper (cf. above, p. 1, n. 2), in its present imperfect state, contains an account of only 1124 a. 2 r. and some 550 'perches' of meadow. The list of tenants' holdings and the Court Rolls give information concerning 156 a. 2 r. more, making a total of 1281 a.

[2] 24 acres in XII. 6 are estimated as woodland.

In the Norfolk Domesday the holdings are regularly rated in terms of carucates and acres. These were probably fiscal rather than areal[1]. The arable area might be calculated from the number of ox-teams if we knew how many acres to reckon to a team, but the size of the team land probably varied from place to place[2]. It is clear from the following table that there was no room in the Forncett parishes for team lands of 120 acres, or 15 acres to each ox.

Forncett St Mary.

	1565	1086	1066	1086
Arable	473 a.	60 oxen	84 oxen	324 fiscal acres
Meadow	106 a.			27 a.
Wood	75 a.			wood for 8 'porc'

Twanton and Middleton.

Arable	765 a.	84 oxen	92 oxen	364½ fiscal acres
Meadow	43 a.			21 a.
Wood	34 a.			

Keklington[3].

Arable	599[4] a.	22 oxen	20 oxen	136 fiscal acres
Meadow	35 a.			7 a.
Wood	13 a.			

It was generally the case in East Anglia that manor and vill were not coterminous[5]. They were not coterminous in Forncett. But by far the larger part of the parish of St Mary—691 acres[6]—was held of Forncett manor. The remaining 60 a. 1 r. were held, of Tacolneston 44 a. 3½ r., Williams 9 a. 2½ r., Clavers 5 a., Tharston 3 r.

The parish of St Peter's was held of 14 manors: Forncett (about 1000 acres[6]), Clavers, Richmond (as of manor of Cossey), Jermyes, Tacolneston, Moulton, Williams, Tharston, Haydon, Aslacton Park's, Wacton, Bunwell, Aslacton Priory, Banyarde's Hall.

[1] Maitland, *Domesday Book and Beyond*, 429 ff.

[2] Maitland, *op. cit.* 433–5. But cf. Vinogradoff, *Growth of Manor*, 156 ff., 254 ff., where arguments are advanced in favour of an average plowland of 120 acres throughout England.

[3] The dimensions of Keklington are not given in Domesday and the number of acres at which it was rated is very small in proportion to its area of arable at a later time. The amount of geld with which it was charged is not stated. Either the Domesday account of Keklington is incomplete or else Keklington was a very small hamlet in 1086. It is noteworthy that Westwood is not included in the Domesday account of Keklington.

[4] Including Westwood Ridding (91 statute a, 120 a local measure).

[5] With the possible exception of Ashwellthorpe, there was not a vill in Depwade Hundred in 1086 that was not held of more than one lord. Blomefield, *op. cit.* v. 125–312. Maitland, *op. cit.* 22, 23.

[6] Not including the commons.

The lands of each of these manors did not, of course, lie together, but were interwoven with the lands of other manors[1]. The inter-weaving of the lands of different manors in the fields of the vill would naturally result from the multiplication of lordships within the vill. As a rule the lands of each tenant were scattered, and when within a vill some held of one lord and some of another the different manors of which they held would be interwoven.

Bringing together the entries in Domesday Book pertaining to Forncett vill[2], we find that manorial relations within the vill under-went considerable alteration between 1066 and 1086, and were very different in 1086 from what they were in 1565. Thus, the two manors[3], Olf's and Colman's, that existed in 'Fornesseta' in 1066, were evidently united by 1086. Oslac's and Hardekinc's—later Walter's—manors cannot be identified with any of the manors that extended into the vill in 1565. There seems to be no reason for believing that many of the holdings of freemen and sokemen formed part of any manor until, as is probable, they were united by Bigod to Forncett. In 1086 part of the manor of Tasburgh, later Uphall's (Terrae Osberni Episcopi) lay in this vill[4], and Earl Alan of Richmond had tenants there. But of the fourteen manors that extended into the vill in 1565 only Forncett and Richmond clearly lay there in 1086. In 1565 Uphall's manor apparently did not extend thither.

2. *The territorial development of Forncett manor.*

In the Survey of 1565 some 2700 acres[5] are recorded as belonging to Forncett manor, of which about 1700 lay within the vill of Forn-cett, and the remaining 1000 in seventeen neighbouring vills: Moulton, 242 a., Tacolneston, 216 a., Aslacton, 195 a., Wacton, 92 a., Stratton, 74 a., Carleton, 51 a., and smaller areas in Tivetshall, Tasburgh, Flordon, Saxlingham, Tharston, Tibenham, Bunwell, Wymondham, Hapton, Fundenhall, and Hethel.

The attempt to determine what lands belonged to the manor of Forncett in 1086 is attended with difficulties; but our knowledge of the extent of the manor at a later time throws light on the Domesday Record.

The principal entries in Domesday Book relating to the lands that in 1086, or soon after, seem to have belonged to the manor of Forncett are in three groups. In the first group the nucleus

---

[1] See Appendix II.   [2] Appendix III.   [3] Holdings with demesne teams are here reckoned as manors.   [4] Blomefield, *op. cit.* v. 214.   [5] Not including commons.

of the manor is described. It lay in Fornesseta (St Mary's), was held T.R.E. by Colman, a freeman, under Stigand, and T.R.W. by Roger Bigod. Connected with this manor were two berewics—one in Aslacton and one in Twanton—and sokemen in Keklington and Halas[1]. All these were valued at £6 and formed part of Bigod's demesne lands which he held directly from the King.

The second group of entries describes a second manor in Fornesseta. T.R.E., it had been held by Olf—probably the same Olf that held the neighbouring manors of Ketteringham and Carleton. Then there were demesne teams, but T.R.W. there were none. T.R.W., Bigod also held this in demesne directly from the King. The manor was doubtless already, or soon after, joined to Forncett manor. Sokemen, holding in 11 vills, were valued with this manor. The whole was worth £5. 0s. 10d.

The third group is the long list of Bigod's freemen in Depwade Hundred. Their lands lay in 16 vills. Their value was lumped together at £22. 2s. 8d., though the men of Tasburgh, the claim to one of whom was disputed, have a separate valuation. Now, there is no clear evidence that in 1086 these freemen were connected with Forncett or with any other manor. But since at a later date lands in nearly all of these vills were held of Forncett manor, and since in several of these vills in 1086 Bigod had no tenants except these freemen, it is practically certain that these freemen or their successors were connected with Forncett manor—the only manor in Depwade Hundred of which Bigod was the immediate lord[2].

The following table shows in greater detail, though perhaps imperfectly, the composition of Forncett manor in 1086.

	Freemen	Sokemen	Villeins	Bordiers	Slaves
FORNCETT ST MARY.					
Colman's manor (T.R.E.)		3	2	14	
Olf's manor (T.R.E.)			1	3	1
Bigod's freemen	7				
TWANTON.					
Berewic of Colman's manor (William holds, 1086)		1		3	

[1] Blomefield, *op. cit.* v. 223, VIII. 16, identifies Halas with Hales in Loddon or Clavering Hundred. But since it is entered under Depwade Hundred it seems more probable that it was near the hamlet of Overhales into which Forncett manor extended (Court Roll, Pentecost, 2 Henry IV.). This hamlet was probably in Tacolneston. Haleswong, also part of Forncett manor, was in Tacolneston.

[2] Thus the only tenants that Bigod had in Carleton in 1086 were 21 freemen and their 10 bordiers, while a list of the suitors of Forncett court, 17 Henry VIII., names 29 suitors from Carleton.

	Freemen	Sokemen	Villeins	Bordiers	Slaves
Valued with Olf's manor		2			
Bigod's freemen	1[1]	4[2]		10[2]	1[2]
Bigod's freemen (William holds, 1086)	12			3[3]	
Bigod's freemen	4[4]				
Bigod's freemen	3				

KEKLINGTON.

	Freemen	Sokemen	Villeins	Bordiers	Slaves
Valued with Colman's manor		2			
Valued with Olf's manor		2			
Bigod's freemen		5			

ASLACTON.

	Freemen	Sokemen	Villeins	Bordiers	Slaves
Berewic of Colman's manor		3		6	
Valued with Olf's manor		1		2[5]	
Bigod's freemen (Hugo holds, 1086)	11				
Bigod's freemen	1				

HALES.

	Freemen	Sokemen	Villeins	Bordiers	Slaves
Valued with Colman's manor		3			
Bigod's freemen	4				

TACOLNESTON.

	Freemen	Sokemen	Villeins	Bordiers	Slaves
Bigod's freemen	1			3	

WACTON.

	Freemen	Sokemen	Villeins	Bordiers	Slaves
Valued with Olf's manor		1			
Bigod's freemen (Durand holds, 1086)	6			5[3]	
Bigod's freemen	4[6]				
Bigod's freemen	2				

MOULTON.

	Freemen	Sokemen	Villeins	Bordiers	Slaves
Valued with Olf's manor		1			
Bigod's freemen (Alger holds, 1086)	$9\frac{1}{2}$			15	
Bigod's freemen	$2\frac{1}{2}$[7]				
Bigod's freemen	1			7	
(Alger holds, 1086)	14				
Bigod's freemen	4				
Bigod's freemen	3				

TIBENHAM.

	Freemen	Sokemen	Villeins	Bordiers	Slaves
Valued with Olf's manor		2		8	
Bigod's freemen	3			7	
Bigod's freemen	5				

[1] Oslac.   [2] Under Oslac.   There was a demesne team and a team of men.
[3] Under the freemen.   [4] These 4 freemen were under the 12 freemen.
[5] Under the sokeman.   [6] Under the 6 freemen.   [7] Under the $9\frac{1}{2}$ freemen.

	Freemen	Sokemen	Villeins	Bordiers	Slaves
THARSTON.					
Valued with Olf's manor		2			
STRATTON.					
Valued with Olf's manor		1			
Bigod's freemen	8				
SHELTON.					
Valued with Olf's manor		1	6	14	1
Bigod's freemen	9½			3	
(Durand holds, 1086)	4[1]				
HARDWICK.					
Valued with Olf's manor		2		5	
FRITTON.					
Valued with Olf's manor		1			
Bigod's freemen	3½	1½		13	
CARLETON.					
Bigod's freemen	5				
Bigod's freemen	16½			10	
FUNDENHALL.					
Bigod's freemen	1				
Bigod's freemen					
(Osbertus holds, 1086)	2			2	
HAPTON.					
Bigod's freemen				2	
Bigod's freemen	4				
TASBURGH.					
Bigod's freemen					
(Berardus and Aselinus hold, 1086)	7				

It will be noticed that among the tenants of this manor there were freemen and sokemen who had tenants under them. In Moulton and in Shelton holdings of this sort apparently developed into distinct manors, but in other cases there was no such development[2]. What was the relation to Forncett manor of the bordiers and villeins who were under free tenants and sokemen? To this question the later Forncett records suggest an answer.

From these records it appears that there were two classes of unfree tenants connected with the manor:

(*a*) The 'customers,' who rendered week-work throughout the year,

(*b*) Bond sokemen, who were in general exempt from week-work

[1] Under the 9½ freemen.   [2] Cf. Blomefield, *op. cit.* v. 204, 263.

and rendered only three plowings yearly and a few other light labour services.

The customers were not numerous. Week-work seems to have been charged upon only 21½, later upon 25, out of some 135 bond tenements[1]. It seems highly probable that these few customers were the successors of the villeins and bordiers—20 in number—who held directly of Bigod, and whose representatives T.R.E. belonged to Colman's and to Olf's manors. And it seems equally probable that the bond sokemen represent the bordiers and villeins who were under some tenant freeman or sokeman, to whom they probably owed food-rents, or other dues, though in some cases their immediate overlord seems to have had no demesne land on which they could have been employed. But they pertained to the manor of Forncett, their land could be conveyed only with the license of the lord of Forncett, and they owed the lord of Forncett a few days' plowing yearly[2].

About the year 1086 there seems to have been a tendency toward the bringing together of many estates into one lordship and the consequent growth of large manors; while later the process of subinfeudation worked opposite results. These tendencies are illustrated in the history of Forncett manor. After 1086 the manor of Clavers in Forncett was carved out of land that had previously formed part of the manor of Forncett[3], and the manors of Aslacton Park's and Aslacton Priory out of Aslacton, a berewic to Forncett manor[4]; while among the holdings of Bigod's freemen were estates that seem to have developed into the manors of Moulton and of Shelton[5].

In Depwade Hundred in 1086 we count 24 manors and 4 berewics; some of the manors are very small and cannot be identified with later manors.

---

[1] See below, pp. 67, 68.

[2] The number of bond sokemen in the later period cannot be determined; for among the holders of the 135 bond tenements there were apparently not only customers and bond sokemen but also some free sokemen and the tenements of the two classes of sokemen cannot be distinguished from one another. For evidence of this see below, p. 83 ff. Since many Domesday entries prove that there were in 1086 sokemen and even freemen who could not sell their land 'sine licentia domini' (Round, *Feudal England*, 28 *passim*, and Maitland, *Domesday*, 105), it is not strange that free sokemen should be found among the holders of 'terra nativa.' Like the bond sokemen the free sokemen appear to have rendered light labour services to the lord of Forncett. It seems probable that the free sokemen represented 'sochemanni' of 1086, who could not withdraw from their land without license from their lord. Of course, other of the Forncett 'sochemanni' of 1086 may have been represented at a later period by 'libere tenentes.'

[3] Blomefield, *op. cit.* v. 259.   [4] Blomefield, v. 177.   [5] Blomefield, v. 204, 263.

In 1300 there were 52 manors in the 19 vills of this hundred. Of the 14 manors extending into Forncett vill, at least 7 cannot be reckoned as manors till after 1086[1].

3. *The distribution of homesteads considered in relation to the tenures by which they were held.*

In 1565, in Forncett St Mary, east of the Norwich road and north of the site of Forncett manor house, were seven dwellings, five held by free and two by servile tenure. In Galgrym, in the south-west part of the parish, were 15 messuages of servile tenure, ten built and five vacant, and one free messuage. The only other dwellings standing in St Mary's appear to have been one near Cawdwell Green, built upon land that was once the lord's demesne; and two near Bowford common that had been free but were now soiled[2]. Not far from these, on Lound Lane, was a vacant messuage that had formed part of the servile tenement of Roger at the Lound.

The percentage of servile messuages in Forncett St Mary, counting vacant sites, was 70.

In Twanton, along the western side of the main Norwich road, was a row of 16 messuages, eight built and eight vacant. On the east of the road were the rectory, the town house, a vacant site, the vacant site of Clavers manor house, and beyond Southgate common and extending into the present parish of St Mary's, four dwellings, one unoccupied site, and the old Gild House. The other houses in Twanton were in small scattered groups or isolated. These were 21 messuages, 14 built and seven vacant, of which four were east of Southgate or Carr Hill common; four were near Moorgate Green and a fifth not far from this group; nine were near Twanton Green, two standing apart from the rest and from one another; the remaining two seem to have been isolated homesteads. Of these 43 messuages (exclusive of the rectory, Clavers manor site, the town and gild houses), 14 were servile, 27 free; the tenure by which the other two were held is doubtful. Leaving the doubtful two out of account, the percentage of servile messuages was 34. Counting only the homesteads in eastern Twanton, *i.e.* in precincts X., XI., XII., but 15·8 per cent. were held by servile tenure.

Of the 38 messuages in Keklington, of which 34 were built, there

---

[1] These are, Clavers, Aslacton Park's, Aslacton Priory, Wacton, Moulton, Williams, Tacolneston. In 1086 Tacolneston was a berewic of Wymondham.

[2] For 'soiled land' see p. 70 and '*Terra Soliata*' (*Eng. Hist. Rev.*, XIV. 507).

were 20 free and soiled and 18 servile.   Thus the percentage of originally servile homesteads was 47·4.

Not counting the two manor sites, the rectory, or the town and gild houses, there were mentioned in the Survey in both parishes together 108 messuages, including 27 vacant and 81 built.   Omitting the two doubtful cases, the servile messuages were 48 per cent. of the total number.

Turning to Domesday Book, we find that a rough correspondence[1] exists between the relative numbers of freemen and sokemen on the one hand, and of villeins, bordiers and slaves on the other hand, mentioned in connection with a given hamlet in 1086, and the relative numbers of free and servile messuages in the same locality as indicated in the Survey of 1565.   This appears from the following tables :

1565. *Messuages.*

	Free and soiled	Servile	Doubtful	°/₀ of servile messuages
St Mary's	8	19		70
Twanton and Middleton	27	14	2	34
Keklington	20	18		47·4

Total, 108 messuages.   Per cent. of servile, 48.

1086. *Persons.*

	Freemen and sokemen	Villeins, bordiers, slaves	°/₀ of unfree[2] persons
St Mary's	12	23	65·7
Twanton and Middleton	42	23	35·4
Keklington	12	3	20

Total, 115 persons.   Per cent. of unfree, 42·6.

The tables show that in 1086 there was a large proportion of unfree persons in the parish of St Mary's, and a large proportion of freemen in Twanton, especially (as the Survey of 1565 indicates) in East Twanton.   Now it is just in this eastern part of Twanton that the houses, instead of being in comparatively closely-built rows, as in other parts of Forncett, are scattered either in very small loose clusters near Twanton, or Middleton, or Moorgate or Southgate common, or are quite apart and isolated.

[1] For many reasons we should not expect to find the correspondence exact, for some of the sokemen of 1086 probably held bond land.   See below, p. 12, n. 2.

[2] It is perhaps permissible to use the term 'unfree' as a convenient one, under which to include villeins, bordiers and slaves, in contrast to 'liberi homines' and 'sochemanni.'   Cf. Maitland, *Domesday*, 24–79.   It is not of course to be understood to imply that the villeins of the eleventh century were serfs.

These facts seem to indicate a connection in this locality between the distribution of dwellings and the status of the population, and seem to show that while the unfree were grouped in villages many of the freemen ' dwelt apart and scattered[1].'

It is also significant that the hamlet which contained by far the largest proportion of servile messuages (Galgrym in Fornesseta) was situated close to the manor house (Fornesseta)[2].

4. *The extent of land in Forncett vill held of Forncett manor by each kind of tenure.*

The Survey, supplemented here and there by the Court Rolls, designates, as a rule, the 'terra libera,' 'terra nativa,' 'terra soliata,' and the original demesne. Before 1565 all of the arable demesne had come into the hands of the tenants of the manor, who held it at fee farm rents. But the Surveyor usually states what land had been demesne, and where he does not do so it may be identified from the Court Rolls. In some cases the Surveyor was unable to determine by what tenure a given piece of land was held. Such land is classed in the following tables as 'doubtful,' *i.e.* of doubtful tenure. As the tenures of land held of Forncett manor seem to have been ascertained with more care than the tenures of land of other manors in Forncett vill[3], only that part of Forncett vill that was held of the manor of Forncett will be considered.

[1] In his paper on ' Elizabethan Village Surveys,' based upon a study of the surveys of eighteen Norfolk villages, Mr Corbett says, 'as a rule the messuages in these Norfolk villages are not collected into streets, but lie scattered about along the various ' gates' or lanes.' (*Transactions, Royal Historical Society*, N.S. XI. 78, 1897.) It is well-known that Domesday Book ascribes an unusually large proportion of freemen and sokemen to Norfolk. There is a temptation to conjecture that what was true of Forncett was true of other Norfolk villages and that it was the freemen and sokemen—possibly descendants of the invading Norsemen—who occupied the scattered homesteads.

[2] The place-name Fornesseta suggests that the hamlet of Galgrym may have been a village of Englishmen which had become subject to the Norseman Forn. Mr W. H. Stevenson has kindly supplied the following information regarding the meaning of the place-name: Forn is an old Norse name, originally a nick-name meaning 'the old,' not a native Old English name. The meaning of the suffix is not clear. Perhaps it is old Norse *setr*, seat, residence. The Rigneseta in Suffolk of Domesday Book appears to be identical with Ringshall, and here we have again an old Norse name, Ringr. But whatever its origin *sete* was sometimes used in the sense of village or hamlet.

[3] This appears from a comparison of the Moulton Court Rolls with the Survey; and the Surveyor himself says, with regard to XI. 1, strip 22, ' Thomas Denne dicit se tenere native de Tharston et quia nulla intentione huic manerio (*i.e.* Forncett) pertinere potest per aliquas evidencias adhuc ostentas minorem curam habeo ad titulum.'

Forncett Manor in St Mary's (691 *a.*).

Demesne   229 a., 3 r.   { Site of manor house   7 a.
                           Arable   ...   ...   IOI a., 2½ r.
                           Meadow and pasture   19 a., ½ r.
                           Woods and hill pasture   102 a.

Free   112 a., 2 r. ⎫
Soiled   63 a., 3 r. ⎬ 176 a., 1 r. ⎫
Bond   261 a., 2½ r. ⎬ 59 °/₀ of tenants' land was servile[1]
Doubtful   23 a.   ⎭

Forncett Manor in St Peter's (892 *a.*)[2].

In Twanton (481 *a.*, 1 *r.*).

Demesne   42 a., 2½ r.   { Arable 14 a., 3 r.
                          { Meadow 27 a., 3½ r.

Free   226 a., 2½ r ⎫
Soiled   77 a.   ⎬ 303 a., 2½ r. ⎫
Bond   106 a., 1½ r. ⎬ 26 °/₀ of tenants' land was servile[1]
Doubtful   28 a., 2½ r.   ⎭

In Keklington (410 *a.*, 3 *r.*)[2].

Demesne   47 a., 3 r.   { Arable   39 a., 2 r.
                         { Meadow   1 r.
                         { Wood   8 a.

Free   151 a.   ⎫
Soiled   33 a., ½ r. ⎬ 184 a., ½ r. ⎫
Bond   116 a., 3½ r. ⎬ 38·9 °/₀[3] of tenants' land was servile[1]
Doubtful   62 a.   ⎭

From this analysis it appears that in St Mary's, where the ratio of servile messuages was largest, the ratio of land held by servile tenure was also largest, and the arable demesne comparatively extensive; whereas Twanton, which had the smallest number and ratio of servile messuages, had the smallest ratio of servile land and the smallest area of arable demesne.

It is noteworthy that in each of these hamlets the percentage of tenants' land held by servile tenure was smaller than the percentage of servile messuages.

[1] Land of doubtful tenure is not included.

[2] But this is incomplete, see p. 6, n. 1. Westwood Ridding, comprising 91 acres of arable demesne, is omitted. The land in St Peter's held of Forncett manor may be roughly estimated as 1000 acres.

[3] But owing to the large amount of 'doubtful' land this figure cannot be depended upon as more than a rough approximation.

	°/₀ of servile messuages held of Forncett manor, 1565 ('soiled' not included)	°/₀ of land held of Forncett manor by servile tenure (former demesne and ' soiled ' land not included)
St Mary's	70	60
Twanton	38·3	26
Keklington	58	39[1]

Hence the acreage of an average servile tenement was less than that of the average free holding; the free holding would perhaps average roughly about 50 °/₀ more than the servile[2].

5. *The bond tenements*[3].

The holdings in Forncett manor at an early period seem to have been extremely small. The list of bond tenements given in the Survey of 1565[4] reflects, of course, the conditions of a much earlier time. By 1565 the location of some of the tenements had been forgotten. The money payments which each tenement ' was accustomed to render ' are recorded; but the ' other services,' *i.e.* the labour dues and payments in kind, are not described. Some of the same tenements are mentioned in the Account Roll of 1376–7. The names of some appear as personal surnames in the Subsidy Rolls of 1327 and 1332[5], and not in the later records; but the documents are wanting in which the tenements might be traced to an earlier time. It is, however, very probable that the names date from the late thirteenth century[6]; while the tenements as fixed areas chargeable with a fixed amount of dues date from an earlier period. From the fact that each bears a person's name and includes one messuage and often a certain number of acres of meadow as well as of arable, it seems clear that each represents the entire area of *terra nativa* held of Forncett manor by a single tenant.

---

[1] This figure is not very trustworthy, see above, p. 16, n. 3.

[2] The bearing of this fact on the question of population appears on p. 105.

[3] As the Survey of 1565 shows, only the *terra nativa* was divided into 'tenements,' which preserved through many generations an ideal unity and a name.

[4] See Appendix IV., Nos. 1–122.

[5] See Appendix V.

[6] Perhaps the tenement known as Ivo Charyers was held by 'Ivo le Carcectarius' mentioned in the Account Rolls of 1300 ff.

The following table shows the arable area included in each of the 122 tenements listed in the Survey[1].

No. of tenements	Arable acreage	No. of tenements	Arable acreage
1	30 a.	8	8 a.
1	24 a.	1	7 a. 2 r.
1	19 a. 1½ r.	1	7 a. 1 r.
7	18 a.	14	7 a.
1	16 a.	2	6 a. 2 r.
1	15 a.	1	6 a. 1 r.
1	14 a. 1 r.	3	6 a.
1	13 a.	1	5 a. 2 r.
2	12 a.	37	5 a.
1	11½ a.	1	4 a. 2 r.
1	11 a. 1½ r.	2	4 a.
1	11 a. 1 r.	1	3 a. 2 r.
2	11 a.	3	3 a.
1	10 a. 1½ r.	1	2 a. 3 r.
7	10 a.	1	2 a. 2½ r.
2	9 a.	10	2 a. 2 r.
1	8 a. 3 r.	2	2 a.
1	8 a. 2 r.	122	917 a. 1 r.

Fifty-eight tenements were 5 acres or less; 42 were from 5 to 10 acres; 20 from 10 to 20 acres; 2 from 20 to 30 acres. The average tenement included only 7·5 acres of arable land; the typical customers' tenement was only 5 acres.

Very small tenements were also the rule in Forncett vill in 1086. The population of Forncett in King William's time is recorded in Domesday as follows:

	Freemen	Sokemen	Villeins	Bordiers	Slaves	Total
St Mary's	9	3	3	19	1	35
Twanton and Middleton	33	9	—	20	3	65
Keklington	8	4	—	3	—	15
	50	16	3	42	4	115

As it is only in the case of St Mary's that both the Domesday record and the Survey appear to be complete, most weight must be attached to the statistics of that parish. The population of St Mary's, as given in Domesday, was 34 (not counting the slave). The arable area in St Mary's in 1565 was 473 acres. It could not have been more in 1086. In 1565 the arable demesne was 100 acres; in

---

[1] Since at least 13 additional tenements are mentioned in the Court Rolls, there were altogether about 135 tenements. See Appendix IV., Nos. 123–135.

1086 there were two teams in demesne.   Therefore it is practically certain that the area of arable in the tenants' hands in 1086 could not have exceeded 373 acres.   Dividing this by 34, we find that the average holding must have been less than 11 acres.

The maximum arable area that it seems possible to concede to Twanton is 765 acres.   There were three teams in demesne in 1086; allowing 50 acres to the team, 615 acres are left as tenants' land; dividing by 62, we get 9·9 acres as the average holding.

But before accepting these small numbers as correctly representing the area of the average tenement, we have to consider whether some of the recorded population have not been counted twice.   Thus, Professor Maitland, in his analysis of Domesday, says, ' There is reason to think that some of the freemen and sokemen of [Norfolk and Suffolk] get counted twice or thrice because they hold land under several different lords[1].'

But in Fornesseta (St Mary's) only two persons could have been counted a second time, for the three sokemen were connected with Bigod's manor, and of the nine recorded freemen seven were Bigod's men and two were connected with Bishop Osbern's manor. Assuming that the latter were also Bigod's men, the number of persons would be reduced by two, and the area of the average holding increased to 11·7 acres.   This is the maximum area possible. There is reason to believe that the actual area was less than this.

Of the 42 freemen and sokemen in Twanton, four 'and a half' held of Earl Alan; the rest held of Bigod, some immediately and others, apparently, through mesne lords.   It is impossible to determine certainly how many of them may have been counted more than once; but the weight of probability strongly favours the assumption that the average tenement in Twanton was not more than 11 or 12 acres.

We are prepared to find many small servile tenements in a district where the *bordarii* were so numerous[2], but the holdings of the freemen must also have been very small[3].

[1] *Domesday Book and Beyond*, 20.

[2] Maitland, *Domesday*, 40.   Cf. Vinogradoff, *Growth of Manor*, 338.

[3] Very small tenements seem to have been characteristic of East Anglia generally.   Light on this point is obtained from the 'Three Manorial [East Anglian] Extents of the Thirteenth Century,' printed in translation by Rev. W. Hudson in *Norfolk and Norwich Arch. Soc.*, *Norfolk Archaeology*, XIV. 1–56 (1899).

CHAPTER II.

THE DEMESNE. 1270—1307.

FORNCETT was one of a large number of East Anglian manors held by the Earls of Norfolk. From the chief seat of the Earls, at Framlingham, Suffolk, these manors were administered partly as distinct units, partly as members of one great estate. The local officers of Forncett were in constant touch with the officers of the central administration and with local officers of other of the Earls' manors in Norfolk.

Considered from the Earls' standpoint, the manor of Forncett was, primarily, a source of revenue in money and in kind. It helped to fill their treasury and to supply food for their great household. Some of the cash receipts were paid by the local officers to the collector of Framlingham or to itinerant accountants; but much of the money never reached the central treasury but was disbursed by the local officers, upon order of the Earl, to his creditors in Norwich or the vicinity[1]. Thus the scattered manors, each with a fisc of its own, facilitated the payment of debts, while the necessity of transferring cash over a long distance was avoided.

Material for a study of the relations of the manors to the Earls' household and to one another is furnished in the valuable series of Bigod's Account Rolls, preserved in the Public Record Office, but in this volume we are only concerned with the internal economy of one of these manors.

Judged by the standards of the thirteenth century, the Forncett manor-house seems to have been almost palatial[2]. For while the

---

[1] Instances of such payments occur in nearly all of the rolls, e.g.:

'In expensis militum hundredi coram justiciariis apud Norwicum pro negotio Comitis et libertatibus suis salvandis xv*s.* iii*d.*' Min. Acc'ts, 935/6.

'Liberati W. H. praeposito de Parva Framingham ad opus mercatorum xxiiii*l.* per i. talliam. Item lib' W. C. praeposito de Sudfeld ad opus mercatorum xx*l.* per i. talliam. Item lib' R. H. praeposito de Dichingham ad opus mercatorum xxi*l.* vi*s.* per i. talliam. Item lib'. R. B. praeposito de Hanewrthe ad opus creditorum xliii*l.* xviii*s.* per i. talliam.' Min. Acc'ts, 935/8.

[2] See description of houses of Henry III. and Edward I. in Wright, *Homes of other Days*, 152.

ordinary house of the period contained only a central hall with a chamber on one side and a stable on the other[1], there were at Forncett some dozen chambers and outbuildings more or less separated from the main room—the hall[2], and some half-dozen barns and stables.

Besides the hall, there were the Earl's chamber[3], the knights' chamber[4], with an upper room or soler[5].—a place of special honour and safety[6]—the chapel[7], the bailiff's chamber[8], the house of the plowmen and carter[9], the kitchen[10], salser[11], buttery[12] and larder[13], the bake-house, with an oven for melting lead[14], the dairy[15], at least three stables[16], a cattle-house[17], grange[18], granary[19], hay-house[20], goose-house[21], hen-house[22], and pin-fold[23].

The buildings were of clay[24]; in most cases the roofs were thatched with straw stubble[25], which the prevalent mode of reaping left long; but the hall was thatched with reeds cut from the pond (*stagnum*)[26]. The walls were also of clay[27], with thatched tops. They surrounded both the outer court[28], and at least in part the inner court or courts[29].

[1] Wright, *op. cit.*, 141, 142.

[2] It is hard to fix the position of the *camerae* relatively to each other and to the hall. The thatching accounts show that they were under different roofs; *camera servientis* and *domus servientis* appear to be used as equivalent terms. The buildings probably stood about the inner court. In 1293 the officers of the manor account for expenditure 'in factione i. muri inter cameram servientis et domum famulorum, in longitudine i. perticatae et vii. pedum'; 'in factione i. muri de novo inter aulam et domum sauserii longitudine ii. perticatarum.' Possibly the walls connecting these buildings were the walls of the inner court.

[3] Appendix VIII., xxxv., xl.

[4] Appendix VIII., xxxv.

[5] Appendix VIII., xxxv., 'forinseca camera super cameram militum.' Min. Acc'ts, 935/12.

[6] Wright, *op. cit.* 148.   [7] Min. Acc'ts, 935/10.

[8] Appendix VIII., xl.

[9] Min. Acc'ts, 935/4, 'domus famulorum.'

[10] Appendix VIII., xl.   [11] Appendix VIII., xxxv., xl.

[12] Min. Acc'ts, 935/14.   [13] Appendix VIII., xxxv., xl.

[14] Min. Acc'ts, 935/14. Lead was used for roofs, cisterns, conducting pipes and nails. Rogers, *Agric. and Prices*, i. 500, 599.

[15] Appendix VIII., xxxiv.

[16] Appendix VIII., xxxv., xl., and Min. Acc'ts, 935/13, 'longum stabulum juxta ecclesiam; longum stabulum juxta faldam.'

[17] Appendix VIII., xxxiii., xxxiv., xl.   [18] Appendix VIII., xxxiii., xxxiv.

[19] Min. Acc'ts, 935/4.

[20] Min. Acc'ts, 935/4.   [21] Min. Acc'ts, 935/11.

[22] Appendix VIII., xxxiv.   [23] Appendix VIII., xxxiv., xl.

[24] Appendix VIII., xl., etc.

[25] Appendix VIII., xxxiv., xl.   [26] Appendix VIII., xxxiv., xxxv.

[27] Appendix VIII., xxxiv., xl.

[28] Min. Acc'ts, 935/6.   [29] Appendix VIII., xxxiv.

When the buildings and walls needed repair hired labourers and customary tenants joined in the work of restoration. Such part of the work as required greater skill—the carpentry[1], thatching[1], and interior plastering[1]—was done by hired labour. The rougher part was done by the customary tenants, who tore down old walls[2], dug the clay[3], and fetched water to 'temper' it[2], pulled off the old thatch[2] and cut and brought stubble for the new[2]. The labour of daubing the clay walls of the buildings was shared by both classes of workmen[4].

The most important resident within the manor court was the bailiff[5]. He was appointed by the lord to have general oversight of all that went on in the manor and to protect the lord's interests. It was his duty to see that the lower officers were faithful and active, that the demesne was properly tilled, the grain properly garnered, the stock cared for, and the produce sold in the best market[6]. If he needed advice he consulted with the steward[7]. He received guests —knights, grooms, and officers of the lord—but unless they were introduced by the lord's writ the bailiff ran the risk of not being refunded for the expense of their entertainment[8]. The bailiff was not directly maintained from the estate, but received yearly wages. In the thirteenth century he usually received 52s. annually and a robe worth 20s.[9] Later, his wages amounted to 104s. a year[10]. He also had his dwelling, which was repaired at the cost of the lord[11], and, for his horse, stabling, and the allowance of a peck of oats a day[12].

Besides this resident agent, the lord had many travelling agents, who made their eyres from one to another of his scattered manors. Not many weeks passed at Forncett without a visit from one of these officers. The most frequent visitor was the steward. It was usually the business of holding court that brought him to the manor[13]. His special province was to protect the legal rights of the lord[14], and he had also to acquaint himself with the economic administration of the estate[15]. Sometimes his expenses were allowed him from the manor[16]; at other times, as the records incidentally tell us, he was paid a fixed

---

[1] Appendix VIII., xxxiii.–xxxv.   [2] Appendix VIII., xl.
[3] Appendix VIII., xxxix.–xl.   [4] Appendix VIII., xxxiii.–xxxv., xxxix.–xl.
[5] Serviens or ballivus. The words are used interchangeably.
[6] Lamond's edition of Walter of Henley, etc., 87–97.
[7] Walter of Henley, 84, 90.   [8] Walter of Henley, 92, 102.
[9] Min. Acc'ts, 935/5, Walter of Henley, 92.
[10] Min. Acc'ts, 935/15.   [11] Appendix VIII., xl.
[12] Min. Acc'ts, 935/10, 935/15.
[13] Min. Acc'ts, 935/13.   [14] Walter of Henley, 84.
[15] Walter of Henley, 86.   [16] Appendix VIII., xxxv.

fee, and no such allowance was made[1]. Not infrequently bond tenants discharged some of their labour dues by carrying to distant manors the steward's letters concerning distraints, holding of court, and other matters pertinent to his office[2].

As the steward acted as a check upon the bailiff and other officers, so did the accountants upon the officers of the manor, including the steward himself[3]. Before threshing time, they sometimes came to the manor to examine into the condition of the estate, and to estimate the quantity of grain[4]. But their most important visit was made after Michaelmas, when the subordinate officers rendered account of what they had purchased, or spent, or received, either of produce or of money, and the clerks drew up the final account. 'Views of account' were also taken at other times of the year, especially in the spring[5]. Among the auditors or accountants were John Bigod, brother of the Earl[6], and the Abbot of Tintern[7]. One of their chief duties was to collect the money that was due; for it was not considered wise to leave the lord's money in the hands of bailiff or of reeve[8].

Besides these regular visitors, some half-dozen casual guests might be expected at the manor yearly. Thus in 1274 came Eborard, the hunter, with two men and four grey hounds and twenty-five of the earl's dogs, and spent three October days at Forncett[9]. In 1277, just after Michaelmas, Walter de Vilers, Nicholas Peche and Gilbert, falconers, came with three lads and five falcons belonging to the Earl, and stayed six days[10]. At the same time Eborard, the hunter, with a man and dogs, was also there[10]. Sometimes the guests stopped for only one night; lawyers journeying to Norwich on the Earl's behalf[11], itinerant bailiffs[12] on their way to Lopham[13], grooms with horses of the Earl[14], knights and clerks travelling on the Earl's business, found this a convenient resting-place[15].

The Earl and Countess seem to have visited Forncett at irregular intervals, which would perhaps average three or four years. In the

---

1 Min. Acc'ts, 935/13, 935/15. 2 Appendix VIII., xli.
3 Min. Acc'ts, 935/15, Walter of Henley, 108.
4 Min. Acc'ts, 935/15, Walter of Henley, 126.
5 Appendix VIII., xxxvi. Min. Acc'ts, 935/15.
6 Rogers, *Agric. and Prices*, i. 165.
7 Appendix VIII., xxxvi. For the relation of the Bigods to Tintern Abbey see Dugdale's *Monasticon Anglicanum*, v. 265 ff.
8 Min. Acc'ts, 935/13, 935/15.
9 Min. Acc'ts, 935/4.
10 Min. Acc'ts, 935/5.
11 Min. Acc'ts, 935/11.
12 Min. Acc'ts, 935/13.
13 Min. Acc'ts, 935/15.
14 Min. Acc'ts, 935/5.
15 Min. Acc'ts, 935/13, 935/16.

spring of 1273 they spent nine weeks there[1], and the very large number of retainers and of horses that they brought with them were a heavy charge upon the estate[2].

Besides the bailiff, some eight or nine servants of inferior rank lived in the manor court[3]. These were four plowmen, a carter, a cowherd, a swineherd, a dairymaid, and, during three or four months in the year, a harrower. From year to year there was some change in the number of these servants. Sometimes no pigs were kept, and the swineherd was not needed. In the later years of the period, a few servants were added to those already enumerated—a *grangiarius*[4], a warrener[5], and a second maid who prepared the servants' pottage[6].

Unlike the bailiff, who received money wages, these servants were chiefly paid in kind, and thus directly maintained from the produce of the estate. Their wages varied slightly in different years, but, as a rule, the *grangiarius* was allowed a quarter of wheat every eight weeks[7], the warrener a quarter of wheat every ten weeks, throughout the year[8]. Each of the plowmen and the carter had a quarter of barley every twelve weeks, besides which they together consumed during the year twelve bushels of oats made into pottage[9]. The daye and cowherd were allowed a quarter of barley every fourteen weeks[10], the swineherd every sixteen weeks[11]. The money wages of plowmen and carter were 3s. yearly[12]; the daye and cowherd received 1s. a year[13].

From 1272–1293 the miller was a stipendiary of the lord, though not resident within the court. He received 2s.[12], later 1s., and, apparently, an allowance of grain[9] annually; and his house was repaired at the lord's expense. After 1300 the mill was 'farmed' and the miller no longer received a fee.

Certain tenants of the manor were elected or appointed from year

---

[1] Appendix VIII., xxxvi.

[2] Appendix VIII., xxxv.–xxxvii. The Earl seems also to have been at Forncett in 1281–2, 1285–6, 1292–3 and 1299–1300.

[3] As there is frequent mention of the *domus famulorum*, which was situated near the *camera servientis* in the manor court; and as a maid was hired by the year to prepare pottage for the *famuli*, it seems probable that the plowmen and carter at least, the principal *famuli*, were unmarried men, resident within the court ; but see Rogers, *Agric. and Prices*, i. 286–289.

[4] Min. Acc'ts, 935/12.   [5] Min. Acc'ts, 935/12, 935/13.

[6] Min. Acc'ts, 935/14.

[7] Min. Acc'ts, 935/12. In Bishop Grossteste's household, one quarter of wheat made 180 loaves, weighing five marks (2¾ lbs.) each. Walter of Henley, 139.

[8] Min. Acc'ts, 935/13. But in some years the warrener's fees were similar in kind to those of the bailiff. Thus, in 1303, he received the yearly wage of 45s. 6d. and a robe worth 13s. 4d.

[9] Appendix VIII., xxxvii.

[10] Appendix VIII., xxxvii. Cf. Walter of Henley, 73–5.

[11] Min. Acc'ts, 935/16.   [12] Appendix VIII., xxxiii.

[13] Appendix VIII., xxxiv.

to year to act as officers of the lord.   These were a reeve (*praepositus*), several beadles or messors (*bedelli, messores*), a cart-reeve, a reap-reeve, and one or more collectors of rents.

By far the most important of these officers were the reeve and the messor of Forncett.   They were serfs, apparently appointed by the lord to these oner̀ous and responsible positions[1].   It was they who rendered the yearly accounts[2] of all receipts and expenditures, whether of money, grain, or stock, connected with the manorial administration, and hard might be their lot if they failed to produce evidence in the shape of *talliae, brevia,* or *billae* sufficient to convince the auditors of the correctness of their returns[3].   The duties of the *praepositus* seem to have consisted largely of the care and sale of stock and grain[4].

The terms *bedelli* and *messores* are used interchangeably in the rolls.   Besides the messor of Forncett, there were messors of Moulton, Carleton, and Stratton.   It has been shown that the manor of Forncett extended into these vills, and the groups of tenants, or homage, from Carleton, Stratton, and probably from Moulton, present in the Forncett manor court, severally chose the messor for their own vill.   The beadles or messors were prominent in connection with the court[5].   Conveyances of bond land were made through their hands ; they received complaints, made attachments and answered for amercements[6].   They also answered for receipts from the sale of 'works,' rents in kind, and agistment[6].

---

[1] This appears from the facts that the surnames of most of the reeves and messors are recognisable as the surnames of servile families ; and that, in the extant Court Rolls dating from before 1350, no election of reeve or of messor of Forncett is recorded, although for the year 1332–3 the series of rolls is complete.   Since the offices were held by the same persons in successive years they could not have been filled by rotation.   From the fact that autumn-works and averagia, but not winter-works, were 'allowed' to these officers, it may perhaps be inferred that they were selected from among the bond sokemen rather than from among the customers.   See below, p. 66 ff.

[2] The heading of the compotus rolls varies from year to year, but the typical formula runs as follows:

'M. N. praepositus et M. N. messor...reddunt compotum...tempore M. N. ballivi.'

[3] Thus, in 1300 (Min. Acc'ts, 935/14) Roger of the Hill, reeve in 1294 'sought allowance' of £7. 7s. 7d. charged against him by the accountant in 1294, because Roger had sold grain to that value without a writ.   Roger states that the steward had enjoined the bailiff and him 'sub immensa poena' to sell the grain in order to raise money for part of the expenses of the Earl and Countess at Bungay.

In the same account roll, Simon Herberd, reeve in 1296, 'sought allowance' of £3. 6s. 8d. charged against him for grain sold to Reginald of Shottisham.   Reginald would not pay because he claimed that this debt had been discharged by services performed by him for the Earl.   Two other similar petitions were made by former reeves of the manor in 1300.   In 1303 the claim of Simon Herberd for the sum paid by him in 1296 was allowed.

[4] See Walter of Henley, pp. 96, 98 *et passim,* for an account of the reeve's duties.

[5] Cf. below, p. 75, n. 2.   [6] Appendix IX., lxx., lxxi.

The reap-reeve and cart-reeve were charged with humbler agricultural services, the performance of which was limited to the harvest season. They were elected in the manor court.

Near the church and between the manor court and the meadow that bordered on the beck, lay the gardens[1]. They were surrounded by walls[2]; a ditch ran between one garden and the meadow[3]. They were as much orchards as gardens in the modern sense, for their chief marketable products were apples and cider[4]. The yield of these was very irregular. In some years the bailiff and townspeople testified that no cider had been made[5]; often nothing was sold from the gardens[6]. On the other hand, in 1273, 351 gallons of cider were sold for over £1[7], and in another season 76 bushels of apples were gathered[8]. As a rule the apples were either sold or sent to Lopham[9]. Not far from the hall was a vineyard[10].

The chief source of income to the lord of the manor was the produce of the arable demesne. This lay for the most part in Forncett, though there were a few acres in Tacolneston, Moulton, and Wacton.

Its location, in so far as it lay in Forncett, is shown on the map, and exhibits some noteworthy features.

First, near the manor house in St Mary's, near, that is, to the nucleus of Forncett manor, was a large block of land known as the Hall Close, or Hall Croft, while not far off were other blocks, each of several acres.

Second, excepting these pieces, a very large proportion of the arable demesne lay on the outskirts of the manor, and was assart, *i.e.* land brought into cultivation at a comparatively late period[11]

Third, only a very small proportion of the demesne consisted of scattered acre or half-acre strips, the rest being in blocks of considerable size.

Fourth, as has been said, there was very little demesne in the free hamlets of Eastern Twanton.

The fields (*campi*) of Westwood Ridding and of Hall Close were

Two gardens are mentioned, the 'magnum gardinum,' and 'gardinum juxta ecclesiam.' Min. Acc'ts, 935/12.

[2] Min. Acc'ts, 935/12, 935/13, 935/14.   [3] Min. Acc'ts, 935/4, 935/17.

[4] Cf. also 935/16, '6s. de veteribus pomariis...in gardino de Tacolneston.'

[5] Min. Acc'ts, 935/12.   [6] Min. Acc'ts, 935/14.

[7] Appendix VIII., xxxii.   [8] Min. Acc'ts, 935/5, 935/8.

[9] Min. Acc'ts, 935/5, 935/15.   [10] Min. Acc'ts, 935/4, 935/12.

[11] For example, Westwood Ridding, the piece near Tharston Wood (XII. 6, St Peter's), Bolkarridding (III. 2, St Mary's), the strip west of Bromewood (IV. 7, St Mary's) and probably the strips south of Bromewood (IV. 6, St Mary's).

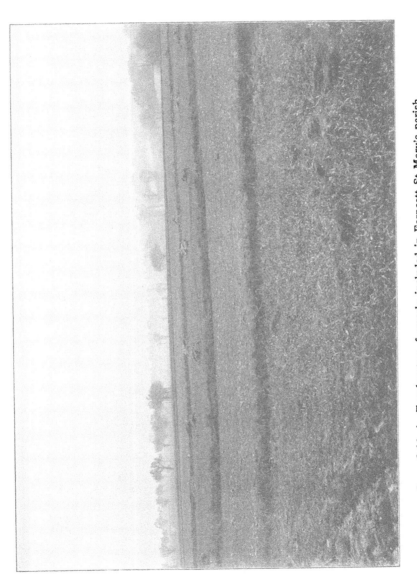

Open fields in Tacolneston, formerly included in Forncett St Mary's parish.

Compare Map, IV. 1, and Appendix II.

surrounded by ditches, which, used as pasture, were a considerable source of income[1]. These fields and five or six of the smaller pieces of the demesne were also inclosed 'ad defensionem bladi comitis' by 'fossat[a]' annually erected and removed by the customary tenants[2].

The arable demesne was about 300 acres in extent, or about one-ninth of the total acreage of the manor[3].

Probably Forncett was a three-course manor, but the rolls contain no clear indications that there were within the vill three great fields, cultivated in rotation[4]. 'Campi' are mentioned ; but they were numerous and small.

It is somewhat surprising to find that the area of the demesne in cultivation in different years was, as a rule, considerably more than two-thirds of its total acreage. In the Account Rolls returns are made of the number of acres sown with each kind of grain, and of the (same) number of acres harvested. The figures are as follows :

Year	Number		Year	Number
1273	205		1290	241
1275	232		1293	249
1278	232		1300	206
1279	202		1303	189[6]
1280	232		1304	182[6]
1284[5]	216		1306	208
1286	210		1308	161

The large number of acres sown in 1293 and other years cannot, apparently, be accounted for by any increase in the amount of land in the lord's hands. It seems to have been the case that, as the language of the rolls implies, some of the demesne was cultivated

---

[1] Cf. p. 32. In 1286, 30s. 4d. were spent 'in i. fossato circa Bone Welleridingg faciendo de longitudine clxii. perticatarum.' In the same year only 3s. were received from the sale of the herbage of the ditches about the ridding, 'et non plus pro fossatura impediente herbagium ibidem.' In 1290, 5s. 4d. were received, which seems to be somewhat above the average amount.

[2] Appendix VIII., xxxix., and the later Min. Acc'ts.

[3] In the Account Rolls of 1376–8 it is stated that the arable demesne consisted of 166½ acres besides Westwood Ridding. From a Court Roll of 1406, it appears that Westwood Ridding was 120 acres in extent. This would make the total arable 286½ acres. By adding together the areas of all the pieces described as former arable demesne in the conveyances of the fifteenth and sixteenth centuries up to 1565, a total is obtained of about 175 acres plus the 120 acres of the Ridding or a grand total of about 300 acres. The inquisition post-mortem of 1270 gives 180 acres as the area of the arable demesne, but this doubtless refers only to the acreage under cultivation in that year. If two-thirds of the demesne were cultivated in 1270 its total area must have been 270 acres.

[4] For an account of the three-field system, see Cunningham, *Industry and Commerce*, 4th ed., i. 74, and Walter of Henley, 6, 8 *et passim*.

[5] The account for 1282 is too much damaged for the number to be ascertained.

[6] Cf. below, p. 48, n. 1.

in more than two successive years[1]. This doubtless necessitated artificial enrichment of the soil, but for this provision was made[2].

The crops raised were barley, wheat, oats, and peas. The areas assigned to the different kinds of grain varied somewhat from year to year, but generally some 80 acres were sown with barley ; 50 with wheat ; 35–45 with oats, and as many with peas.

Most of the plowing was done by the three[3] demesne teams of stotts and oxen[4]. Two of these teams seem to have been driven by hired plowmen[5], while customary tenants assisted in driving the third[6]. The tenants also plowed some fifty acres with their own teams. 'Plowing for seed' took place at three seasons of the year : for wheat, between Michaelmas and Christmas; for oats and peas, between Purification (February 2) and Easter ; for barley, between Easter and Pentecost. Between Purification and Pentecost there was a 'second plowing,' in preparation for the barley (rebinatjo ad ordeum)[7]. It was so late in the spring when the barley was sown that the earth had become dry and hard, and the clods had to be broken up—a task performed by the tenants[8] or by the plowmen[9].

The harrows were usually drawn by demesne teams ; very rarely

---

[1] Thus, in the rolls of each of the three successive years 1278–80, it is recorded that 'fossat[a]' were 'erected' 'ante bladum comitis' at Smallbusk (II. 1, St Mary's, near Langmoor Common), Cawdwellwong (III. 6, St Mary's, near Cawdwell Common), at Hane's gate (II. 4, St Mary's, near Cawdwell Common), at Deknesgate, at Hallcroft (V. 3, St Mary's) and at Hallswong. Apparently these lands needed special protection from trespassing cattle because they were near commons. But, if these lands were fallow in any of the three successive years mentioned, what need was there for inclosing them? And it does not seem probable that the phrase 'ante bladum comitis' is meaningless. Walter of Henley, p. 19, speaks of 'lands which are sown yearly'; and cf. Vinogradoff, *Growth of Manor*, p. 182.

[2] See below, p. 32.

[3] 1270. 'In ii. vomeribus emptis ii*d.*' 'In i. vomere fabricando i*d.*' 'In iii. carucis reponendis iii*d.*' Since the demesne comprised about 300 acres of arable and 50 acres were plowed by tenants' teams, a team-land must have been about 80 acres in extent. This is larger than it was in 1086, but far short of the 180 acres which Walter of Henley thought might be plowed by a single team in a three-course manor. For a discussion of the team-land see Maitland, *Domesday*, 397.

[4] Appendix VIII., xxxiii. 'In i. stotto empto ad carucam.' Allowing six or even but four stotts to a team there were not enough stotts on the manor to pull three plows. The team doubtless consisted partly of oxen, a considerable number of which were constantly retained on the manor. For mixed teams of horses and oxen, cf. Walter of Henley, 11.

[5] There were four hired plowmen; probably two went with one plow.

[6] Min Acc'ts, 935/6, 935/7, 935/10, 'In tertia caruca fuganda temporibus seminationis hoc anno, lxvi. opera.'

[7] Appendix VIII., xxxi., xxxix. The Forncett rolls do not mention the *warectatio*, or first plowing of the fallow; but since the rolls furnish detailed information only in regard to the plowings performed by the tenants' teams, it may, perhaps, be inferred that the *warectatio* was performed by the teams of the demesne.

[8] Appendix VIII., xxxix.

[9] Min. Acc'ts, 935/15, 'In glebis frangendis nil, quia per carucarios.'

by horses of the bondmen[1]. A harrower was hired for three or four months in the spring, when the land was being prepared for oats, peas, and barley[2]. Tenants aided in driving the teams[3].

The wheat, oats, and barley were weeded by the tenants, usually in July[4]. The tenants also reaped, bound and gathered all the crops[5]. The harvest was carried from the fields by carter and tenants in carts of the tenants as well as in those of the lord[6]. Tenants also helped to stack the corn in the granary[7]. The threshing seems to have taken place in the grange or in the hall[7]. In the earlier years for which we have information the threshing was largely performed by hired labour, but after 1280 it was almost entirely the work of the tenants[8]—a change which was advantageous to the lord, since the money received from commuted labour dues did not equal the threshers' wages. The winnowing was done by the tenants, with more or less assistance from the daye. After it had been threshed the straw was carried from the grange and stacked in the hall, or in the chamber of the knights[9]. Much of the grain was sold in Norwich, whither it was carried in the carts of the tenants, as well as in those of the lord[10].

The principal crop was barley. The yield was remarkably small. According to the anonymous treatise on 'Husbandry' the return should have been eight-fold[11], but in 1280 it was less than two-and-a-half-fold; not infrequently it was over four-and-a-half-fold; but four-fold, or sixteen bushels to the acre, seems to have been an average yield[12]. In many years the issue from the field was

---

[1] Min. Acc'ts, 935/10, 'In terra hercianda de equis nativorum, vi. opera.'

[2] Appendix VIII., xxxiii. [3] Appendix VIII., xxxix.

[4] Appendix VIII., xl., Min. Acc'ts, 935/4, etc. [5] Appendix VIII., xl.

[6] Appendix VIII., xli. [7] Appendix VIII., xl.

[8] 1273. 240 quarters by hired labour. 69 quarters by the tenants.

1275.	260	,,	,,	23	,,	,,
1278.	40	,,	,,	260	,,	,,
1279.	68	,,	,,	248	,,	,,
1280.	140	,,	,,	125	,,	,,

1280. 'Memorandum quod de caetero nichil trituretur nisi per opera.'

[9] 1279. 'In stramine portando extra grangiam usque in aulam et in eodem stramine reportando extra aulam et extra cameras ad ponendum et tassandum in camera militum.' See also Min. Acc'ts, 935/8, 935/4.

[10] Appendix VIII., xli. [11] Walter of Henley, 66 and 70.

[12] In the rolls of 1290–1306 the return of grain was noted. In the few cases where rolls of successive years are extant the return can of course be calculated by a comparison of the harvest of one year with the amount sown in the year preceding.

In 1290 the return for barley was to the 4th grain + 6 qr. 3 bu.

,, 1293	,,	,,	,,	$3\frac{1}{2}$	,,	+3 qr. $4\frac{1}{2}$ bu.
,, 1300	,,	,,	,,	$4\frac{1}{2}$	,,	+$5\frac{1}{2}$ qr.
,, 1303	,,	,,	,,	3	,,	+1 qr. 5 bu. 3 pecks
,, 1304	,,	,,	,,	4	,,	+3 qr. $1\frac{1}{2}$ bu.
,, 1306	,,	,,	,,	4	,,	−2 qr. 5 bu.

supplemented by some 200 bushels of toll from the mill. This multure, with some 50 bushels additional, was given to the servants of the court. In some years several bushels were given to the pigs and fowls that were to be fattened for killing, or were mixed with oats and fed to the stotts. Four bushels were allowed for the annual reap-sheaf of the customary tenants. About one-fourth of the issue was retained as seed for the following year. Rarely, as many as 480 bushels were brewed, partly by the customary tenants, and partly by the servants of the court; and the beer was either sold or distributed among other of the Earl's manors. The remainder averaged some 700 bushels, which were sold for some £20.

The return from wheat was about five-fold[1], which, as two bushels or a trifle over were sown to the acre, amounted to 10 bushels as an acre's produce. The yield of wheat, therefore, reached the standard of the treatise on Husbandry[2]. Occasionally a few bushels were bought, and during the years that the manor of Moulton was in the Earl's wardship, some 240 bushels were added from this source. About a fifth of the issue was used for seed; the remainder was generally sold, though some quarters might be sent to Attleborough or to Lopham, or paid to the bailiff of the hundred, or, in the case of the coarser grain, be added to the servants' portion of barley.

In general, however, such wheat as was not used for seed was sold; this usually amounted to about 400 bushels, worth some £15.

The demand for oats on the manor was far greater than for the other kinds of grain. A much smaller proportion was sold, and when large numbers of horses were stabled at Forncett, as during the Earl's visits, the purchases of oats were large. It was doubtless in consequence of the demand for this kind of grain that certain tenements paid oat-rents, amounting altogether to 344 bushels yearly.

The yield was from three to four-fold[3], or from 12 to 16 bushels from the acre, the average thus falling somewhat below the four-fold

---

[1] In 1290 the return for wheat was to the 5th grain + 1½ bu.
  ,, 1293 ,, ,, ,,   4th ,, and a half + 3½ bu.
  ,, 1300 ,, ,, ,,   5th ,, − 2 qr. 7 bu.
  ,, 1303 ,, ,, ,,   5th ,, and a half + 2 qr. 6½ bu.
  ,, 1306 ,, ,, ,,   5th ,, − 4 bu.

[2] Walter of Henley, 70.

[3] In 1290 the return for oats was to the 3rd grain − 1 bu.
  ,, 1293 ,, ,, ,,   4th ,, − 6 qr. 7 bu.
  ,, 1300 ,, ,, ,,   3rd ,, + 5 qr. 7 bu.
  ,, 1303 ,, ,, ,,   3½ ,, + 3½ bu.
  ,, 1304 ,, ,, ,,   3½ ,, + 3 qr. 3½ bu.
  ,, 1306 ,, ,, ,,   3rd ,, − 3 qr. 5 bu.

return, which, as the author of 'Husbandry' asserts[1], might have been looked for. In some years oats were sold to the value of £3 or £4, but the large purchases of other years, amounting sometimes to £10 or £12, in the long run overbalanced the receipts from this source.

The return from peas was small[2] and extremely irregular, ranging from less than two to nearly six-fold, or from 4 to 12 bushels from the acre[3]. Except what was kept for seed, and perhaps some half-dozen bushels or more fed to the pigs, the issue was sold. In the more abundant years some 200 or 300 bushels brought from £5 to £6; while in the less productive years so much was retained for seed that not more than a few shillings' worth reached the market.

In general, it may be said that while the oats were consumed on the manor, the greater part of the wheat, barley and peas were sold, and that the receipts from the sale of grain were far larger than those from any other single source. The grain that was not sold was used for seed, or sent to other of the Earl's manors, or given to the servants and live-stock.

Acre for acre the low-lying meadows far surpassed the arable in value. Though they were the only hay-producing lands their yield sufficed for the demesne stock. As a rule, however, no hay was sold; but in 1307, when the manor was in the king's hands, and little live-stock was left upon it, more than £2 worth of hay was sold; and in 1273 hay was sold to the value of £1. 12s. During the period under consideration some of the low wet lands of the manor were being drained and converted into meadow[4]. In 1376 the demesne meadow was 30 acres in extent[5].

The mowing of the demesne meadows was mostly performed by the bond tenants, as part of their labour dues.

While grain-fields and meadows thus contributed to the sustenance of the stock, they chiefly depended on the pastures for food. The grazing grounds were of many kinds : common and several pastures, fallow, meadow after the hay had been cut, waste, woodland, ditches and roads. The lord sold the herbage of the commons and woodland, as well as of the lands in which he had sole rights.

---

[1] Walter of Henley, 70.

[2] Peas should yield to the sixth grain according to the treatise on Husbandry. Walter of Henley, 70.

[3] In 1290 the return for peas was to the 3rd grain + 2 qr. 2½ bu.

	1293	,,	,,	,,	3½	,,	− 4 bu.
	1300	,,	,,	,,	6th	,,	− 2 qr. 7½ bu.
	1303	,,	,,	,,	4th	,,	+ 1 qr. 2 bu.
	1304	,,	,,	,,	4th	,,	+ 3 qr. 1½ bu.
('altero')	1306	,,	,,	,,	2nd	,,	− 2 qr.

[4] Min. Acc'ts, 935/5.   [5] Appendix IX., xlix.

Thus, in 1278, he was paid 4*s.* 6*d.* for permitting 61 cows, 7 affers, 14 pigs, and 25 sheep to common on Langmoor, the principal common of Forncett St Mary[1]. A few pence were also received from the herbage of Lound common. Who were the owners of these cattle? Not the free tenants, probably, since they had free common; nor is it likely that strangers would have had so large a number of cattle there. It would seem as though some of the customary tenants lacked sufficient common rights. And it may also have been these tenants who paid between them a few shillings yearly to the lord in return for pasture in Bromwood and in Gilderswood. The fallow land, the herbage of which rented at from 2*d.* to 3½*d.* an acre, was probably enclosed. The ditches were important grazing grounds; thus the herbage of the ditches about Bunwell (Westwood) Ridding was sold for 4*s.* 10*d.*, and other ditches about the woods and about Hallcroft (V. 3, St Mary's) brought about a shilling. The pasture of a road in the Ridding was worth 8*d.*, and waste lands fallen into the lord's hands a few pence more. Altogether, the lord received annually some 16*s.* from the sale of herbage.

Turf used as fuel was sometimes sold from the common; ferns and stubble were also sold.

At irregular intervals large sales were made of underwood and of alders, amounting sometimes to £6 a year. Other sources of income were dead trees and the branches and bark of trees that had been felled for the repair or construction of the demesne buildings and implements.

The demesne live-stock served divers purposes. Horses, stotts[2], and oxen laboured on the demesne; cattle, especially calves, were sold or sent to other of the Earl's manors; cattle and pigs were slaughtered for the larder; hides of cattle and of stotts were sold. Before 1300, after each Michaelmas the tenants were accustomed to come with 43 carts to carry the manure from the court-yard (curia) to the fields[3]. In 1300 this carrying service was commuted by the tenants, who now merely scattered the manure over the fields, whither it was carried in the carts of the lord[4]. The fallow was

---

[1] At the rate of ½*d.* for a cow, 1*d.* for an affer, 1*d.* for a pig, and 1*d.* for 10 sheep. From 1270–1300, the lord's annual receipts from the sale of herbage in Langmoor were usually from 3*s.* to 4*s.* 6*d.*, though they fell off toward the end of the period, and after 1300 did not rise above 2*s.*

[2] A stott or affer was an inferior kind of horse, commonly used for plowing. Cf. Min. Acc'ts, 935/5, 935/6, 935/12 under title *Stotti*.

[3] Appendix VIII., xli.

[4] 'De cariagio fimi ad festum Sancti Michaelis, xviii*s.*' Min. Acc'ts, 935/14. 'In x. acris fimo spargendis tempore seminationis frumenti cum auxiliis carucariorum, v. opera.' Min. Acc'ts, 935/15.

sometimes enriched by folding sheep upon it. Thus, in 1293 the herbage of 13 acres of fallow in Bunwell Ridding was granted to a shepherd in exchange for the fold[1].

The following tables show how many cattle and stotts were on the demesne during each year, how many remained at each Michaelmas, the causes of loss, and, apart from natural increase, the sources of supply. The cart-horses, *carectarii*, usually two in number, are enumerated among the *stotti*; *bovetti* and *juvencae* were two-year-olds; *bovunculi* and *juvenculae* were yearlings.

1272–3

	During the year	At Michaelmas	Sold	Died	Tithe	Sent to other manors	Killed for larder	Bought	From other manors
Stotti	11	10	1	—	—	—	—	1	—
Boves	11	11	—	—	—	—	—	—	—
Vaccae	23	19	4	—	—	—	—	2	3
Bovetti	4	4	—	—	—	—	—	—	—
Juvencae	3	3	—	—	—	—	—	—	—
Bovunculi	2	2	—	—	—	—	—	—	—
Juvenculae	4	4	—	—	—	—	—	—	—
Vituli	17	9	6	1	1	—	—	—	—
Total	75	62	11	1	1	—	—	3	3

1274–5

	During the year	At Michaelmas	Sold	Died	Tithe	Sent to other manors	Killed for larder	Bought	From other manors
Stotti	11	10	1	—	—	—	—	1	—
Boves	15	14	1	—	—	—	—	—	—
Vaccae	23	21	2	—	—	—	—	—	—
Bovetti	3	3	—	—	—	—	—	—	—
Juvencae	6	5	1	—	—	—	—	—	—
Bovunculi	3	2	—	—	—	—	—	—	—
Juvenculae	3	3	—	—	—	—	—	—	—
Vituli	17	8	5	4	1	—	—	—	—
Total	81	66	10	4	1	—	—	1	—

1277–8

	During the year	At Michaelmas	Sold	Died	Tithe	Sent to other manors	Killed for larder	Bought	From other manors
Stotti	13	10	3	—	—	—	—	—	3
Boves	18	17	1	—	—	—	—	—	1
Vaccae	24	17	4	—	—	3	—	—	—
Bovetti	5	4	—	1	—	—	—	—	—
Juvencae	4	2	—	2	—	—	—	—	—
Bovunculi	6	6	—	—	—	—	—	—	—
Juvenculae	5	5	—	—	—	—	—	—	—
Vituli	16	11	4	—	1	—	—	—	—
Total	91	72	12	3	1	3	—	—	4

1278–9

	During the year	At Michaelmas	Sold	Died	Tithe	Sent to other manors	Killed for larder	Bought	From other manors
Stotti	13	9	3	1	—	—	—	3	—
Boves	21	19	2	—	—	—	—	—	—
Vaccae	19	16	3	—	—	—	—	—	—
Bovetti	6	5	—	1	—	—	—	—	—
Juvencae	5	5	—	—	—	—	—	—	—
Bovunculi	7	6	—	1	—	—	—	—	—
Juvenculae	3	3	—	—	—	—	—	—	—
Vituli	14	8	4	1	1	—	—	—	—
Total	88	71	12	4	1	—	—	3	—

[1] '[Herbagium.] De xiii. acris warecti in Bonewelle Rydinge nihil respondet in denariis quia testiatur per ballivum quod bercarius habuit dictum warectum ex conventione quia compostabat xiii. acras cum falda.' Min. Acc'ts, 935/13.

1279-80

	During the year	At Michaelmas	Sold	Died	Tithe	Sent to other manors	Killed for larder	Bought	From other manors
Stotti	12	10	1	1	—	—	—	—	—
Boves	24	21	3	—	—	—	—	—	—
Vaccae	21	21	—	—	—	—	—	—	—
Bovetti	6	6	—	—	—	—	—	—	—
Juvencae	4	3	—	1	—	—	—	—	—
Bovunculi	2	2	—	—	—	—	—	—	—
Juvenculae	6	6	—	—	—	—	—	—	—
Vituli	19	9	7	1	2	—	—	—	—
Total	94	78	11	3	2	—	—	—	—

1283-4

	During the year	At Michaelmas	Sold	Died	Tithe	Sent to other manors	Killed for larder	Bought	From other manors
Stotti	10	8	—	2	—	—	—	2	—
Boves	19	14	—	5	—	—	—	—	—
Vaccae	25	23	—	1	—	1	—	—	—
Bovetti	3	—	3	—	—	—	—	—	—
Juvencae	7	5	2	—	—	—	—	—	—
Bovunculi	6	6	—	—	—	—	—	—	—
Juvenculae	3	3	—	—	—	—	—	—	—
Vituli	22	10	10	—	2	—	—	—	—
Total	95	69	15	8	2	1	—	2	—

1285-6

	During the year	At Michaelmas	Sold	Died	Tithe	Sent to other manors	Killed for larder	Bought	From other manors
Stotti	11	10	1	—	—	—	—	1	1
Boves	21	14	—	—	—	2	5	—	4
Vaccae	33	19	—	—	—	4	13	—	13
Bovetti	9	6	—	—	—	—	3	—	3
Juvencae	5	4	—	—	—	—	1	—	1
Bovunculi	6	6	—	—	—	—	—	—	—
Juvenculae	2	2	—	—	—	—	—	—	—
Vituli	20	9	7	3	1	—	—	—	—
Total	107	70	8	3	1	6	22	1	22

1289-90

	During the year	At Michaelmas	Sold	Died	Tithe	Sent to other manors	Killed for larder	Bought	From other manors
Stotti	9	9	—	—	—	—	—	—	—
Boves	14	11	1	—	—	—	2	2	—
Vaccae	20	19	—	—	—	—	1	—	—
Bovetti	4	3	1	—	—	—	—	—	—
Juvencae	4	4	—	—	—	—	—	—	—
Bovunculi	4	4	—	—	—	—	—	—	—
Juvenculae	3	2	1	—	—	—	—	—	—
Vituli	20	10	8	2	—	—	—	—	—
Total	78	62	10	3	—	—	3	2	—

1292-3

	During the year	At Michaelmas	Sold	Died	Tithe	Sent to other manors	Killed for larder	Bought	From other manors
Stotti	8	7	—	1	—	—	—	1	—
Boves	16	12	1	1	—	—	2	—	—
Vaccae	22	17	2	1	—	—	2	—	—
Bovetti	4	4	—	—	—	—	—	—	—
Juvencae	3	3	—	—	—	—	—	—	—
Bovunculi	6	6	—	—	—	—	—	—	—
Juvenculae	2	2	—	—	—	—	—	—	—
Vituli	15	4	6	2	1	2	—	—	—
Total	76	55	9	5	1	2	4	1	—

1299-1300

	During the year	At Michaelmas	Sold	Died	Tithe	Sent to other manors	Killed for larder	Bought	From other manors
Stotti	8	7	—	—	—	1	2	1	—
Boves	13	9	—	—	—	2	2	1	—
Vaccae	24	16	1	2	—	4	1	—	—
Bovetti	3	3	—	—	—	—	—	—	—
Juvencae	2	2	—	—	—	—	—	—	—
Bovunculi	7	7	—	—	—	—	—	—	—
Juvenculae	2	2	—	—	—	—	—	—	—
Vituli	20	11	4	—	2	—	3	—	—
Total	79	57	5	2	2	7	6	2	—

	1302-3									1303-4								
	During the year	At Michaelmas	Sold	Died	Tithe	Sent to other manors	Killed for larder	Bought	From other manors	During the year	At Michaelmas	Sold	Died	Tithe	Sent to other manors	Killed for larder	Bought	From other manors
Stotti	10	7	3	—	—	—	—	2	—	7	7	—	—	—	—	—	—	—
Boves	23	21	—	—	—	1	1	—	—	26	12	6	—	—	8	—	—	—
Vaccae	24	22	—	—	—	—	2	—	—	28	21	—	2	—	5	—	—	—
Bovetti	5	5	—	—	—	—	—	—	2	2	2	—	—	—	—	—	—	—
Juvencae	6	6	—	—	—	—	—	—	—	7	6	—	—	—	1	—	—	—
Bovunculi	3	2	1	—	—	—	—	—	2	1	1	—	—	—	—	—	—	—
Juvenculae	7	7	—	—	—	—	—	—	1	6	5	—	1	—	—	—	—	—
Vituli	22	7	13	—	2	—	—	—	—	20	4	12	2	2	—	—	—	—
Total	100	77	17	—	2	1	3	2	5	97	58	18	5	2	14	—	—	—

	1305-6								
	During the year	At Michaelmas	Sold	Died	Tithe	Sent to other manors	Killed for larder	Bought	From other manors
Stotti	7	6	1	—	—	—	—	—	—
Boves	12	10	—	1	—	—	1	—	—
Vaccae	29	23	1	1	—	—	4	—	—
Bovetti	1	1	—	—	—	—	—	—	—
Juvencae	3	3	—	—	—	—	—	—	—
Bovunculi	4	4	—	—	—	—	—	—	—
Juvenculae	1	1	—	—	—	—	—	—	—
Vituli	20	6	12	—	2	—	—	—	—
Total	77	54	14	2	2	—	5	—	—

Less than 4 % of the horses and only 3·75 % of the cattle were lost by death[1].

Pigs were kept in seven out of these thirteen years. In some years the number of pigs was small—from 5 to 10; in 1303 and 1304 it was 100 or more. In 1286, 48 pigs were received from the reeves of Haneworth, Lopham, Halvergate[2], and Framlingham Parva. These were killed for the earl's larder, and, together with the carcasses of 22 cattle, also from other manors, delivered to the reeve of Caister. This instance illustrates how, in case of necessity, the earl might collect a considerable quantity of provisions from his scattered manors without seriously burdening any one of them. The

[1] Compare with conditions on the manors of the Bishop of Winchester in 1208–9, where about 14 % of the horses were lost by murrain and a little more than 10 % of the cattle died. Hall, *Pipe Roll of the Bishopric of Winchester*, pp. xxxxi.–xxxii.

[2] 20 pigs from Halvergate were kept two weeks and consumed 41½ bushels of peas; 14 pigs from Haneworth were kept one week and were fed 5 bushels of peas. 12 bushels of coarse barley were also consumed by the pigs that were being fattened for the larder, presumably these same 34. Min. Acc'ts, 935/11.

animals were driven or carried from the more distant manors to
Forncett, there fattened, slaughtered, and the meat carried to Caister
—a distance of some six or seven miles.   In 1290, 96 geese, 60 hens,
and 89 pullets[1] were bought, fattened, and sent for the use of the
earl to Framlingham, and in the same year 2700 eggs were bought
and carried to the same place.   Geese and hens were raised for sale,
and in most years from 25 to 50 of each kind of fowls were brought
to market.   Hens to the number of 170, due from the tenants as rent,
30 or 40 capons, partly from the demesne farm and partly from
rents, and eggs from the same two sources, were also sold.   A small
number of peacocks and peahens was often kept, and in 1278 five
were sent to Lopham, where the king was expected[2].   The proceeds
from the sale of poultry ranged from 14s. to £1. 15s. yearly; they
were of course diminished when, as occasionally happened, a large
proportion of the fowls were sent from Forncett to other manors[3].

The dairy was an important source of income.   In 1300 and
afterwards the milk was farmed at the rate of 4s. 6d. for the milk of
each cow.   As some 20 cows were usually kept, the receipts from
this source averaged about £4. 10s. a year.   Before the milk was thus
farmed, the proceeds from the sale of butter and cheese sometimes
exceeded and often fell considerably below this amount.   The income
from the sale of stock about equalled that from the dairy.

The windmill was also profitable.   Although mill-stones were
expensive[4] and were frequently renewed, yet the yearly expenses
connected with the maintenance and operation of the mill were, as a
rule, from £3 to £5 less than the value of the barley and wheat
which constituted the receipts from the mill, and which, in the
earlier years, seem to have been a certain proportion of the grain
ground at the mill.   In 1300 and later the mill was farmed for a
yearly payment of 24 or 25 quarters of barley.   While the bondmen
were obliged to bring their grain to the mill, free tenants sometimes
had theirs ground elsewhere[5].

It was probably at Norwich that the manor produce was sold.

[1] The geese and pullets together consumed 32 bushels of oats and 6 bushels of coarse
barley, or 6¼ quarts of grain each. Min. Acc'ts, 935/12.

[2] Min. Acc'ts, 935/6.   In Advent, 1278, the king was present at the dedication of
Norwich Cathedral.   Gough, *Itinerary of King Edward the First*, i. iii. 89, 90.   Lopham is
not mentioned in the Itinerary.

[3] Min. Acc'ts, 935/6, 935/12.

[4] In 1275 a mill-stone was bought for £1. 13s.; in 1278, two stones cost £1. 8s. and
£1. 10s. respectively; in 1290 a stone cost £1. 10s., etc.

[5] In 1279 the reeve accounted for 26 quarters 2 bushels of barley from the mill. 'Et ideo
non plus hoc anno pro debilitate molendini et quia alii (sic) ii. molendina de novo erecti (sic)
sunt prope et liberi homines noluerunt sectare molendinum comitis pro debilitate.'   Min.
Acc'ts, 935/7.

At least part of the grain was carried there, and it is very likely that the cheese, butter, poultry, and eggs were also sold at the Norwich market, though they may have been taken to the nearer markets of Stratton, Aslacton, or those of other of the neighbouring villages[1].

To complete the account of the various sources from which the lord's income was derived, it is necessary to add to the description of the demesne land and stock an account of the payments made to him as lord of the soil and feudal superior. Of these payments the most important were the fixed money rents paid by both bond and free tenants[2], usually at the terms of St Andrew, Easter, and Michaelmas; amercements and fines known as 'perquisites of court'; money paid in lieu of labour dues; and the yearly tax imposed upon the bondmen. Minor payments were chevage, foldage, and market tolls. The following tables give the value of the different sources of income and the expenses incurred in carrying on the estate.

Receipts.

	1272–3			1274–5		
	£.	*s.*	*d.*	*£.*	*s.*	*d.*
Fixed rents	18	3	7¾	18	3	7¾
Farm of market		2	6		2	6
Chevage		8	6		8	7
Foldage		3	9½		2	9½
Sale of works	5	13	2¾	5	7	5
Herbage	1	0	4		17	4
Hay	2	12	11			
Turf etc.	1	13	6½		4	5
Underwood	5	10	2	4	8	½
Grain	61	12	3¼	50	6	1¾
Cider	1	1	11¼			
Stock	5	3	0	2	15	8
Dairy	4	3	0¾	3	17	0
Pleas	14	0	0	22	5	4
Tallage	6	13	4	8	0	0
Total	128	2	2¾	116	18	10½

Expenses.

	1272–3			1274–5		
	£.	*s.*	*d.*	*£.*	*s.*	*d.*
Rents paid and allowed		3	2½		5	9
Plows and carts	2	17	4	3	2	5½
Buildings and walls	4	5	10½	3	19	8½
Small necessaries		7	10¾		12	8¼
Dairy		4	3¼		4	11
Threshing	1	15	5½	2	0	11¾
Meadow and autumn expenses		1	4			
Stock		16	7		9	0
Bailiff	1	19	0	2	12	0
Steward	1	6	9½	1	6	11¼
Grain	8	2	4¼			
Expenses of Acc't	1	0	8½		18	2
Total	23	0	9¾	15	12	7¼

[1] In the early years of the 14th century there were weekly markets at 5 out of the 19 vills situated in Depwade hundred: viz. Tacolneston, Aslacton, Hempnall, Stratton, and Fritton. Annual or semi-annual fairs were also held at these places. Blomefield, *History of Norfolk*, v. 166, 177, 184, 188, 190, 310.

[2] According to an Inquisition-post-mortem of 54 Hen. III. (File 38, No. 17), the fixed rents of the free tenants were worth £6. 19*s.* and the fixed rents of the customary tenants £4 exclusive of the £4. 10*s.* from 'the homage called Hadesco.' Like most of the values assigned by the inquisition, these fall short of the truth, but the actual proportions paid by free and by customary tenants are very likely maintained.

Receipts.

1277–8

	£.	s.	d.
Fixed rents	18	3	7¾
Farm of market		2	6
Chevage		8	8
Foldage		2	11½
Sale of works	4	18	7¼
Herbage		18	10½
Hay		6	2½
Turf		1	9½
Underwood	1	11	6
Grain	52	6	8
Cider			
Stock	4	18	3½
Dairy	3	13	6
Pleas	13	12	0
Tallage	8	0	0
Total	109	5	2½

Expenses.

1277–8

	£.	s.	d.
Rents paid and allowed		3	2½
Plows and carts	2	9	9
Buildings and walls ...	3	15	6½
Small necessaries ...		5	1½
Dairy		4	7½
Threshing		8	4
Meadow and autumn expenses		2	4
Stock			
Bailiff	3	12	0
Steward	1	12	7
Grain			
Expenses of Acc't ...		15	7
Total	13	9	1

Receipts.

1278–9

	£.	s.	d.
Fixed rents	18	3	7¾
Farm of market		2	6
Chevage		8	8
Foldage		3	3
Sale of works	4	9	4¾
Herbage	1	18	8
Hay		2	3
Turf		2	7
Underwood and Escheats	2	12	4
Grain	38	8	3½
Cider			
Stock	4	10	9¾
Dairy	3	11	1
Pleas	15	9	8
Tallage	9	13	4
Total	99	16	5¾

Expenses.

1278–9

	£.	s.	d.
Rents paid and allowed		3	2½
Plows and carts	2	17	7
Buildings and walls ...	6	11	10¼
Small things		10	1½
Dairy		4	6½
Threshing		9	4½
Meadow and autumn expenses			
Stock	3	8	2½
Sergeant, steward, and accountants	6	11	2½
Grain	2	16	7
Total	23	12	8¼

Receipts.

1279–80

	£.	s.	d.
Fixed rents	18	9	3
Farm of market		2	6
Chevage		8	8
Foldage		3	5½
Sale of works	5	4	3½
Herbage		14	2½
Hay			
Turf		1	6
Underwood	7	6	4
Grain	48	1	8
Cider			
Stock	3	19	11
Dairy	4	0	0
Pleas	18	13	3
Tallage	9	13	4
Total	116	18	4½

Expenses.

1279–80

	£.	s.	d.
Rents paid and allowed		3	2½
Plows and carts	2	14	11½
Buildings and walls ...	11	16	8½
Small necessaries ...		3	10
Dairy		3	5½
Threshing	1	0	1
Meadow and autumn expenses			
Stock	1	18	9
Sergeant and steward ...	7	3	1
Grain	2	0	0
Total	27	4	1

Receipts.

1283–4

	£.	s.	d.
Fixed rents	18	15	8
Farm of market		2	6
Chevage		8	8
Foldage		2	10½
Sale of works	5	8	11¾
Herbage		12	8
Hay			
Turf		1	10
Underwood	3	2	4
Grain	39	1	8½
Cider			
Stock	6	2	½
Dairy	4	11	0
Pleas	15	16	7
Tallage	9	13	4
Total	104	0	2¼

Expenses.

1283–4

	£.	s.	d.
Rents paid and allowed		7	10½
Plows and carts	2	5	7
Buildings and walls ...		11	6½
Ditches		12	3½
Small things		3	5½
Dairy		3	5
Threshing	1	2	5¾
Meadow and autumn expenses		1	1
Stock		19	1½
Sergeant	3	12	0
Grain	2	11	2¾
Expenses of acc't ...		15	2½
Purchases of land ...	2	4	6
Total	15	9	9½

Receipts.

1285–6

	£.	s.	d.
Fixed rents	18	16	2¼
Farm of market		2	6
Chevage		8	6
Foldage		2	½
Sale of works	4	14	0
Herbage	1	10	½
Hay			
Turf		1	8
Underwood	2	2	0
Grain	30	17	3¼
Cider			
Stock	5	16	9
Dairy	4	16	0
Pleas	6	15	6
Tallage	9	13	4
Total	85	15	9½

Expenses.

1285–6

	£.	s.	d.
Rents paid and allowed		2	10½
Plows and carts	2	16	6½
Buildings and walls ...	1	17	8½
Ditches	1	10	11
Small things		11	9
Dairy		3	1½
Threshing		11	1½
Meadow and autumn expenses		2	6
Stock	1	3	11¼
Fees to officers	4	2	11
Grain			
Expenses of acc't ...		14	6
Total	13	17	10¾

Receipts.

1289–90

	£.	s.	d.
Fixed rents	18	16	2¼
Farm of market		2	6
Chevage		8	0
Foldage		1	10½
Sale of works	5	2	4¼
Herbage	2	1	3½
Hay			
Turf			8
Underwood	5	14	2
Grain	34	14	3¼
Apples			4
Stock	2	11	9½
Dairy	3	8	0
Pleas	8	17	8
Tallage	9	13	4
Total	91	12	5¼

Expenses.

1289–90

	£.	s.	d.
Rents paid and allowed		2	10½
Plows and carts	2	11	5
Buildings and walls ...	3	16	6¼
Small things		8	1¾
Dairy		3	10
Threshing		15	6
Meadow and autumn expenses		1	5
Stock	2	7	1
Sergeant	2	12	0
Steward		6	7
Grain		5	11
Expenses of acc't ...		8	2
Total	13	19	5½

Receipts.

1292-3

	£.	s.	d.
Fixed rents	18	16	8¼
Farm of market		2	6
Chevage		8	0
Foldage		1	4
Sale of works	4	8	8¾
Herbage	1	8	9
Hay			
Turf		1	2½
Underwood	6	10	1
Grain	36	19	10
Garden			
Stock	2	8	4¾
Dairy	3	2	0
Pleas	6	7	11¾
Tallage	9	13	4
Total	90	8	10

Expenses.

1292-3

	£.	s.	a.
Rents paid and allowed		3	4½
Plows and carts	2	9	9
Buildings	1	11	7½
Small things		11	5½
Dairy		3	2
Threshing		13	9
Meadow and autumn expenses		3	1
Stock		11	¼
Sergeant	2	12	0
Grain	11	0	8
Expenses of acc't ...		8	8½
Total	20	8	7¼

Receipts.

1299-1300

	£.	s.	d.
Fixed rents	18	18	¼
Farm of market etc. ...		4	3
Chevage		8	0
Foldage		1	10½
Sale of works	6	17	1¼
Herbage	2	1	3
Hay			
Turf			10
Underwood	6	11	11
Grain	30	4	¼
Dove-house		1	6
Stock	3	2	1¼
Dairy	4	1	0
Pleas	14	7	3
Tallage	10	13	4
Total	97	12	5½

Expenses.

1299-1300

	£.	s.	d.
Rents paid and allowed		1	9½
Plows and carts	2	5	10½
Buildings and walls ...	1	6	6½
Small things		6	4¼
Dairy		8	9
Threshing			
Meadow and autumn expenses		2	9
Stock	1	13	0
Sergeant	4	18	0
Warrener	1	13	7½
Grain	12	3	10½
Expenses of account ...		15	7
Total	25	16	1¾

Receipts.

1302–3

			£.	s.	d.
Fixed rents	...	...	18	18	3¼
Farm of market etc.	...			4	9
Chevage	...	...		8	0
Foldage	...	...		1	10½
Sale of works	...	...	7	5	3
Herbage	...	...		18	4
Hay	...	...	...			
Turf	...	...	...		4	3
Wood	...	...	...	41	1	6
Grain	...	...	...	34	1	6½
Garden	...	...	...		1	6½
Stock	...	...	...	5	8	9¾
Dairy	...	...	...	4	19	0
Pleas	...	...	...	13	9	9½
Reliefs	...	...	...	10	0	0
Tallage	...	...	...	9	13	4
Total	...	...	...	146	16	3

Expenses.

1302–3

			£.	s.	d.
Rents paid and allowed				1	9½
Plows and carts ...		...	2	13	4¼
Buildings ...	...	...	2	15	8
Small things	...	...		3	2½
Dairy	...	...			7	9¾
Threshing	...	...			
Meadow and autumn expenses ...	...	...		3	3
Stock	...	...		1	16	5¾
Sergeant and warrener ...			8	2	10
Grain	...	...	...		16	3
Expenses of account	...		2	9	9¾
Total	...	...	...	19	10	5½

Receipts.

1303–4

			£.	s.	d.
Fixed rents	...	...	18	18	3¼
Farm of market etc.	...			4	9
Chevage	...	...		8	0
Foldage	...	...		2	½
Sale of works	...	...	8	3	2¼
Herbage	...	...	2	4	2¾
Hay	...	...			
Turf	...	...	...		1	6
Underwood	...	...	8	7	6¾
Grain	...	...	...	41	3	2
Cider	...	...	...			
Stock	...	...	...	5	3	5¼
Dairy	...	...	...	4	10	0
Pleas	...	...	....	12	5	5½
Tallage	...	...	...	9	13	4
Flax	...	...	...			8
Total	...	...	...	111	5	7¼

Expenses.

1303–4

			£.	s.	d.
Rents paid and allowed				1	9½
Plows and carts ... ·		...	2	3	10
Buildings ...	...	...		13	4
Small things	... ··	... ·	1	11	2¼
Dairy	...	...	...		10	0
Threshing	...	...			
Meadow and autumn expenses ...	...	...		3	3
Stock	...	...			
Sergeant	...	...	...	5	4	0
Grain	...	...	...	18	9	4
Expenses of account	...		1	6	10¾
Warrener ..	...	...		2	5	6
Total	...	...	...	32	9	1½

Receipts.				Expenses.			
1305-6				**1305-6**			
	£.	s.	d.		£.	s.	d.
Fixed rents	18	18	7	Rents paid and allowed		1	9½
Farm of market etc. ...		4	9	Plows and carts	3	3	6½
Chevage		8	0	Buildings	3	13	3¼
Foldage	1	11½		Small things	3	5	4¼
Sale of works	7	15	1¾	Dairy		8	7
Herbage	2	18	8	Threshing			
Hay				Meadow and autumn ex-			
Turf		1	11	penses		6	3
Wood	12	5	5	Stock		8	0
Grain	24	6	8½	Sergeant			
Cider				Grain			
Stock	3	14	¾	Expenses of account ...		14	3½
Dairy	4	10	0	Ditches		2	3½
Pleas	12	17	7½				
Tallage							
Issue of manor[1]		16	6				
Total	88	19	4	Total	12	3	4½

In attempting to determine approximately the annual net profits from the manor, the items relating to grain and stock present special difficulties. Sometimes the grain and stock supplied to the earl's household were accounted for as 'sold' to the earl, and the money receipts were entered in the same fashion as the receipts from sales at Norwich market. At other times no money was received for the commodities supplied to the earl. Often both grain and stock were received from, or sent to, other of the earl's manors, no money payments being made. In calculating the net profits, the stock and grain sent to other manors or used by the earl have been valued as receipts, and the stock and grain received from other manors have been valued as expenses. The prices of these commodities have been calculated for each year from the prices entered in the account rolls of that year, or where these prices were too few to form the basis of a trustworthy average, Thorold Rogers' average prices have been used.

---

[1] Under this head sales of various articles are recorded, an old pair of wheels, etc.

The first column of the table gives the net money profits according to the bailiff's reckoning[1]; the second column includes the value of grain and stock, reckoned in the way just explained[2].

Net profits.

	£.	s.	d.		£.	s.	d.
1273	105	1	5		101	9	10½
1275	101	6	3¼		105	1	½
1278	95	16	1½		93	11	1¼
1279	76	3	9½		80	9	3½
1280	89	14	3½		89	14	3½
1284	88	10	4¾		90	16	7¼
1286	71	17	10¾		78	9	2¼
1290	77	12	11¾		84	19	1¼
1293	70	0	2¾		87	14	4¼
1300	71	16	3¾		80	3	1¾
1303	127	5	9½		125	1	1¼
1304	78	16	5¾		100	7	¼
1306	76	15	11½				

Average : about £87.　　　Average : about £93.

The expenses consisted of a few small rents, the largest being a payment of 16*d.* as waite-fee[3] for the guard of Norwich castle; of some insignificant customary payments, e.g. 4*d.* to the plowmen on Lammas-day; of wages to the lord's agents and to the inferior officers of the manor, as well as to the smith, carpenters, thatchers, plasterers, coopers, and other workmen employed on the demesne; of purchases of iron, steel, salt, grease, tallow, and sundry manufactured articles. These last included plow-shares, wheelbarrows, wheels for plows and wheelbarrows, forks, spades, hoes or mattocks, axes, clouts, strakes, axle-irons (hurthirons)[4], wer-irons[5], nails of various kinds, hinges, boards, laths, saddles, saddle-bags, leather

---

[1] 'Liberationes' or payments made in the lord's behalf to persons not connected with the manor are, of course, left out of account.

[2] At Forncett, the average price of a quarter—eight bushels—of wheat in the ten years for which we have information was 5*s.* 10¼*d.* Calculated from Thorold Rogers' tables, the average price of a quarter of wheat in the same ten years was 5*s.* 6½*d.* But Rogers has omitted the low prices of inferior grain while the Forncett average is based on all the prices quoted, including the low prices at which grain was sold 'ad opus comitis.' It may therefore be concluded that the price of wheat was high in Forncett.

[3] For waite-fee, see *Memorials of S. Edmunds*, R.S., I. 269, 271, and *Red Book of Exchequer*, R.S., ccxl.

[4] Probably connected with *hurter*, the iron ring in the axle of a cart. Halliwell, *Dict. of Archaic and Provincial Words.*

[5] The meaning of this term is not clear to me.

collars, traces, halters, curry-combs (strigils), cord, sacks (probably for measuring grain), canvas for the windmill-sails and for sacks, cloth for winnowing, small cloths used in straining milk and making cheese, hair-cloth for the malt-house[1], pots and pans of earthenware and of brass, buckets, vats, small vessels for the dairy, stamps for butter or cheese, sieves, hurdles for harvest carts, hurdles for sheep, a key for the grange, and a bolt for the hay-house[2].

But while many articles were thus procured from outside the manor, some of the more important implements of the farm were made on the estate itself by the labour of the smith and of carpenters. Thus, in 1275, two carpenters were hired for three days to prepare timber for the plow and to make three harrows and yokes. The frame of the plow was put together by carpenters and fitted with iron by the smith. The carts were also made within the manor, as were also the ladders and some of the wooden vessels, though these latter seem to have been more frequently bought. In 1300, when the earl was about to visit the manor, several men were hired for 18 days to prepare 'divers vessels.'

The material in print affords a very insufficient basis for comparison between this and other manors, but such a comparison seems to indicate that the more unusual features of the Forncett accounts were the number of chevage-paying bondmen, the tax annually levied upon the tenants, and the sums paid as rent, and as fines and amercements—sums not only absolutely large, but relatively as compared with the proceeds from grain and stock[3]. About 100 persons annually paid chevage. They are called in some rolls

[1] Used for drying the malt after it had been made to germinate. Rogers, *Agric. and Prices*, I. 572.

[2] These articles were probably obtained at Norwich where a number of industries had arisen, and the large market created by a populous town in a well-peopled district permitted the division of employments to be carried comparatively far. At about this time there were in Norwich gilds of saddlers, tanners, cobblers, and fullers. In the extracts from the Leet Rolls of Norwich (1288–1313) printed on pp. 1–61, vol. v. (1891) of the Selden Soc. publications, some 60 or 70 different trades are mentioned. To illustrate the sources from which the articles purchased for Forncett may have been supplied, as well as to show how minute was the division of employments in Norwich, a few of the occupations noticed in the leet rolls may be enumerated: viz. turners, basket-makers, lock-smiths, mustard-men, mitten-makers, girth-makers, bell-founders, makers of knife-handles, bird-snare makers, lace-braiders, chaloners (blanket-makers), hatters, and barbers.

[3] For example, in Forncett fixed rents averaged about £18. 10s.; perquisites of court were usually between £10 and £20; sales of grain between £30 and £60.

In Wilburton, temp. Ed. II., 'rents of assize' were about £2; perquisites of court somewhat more; sale of crops £8 to £54. Maitland, 'History of a Cambridgeshire Manor,' *Eng. Hist. Rev.*, July, 1894.

In Cuxham, Oxford, 1316–17 (a year of great scarcity) rents were less than £2; fines and pleas, £3. 15s.; grain, £19. 5s. Rogers, *Agric. and Prices*, II. 617–630.

On the other hand, other of Bigod's Norfolk manors present the same peculiarities as

anlipimen[1]; in other rolls, *nativi manentes extra manerium*. It is somewhat surprising that, while the number of bond tenements was only about 135, so many Forncett bondmen should have been *extra manerium*. But the bond tenements were extremely small, and there was little room for additional servile tenants. There must have been many younger sons of full age, who, though resident in Forncett vill, were not tenants of Forncett manor, and might therefore be considered *extra manerium*[2]. To these, as being in most cases unmarried, the term *anlipimen* would also apply. Doubtless some of the bondmen who held no land of Forncett manor went to Norwich or other large towns, or to neighbouring villages where they might even become tenants of other manors[3].

The tallage[4] levied was always a round sum imposed upon the manor as a whole, and divided among the bondmen, possibly in proportion to the number of their cattle[5]. In 1273 ten marks were levied; in 1275 and 1278 twelve marks, and in each of the following years up to 1306 for which there is evidence fourteen and a half marks, except in 1300, when an additional pound was paid by the bondmen as a 'gift' (*donum*).

The large sum annually paid as rent is probably to be explained by the large number of free tenants and sokemen and the small number of customary tenants (exclusive of sokemen), and by the comparative abundance of money in the vicinity of such a centre of trade and industry as Norwich.

As the account rolls extend over thirty-five years (1272–1306) we might expect that a comparison of the later with the earlier rolls would show that changes had taken place within the period. But

Forncett. Thus, in Ditchingham, 1273, 32 *anlepimen* paid chevage; a tallage of £12. 13s. 4d. was levied; rents were over £11; pleas, £10. 11s.; grain, £48. 6s. In 1275, pleas were £18 and sales of grain £31; in 1276, pleas were £11. 13s.; grain, £26. 8s. Min. Acc'ts, 933/22, 933/23, 933/24.

In Parva Framlingham, 1275, 93 *nativi* paid chevage; a tax of £15. 6s. was collected. In this and the two following years for which there are records, rents were £18. 10s.; pleas, about £12; sales of grain, about £20–34. Min. Acc'ts, 935/25—935/27.

[1] A.S. *anlepi*, alone, single, unmarried. Halliwell, *op. cit.* See also, Maitland, *Court Baron*, 146; Vinogradoff, *Villainage*, 213; Ramsey Cartulary (R.S.) 1. 50.

[2] From 1501–1503, a bondman who lived within Forncett vill, but was not a tenant of the manor, paid chevage; and in an extent of the Honor of Richmond in the county of Norfolk, 8 Edw. I., we read that 'chevagium commorantium in manerio qui non tenent terram nec domicilium valet per annum 3s.' *Registrum Honoris de Richmond* [ed. Rog. Gale], Appendix, p. 47.

[3] In the Norwich leet rolls of 1312/13, a William of Forncett is mentioned as a citizen, and the wife of Richard of Forncett is amerced. Hudson, *Leet Jurisdiction*, 57–8.

In 4 Edw. [II.?] an 'Earl's bondman' whose surname indicates that he was appurtenant to Forncett, held land in Moulton, and of Moulton manor. Moulton Court Rolls, ms.

[4] The Latin terms used are *talliagium, recognitio, misa,* and *auxilium*.

[5] Vinogradoff, *Villainage*, 293.

the differences between the earlier and later years seem few and of little general significance.

Rents show a small and gradual increase. In 1306 they amounted to 15s. more than in 1273, a rise of over 4 per cent. But this does not necessarily denote an increase in the number of tenants, in the area of land let, or in the value of the land. A large part of the increase, at least, was due to payments made by bondmen who had purchased free land, or to small sums paid to the lord in return for the grant of special privileges[1]. The amount of such payments as salt-penny, forth-ward (ward-penny), scor-fee[2] and the like remained unaltered. It is to be noted that the lord seems to have had little difficulty in finding tenants during this period, and few of the rent-paying lands remained in his hands.

One-fourth of the tolls of Stratton market were farmed for 2s. 6d. from 1273 to 1293, for 3s. 6d. in 1300, and 4s. in 1303 and later.

Foldage payments declined, as a rule, after 1290.

The following table shows that in the first years of the fourteenth century more ' manual ' works were annually sold than at an earlier date. This difference, however, does not appear to be a consequence of the working of general causes, or to indicate an advance toward complete commutation. On the contrary a close examination of the rolls seems to show that local and temporary causes suffice to explain the change.

Number of ' works ' due each year.

Winter works	Summer works	Autumn works	Total
1505	245	1223	2973

Number of works sold.

	Winter works	Summer works	Autumn works	Total
1273	60	45	500	605
1275	464	51	328	843
1278	18	0	281	299
1279	69	0	441	510
1280	58	24	286	368
1284	654	59	384	1097
1286	287	25½	387	699½
1290	468	114½	368	950½
1293	383	26	311½	720½
1300	101½	173	636	910½
1303	325½	148	600	1073½
1304	830	151	678	1659
1306	693½	78	586	1357½

[1] Thus, a tenant pays 4d. that his son may become a chaplain. Min. Acc'ts, 935/14.
[2] For the meaning of this term cf. Appendix VIII., p. xxx., n. 1.

Thus, in 1278, fewer works were sold than in any other year of which we have record. But the great demand for labour rents in this year is to be explained by the fact that at this time 33 acres of the Moulton demesne which were in the earl's hands during the wardship of the heir of Moulton manor, were cultivated by the customary labour of the tenants of Forncett manor. In 1304, on the other hand, the large sale of works is accounted for by the fact that in this year much of the grain from the demesne was sold in the sheaf, and some 500 'diets' usually needed for threshing were not demanded. In 1303 and 1304 part of the arable was left unsown[1] which was another reason for the diminished demand for labour in these years.

Moreover, if the increase in the fourteenth century of the number of cases in which tenants paid money in lieu of rendering service, denoted a change from an earlier system of 'natural husbandry' to a 'money system,' we should expect to find an increase in the amount of unskilled labour hired, corresponding to the decrease in the quantity of customary labour rendered. As a matter of fact, however, less unskilled labour was hired in 1304 than in 1278[2].

There was an increase in the sales of trees and underwood toward the end of the period, when large numbers of trees were felled[3].

On the whole the changes that appear after 1300 seem, as has been said, to have a merely local significance, and may possibly be accounted for by the fact that in 1302 the earl surrendered his estates to the king, and on receiving them back had only a life interest in them[4]. In December 1306 Earl Roger died[5], and in June 1307 the manor passed into the charge of officers of the king[6].

---

[1] 'De herbagio xviii. acrarum terrae arrabilis non seminatarum.' Min. Acc'ts, 935/15 (1303). 'De herbagio xxv. acrarum dim. non seminatarum hoc anno.' Min. Acc'ts, 935/16 (1304). Cf. above, p. 27.

[2] In 1278, payments to unskilled labourers in yearly and daily wages and in customary fees amounted to £1. 19s. 7½d., of which 10d. was paid for work done on Moulton demesne. In 1304 similar payments amounted to £1. 8s. 4½d. The difference is due to the small quantity of day labour employed in the latter year.

[3] 'De siccis arboribus venditis...£35. 9s.' Min. Acc'ts, 935/15.

[4] Stubbs, *Const. Hist.*, II. 154.

[5] *Dict. Nat. Biog.*

[6] Min. Acc'ts, 937/10.

CHAPTER III.

THE DEMESNE. 1376—78.

THE records dating from between 1307 and 1376 are not sufficiently abundant to enable us to reconstruct the history of that period, but light is thrown on the years 1376–78 by two Account Rolls that have fortunately been preserved[1].

It has been seen that during the thirty-five years from 1272 to 1306, few changes occurred in the manorial organization and management; but within the seventy years between 1306 and 1376 the organization of the manor and the administration of the demesne were revolutionized.

In the court-yard, as at the beginning of the century, stood the demesne buildings. By 1376 some had fallen to decay[2], but in the two years now under consideration considerable activity was shown in the erection and repair of buildings. Thus a stable and cowhouse, eighty-four feet long[3], and a chamber for the steward[4], besides gates and walls[4], were newly constructed. The hall[4], wardrobe[4], kitchen[4], dairy[4], hay-house[4], grange[3,4], stables[4], and gate-house[4], as well as the mill[3], which, unlike most of the demesne buildings, stood outside the court-yard, were repaired. A 'chamber called the wardrobe' was moved from the hall and placed next to the steward's chamber[4].

As in the earlier period, the work of building and repair was performed by hired labourers assisted by the customary tenants[5]. The houses seem to have been built of about the same materials as before; the court-yard was partly inclosed by clay walls[6], and partly by ditches and dead hedges[7].

But though it is possible that no very great change had occurred since the beginning of the century in the appearance of the buildings

---

[1] Printed as Appendix IX.
[2] Appendix IX. l.
[3] Appendix IX. lv.
[4] Appendix IX. lvi.
[5] Appendix IX. lv., lvi., lxii., lxiii.
[6] Appendix IX. lvi., lxiii.
[7] Appendix IX. lxiii.

within the court-yard, a decided change had taken place in the relation of the occupants to the manorial organization. Formerly, as has been said[1], the permanent residents in the court-yard consisted of the bailiff and several servants of inferior rank ; but from 1376 to 1378 the only demesne servants of this class in the manor were a warrener[2] and a shepherd. There is no clear evidence as to their place of residence. The money wages of the shepherd were 6*s.* 8*d.* yearly[3], or more than twice those of the plowmen or carters in the earlier period ; his wages in kind also—a quarter of grain every ten weeks besides a yearly allowance of several bushels of oats for pottage[2]—were liberal, judged even by the standard of the thirteenth century. There was no resident bailiff, at least in the old sense of the term, now exercising the functions of his office in the manor. Most of the duties formerly discharged by the bailiff had no longer to be performed ; those that still remained seem to have devolved chiefly upon an officer named William Gunnyld, a sort of itinerant bailiff, and perhaps to some extent upon the reeve, who is sometimes called the bailiff of the manor[4]. Gunnyld made contracts for the erection of new buildings[5]; bought, in 1377, sheep to stock the demesne[6] ; arranged for the housing of the sheep in the court-yard[7], and, in short, introduced the innovations and bore the heavier responsibilities in the management of the demesne[8]. His supervision apparently extended over other of the countess's manors[9]. He did not live in the manor; occasional brief visits are noted[10]. Matters calling for less exercise of discretion than those undertaken by Gunnyld—as the repair of buildings and small purchases—seem to have been entrusted to the reeve, who accounted for the expenses involved therein as well as for the receipts from most of the principal sources of income. For certain of the receipts, however, the messor was responsible. In selecting the reeve and messor of Forncett, what appears to be a new method was now employed. One large or several small bond tenements were elected by the homage to bear the pecuniary burden of each of these offices. Twenty acres, charged with 2*s.* an acre, was

---

[1] See above, pp. 22, 24.   [2] Appendix IX. lx.

[3] Appendix IX. lvii.

[4] In 1376–77 the reeve was William Hernynge, Appendix IX. xlii. But William Hernynge is also spoken of as bailiff and in a connection that seems to show that the reeve is intended, Appendix IX. lxxi. In 1377–78, John ate Lound was reeve, Appendix IX. xlii. A John Lound is also spoken of as bailiff of the manor of Forncett, Appendix IX. lxviii. Thus it appears that the distinction earlier made between bailiff and reeve was now obscured.

[5] Appendix IX. lv., lvi.   [6] Appendix IX. lix.

[7] Appendix IX. l.   [8] Appendix IX. l., *et passim.*

[9] Appendix IX. lvii., lviii., lix.   [10] Appendix IX. lvii., lviii.

the area generally chosen to support the reeveship ; and fifteen acres, charged at the same rate, to support the office of messor. Many of the tenements thus burdened were divided among several different tenants, free as well as bond. The person who acted as officer was sometimes one of the tenants of the elected tenements and sometimes not. He was usually but perhaps not invariably a serf. His stipend consisted of the money charged upon the tenements[1].

Though the number of demesne officers resident in the manor had diminished, the itinerant officers—the steward and accountants— seem to have visited. the manor with about the same frequency as before[2].

One of the most striking changes that had occurred in the economy of the court-yard was the leasing of some of the demesne buildings to tenants, and even to bondmen of the manor. The hall and many of the other buildings were still in the lord's hands, but in 1376–77 the sheep-house and fold[3], the chambers east and west of the gate[3], the cart-house[4], grange[3], and stotts' stable[3] were let, either for terms of years, or from year to year. In 1377–78, however, Gunnyld stocked the demesne with some two hundred sheep[5]. The sheep-house had then fallen[3], the fold and the chamber west of the gate[3] were occupied by the demesne sheep, and the chamber east of the gate[4] and the cart-house[4] were no longer farmed, as Gunnyld had ordered that no beasts should be kept in the court-yard except those belonging to the countess.

The pasture and fruit of the garden, the herbage of the pound-yard and kitchen yard, the orchard, and a close called Cornescroft were also farmed[3].

But the changes already noted were but the natural results of a far more important change in the method of manorial administration —the leasing of the arable land[6]. Formerly, as has been seen, the produce of the arable demesne was the lord's chief source of income ; the demesne was cultivated largely by the labour services of the customary tenants, though plowmen and carters were hired[7]. But by 1376 the number of tenants owing labour rents was far less than at the beginning of the century, for much of the land held by this tenure had fallen into the lord's hands, either upon the death of the tenant without heir or because he had waived his holding. Thus out

---

[1] Appendix IX. li., lvii.   [2] Appendix IX. lvii., lviii.
[3] Appendix IX. l.   [4] Appendix IX. li.
[5] Appendix IX. lix.   [6] Appendix IX. xlix.
[7] See above, p. 26 ff.

of 3219 winter, summer and autumn diets charged upon the land, 1452 diets in 1376–77 and 1722 diets in 1377–78 were no longer available since the tenements from which they had formerly been due had come into the lord's hands[1] or, as in a single instance, were exempt from labour services on account of a payment made by the tenant[2]. And some ten to twenty additional works—as from tenements elected to bear the offices of reeve or messor, and thus temporarily freed from labour-rents—could not be demanded[3]. Under these circumstances the customary labour of the tenants was no longer sufficient for the cultivation of the demesne, and it is extremely probable that even such services as were due would in many cases have been very unwillingly rendered[4]. It may be noticed here that the 250 acres which had escheated to the lord, and a large part of which was formerly charged with labour dues, was farmed by the lord to a number of tenants, at money rents for terms of years[5]. So that about half of the labour rents once due could not henceforth be claimed, since the land upon which they were charged was held by a new tenure, and some 250 acres, a large part of which was once bondland, had now been converted into leasehold.

With regard to the cultivation of the demesne under these new conditions, several alternatives presented themselves to the lord; either the demesne might be cultivated under the direction of the bailiff as before, but largely by means of hired labour; or the lord might give up the cultivation of the demesne, either leasing it to tenants or retaining it as pasture land in his own hands. As a matter of fact, the lord ceased to cultivate the demesne. He let for a term of years $166\frac{1}{2}$ acres of arable[6] and the right of pasture on Westwood Ridding[7].

In adopting this new policy of leasing the arable demesne, the lord was probably influenced by the following considerations. As has already been said, if the demesne had been cultivated as formerly under the direction of the bailiff, a large amount of labour must necessarily have been hired. But since the beginning of the century there had been a very considerable rise in the price of labour relative to the price of grain[8]. The profits of agriculture would therefore

---

[1] Appendix IX. lxii.

[2] 'Tenementum Thomae Southauwe,' lxii., lxv., lxvi., cf. p. xliii.

[3] Appendix IX. lxii., lxiv–lxvi.   [4] See below, pp. 72, 74, 75.

[5] Appendix IX. xliv ff.   [6] Appendix IX. xlix.

[7] Appendix IX. li.

[8] For wages, see Appendix IX. lv., lvi. and below, p. 56, n. 2.

have been less than in the earlier period. It might indeed be
supposed that the increased price of labour would have been felt by
the farmer as well as by the lord, and that consequently the rent that
the farmer could have afforded to pay would not have exceeded
the reduced profits that the lord might have obtained by cultivating
the demesne for his own benefit. But it is probable that the increased
price of labour affected the profits of the farmer far less than it
affected the profits of the lord. The 166½ acres of the arable
demesne were leased to two bondmen, who doubtless themselves
performed much of the agricultural labour, though they bought
from the lord 40 autumn diets. Moreover, other things being
equal, the net profit of the tenant farmers would have been greater
than that of the lord, since they superintended in person the management of their estate, and not, as did the lord, through a staff of
agents whom it was expensive to maintain and who often sacrificed
the lord's interests to their own. It is also possible that the farmers
sought immediate profits from the cultivation of the land, avoiding,
for example, the expense of manuring the soil ; though such management would be ruinous in the end, the loss would fall upon the lord
of the manor rather than upon the tenant. The diminished population of the manor, the consequent decay of labour services, the
refractory spirit of the tenants and their increased prosperity, the fact
that tenants could afford to pay a rent for the demesne that was
greater than the net profits to be derived from its cultivation by the
bailiff under the new conditions of high wages and relatively low
prices, were circumstances that, acting together, brought about the
leasing of the arable demesne and the breaking up of the old
manorial organization. The date of the adoption of this policy of
leasing the arable demesne cannot be exactly determined, but there
can be little doubt that it was within the period 1358–73[1].

The 30 acres of meadow and the customary labour of the tenants
that mowed the meadow were farmed to the two bondmen who had
also farmed the arable demesne.

As a result of the breaking up of the unity of the demesne, the
lord had less use than before for labour rents and rents in kind,
since there remained in his possession only some of the buildings
in the court-yard, part of the pasture and the waste. A few of the
labour rents were sold at a profit to one of the farmers of the

---

[1] The lease in force in 1376–78 was granted in 1373. It is possible that the demesne was
first leased somewhat earlier. The court rolls, 1332–58, record no instance of the leasing
of land by the lord for terms of years. For the period between 1358 and 1373 the rolls are
missing. After 1373, numerous leases by the lord are entered upon the rolls.

demesne[1]; others were employed in repairing demesne buildings and walls[2], making hedges[2], cutting underbrush[2], and in performing a variety of carrying services (*averagia*)[3].

A question of prime importance to the lord—the effect of these changes in administration and organization upon the net profits from the manor—must be next considered. On this question a comparison of the following table with those already given on pp. 37–44 will throw some light. Only a brief comment upon the various items of the table need be added.

Receipts.

	1376–77				1377–78			
	£.	s.	d.	q.	£.	s.	d.	q.
Fixed rents	20	15	6	1	20	14	6	0
Farm of market		6	8	0		6	8	0
Farm of lands	17	16	10	2	18	12	4	2
Farm of Demesne	14	7	11	0	14	6	9	0
Sale of uncertain rents and works	8	12	1	1	6	17	9	2⅓
Office of reeve	2	0	0	0	2	0	0	0
Sale of pasture	1	18	9	0	1	14	11	0
Sale of underwood		6	4	0		3	6	0
Sale of grain	4	6	4	0	1	15	7	2
Perquisites of court	21	11	6	0	13	4	5	0
Sales on account		5	1	2		2	11	0
Total	92	7	1	2	79	19	5	2⅓

Expenses.

	1376–77				1377–78			
	£.	s.	d.	q.	£.	s.	d.	q.
Tithe		3	6	1		3	8	3
Rents paid and decayed	2	10	4	1½	2	2	3	1½
Buildings, gates, and walls ...	8	2	11	2	5	11	2	2
Cost of fold and sheep					1	11	9	2
Necessary expenses		3	10	0		12	9	2
Wages	2	0	0	0	2	5	3	0
Steward and visitors	4	9	6	2	1	13	11	2
Sheep					14	6	6	0
Total	17	10	2	2½	28	7	6	0½
Net profit	74	16	10	3½	51	11	11	2

The increase since 1307 in the amount of fixed rents was relatively greater than the increase between 1273 and 1307. A few of

---

[1] Appendix IX. li.   They were sold to the farmer of the demesne at 3*d.* apiece. Had they been commuted by the tenants they would have brought but 1*d.* apiece.

[2] Appendix IX. lxii., lxiii., lxvi., lxvii.   [3] Appendix IX. lxv.

the new payments are noteworthy. Two men paid that they might be 'unburdened' of their 5-acre holdings[1], and 5-acre tenements were held by a peculiarly onerous tenure[2]. The wife of Thomas Southauwe paid 15s. yearly that she might be excused from the performance of all works and customs[1]. A bondman paid 18d. for license to live outside the demesne[1]. There were many payments ('increments') from bondmen who had purchased land originally free[3].

The 250 acres or thereabouts of farmed land had come into the lord's hands in the two ways already noted[4]. Some of the leases recorded were granted in 1370. There is no evidence of earlier leasing of demesne land for terms of years. There are, however, many early instances of leasing. Thus the manor of Witlingham, which was in Earl Bigod's hands during the minority of the heir, was farmed from 1278–80, and there are many similar cases recorded on the early account rolls. Market tolls were farmed as was also the milk of cows. In 1300 a payment was made for land which had been granted for the term of life. In the court roll of 1358 a similar grant was entered. In 1332 a tenant paid a fine for 'having his term' in land hired from another tenant for the term of six years. But as has been said there is no instance of the farming of demesne land for a term of years prior to 1370. Now, in some cases, where the land had been heavily burdened with labour services, the rent paid by the lessee to the lord did not equal the value of the labour services previously due from the land. On the other hand, some of the land which had fallen into the lord's hands had apparently been very lightly charged, either with money rents or with services. In the case of such land the lord gained by letting it on the new terms. On the whole these 250 acres now brought to the lord nearly as much as before. The demesne, however, leased partly as arable, partly as pasture, was distinctly less valuable than before.

In comparing the net profits from the manor in 1376–77 with those accruing between 1272–1307 it must be remembered that in the earlier period some of the grain and stock were used in provisioning the earl's larder, or were sent to other of the manors of the earl. In 1376–78, on the contrary, the net profits represent the whole of the income from the manor.

Allowing then for the value of stock and grain used by the earl in the earlier period, the decrease in the value of the manor of Forncett by 1376–77 may be estimated as about £30.

---

[1] Appendix IX. xliii.   [2] See below, p. 65.
[3] Appendix IX. xlii ff.   [4] See above, p. 51.

CHAPTER IV.

THE DEMESNE. 1400—1605.

In 1400 a jury made presentment that during the time of Countess Margaret (1372–99) the buildings within the manor court had suffered waste and had decreased in value more than £33[1].

The decline in value was itemized as follows:

							£.	s.	d.
The great hall	...	...	...	...	...	...	2	0	0
The long house	...	...	...	...	...	...	5	0	0
Kitchen and stable...	...	...	...	...	...		6	8
Granary	...	...	...	...	...	...	2	0	0
Small hall with chamber annexed ...	...	...	...	...	2	0	0
Grange	...	...	...	...	...	...	20	0	0
House next the gate ...	...	...	...	...	...	2	0	0
Total ...	...	...	...	...	...	...	33	6	8

The loss was most considerable in the case of the grange. Since the arable demesne was no longer in the lord's hands this building had ceased to be of use.

In 1432–33 the hall, kitchen, and other 'houses' were still standing[2].

---

[1] Appendix X. lxxiii.

[2] This appears from a presentment made by the jury in the court of August, 1433, concerning the expenses of the bailiff during the time of Lady Katherine, i.e. after October, 1432. The presentment was as follows:

In fensura et clausura manerii, vis. vid.

In stramine empto pro coopertura domorum manerii cum cariagio ejusdem straminis, vis.
In coopertura dictarum domorum per vi. dies cum i. homine et serviente suo, iiis. vid.
Item in broches et swethis pro eodem, iid.
Item in i. porta pro le Dammedewe, vid.
Item soluti i. homini pro emendatione cepi circa dictum pratum vocatum Dammedewe per iii. dies, xiid.
Item soluti i. homini pro emendatione cepi circa boscum dominae vocatum Gyldriswode per iii. dies, xiid.
Item in Hokys et Hengelys pro aula et coquina in manerio, xvid.
Item soluti uno carpentario conducto per iii. dies faciendum hostia aulae et coquinae et le trestelle, xiid.
Item uno homini falcando pratum dominae vocatum Stubbyng, videlicet scar pro coopertura domorum manerii per ii. dies, xvid.
Item pro factura et vertura ejusdem, vid.
Item pro cariagio ejusdem usque manerium, vid.
It is to be noted that the wages of labour in 1433 were the same as in 1376–78, sixty years

No later reference to the manor-house has been found in the rolls. There is evidence that before 1491 the manor-house had disappeared, for in that year a tenant held "scitum manerii vocatum le Maner Yerd cum i. domo in eodem scitu vocata le Incethous[1]."

It has been seen that some 180 acres of arable demesne lay in scattered pieces of various sizes, while 120 acres formed the single piece known as Westwood Ridding.

In 1373 the scattered arable was leased as a whole. Later it was let in small parcels to many tenants. Thus in 1412, 7 acres were let to one tenant, 3½ acres to a second, 3 acres to a third, and one acre to a fourth. Some of the pieces were let for terms of years, others from year to year[2].

In the case of the demesne, as of other lands that were let to farm, leases for six or seven years were followed by leases for longer terms of 12, 20, or 40 years. Toward the end of the fifteenth century the system of leasing former demesne for terms of years, or from year to year, was practically abandoned. Lands formerly held by this tenure were granted to be held 'at fee farm,' i.e. at a perpetual money rent. They were conveyed in the manor court like copyhold, and like copyhold were held "ad voluntatem domini secundum consuetudinem manerii."

To illustrate these changes in tenure the conveyances relating to one small parcel of the demesne are appended[3]. The history of this piece is that of the whole demesne, except that some of the pieces were for a time let from year to year.

Although in the thirteenth century Westwood Ridding had been arable, in the latter fourteenth and in the early fifteenth century it was used for pasture. In 1373 the pasturage of the Ridding was let for seven years. In 1406 'one piece of pasture called le Redyng,' and containing 120 acres, was let for seven years at 30s. In 1411 it was again farmed as a whole for 33s. 4d. In 1431 'one half of the close called Ridding' was farmed. In 1467 this piece was divided into halves, which were granted to different tenants to hold at fee farm. In 1431 a parcel of 25 acres was farmed for 10 years. In

---

before. In both years a carpenter received 4d. a day, and a thatcher and his assistant 7d. between them. In 1433 the work of repairing hedges was paid at the rate of 4d. a day. In 1376–78 the wages paid for ditching and plastering were 3d. or 4d.

[1] From a later conveyance of this property it appears that the 'incet house' was a stable.

[2] 1497. Grant to W. F. of 6 a. 2 r. lately demesne which W. F. lately took to farm 'de anno in annum.' There are other similar entries.

[3] Appendix XI. lxxv, lxxvi.

1478 this was granted in parcels of 20 and of 5 acres respectively to different tenants to hold at fee farm. In 1438, 30 acres were farmed for 12 years, and in 1474 this piece "jacens pro xxx. acris" was granted in fee farm.

During the thirty years following the period dealt with in the last chapter, land held by labour services continued to revert to the lord, and to be leased by him at money rents. By 1406 nearly all of the land that had once rendered week-work had thus been converted into leasehold, which finally, as has been shown, came to be held at fee farm rents. In this year, out of the 3219 winter, summer, and autumn diets formerly charged upon the manor, only 195 were available; and out of the 1505 winter-works for which the customers had once been accountable, only 45, or less than those formerly due from a single typical customers' tenement, were still owed[1].

We have seen[2] that the net profits from the manor were considerably less in 1378 than they had been in the thirteenth century. In 1409–10 the manor was let to farm for the yearly rent of £60[3].

A statement of the receipts from the manor in 1527–28[4] gives the following particulars:

1527–8

							£.	s.	d.
Rents and farms	...	...	...	...	...	...	55	5	11
Courts	...	...	...	...	...	...	12	2	4
Fines from two bondmen	...	...	...	...	...	10	0	0
Total receipts	...	...	...	...	..	...	77	8	3

---

[1] An Escheators' Inquisition for 1406 states the number of works due in that year from the manor. The following entry from a Court Roll of 1439 affords further evidence that this land was let to farm: 'Jur' praesentant quod omnia terrae et tenementa hujus manerii quae reddere solebant reddita avenarum sunt decasa in manu dominae et dimittuntur parcellatim diversis tenentibus hujus dominii ad firmam pro quibus officiarii dominae debent allocari de redditu et servitiis dictorum terrarum et tenementorum causa praedicta.' Since oat-rents were paid by nearly all of the tenements that rendered week-work (see table, pp. 60, 61), it is evident that all or nearly all of these tenements must have been in the lord's hands by 1439. The presentment of the jury in 1433 (see footnote, p. 56) shows that services formerly rendered by customary labour were now performed by hired labour.

[2] p. 55.

[3] 'Firma manerii de Fornsete. Willelmus Rees et Jacobus Billyngford firmarii manerii de Fornesete respondunt de lx. *l.* de firma sua ejusdem manerii per litteras Regis patentes eisdem concessas solvendis ad terminos Paschae et Sancti Michaelis.' Min. Acc'ts, 1093/1.

[4] Heralds' College. Arundel MSS., no. 49, folio 24. The items regarding the fines of bondmen read as follows:

'It'm le xxv. iour de Marcz rec' de Wauter Bolyaute de fyn qil ne portera plus d'office vers ma dame en la ser[iant]ie de Fornesete, c. *s.*...... It'm receu de la fyn William Hernyng pur avois fait a ma dame, c. *s.*'

An account roll of 1604–5 shows that the net profits from the manor in that year were £50.

1604–5

Receipts.

	£.	s.	d.
Fixed rents	39	9	0¾
Farm of demesne meadow, woods, etc.	7	15	0
Courts	7	13	9
Total	54	17	9¾

Expenses.

	£.	s.	d.
Rents paid (Castleward)		1	4
Steward and accountant	4	15	8
Total	4	17	0
Net profit	50	0	9¾

Our evidence, then, points to the conclusion that during the period 1400–1605 the net profits of the manor continued to decline.

The rents were for the most part fixed in amount, and, with the fall in the value of money in the sixteenth century, became less valuable to the lord. With the extinction of serfdom, which was complete in Forncett manor in the year 1575, a source of revenue ceased. Tallage, and such payments as merchet, chevage, and fines to administer the goods of deceased serfs, were no longer rendered. The courts also were less profitable than in earlier times, and the mill was no longer a source of income[1].

---

[1] Escheators' Inquisition, 1406. Mill used to be let for 20*s.* Out of repair and worth nothing.

Table based on Account Rolls of 1376—8, Appendix IX.

	Lands and tenements 1376–8	Area		Former money rents (App. IX., liii ff.)		Misc. money payments	Carriage of manure	Saltpenny	Oats		Hens	Eggs	Winter works	Summer works	Averagia	Malt	Autumn works	Autumn carriages	Misc. services	Money value of services and payments		Ditto per acre		Rent 1376–8		Ditto per acre		Gain or loss to lord + = Gain − = Loss		Ditto per acre	
		a.	r.	s.	d.	d.			qr.	bu.										s.	d.	s.	d.	s.	d.	s.	d.	s.	d.	s.	d.
1	Stalon		2	1	0	—	—	—		—	1	5	—	—	—	—	—	—	—	1	2¼	2	4½		—		—		—		—
2	Ivo Charer	—		3	8¾	—	—	—		—	—	—	—	—	—	—	—	—	—	3	8¾		—		—		—		—		—
3	J. Hors	[2	2][1]		2¾	—	—	—		6	1	5	35	10	3	—	16	—	—	5	5	2	2	1	8		8	−3	9	−1	6
4	R. Fledede	—			9¼	—	—	—		—	½	2½	—	—	1½	—	1½	½	—	1	1⅝		—		—		—		—		—
5	R. Agas	—			4	—	—	—		—	1	5	—	—	—	—	—	—	—		6¼		—		—		—		—		—
6	D. Toward	4	0	1	0	—	—	—		—	1	5	—	—	—	—	—	—	—	1	2¼		3½	1	4		4		+1¾		+½
7	M. Hippele	—			6½	—	6}	2¼	1	4	1	5	70	10	3	1	24	—	—	10	2¼		—		—		—		—		—
8	Tedgor	[5][2]	0		10	—	6}		1	4	1	5	—	10	1½	1	—	—	—	6	2¼	1	2¾	3	4[3]		7¾	−2	11		−7
9	R. Petyfer	2	0		4	—	—	—		—	—	—	—	—	—	—	—	—	—		4		2		—		—		—		—
10	Rust voc. Bert	—			7½	—	—	—		—	1	5	—	—	3	—	24	—	3[4]	3	5¼		—		—		—		—		—
11	Elred	[5]	0		6½	—	6	1¾		—	1	5	70	10	3	1	—	—	—	4	2¼		10	4	6		10¾		+3¾		+¾
12	Lestan	[2	2][5]		2¾	—	—	—		6	1	5	35	10	3	—	16	—	—	5	5	2	2	2	8	1	¾	−2	9	−1	1¼
13	J. Asshewelle		3		2	1½[6]	—	—		—	—	—	—	—	—	—	—	—	—		3½		4¾		—		—		—		—
14	J. Kyng	5	0		6½	—	6	1¾	1	4	1	5	70	10	3	1	24	—	—	10	2¼	2	½	5	8	1	1½	−4	6¼		−10¾
15	R. Jebat	5	0		6½	—	6	1¾	1	4	1	5	70	10	3	1	24	—	—	10	2¼	2	½		—		—		—		—
16	J. Ulfi or Ulsi	5	0		6½	—	6	1¾	1	4	1	5	70	10	3	1	24	—	—	10	2¼	2	½	[5	2½][7]	[1	½][7]	[4	11¾][7]	[1][7]	
17	J. de Fornecete q. Elfled	5	0		6½	—	6	1¾	1	4	1	5	70	10	3	1	24	—	—	10	2¼	2	½		—		—		—		—
18	voc. Wrong	[5]	0		11¼	—	—	—		—	—	—	—	—	—	—	—	—	—		11¼		2¼	4	6		10¾	+3	6¾		+8½
19	Warde	5	0		6½	—	6	1¾	1	4	1	5	70	10	3	1	—	—	—	8	2¼	1	7¾		—		—		—		—
20	T. Southawe	10	0		6½	—	12	1¾	3	0	1	5	70	10	3	2	40	—	—	16	2¼	1	7½	15	0	1	6	−1	2¼		−1½
21	Bagfens		3		—	4[8]	—	—		—	—	—	—	—	—	—	—	—	—		4		5¼		—		—		—		—
22	Dewey nuper Toly	1	0		—	2[8]	—	—		—	—	—	—	—	—	—	—	—	—		2		2		—		—		—		—
23	R. Galgrim	5	0		6½	—	6	1¾	1	4	1	5	70	10	3	1	24	—	—	10	2¼	2	½	6	8	1	4	−3	6¼		−8½
24	S. Spellere	5	0		6½	—	6	1¾	1	4	1	5	70	10	3	1	24	—	—	10	2¼	2	½	}							
25	S. Spellere	1	3		4	9¼[9]	1	—		—	—	—	—	—	—	—	—	—	—	1	2¼		8¼	} 4	11		8¾	−6	5½		−11½
26	Gallard nuper Raven	—			6½	—	—	—		—	—	—	—	—	—	—	—	1	—		7½		—		—		—		—		—
27	W. Florance[10]	2	2		6½	—	—	—		6	1	5	—	—	3	—	16	—	—	4	5¼		—	3	2		—	−1	3¼		—
28	Bretone	—			6	—	—	—		—	1	5	—	—	1	—	1	½	—		11¼		—		—		—		—		—
29	W. Pote	5	0	1	2	—	—	—		—	—	—	—	—	—	—	—	—	—	1	2		2¾		—		—		—		—
30	H. Baroun	5	0		6½	—	6	1¾	1	4	1	5	70	10	3	1	32	—	—	10	10¼	2	2		—		—		—		—
31	Toly		[11]		6	—	—	—		—	—	—	—	—	—	—	—	—	—		6	10	0	10	0		—	+9	6		—
32	Geyres[12]	2	2[13]		6¾	—	—	—		—	1½	7½	—	—	3	—	11	1½	—	2	3¼		—		—		—		—		—
33	Elfled	—			2¾	—	—	—		—	3	15	—	—	—	—	—	—	—		9½		—		—		—		—		—
34	Clerkes	¼ of lands			10½	—	9[14]	—		—	—	—	—	—	—	—	—	—	—	1	7½		—	7	0		—	+5	4½		—
35	A. Baldewyne	1	0		1½	—	—	—		—	—	—	—	—	—	—	—	—	—		1½		1½	1	0	1	0		+10½		+10½
36	Durraunt	2	2		3¼	—	3	—		6	1	5	33	5	1½	—	16	—	—	5	3¾	2	1½	2	2		10½	−3	1¾	−1	3
37	Carletone	4	0	1	0	5⅝[15]	—	—		—	—	—	—	—	—	—	—	—	—	1	5⅝		4½		—		4		—		−½
38	Hapton q. Unwyne		2		1	—	—	—		—	—	—	—	—	—	—	—	—	—		1		2		2		4		+1		+2

39	Grey
40	T. Avelyn
41	Lythfot
42	Clyre
43	R. de Wode q. H. Raven
44	W. Scrape
45	Hulot
46	A. Baldewyne
47	Gosses
48	Bygges
49	Bacon
50	Herberd or Crowes
51	W. Gallard
52	Sot
53	Bottes
54	Schacheloke
55	Ten. retro stabulum
56	A. Lavendre
57	Mones
58	Pote in Wacton
59	Edwardes
60	Broketothe
61	Redynge or atte Hill
62	Coleman
63	Rougheye n. Baroun
64	q. R. Galgrym
65	Raven q. Scathelok
66	Splyttes
67	Spyr
68	R. Hulle
69	R. Gallard

[1] In the list of tenements in the survey of 1565, the area of tenement Hors is given as 2 a. 2 r. pertaining to this tenement were leased. The area that had reverted to the lord is therefore reckoned as 2 a. 2 r. In 1376–7, 2 a. 2 r.

[2] This was the area farmed in 1376–7.

[3] Includes rent for two messuages.

[4] Harrowings worth 1d. apiece.

[5] This was the amount farmed in 1376–7.

[6] 'Ex de aliis consuetudinibus 11½d.' apiece.

[7] 5 acres ten. Ulfi and 3 rods ten. Hippel were let together for 6s.

[8] 'pro omnibus servitiis.'

[9] 'Et pro aliis operibus [consuetudinibus] extra non computatis.'

[10] It is assumed that 'Tenementum Willelmi Florance' is the same as the two (or two-and-a-half) acres 'quondam Florance.'

[11] It is not quite clear whether 25 acres or 12½ acres were farmed.

[12] = Greyes (?).

[13] Sometimes given as 3½ acres.

[14] 'Et operibus extra non computatis.'

[15] 'Et de aliis operibus extra non computatis.'

[16] 1 r. and a messuage were rented.

[17] Of which 1 a. 1 r. were meadow. Note that this tenement paid 'medweerth.'

[18] Medweerth, worth 3d.

[19] 'Et pro consuetudinibus extra non computatis.'

[20] No allowance is made for these services and payments in the roll of 1376–7. They are however allowed for as decayed in the roll of 1377–8.

[21] ½ a. was farmed for 3d. or at a gain of 4½d. per acre.

[22] Capons worth 4d. apiece.

[23] 2 r. 'quondam Hugonis ate Hill' were let for 4d.

CHAPTER V.

THE TENANTS AND THEIR LAND. 1272—1306.

LITTLE direct evidence has been found concerning the number and economic condition of the tenants of Forncett manor in the thirteenth and fourteenth centuries, but the Account Rolls, though primarily treating of the demesne, incidentally furnish material from which some inferences regarding the economic position of the tenants of the manor may be drawn.

From the table on pp. 60, 61, it appears that the lands that, by 1376, had fallen into the lord's hands, had previously been burdened with payments and services of various kinds. Some were probably free lands[1], but by far the larger part were bond tenements or portions of bond tenements.

The tenements may be roughly classified according to the nature and amount of the services with which they had been charged. On these grounds two main classes of tenements may be distinguished, and these again may be further subdivided.

The first main class comprises such tenements as either rendered no week-work at all, or else rendered it only during the autumn. Tenements in this class would fall into one or the other of two groups. First, tenements that did not render labour services, but paid either money rents only, or in addition such insignificant rents in kind, as a hen and a few eggs yearly; this group was a very small one, and probably consisted only of such tenements as had been freed from their labour dues, through commutation or otherwise[2]. Second, tenements rendering such labour services as *averagia*, autumn cartings, occasional autumn day-works, and, in some instances, week-work in the autumn. This group was very large.

---

[1] For example, no. 49, p. 61, the 'divers lands' of Robert Bacon. Bacon had been outlawed for felony. He held 60 acres in chief of Forncett manor and 16 acres of Moulton manor. Inq. p. m. 46 Edw. III., 2nd nrs., no. 57 a, and 50 Edw. III., 2nd nrs., no. 6.

[2] No. 2, p. 60 falls within this group. The large money rent paid by this tenement suggests commutation.

The second main class consisted of the tenements that rendered week-work during the winter, spring, and summer. This class may be divided into two groups. First, the tenements rendering the heavier week-work, *i.e.* two days' work weekly from September 29 to August 1, with the exception of four holiday weeks; and three days' work weekly from August 1 to September 29[1]. These tenements were, as a rule, five acres in area, and were held by what was called "five-acre tenure." One tenement, charged with exceptionally heavy services, included 10 acres[2]. The second group consisted of tenements rendering lighter week-work—one day weekly from September 29 to June 29, with four holiday weeks; one or in some cases two days' work weekly from June 29 to August 1, and two—in some cases three—days' work weekly from August 1 to September 29. These tenements had an area of two and-a-half acres.

A classification of tenants roughly parallel to that of the tenements gives the following groups: Sokemen, occupants of tenements of the first class; customary tenants of five-acre holdings, customary tenants of two-and-a-half-acre holdings, occupants of tenements of the second class[3].

The free tenants performed few labour services, and these services seem to have been charged upon the individual tenants, rather than upon their holdings. When the barley, the principal crop, was being sown, and there was an unusual demand for plow-teams, the teams of the free tenants as well as those of the customary tenants and of the sokemen were called upon for a day's boon work. On this occasion the lord provided food for the plowmen. Between 1272 and 1306 the teams of the free tenants seem actually to have performed the work. But their service was *nullius pretii*, and when, as in 1376, this kind of service was no longer demanded, the free tenants would not pay a money equivalent for the work that they were no longer called upon to do[4].

---

[1] Winter works extended from September 29 to June 29, a period of 39 weeks. As either 70 or 35 works of this kind were usually charged upon a tenement (see table, pp. 60, 61) there would seem to have been four holiday weeks during this season. These were probably two weeks at Christmas, one week at Easter, and one week at Whitsuntide (cf. Cunningham, *Growth of Eng. Ind.*, 3rd edition, I. 585, also I. 583). Summer works extended over the five weeks from June 29 to Aug. 1, autumn works over the eight weeks from Aug. 1 to Sept. 29. Min. Acc'ts, 935/11.

[2] No. 20, p. 60.

[3] For a somewhat similar though more elaborate classification dating from the thirteenth century, see Vinogradoff, *op. cit.*, 186. For classes of sokemen, see below, p. 83 ff.

[4] 'Et de ii. precariis ad ordeum de exitu custumariorum de sokemennis…pretium precariae iiii*d*. Et de ii. precariis nullius pretii de exitu liberorum tenentium…De quibus in venditione …ii. De residuo nihil quia licet non faciant nihil dominae dabunt.' Appendix IX, lxiv.

Sokemen are frequently and consistently distinguished from free tenants on the one hand, and from customary tenants on the other hand. Unlike the free tenants, the bond sokemen paid a money equivalent for such labour dues as they did not perform. Unlike the customary tenants, the sokemen did not perform week-work, at least throughout the year. Like the customary tenants, the sokemen assisted in ploughing the demesne. But while each of the teams of the customary tenants, which during this period numbered from four-and-a-half to two, ploughed once every week from Purification to Pentecost, the sokemen's teams, numbering from twenty-three to fourteen, made but three ploughings each during the year. The ploughings of the customary tenants were simply that form of labour by which, in the spring, a part of their regular week-work was discharged ; so that the reeve, in making his annual account, 'allowed' to the tenants a number of week-works corresponding to the number of customary ploughings performed. But the reeve made no such allowance for the ploughings of the sokemen ; so that either the ploughings of the sokemen were additional to the week-work rendered by them, or else the sokemen were not burdened with winter week-work. The latter explanation is doubtless the true one, for the number of tenements rendering week-work was so small[1] that, at most, week-work could have been charged upon only a very small proportion of the tenements of the sokemen. It would seem, therefore, that the sokemen were not burdened with week-work, at least during the greater part of the year, and that in just this fact lay a principal line of demarcation between them and the customary tenants. Besides the ploughings, the sokemen performed carrying services (*averagia*) ; three was the number of these usually charged upon a tenement. At an earlier period than that now under consideration they took part in the autumn *precariae*[2]. But from 1272 to 1306 the autumn *precariae* were not demanded, but were 'sold' to the tenants. With the exception of autumn cartings, the other forms of labour-rents are registered as due from the customary tenants. The light labour-rents of the sokemen were not complemented by heavy payments in money or in kind. Yet for one privilege they paid more highly than the customary tenants ; for, while the sokemen paid 1*d.* for every cow and for every five sheep not sent to lie in the lord's fold, the customary tenants paid only half as much for the privilege of folding their own beasts.

[1] Cf. table, p. 67.   [2] Min. Acct's, 935/2.

In contrast to the more lightly burdened tenements of the sokemen, stand the tenements that rendered week-work. Besides the week-works the tenement of five-acre tenure seems usually to have been charged with the following annual dues : three *averagia*, the carting of manure—a service that after 1300 seems always to have been commuted ; the making of a quarter of malt; the payment of twelve bushels of oats; of a hen and five eggs ; of $1\frac{3}{4}d$. as salt-penny ; and of a money rent of $6\frac{1}{2}d$. Now, estimating the value of these services and payments in kind at the amounts for which they were 'sold' to the tenant, when not rendered, a tenement of five-acre tenure was worth more than 2*s.* an acre[1]. But in 1376 these same tenements were being leased at half this rent per acre. Unless the value of the land had fallen by more than one-half between the beginning of the century and 1376, it would seem that the customary tenants of the earlier period were heavily burdened.

What were the number and area of the tenements that rendered winter and summer week-work, and in what ratio do their number and area stand to the number and area of the less burdened tenements? In attempting to find an answer to these questions a series of proportions is employed. These proportions are formed from the following known quantities :

(1) The number of tenements that formerly owed a given service, but by 1376 had decayed.

(2) The total number of services of this kind that by 1376 had decayed.

(3) The total number of services of this same kind that were charged upon the manor as a whole.

It is assumed that the ratio between the number of decayed tenements formerly owing a given service, and the total number of decayed services of this kind, is identical with the ratio between the whole number of tenements upon which this service is charged

---

[1] There was no fixed sum for which the oat-rent might be commuted. The value of this form of rent varied from year to year. The valuation adopted in the tables is 4*d.* a bushel, which is $1\frac{1}{2}d$. more for a quarter of oats than the average price per quarter between the years 1271 and 1380 according to Rogers, *Agric. and Prices*, I. 245. From 1272 to 1306, hens were worth 1*d.* a piece instead of 2*d.* as in 1376-8; and eggs were worth $3\frac{1}{2}d$. or 4*d.* instead of 5*d.* as in 1376-8.

With the possible exception of the service of carting manure, the value of which is not stated in the rolls of 1272–1306, labour services were commuted at the same price in the later as in the earlier period. In 1376, and apparently, though to a less degree, in 1272, the sums for which labour services might be commuted fell short of their actual value to the lord. Therefore the real value of the rent paid for these tenements was even higher than it is here estimated.

D.   5

and the whole number of services of this kind due from the entire manor[1]. Granting this assumption, a proportion may be formed from the three known quantities that will give the total number of tenements upon which a given service was formerly charged. The data required for forming the proportion are obtained from the account rolls.

$°/_o$ *of works and payments decayed.*

		1376–7	1377–8
Winter works		71·8	83·4
Summer works	$°/_o$ decayed of works charged in 1272—		
	1306	61·2	71·5
	Ditto in 1376	30·6	35·7
Salt-penny		61·7	61·7
Malt		60	74·4
Oats		52·6	57·7
Autumn works		33	39
Hens		21·6 or 31·2	24·4 or 37
Averagia		20	23·6
Autumn cartings		9·3	21

In drawing up that part of the account that relates to the services and customs due from the tenants of the manor the method was regularly followed of first setting down the total number of services of any kind with which the whole manor was charged, and then recording how many of these services had been performed or sold or were decayed. The number of the different sorts of services thus charged upon the manor varied little from year to year. A comparison of the rolls of 1272 and 1376 shows that, except in the case of summer works, there was little change in this respect for more than a century. This the following table shows.

[1] It would be difficult to prove positively the validity of this assumption, unless precisely what is sought for were already known, viz. the total number of tenements charged with a given service; but certain considerations make it probable that the ratios in question do not differ very widely from one another. For, first, in the case of certain services and payments the amount rendered by the several decayed tenements was uniform. Hence it seems probable that the tenements that had not decayed likewise rendered, severally, the same amount of these kinds of services. If this were so the ratios in question would clearly be the same. Further, in most of the cases where the burden was not laid upon the several tenements with exact uniformity, it was nevertheless imposed with a high degree of regularity. Again, as the above table indicates, the number of decayed services is a large proportion of the total number of services charged upon the manor.

Services and payments in kind charged upon the manor.

	1272	1376
Oats	43½ qr.	43½ qr.
Hens	170	176
Eggs	910[1]	1010
Winter works	1505	1505
Summer works	245	490
Averagia	341	341
Malt made	21 qr.	21½ qr.
Autumn works	1223	1224
Autumn cartings	43	43
Carting of manure	43	Not separately accounted for

The number of tenements that had formerly owed a given service but by 1376 had decayed, as well as the total number of services of this kind that by 1376 had decayed, can be readily ascertained from the table on pp. 60, 61. Thus it is found from this table that in 1376–8 18 decayed tenements were charged with 1081 winter (week-) works. Now the total number of winter works due from the manor was 1505. It is therefore probable that these 1505 works were formerly borne by some 25 tenements. In like manner the number of tenements owing the several sorts of payments in kind and services may be found. The following table gives the results obtained :

Salt-penny was due from 18 tenements
Malt was made by 21½ tenements
Winter week-works were due from 25 tenements
Summer   „   „   26   „
Oats were due from 36 tenements
Autumn cartings were due from 64½ tenements
Autumn works   „   78   „
Hens   „   116[2]   „
Averagia   „   134   „

The table shows the approximate distribution of the different kinds of services upon the tenements about 1376. There is, however, reason to suppose that at a much earlier time, a century or more before, the distribution was somewhat different. For the original

---

[1] In 1278, 1010 eggs.

[2] From 1272–1306, 60 additional hens were paid as 'lok silver.' These were probably a fixed charge upon the whole manor and not divided among the different tenements.

holdings would tend to become divided, and the services formerly rendered by a single tenement would later be performed by two or more. The account rolls indeed bear traces of a time when the number of tenements rendering week-work was smaller than that indicated in the table. According to the table, 25 or 26 tenements owed week-work from September 29 to August 1. But it is noticeable that in computing the number of the several kinds of services and payments due from the manor the number 21½ was, in many cases, taken as the basis of calculation. Thus 1505 winter works were due from the manor, that is, 70 works from each of 21½ tenements[1]. The 245 summer works charged upon the manor are not so evidently calculated upon this basis ; 10 summer works seem to have been the full quota due from a single tenement[2]. It would have taken 21½ + 3 tenements to perform the whole number laid upon the manor. Forty-three summer works were allowed for the mowing of the demesne meadows, perhaps two works from each of 21½ tenements. Forty-three cartings of manure were also due ; 21, later 21½ quarters of malt were due, and the table on pp. 60, 61 shows that 1 quarter was regularly paid by a single tenement; 43½ quarters of oats were due, but, in this case, 1½ quarters was the full amount usually imposed upon one tenement. Forty-three autumn cartings were due, but here again it must be admitted that the evidence of the rolls of 1376–8 does not point to the distribution of this form of service among only 21½ tenements, but among a considerably larger number. *Averagia*, autumn works, and payment of hens were certainly rendered by sokemen[3]. It is not therefore surprising that they are not calculated upon the basis of 21½ customary tenements.

The table on p. 67 indicates that the number of tenements charged with winter and summer week-work was considerably less than the number of tenements charged with such dues as *averagia* and autumn cartings.

The area burdened with week-work may be roughly estimated at 125 acres, while the area charged with lighter labour dues, but free from week-work during at least three-fourths of the year, may be

---

[1] Cf. table, pp. 60, 61 which shows that 70 was the number of winter works regularly due from a tenement.

[2] See table, pp. 60, 61.

[3] Cf. above, p. 64, Appendix VIII. xl., xli. and other Ministers' Accounts. The Account Rolls of 1376–8, Appendix IX. lxi., and a few of the earlier Rolls fail to make the usual and doubtless correct distinction between works rendered by customers and works rendered by sokemen. This failure probably signifies nothing more than carelessness on the part of the accountants' clerks.

estimated at 875 acres[1]. The tenants of the 125 acres appear to have been known as customary tenants, the tenants of the 875 acres as sokemen.

The evidence regarding the number of plough teams owned by sokemen and 'customers' respectively, supports the conclusion that has been reached regarding the acreage held by these two classes. The customary tenants, as has been said, furnished from 2 to $4\frac{1}{2}$ teams for the demesne ploughing ; the sokemen furnished from 14 to 23 teams ; the free tenants, in 1272–3, $16\frac{1}{2}$ teams. The area held by each of these classes cannot be precisely stated on account of the fact that some of the free land had been soiled. It is impossible to determine precisely the quantity of land that had been soiled by 1272, but it may be very roughly estimated at about 200 acres[2]. If this estimate be correct the customary tenants must then have held about 150 acres, including 25 acres 'soiled'; the sokemen 1050 acres, and the free tenants 1050 acres.

The lack of court rolls prevents us from speaking with certainty of the legal tenure by which sokemen held their land during the period dealt with in this chapter ; but by the end of the fourteenth century, at all events, the land that during the thirteenth century had been held by sokemen and by customers was classified as *terra nativa*. In the method of conveyance, and in the legal nature of the tenure by which they were held, it does not appear possible to distinguish in the later records between what had been the lightly-burdened tenements of the sokemen and the heavily-burdened tenements of the customers. By 1400 both were 'copyhold.'

On the important question of the status of the sokemen the documents throw a somewhat uncertain light. The hypothesis that best explains the recorded facts is that there were both free and bond sokemen within the manor[3].

---

[1] In 1376, some 25 tenements were charged with winter week-work. One of these tenements was 10 acres ; the other 17 of which the area is known were either 5 acres or $2\frac{1}{2}$ acres. Therefore it is probable that the area charged with week-work throughout the year did not exceed 125 acres. From the survey of 1565, we learn that some 1000 acres of bond land, exclusive of former demesne, were held of Forncett manor. Deducting 125 acres from 1000 acres we have 875 acres remaining as lightly-burdened bond land. In 1565 free land and 'soiled' land together amounted to about 1250 acres.

[2] In 1565 there were about 525 acres of soiled land.

[3] This question is discussed more fully on pp. 83–85.

CHAPTER VI.

THE TENANTS AND THEIR LAND. 1376—1378[1].

CONCERNING the freeholders (*libere tenentes*) the rolls say little, but they contain several references to free land (*terra libera*). The area of free land (that is, in general, in the case of Forncett manor, land held by charter) continued to decrease as a result of its conversion into *terra soliata*. No bondman of Forncett manor might hold *terra libera*. If land held by charter were purchased by a serf he was obliged to surrender it to the lord's representative in the manorial court, receiving it again to hold at a nominal rent *per virgam ad voluntatem domini*. Henceforth the land was known as *terra tenta per incrementum redditus*, or, more commonly, as *terra soliata (terra solidata)*. The distinction between *terra nativa* and *terra soliata* was regularly maintained, but they were both conveyed in the same way, and if there were any difference in the legal nature of the tenures by which they were held it is not apparent from the rolls. Already in the thirteenth century free land was being converted into 'soiled' land[2]. Between 1358 and 1376, 10½ messuages and some 50 acres were degraded to the lower tenure[3]. By 1378 about one-fourth of the *terra nativa* (250 acres) had reverted to the lady of the manor and had been let for money rents. Among these 250 acres were included some of the lightly burdened tenements of the sokemen, and some of the heavily burdened tenements of the customers. But a far greater proportion of the customers' tenements than of the sokemen's tenements had escheated. Thus, by September, 1377, 15[4] of the 25 customers' tenements had fallen into the lady's

[1] The material for this chapter consists of two bailiff's account rolls, for 1376–8 ; and ten court rolls for the years 1358, 1373 (2), 1374 (4), 1375, 1387, and 1394.

[2] Min. Acc'ts, 935/11.

[3] In the survey of 1565 the total recorded area of soiled land is about 525 acres. 22 soiled messuages are mentioned, but very possibly this list is incomplete.

[4] This is exclusive of no. 50 (p. 61) as the winter works due from this tenement were not accounted for as 'decayed' until the following year.

hands; while by September, 1378, 18 tenements had reverted and had been leased for money rents. Thus by 1378 the number of tenements from which week-work could be demanded during 35 weeks of the year had been reduced from 25 to 7. The area included within these 7 tenements must have been about 30 acres.

Of the 18 tenements fallen into the lady's hands, at least three[1] and probably four or more had been waived by their former occupiers. The tenants of two other tenements (nos. 11 and 14, p. 60) were making annual payments of 1s. and 2s. respectively that they might be 'exonerated' from their holdings. Two tenements (nos. 3 and 30) 'had escheated to the countess after the death of their former tenants,' and one (no. 36) had reverted 'for lack of tenants.' Two tenements (nos. 3 and 20), of which one (no. 3) has already been mentioned as escheating to the countess, had been freed from the performance of labour services, while still in the hands of their former tenants. Of these two tenements one had been freed by a charter from the earl, while 'by special favour' of a former lord of the manor the occupier of the other—a woman—had commuted the 'works and customs' due from all her lands and tenements by an annual payment of 15s. Of the remaining eight tenements it is only known that they reverted to the countess, and in apparently every instance had been let again to other than their former occupiers.

Tenants might 'waive' their holdings for different reasons. Extreme poverty or insufficient physical strength to work the holding and render the labour services might force them to relinquish their tenements, the rent of which they were no longer able to pay. The only cases of the waiving of tenements that appear in the extant Forncett records before 1350 were due to this cause. These cases are entered in the court roll of May 15, 1333. The two tenants who at that time waived their holdings did so *ob inopiam*, but in the latter part of the century the tenants seem to have waived their holdings for other reasons. As the table on pp. 60, 61 shows, the customers' tenements were paying high rents. The average rent per acre at which land was let in Forncett in 1376–8 was 10¾d. But the money value of the services and payments due from the 5-acre tenements of the customers, even when estimated at the very low rate for which the services and payments in kind might be com-

---

[1] These were tenements nos. 19, 44 and 69, pp. 60, 61; and probably also no. 17, for among the fugitive *nativi* named in the court roll of 1373 was a John of Fornesete, and it seems probable that he was the same John of Fornesete that held tenement no. 17 before it fell into the lady's hands, and that on fleeing from the manor he had 'waived' this tenement.

muted, was a little more than 2*s.* an acre[1]. This fact, even when taken by itself, would sufficiently explain why the customers should abandon their holdings.

It is not possible to state even approximately the number of sokemen's tenements that by 1378 had escheated. Many of these tenements had been divided and part of a tenement might fall into the lady's hands, while another part might continue to be held on the old terms. However, we may very roughly estimate the area originally included within sokemen's tenements but by 1378 fallen into the lady's hands, as between 20 and 25 °/₀ of the entire area originally included within the tenements of the sokemen. But of the area included within the tenements of the customers some 76 °/₀ had escheated.

Of the sokemen's tenements or fractions of tenements that had reverted to the lady, ten had escheated after the death of tenants and five had been waived[2]. Why these lands should have been waived is not obvious, for most of them were very lightly burdened and the tenants of some of them were not serfs[3], though the tenants of others may have been.

Though the material likely to contain evidence of the flight of serfs from the manor is very scanty for the period from 1350 to 1400[4], yet the few court rolls that remain show that many of the serfs were seeking to improve their economic or legal status through flight. Thus in a roll of the year 1373 eight bondmen and bondwomen are named as having 'withdrawn' from the manor. It is ordered to 'attach' these and 'all *other* bondmen and bondwomen who have withdrawn[5].' The same roll contains a memorandum to inquire whether a certain serf, not one of the eight named elsewhere

---

[1] Autumn works might be commuted for 1*d.* an acre, but in 1376–8, 40 of these works were let to one of the farmers of the demesne for 3*d.* apiece. If the other works were worth triple the price for which they might be commuted, the actual value of the rent of these customary tenants in case all the services due from them were performed, was 3*s.* 9*d.* an acre.

[2] Nos. 6, 33, 54, 62, and 63. Both nos. 6 and 62 were probably parts of tenement Coleman.

[3] How light were the burdens imposed on these tenements is shown by the fact that the money rent for which they were let in 1378 was greater than the money value of the dues with which they had been charged, estimated at the rate at which those dues might be commuted. See columns 18–22, table pp. 60, 61.

Thus Sir William Germyn, and probably Coleman and Smith were not serfs, but Schacheloke and Raven may have been.

[4] Between 1350 and 1400 from 200 to 250 manor courts must have been held at Forncett, but the rolls of only ten of these courts remain.

[5] 'Praeceptum est attachiare Johannem Baxtere de Multone, et Matthaeum Baxtere fratrem

in the roll, has withdrawn his chattels from the manor[1]. In a roll of
1374 there is an order to 'attach' still another fugitive bondman[2].
An unusually explicit entry occurs in the roll of 1394, where it is
recorded that William Bolytoute is fined 12d. 'because contrary to
the statute and to the prohibition of the steward, for the purpose of
getting greater gain in the autumn season, he withdrew from the vill
and from the lord's domain where he had been dwelling[3].'

Serfs were also paying 'head money' (*chevagium*) for license to
live outside the manor. Thus in 1376–8 John Rougheye made
annual payments of 18d., "pro licentia manendi extra dominium
dominae ad terminum vitae[4]." In 1394 five serfs paid similar fines[5].
In none of the rolls after 1350 are more than 15 serfs recorded as
paying chevage in any one year. Yet we have seen[6] that between
1272 and 1306 chevage was annually paid by some 100 persons
called indifferently *anelipimen* or *nativi manentes extra manerium*.
From 1272–1306, 1d. was the amount received from each of the
chevage-paying bondmen; but in the later fourteenth and in the
fifteenth and sixteenth centuries the fines ranged from 3d. to 3s. 4d.

The distinction between the position of the bondmen who
remained outside of the manor during the period from 1272–1306
and the position of those who fled from the manor during the latter
part of the same century was perhaps as follows: the former
remained outside the manor (i.e. were not tenants of the manor)[7]

ejus, Simonem Herberd Johannem Abotes et Willelmum atte...[nativos] dominae per corpora
eo quod elongant se extra dominium.

Et sicut alias, attachiare Johannem filium Bartholomei de Fornesete, Matildam et
Avelinam filias Johannis de Galgrym nativos dominae per corpora...se extra dominium
dominae. Et omnes alios nativos et nativas dominae qui se elongant, etc.'

1 'Memorandum ad proximam curiam ad inquirendum sive Ricardus Berteram nativus
dominae elongaverit catalla sua extra bondagium dominae necne. [In margin] Compertum
est quod conduxit catalla sua.'

2 'Johannes filius Ricardi Baldewyn manens in Bury, nativus dominae, elongat se extra
dominium dominae. Ideo praeceptum est ipsum attachiare per corpus.'

3 By 25 E. III. stat. II. c. 2, it was decreed that no servant 'go out of the town where
he dwelleth in the winter to serve the summer, if he may serve in the same town, taking
[wages] as before is said.'

4 Appendix IX. xliii.

5 'Fines, viis. xd. Johannes filius Willelmi Pelet (xviii*d*.) nativus dominae de sanguine,
Alicia filia Johannis Haughne (xii*d*.), Willelmus Haughne (xl*d*.), nativi dominae de sanguine,
Johannes filius Walteri Bakefyn (xii*d*.), Johannes de Fornesete (xii*d*.), nativi dominae de
sanguine, dant dominae de fine pro licentia comorandi extra dominium dominae usque festum
Sancti Michaelis Archangeli proxime futurum, etc. Ita quod sint ad curiam hic tenendam post
festum Sancti Michaelis proxime futurum, etc.'

6 pp. 45, 46.

7 See above, p. 46, n. 2.

with the consent of the lord. The manor was overcrowded at this period[1] and the non-tenant serfs represented the surplus servile population. On the other hand, the fugitives of the late fourteenth century left the manor against the will of the lord. The labouring population had diminished. The lord wished to retain his bond tenants within his domain, but the bondmen were attracted from the manor by new opportunities of gain, and the manorial officers could not be depended upon to execute the lord's orders[2].

Of the bondmen that remained within the manor some seem to have prospered. At this period real estate was the form of investment that bondmen would be most likely to make. It therefore throws light upon the condition of the bondmen to inquire to what extent they were renting or buying land.

Of the 73 lessees of land in the years 1376–8, 16 bore surnames that were borne by bond families of the manor, and it may therefore be assumed were serfs. The average amount of land, not including the demesne or the manor of Williams, farmed by the 73 lessees, was $3\frac{1}{2}$ acres. Of the serfs that leased land, nine farmed small amounts of not more than $2\frac{1}{2}$ acres; one farmed $1\frac{1}{2}$ acres of arable, a croft, and the cart-house; another, $2\frac{1}{2}$ acres of arable, the orchard, close, stotts' stable; another, some 6 acres, the chamber west of the gate, and the grange; another, $8\frac{1}{2}$ acres. Of the remaining three, Robert Herberd and Robert Houlot farmed the demesne arable and meadow, besides a few acres of other arable land. Together with William Hernyng, Houlot also farmed the manor of Williams, for which a yearly rent of £8 was paid. Hernyng also farmed the market tolls, and jointly with another tenant—whom we have no reason to suppose a bondman—he farmed some 25 acres in Redelyngfeld. With the exception of the joint lessee of Redelyngfeld, all the lessees of considerable quantities of land were bondmen. With two exceptions the farmers of all the demesne lands and buildings were also bondmen[3].

At this period the bondmen were also purchasing 'soiled land.' Thus between 1358 and 1376 different members of the Bolytoute

---

[1] Evidence for this is the small size of the holdings, see above, p. 17 ff., and the relatively large population at this period, see below, chapter VIII.

[2] Moulton Court Rolls, MS. 1354. 'Misericordia vi. d. De praeposito et messore quia non levaverunt c. s. de Willelmo filio Roberti, Milone Springald, Roberto Elbald et Waltero Bee, manucaptoribus Willelmi Elbald carucarii qui se elongavit a servitio domini sicut habuerunt in praecepto.' For instances from the Forncett rolls see footnotes on p. 75.

[3] This may perhaps be explained by the fact that most of the tenants who lived near the manor house were bondmen. See above, p. 13 ff. and Map.

family—one of the bond families that appears most prominently in the Forncett records—soiled 4½ messuages, 1 pightle, 32 acres, and 9 'pieces' of land.

Besides the flight of serfs from the manor, the rolls, few though they are, contain many other indications of the social disorders which mark this period. Thus, the reference to three 'unknown men' is noteworthy[1]. An unusually large number of persons, including a parson and two chaplains, were amerced for hunting in the lord's warren[1]. There were complaints that three messors had taken from the tenants larger sums than were due; and in general the messors seem to have been particularly untrustworthy in discharging the duties of their office[2].

---

[1] Court roll, 1394.

[2] 1358. The messors of Carleton and Forncett were amerced 'pro contemptu eo quod non custodierunt inquisicionem jur' super diversos articulos prout habuerunt in praecepto senescalli.'

'De W. G. de Carleton electo ad officium cartereve de poena forisfacta eo quod recusavit jurare ad dictum officium faciendum, etc.'

1373. The messor of Carleton was amerced 'quia non fecit officium suum.' The messor of Forncett was amerced 'quia non fect exequit' curiae prout ei injunctum fuit.'

1373. 'De Johanne Dosy messore quia non fecit exequit' curiae prout habuit in mandato.'

1394. 'De Willelmo Barkere (vid.) Johanne Alvard (vid.) Willelmo Grey (vid.) nuper messoribus dominae quia ceperunt de Willelmo Stoktone et de aliis diversis hominibus prout testatur per homagium denarios plus quam levare debuerunt per warantum suum in prejudicium dominae. Ideo in misericordia. Et praeceptum est quod resolvi faciant dictos denarios sic male captos.'

CHAPTER VII.

THE TENANTS AND THEIR LAND. 1400-1575.

THE material for this chapter consists of a series of Court Rolls that begins with 1400 and continues with only two considerable interruptions throughout the fifteenth and sixteenth centuries. For the period between March, 1413, and November, 1422, the record of only a single court remains, and the rolls from 1509 to 1524 were lost as early as 1527[1]. Otherwise the series is fairly complete, though some rolls are missing.

It has been shown[2] that by 1373 the former arable demesne was let in two large parcels at money rents for terms of years, that later it was let in small parcels for increasingly longer terms, and that, by the end of the fifteenth century, it had been granted to divers tenants to hold in fee farm.

In like manner the 250 acres of tenants' land that by 1376-8 had reverted to the lord and had been let by him for terms of years or from year to year[3] were afterwards let for successively longer terms, and were finally granted to many different tenants at fee farm rents.

By 1500 practically all of the land that had reverted to the lord had been let at fee farm[4]. In the sixteenth century the cases are very rare in which the lord lets land for terms of years or at fee farm.

The following tables show the gradual lengthening of the terms and the gradual change from the tenure at terms of years to tenure at a perpetual fixed rent.

[1] See Court roll, 19 Henry VIII., grant of lands of Robert Pyllet to Robert Adams.
[2] See above, pp. 52, 53, 57, 58.
[3] In 1376 nearly equal areas were held at terms of years and from year to year.
[4] The land entered in the extant rolls as granted at fee farm between 1429 when the grants begin and 1500 is about 570 acres, including Westwood Ridding, the other demesne lands and tenants' land.

	No. of cases	Length of term in years.															Fee-farms
		3	5	6	7	8	10	12	16	17	20	24	25	30	40	50	
1376–8	58	0	9	3	38	4	4	—	—	—	—	—	—	—	—	—	—
1401–10	33	1	4	—	22	—	6	—	—	—	—	—	—	—	—	—	—
1422–30	39	1	1	1	8	—	13	2	—	—	11	—	—	—	1	—	1
1431–40	74	—	1	1	9	1	44	3	—	—	10	—	—	—	—	—	5
1441–50	64	—	—	—	—	—	21	4	3	—	26	—	1	1	2	—	6
1451–60	44	—	1[1]	—	—	—	1	4	—	—	20	2	—	1	5	1	9
1461–70	38	—	—	—	—	—	3[2]	1[3]	—	1	5	—	—	—	2	—	26
1471–80	31	—	—	1	—	—	1	—	—	—	4	1	—	—	1	—	23
1481–90	19	—	—	—	—	—	—	—	—	—	1	—	—	1[4]	—	—	17
1491–1500	18	—	—	—	—	—	1	—	—	—	1	—	—	—	—	—	16
		2	16	6	77	5	94	14	3	1	78	3	1	3	11	1	103

Ratio of ' farms' for different terms to total number of ' farms.'

	No. of cases	Length of term in years.															Fee-farms
		3	5	6	7	8	10	12	16	17	20	24	25	30	40	50	
1376–8	58	—	·155	·052	·655	·069	·069	—	—	—	—	—	—	—	—	—	—
1401–10	33	·030	·121	—	·666	—	·182	—	—	—	—	—	—	—	—	—	—
1422–30	39	·026	·026	·026	·205	—	·333	·051	—	—	·282	—	—	—	·026	—	·026
1431–40	74	—	·014	·014	·121	·014	·594	·040	—	—	·135	—	—	—	—	—	·067
1441–50	64	—	—	—	—	—	·328	·062	·047	—	·406	—	·015	·015	·031	—	·094
1451–60	44	—	·023	—	—	—	·023	·090	—	—	·454	·045	—	·023	·114	·023	·205
1461–70	38	—	—	—	—	—	·079	·026	—	·026	·130	—	—	—	·054	—	·684
1471–80	31	—	—	·032	—	—	·032	—	—	—	·129	·032	—	—	·032	—	·742
1481–90	19	—	—	—	—	—	—	—	—	—	·052	—	—	·052	—	—	·895
1491–1500	18	—	—	—	—	—	·055	—	—	—	·055	—	—	—	—	—	·889

The change to longer terms and finally to perpetual fixed rents is perhaps to be connected with the more settled state of society that followed the social disturbances of the late fourteenth century. During the period of upheaval and disorder when the leasing of land by the lord was still novel, both lord and tenant would naturally hesitate to bind themselves by contracts for long terms. Another

[1] Warren.
[2] Including Warren.
[3] Demesne lands leased for 14 years.
[4] 31 years.

reason for the change may be the difficulty that apparently began to be felt in the third decade of the fifteenth century of finding tenants at the rents formerly charged. Longer terms as well as lower rents might serve to attract tenants.

Since the perpetual rents were fixed in amount before the rise in prices that began toward the middle of the sixteenth century, the change to tenure at fee farm must ultimately have resulted in great profit to the tenants and loss to the lord.

In the early fourteenth century rents were determined by custom and not by supply and demand. But in the latter fourteenth century a large amount of land was thrown upon the market and let at competition prices. How thorough was the victory of competition over custom in this field is shown not only by the fact that the bailiff let land at less than the customary rents, *quia non plus potest dimitti*, but much more strikingly by the fact that he took the trouble to state that land was let at the *accustomed* rent because no higher rent could be obtained[1].

The following table[2] shows roughly the fluctuations in the value of the demesne and of the tenants' land that had reverted to the lord and had been let by him for terms of years or at fee farm.

	Area let		Total annual rent of total area let			Average annual rent per acre
	acres	roods	£.	s.	d.	d.
1376–8	327	2	14	11	9½	10¾ −
1401–10	73	2½	2	15	11	9 +
1422–30	103	2	3	7	¾	7¾ +
1431–40	241	2½	8	1	5½	8
1441–50	147	0	4	14	7½	7¾ −
1451–60	110	2	2	17	7½	6¼ +
1461–70	89	0	2	16	10	7¾ −
1471–80	75	3½	2	1	6¼	6½ +
1481–90	30	0		19	9	8 −
1491–1500	57	3	1	14	5¾	7¼

[1] In 1424, 15½ acres were let for 7 years. The tenant used to pay 13s. 2d. but now pays only 10s. 4d. 'testatum est per homagium quod non potest plus dimitti.'

In 1432, 8 acres formerly farmed for 6s. were let for 5s. 'quia non plus potest dimitti.'

In 1438, certain pieces of land were let at 2s. 2d.; in 1450 they were let at 2s. 2d. 'ut soluere consuevit, quia non potest ultra dimitti.'

[2] The table given in the text is based on the fuller table in Appendix VII.

[3] This area includes 166½ acres of arable demesne let at 12d. per acre, and 161 acres of tenants' land at an average rent of 9¼d. per acre. (See account rolls of 1376–8, Appendix IX.)

161 acres instead of 250 acres of tenants' land are used as a basis for determining the rent per acre, because in many instances either the value of messuage and land are lumped together so that the rent per acre cannot be determined or the land is described as a 'croft' or 'pightle' of which the acreage is not given.

In general rents were high in Forncett[1], and from 1376 to 1378, and from 1400 to 1413, they were considerably higher than from 1422–1500.

There are a number of indications that the first fifteen or twenty years of the fifteenth century, together with the latter years of the fourteenth century, form a distinct economic period. Within this period came the Peasants' Revolt. It was a time of social and economic disturbance. Not only the high rental of land, but also the large number of conveyances entered in the rolls of the early fifteenth century point to an unusually active land market[2]. Within

---

[1] This conclusion is based on a comparison of Forncett rents with the statements of economic historians as to the average rental of arable in the fifteenth century. A few quotations will suffice to show that in regard to the value of land in the latter fourteenth and in the fifteenth centuries, the statements of different historians harmonize neither with one another nor with the conclusions arrived at in the text :—

Rogers, *Agric. and Prices*, IV. 128. It is certain that at this time [1455–1530] the rental of average arable land did not exceed, as it did not in the fourteenth century, sixpence an acre. It is probable that it might be even less, for the cost of labour was certainly greater in the fifteenth than it was in the fourteenth century.

W. Denton, *England in the Fifteenth Century*, 153. At the end of the fifteenth century...the fertility of the arable land of England was well-nigh exhausted.... The rent of corn land was scarcely more than nominal. The average rental of an acre of arable land throughout England was less indeed than one day's wages of a carpenter or mason. In many places it did not exceed the wage paid for half a day's work. P. 153, n. 4. Carpenters and masons were then receiving fourpence for a day's work, in country places twopence or threepence ; fair land was then letting at fourpence per acre, and inferior land at not more than half the sum. [At Forncett, in 1376–8 and in 1433, the wages of a carpenter were 4*d*. See above, p. 56, n. 2.]

Cunningham, *op. cit.* (4th ed.), I. 462. Rents in the fourteenth and earlier part of the fifteenth century were exceedingly low. [In note, reference to Rogers, *Agric. and Prices*, IV. 63, 128, and Denton, *Fifteenth Century*, 147.]

Denton, *op. cit.*, p. 147. In the latter part of the thirteenth, and at the beginning of the following century, much corn land had been let at sixpence an acre and occasionally as high as eightpence or even ninepence for the acre.... During the hundred years from 1350 to 1450, we meet with comparatively few notices of so high a rental as this, and when we take into account the decline in the purchasing power of money, this implies a large reduction in the rental of farms. In the latter half of the fifteenth century rents rose again, and were nominally, at least, as high as in 1300, though in reality they were still much lower than in the thirteenth century.

Rogers, *Work and Wages*, 287. During the fifteenth century...the value of land rose rapidly. In the fourteenth century it was constantly obtained for ten years' purchase, the amount of land in the market being probably so abundant, and the competition for its purchase so slight, that it easily changed hands at such a rate. There was also no purchasing as yet on the part of the small proprietors.... Land was valued at twenty years' purchase in the middle of the fifteenth century.

[2] A table showing so far as possible the number of conveyances entered on the extant rolls in each year from 1400–1500 and from 1550–1565, is given in Appendix XII.

Although the number of conveyances annually recorded in the rolls was greater in the early fifteenth century than later, yet the amount of land acquired by single purchases was on the average greater in the sixteenth century than in the fifteenth. Thus in the five years,

this period one tenant—a bondman—accumulated a holding that compared with the holdings of succeeding and of preceding periods was of extraordinary size[1]. Possibly the high rentals of the period are to be connected with the extension of sheep raising. There are several indications that in the late fourteenth century this industry was assuming a new importance in Forncett. Thus, while from 1272 to 1306 there had been no sheep on the demesne, in 1378 the demesne was stocked with 200 sheep, and Westwood Ridding, which had been arable in the early fourteenth century, was leased as pasture. In 1394 three tenants paid fines for having folds for 100 sheep, and the one extant court roll of that year contains a memorandum to inquire at the next court who have folds within the manor, and who of those who have paid fines for having folds have more than 100 sheep without license. Early in the fifteenth century come the first complaints in the extant rolls regarding inclosures. By 1404 a considerable number of tenants had inclosed their lands in the open fields[2], and it is of interest to note that in 1401 one of the

1401 to 1405, we count 122 transfers that appear to be sales. It would not as a rule be possible to assert with regard to any given conveyance that it was based upon a *bonâ fide* sale. But it has seemed safe enough to assume that the conveyances were sales unless they were transfers of property to the heir or near kinsman. Since ' farms' of land, inheritances, and certain other transfers of land have not been counted as sales, the number of ' transfers that appear to be sales' is for a given period considerably less than the number of conveyances. The average amount that passed by means of these 122 conveyances was 1¾ acres. (This does not include the transfer of 50 acres in Redlyngfeld, Hethel. As stated below the relation of this land to the manor of Forncett was peculiar. It was held of other manors as well.) From 1406–10 there were 103 probable sales averaging 1½ acres. From 1491–5, some 79 sales averaged nearly 2½ acres. From 1551—1555, 32 probable sales averaged nearly 4½ acres. From 1556—1560 there were 66 probable sales averaging nearly five acres.

The following table shows more clearly than the averages the tendency towards an increasing proportion of comparatively large sales.

Area sold.

	Under 5 a.	5 a.–5¾ a.	6 a.–10 a.	10 a.–20 a.	20 a.–25 a.	50 a. +
1401–10	207 sales	12	3	3	0	0
1551–60	80 sales	1	6	7	2	2

[1] See below, p. 82.

[2] The following entries appear in a court roll of 1404:

Misericordia iis. iid. Ricardus Horn (xiid.) Robertus May (iid.) Ricardus Cullynge (iiid.) Walterus Colman (vid.) Galfridus Cullynge (iiid.) fecerunt clausuras de terris suis propriis infra dominium et villam de Multone contra consuetudinem dominii per quod tenentes domini communam suam ibidem habere non possunt, videlicet a festo Sancti Michaelis usque festum Purificationis Beatae Mariae Virginis prout de jure habere debuerint et ex antiquo habuerunt. Ideo, etc.

Misericordia iiis. viiid. Et quod Willelmus Florauns (iiiid.) Ricardus Welyard (vid.) Thomas Berd (vid.) Robertus Dosy (vid.) Johannes Skylman (vid.) Willelmus dil Hil, capellanus (vid.) Robertus Sergeante (vid.) Robertus Baxtere (iid.) et Johannes Drylle (iid.) fecerunt similiter infra villam de Fornessete contra consuetudinem dominii. Ideo, etc.

Misericordia iis. Et quod Prior de Thetforde (xiid.) et Robertus de Parke (xiid.) fecerunt similiter infra villam de Aslaktone contra consuetudinem dominii. Ideo, etc.

inclosing tenants, John Skilman, paid for license to have a fold for 100 sheep. The records, then, give the impression that in the later fourteenth century there were many more sheep on the manor than there had been in the early part of the same century. During the fifteenth and sixteenth centuries the tenants continued to inclose their lands[1]. From the Survey of 1565 it appears that at that time from one-third to one-half of the fields of Forncett vill lay within inclosures. Nearly all of these inclosures were between three and fifteen acres in area. The records from 1422 to 1565 afford no clear evidence that during this period sheep-raising was carried on to any very considerable extent. Certainly even by 1565 the sheep-raising industry had by no means become of overwhelming importance. Less than half of the acreage of the fields was in inclosures, and these inclosures were, at least for the most part, arable[2]. The area which they included is described in the survey as *terra*, not as *pastura*, and, as a rule, the inclosed land was divided into separate strips, which were held by many different tenants by different tenures and of different manors. Even when the whole close was in the hands of a single tenant the old division into strips was sometimes maintained[3].

To what extent was there a development in the direction of larger tenancies during the period 1401 to 1565? The court rolls are silent as to freehold. The following table, covering the period from 1401 to 1565, shows the amount of copyhold (including under this head 'soiled' land and fee farm) held at the time of their death by such tenants as died seized of 15 acres or more held by this tenure.

---

[1] 1438. M. vi*d*. d. Jur' infra praesentant quod Thomas Cullyng includit terram suam in campis per quod tenentes domini non possunt habere viam ad terras suas. Ideo ipse in misericordia. Et praeceptum est deponere dictum inclausum citra proximam curiam sub poena xl*d*.

1441. Jur' dicunt quod Robertus Dosy includit communem pasturam de Hylgate et custodit illam communem pasturam pro sua separali pastura in prejudicium dominae. Ideo ipse in misericordia ut in capite, etc. Et praeceptum est illam retro aperire citra proximam sub poena.

[2] The different steps in the process of inclosing the open fields for tillage are set forth in Mr W. J. Corbett's paper on "Elizabethan Village Surveys," *Transactions, Royal Historical Soc.*, XI. 79–87. Conditions at Forncett were closely similar to those on the Norfolk manors described in this paper.

[3] e.g. Forncett St Peter, VIII. 4, and X. 10. 'E. A. tenet totum illud inclausum continens x. acras terrae jacentes in diversis peciis libere.'

	No. of cases	Names of tenants (names of serfs are in italics).	Area of copyhold held at death (including land held at fee farm and 'soiled' land. Leases for terms of years are not included).
1401–1405	1 [1]	*Houlot*	103 a.
1406–1410	0		
1426–1430	1	*Forncett*	15 a.
1431–1435	0		
1436–1440	2	Verdon	17 a. 3 r.
		Hapton	33 a. 3½ r. [2]
1441–1445	0		
1446–1450	1	*Dosy*	52 a.
1451–1455	1	Horn	24 a.
1456–1460	0		
1461–1465	1	May	15 a. 1 r.
1466–1470	3	*Baxter*	16 a.
		Wyght	21 a. ½ r.
		Verdon	26 a.
1471–1475	1	Britief	29 a.
1476–1480	2	*Boole*	22 a.
		Britief	31 a.
1481–1485	3	*Bolitout*	16 a. 1 r.
		Browne	16 a. 1 r.
		Dosy	84 a. 1 r.
1486–1490	3	Baxter [3]	42 a. 3½ r.
		Dosy	60 a.
		Buxton	20 a. 2 r.
1491–1495	3	*Hulle*	28 a. 1½ r.
		Hillyng	20 a. 3 r.
		Wyot	16 a. 2 r.
1496–1500	1	Southawe	40 a.
1546–1550	5	Whitefoot	17 a. 1 r.
		Davy	67 a. 1 r.
		Banaster	44 a. 2½ r.
		Serjeant	70 a. 1 r.
		Swayne	16 a. 3 r.
1551–1555	4	Brown	20 a. 2 r.
		Bolitout	30 a.
		Lincoln	36 a. 2 r.
		Buxton	51 a. 3 r.
1556–1560	7	Baxter [3]	87 a.
		Cok	25 a.
		Dannok	16 a. 1 r.
		Clere	19 a. 2½ r.
		Brightieff	30 a.
		Alexander	43 a. 2 r.
		Horne	31 a.

[1] 50 acres of 'soiled' land in Redlingfeld held by Seuell at the time of his death are omitted. They were later held to the use of the vill of Redlingfeld and bore a unique relation to Forncett.

[2] In connection with J. Baxter, Hapton held for a term of years 'one half of the close called Redding.'   [3] A member of the free family of this name.

During the period under consideration (1401–1500), the copyhold of which a tenant was seized at death is recorded in 286 cases.   In only 23 cases (8 per cent.) did the tenant hold more than 15 acres by this tenure.   After 1450 it is more usual than before to find over 15 acres of copyhold in the hands of a single tenant.   Later, this tendency toward the concentration of larger areas in the hands of individuals becomes increasingly marked.   Thus taking for purposes of comparison with conditions in the fifteenth century, fifteen years in the middle of the sixteenth century (1546–1560), we find that in 16 out of 83 cases (19·3 per cent.) the area of copyhold held at death exceeded 15 acres.   Yet the largest holding of copyhold was but 87 acres.

The rolls afford a much more detailed picture of the condition of the serfs than of the free tenantry, especially the freeholders. But the rolls and the Survey of 1565 both give some information regarding even the last class.

In December, 1400, the first court of Thomas Mowbray was held at Forncett, and many tenants did fealty[1].   These tenants were grouped in three classes :

> *Libere tenentes*, numbering 20,
> *Native tenentes*, numbering 25,
> *Nativi domini de sanguine*, numbering 22.

Since many of the tenants failed to do fealty in this court and either attorned themselves in later courts or omitted the ceremony altogether, the numbers are incomplete, especially for the first two classes.

Comparing these three classes of tenants with the classes found on the manor in the earlier periods, it appears possible to make the following identifications :

The *libere tenentes* of 1400 represent the *libere tenentes* of 1270–1307.

The *native tenentes* of 1400 probably represent the free sokemen of 1270–1307.

The *nativi domini de sanguine* of 1400 represent the customers and bond sokemen of 1270–1307.

The last two identifications require support, and in this connection it will be convenient to present the reasons for believing that there were both free and bond sokemen on the manor.

According to the Survey of 1565 some 1000 acres of bond land (*terra nativa*) were held of Forncett manor.   Of these not

---

[1] Appendix X. lxxii., lxxiii.

more than 125 acres were customers' lands rendering winter week-work, while the remaining 875 acres, or thereabouts, were held by sokemen and were lightly burdened. The 1000 acres of *terra nativa* were divided into some 135 tenements, each of which had been charged with certain dues and bore a name, evidently the name of a quondam tenant, which in many cases persisted unchanged from the fourteenth through the sixteenth century. The customers' tenements numbered about 25[1].

Now 32 family names of serfs are known to us[2], but doubtless more than 32 servile families had been tenants of the manor. We can be sure that our list is complete only for the last few generations of serfdom. For the period before 1400 we have to depend upon a few incidental references in the scanty rolls, so that it is practically certain that the names of many of the old servile families are not included in the enumeration.

Comparing the number of servile families with the number of customers' tenements, it appears that the customers' tenements were too few to maintain the servile families, and that there must have been serfs among the occupants of sokemen's tenements, or in other words that there were bond sokemen. This conclusion is supported by the fact that while 28 of the 32 surnames of serfs appear also as names of tenements, a large proportion of these 28 are the names of sokemen's tenements. Hence, we conclude that the serfs of 1400 represent both the customers and the bond sokemen of 1270–1307.

But there are reasons for believing that some of the sokemen were free, for

(1)   In the account rolls of 1273 and 1275 there is an apparent reference to free sokemen in the entry 'de vi^{xx}. precariis de sokne et non plus quia alii sunt liberi omnes et nichil dabunt.'

(2)   Of the 24 surnames of *native tenentes* (*i.e.* freemen holding bondland) doing homage in 1400, six are also names of sokemen's tenements.

(3)   If the *native tenentes* of 1400 were not as a class representative of a former class of free sokemen it is difficult to explain their origin. Some of them may have been descendants of *libere tenentes* that had ceased to be freeholders and had acquired bond land ; others may have been serfs or descendants of serfs who had

---

[1] p. 67 ff.

[2] These are: Abbott, Aunfrey, Avelyn, Backefenne, Baldwyn, Bartram, Baxter alias Hill, Bole, Brakest, Bullitout, Clerk, Culliour, Dosy, Drill, Edwards, Elfleet, Forncett, Galgrym, Gray, Haughne, Herberd, Hillyng, Hirnyng, Houlot, Hulle, Lound, Mors, Palle, Pelet, Roweye, Rugge, Wronge.

obtained their freedom[1]. But the class is so large, outnumbering apparently each of the other classes, that it seems very unlikely that it should have been altogether derived from them. It may have been considerably augmented by new comers to the manor, but the most probable hypothesis appears to be that the nucleus of this class consisted of representatives of former free sokemen's families.

In 1400 many, probably most, of the freeholders (*libere tenentes*) held a few acres of copyhold land, but none of them apparently held any considerable amount of copyhold of Forncett manor. The holdings of the free copyholders (*native tenentes*) also, in so far at least as they held of Forncett, were, as a rule, very small.

The table on p. 82 indicates the status of the tenants that at the time of their death held an area of 15 acres or more of copyhold[2]. Between 1401 and 1500 in only 23 cases (8 per cent.) did the tenant hold more than 15 acres by this tenure. Of these 23 tenants 13 were freemen and 10 were serfs. In the period 1546–1560 all but one of the tenants of the larger holdings were freemen; and as the Survey of 1565 shows, these largest copyholders were as a rule the large freeholders.

We have next to consider how far the larger properties in copyhold held by freemen were acquired by a process of slow accumulation, lasting through generations, and how far they were acquired by large single investments of capital; and in this connection we have also to consider whether the tenants of these larger properties were of local origin, or were merchants and townspeople.

In Appendix VI. a list is given of the tenants of Forncett manor in 1565, and of their holdings in that year.

Of these 175 tenants, 14 tenants, representing 11 families, held more than 50 acres each.

Now, of these 11 families whose representatives held more than 50 acres apiece, at least nine, if we may safely judge by the continuity of the surnames, had held of Forncett manor since the early years of the fifteenth century. Of these nine, some belonged to the local gentry; others were of humbler social position. In the former class were the Baxters, Brownes, Buxtons, and Reves[3]. Of the two families who entered the manor later, one, the Shermans, was of gentle rank.

---

[1] John Drill, who bears a servile surname, is mentioned among the 'native tenentes,' but there are no indications that any considerable proportion of this class had a servile origin.

[2] 'Copyhold' throughout this chapter includes 'soiled' land.

[3] For the Browne family, who, in the early seventeenth century, were owners of Tacolneston or Dovedale's manor and of Williams' manor in Tacolneston, see Blomefield, *op. cit.* v. 166–169; for the Buxton family, owners of many neighbouring manors, see *Ibid.* v. 276,

In so far as their property consisted of copyhold the amount held by these families in 1565 represented the accumulation of several generations, though the accumulation by these families of land held by copyhold tenure progressed much more rapidly after about 1470 than before.

To illustrate the manner in which the copyhold estates of 1565 had been accumulated, and to indicate the social position of the tenant holding the largest property in that year, the history of the Baxter family will be given[1].

The Baxter Family. In 1400 Robert Baxter did fealty as a freeholder (*libere tenens*). He farmed 120 acres of pasture (Westwood Ridding) for seven years. In 1437 John, probably the son of Robert, held at farm, together with another tenant, half of Westwood Ridding. But the family held little copyhold until toward the close of the fifteenth century.

About 1475 John Baxter died, sole seized of nine acres of copyhold.

In 1485 Richard, son of John, died, seized of six messuages, including three vacant messuages, and some 43 acres of copyhold. This land had been acquired as follows:

9 a. inherited from his father, 1475				
1 a.	acquired by Richard and his father,			1454
1½ r.	„	„	„	1460
2 r.	„	„	„	1461
3 r.	„	„		1470
2 r.	„	„		1472
2 messuages and 5 a.	„	„		1475
3 r.	„	„		c. 1485
3 messuages and 7 a. 2 r.	„	„	and Thos. his son,	1476
1 messuage and 9 a.	„	„	„ „	1480
8 a. 2 r.	„	„	„ „	1482

In 1535 Thomas, son of Richard, died. In 1532 he had surrendered part of his land to one of his sons. At that time he was seized of seven messuages, four of which were vacant, and of 61 a. 1½ r. copyhold. A small part of this holding had been inherited, the larger part he had accumulated, as the following table shows:

283 *passim*; for the Reve family, *Ibid.* v. 260. The Thos. Reve mentioned by Blomefield as lord of Clavers manor was the father of William Reve, tenant of Forncett in 1565. The arms of the Sherman family appear in the windows of Rainthorp Hall. Blomefield, v. 217.

[1] There was also a servile family of this name, whose history is given below on pp. 89-90.

2 messuages and 17 a. 3½ r. inherited from his father, 1487

3	„	and 7 a.	acquired by Thos. and his father,		1476
1 messuage	and 9 a.	„	„	„	1480
	8 a. 2 r.	„	„	„	1482
	2 a.	„	„		1487
	1 a.	„	„		1488
	2 a.	„	„	and Richard his son,	1508
	9 a. 1½ r.	„	„	and his sons,	1511
	1 a.	„	„	„	1511
	1 a. 3½ r.	„	„	„	1514
	1 r.	„	„		1520
1 messuage	and 1 a. 1 r.	„	„		1528

The copyhold that had belonged to Thomas was divided between his sons, Richard and John. About 1557 Richard died seized of 86 a. 3 r. of copyhold. His lands went to his sons Thomas, Richard, and Stephen. The Survey of 1565 states the area of freehold as well as the area of copyhold held by these sons. If as large a proportion of their freehold as of their copyhold was inherited from their father, Richard must have held some 250 acres of Forncett.

In 1565 Thomas, son of Richard, was the largest tenant of Forncett. In right of his wife he held the neighbouring manor of Rainthorp, and he built Rainthorp Hall[1].

It has been said that of the 11 families represented by the 14 largest tenants, all but two had held of Forncett since the early years of the fifteenth century. The two of whom this cannot be asserted are those of Launcelot Smith and John Sherman, 'gentleman.'

The Sherman family cannot be traced as tenants further back than the early years of the sixteenth century. As early as 1515 they held land of Moulton manor. A large share of the copyhold that they held of Forncett manor came to the Sherman family through the marriage of John Sherman (father of the John Sherman who held in 1565) to Margaret, daughter of the bondman Roger Hillyng.

Launcelot Smith acquired his property through a single conveyance. Nearly all of his land, 66 acres, was obtained in 1559 by surrender from the two tenants who had received it in 1556 from the bondman John Dosy on condition that they pay £120 to the lord of the manor[2].

---

[1] Blomefield's *Norfolk*, v. 67, 217. In the church of Forncett St Peter are sepulchral brasses in memory of Richard (d. 1485), and of Thomas (d. 1535). Rubbings of these brasses may be found in the British Museum (Add. MSS. 34, 892, folios 76 and 77). The tomb of Thomas (d. 1611) is in the church of Tasburgh. Blomefield, v. 211.

[2] See below, p. 90, and Appendix XIII. xci.

The landed property of Launcelot Smith seems to represent a single investment of a considerable amount of capital, while all the other larger landed properties of copyhold held in Forncett in 1565 had been gradually accumulated.

Toward the latter part of the fifteenth century freeholders, representatives of the local gentry, began to buy up more considerable amounts of copyhold than formerly, though as early as the beginning of the fifteenth century it was usual for freeholders to have a few acres of copyhold. No ' merchant or townsman ' apparently figured among the larger tenants of the manor[1].

In 1400 nineteen families of servile status held land of Forncett manor; in 1500 not more than eight bond families were tenants; a quarter of a century later there were but five, twenty-five years later only three, and by 1575 serfdom had disappeared.

After 1400 the history of serfdom in Forncett is the history of these nineteen families.

Since the series of court rolls from 1400 to 1575 is fairly complete, it is possible to trace with tolerably satisfactory results the history of each family during the period. The rolls show how much ' soiled ' or ' bond ' land a tenant entered upon or alienated; how much he held of Forncett manor at the time of his death, and to whom it passed; and what land he leased from the lord. They contain lists of chevage-paying bondmen, often naming the place from which the serf is paying chevage, and in a few instances stating his occupation. Eleven wills of bondmen and five manumissions are also entered in the rolls[2].

Besides the nineteen families mentioned, members of five other servile families are referred to in the rolls between 1400 and 1412. In one case a chevage-paying tenant had died, and it was ordered to inquire concerning his heir. In four cases orders were given to seize or distrain bondmen who had withdrawn. As no serfs bearing the surnames of these fugitive bondmen appear in the later rolls, we may assume that the last representatives of these families that were connected with the manor won their freedom by flight.

A brief account of each of the nineteen bond families holding land of Forncett manor after 1400 follows.

The Aunfrey Family. In 1404 John, son of the bondman William Aunfrey, was remaining away from Forncett manor without license from the lord. A few years later his father sold his land and joined

---

[1] Unless Launcelot Smith were such, and of this there appears to be no evidence.
[2] The wills and one manumission are printed in Appendix XIII.

his son. Apparently neither father nor son ever paid chevage or returned to the manor. It looks as if they had freed themselves by withdrawing from Forncett.

The Bakfyn Family. From 1400 to 1444 Nicholas Bakfyn dwelt in Norwich and paid chevage. His father died in 1408, seized of 7 acres of land, which passed to Nicholas. This land Nicholas seems to have alienated within a few years after his father's death. After 1444 the name of Nicholas ceases to appear in the list of chevage-paying tenants, so that his death probably occurred about this time. Either he left no descendants or in some way the ties had been severed that would have bound them as serfs to Forncett manor.

The Baxter Family. About the year 1422 five bondmen of this name were connected with the manor. Of these, two died without male descendants; a third dwelt outside the manor for several years and paid chevage until his death; a fourth fled, and though the order to 'attach' him was repeated at several courts it seems never to have been executed. Thus, in consequence of the failure of male heirs and of withdrawal from the manor, only one branch of the family retained its servile status.

The members of this family held from 10 to 20 acres of land apiece. The wills of John Baxter[1], who died in 1544, and of his widow, who died six years later[2], are both recorded in the rolls, and indicate that the family were in comfortable circumstances. John's real property consisted of two messuages and 10½ acres; his chattels were valued at £8. 4s. 5d. His widow bequeathed two mares, a colt, nine cows, two bullocks, pigs, fowls, clothing, and various household furnishings. John left a son, Thomas. The references that occur to Thomas in his parents' wills give us an unfavourable impression of his character. In 1556 it is recorded that Thomas had been convicted of felonies, and that by reason of his attainture all his lands had escheated to the lord. Thus Thomas ceased to be a tenant of Forncett manor; for one year he paid chevage, and after that we hear no more of him.

In the latter part of the fifteenth century there were two chevage-paying bondmen of this name. William Baxter is also named as remaining in London from 1524 to 1527.

Between 1525 and 1556 John Baxter of Tivetshall and his children paid chevage. In 1556 a writ of manumission was granted by the Duke which freed John, his children, and all their descendants

---

[1] Appendix XIII. lxxxvi–lxxxvii.　　　[2] Appendix XIII. lxxxix–xc.

'from the yoke of servitude.' At the same time four other families, besides the Baxters, were freed, the writs of manumission being practically the same in all cases. Each writ was said to have been granted 'in consideration of certain sums of money.'

We have a probable clue to the amount paid in one instance, for just before his manumission one of the manumitted serfs, John Dosy, surrendered his lands to two tenants on condition that they pay to the Duke the sum of £120[1].

The Bole Family. In 1443 Roger Bole died, seized of one messuage and 1¾ acres. The rather small fines paid by his children for license to marry are explained on the ground of poverty. Shortly before his death in 1467 Roger's son, Robert, was seized of 4½ acres, which passed to Walter Bole. Walter seems to have alienated this land. What became of him afterwards does not appear. His son paid chevage from 1466 to 1472. Between 1428 and 1506 three other bondmen paid chevage.

A second son of Roger Bole died in 1477, seized of a messuage and 22 acres. He was also a lessee of the manor of Williams, for which a yearly rent of £8. 6s. 8d. was paid. Apparently this branch of the family became extinct in the male line in the early part of the sixteenth century.

The Bolitout Family. The most noteworthy circumstances in the records of this family during the fifteenth century are the relatively large amounts of land held by some of its members. Thus in 1410 one tenant had 78 acres and four messuages, and two others, possibly heirs of the first, had 44 acres in 1425 and 1474 respectively. Most of the other tenants, of whom at least eleven may be distinguished, held from 4 to 6 acres, although one held as much as 16 and another less than 2 acres.

In the year 1500 there were four tenants of this name. Of these one seems to have left the manor and to have become a chevage-paying tenant. A second also 'surrendered' his land and paid chevage from a neighbouring village. His will[2], dated 1506, shows that he held a house and land, although not of Forncett manor. His bequests were insignificant—12d. to the parish church, a cow to his wife, and to each of his four daughters 'if it may be borne.' Corn and cattle were to be sold to pay his debts, including a debt of 100s.

---

[1] Appendix XIII. xci. For other instances of the payment of large sums for manumission, see the paper by A. Savine, 'Bondmen under the Tudors,' *Transactions, Royal Historical Society*, N. S. XVII.

[2] Appendix XIII. lxxxi.

This bondman left a son, but the later history of this family cannot be traced, as the rolls from 1508 to 1524 are missing.

In 1524, a few months before his death, the third tenant—Walter —held land to the value of £40. At this time he had two married daughters, but no sons, and bargained with his son-in-law, John Crane, with a view to transferring to Crane all his lands and tenements. But Walter's other son-in-law, John Roo, felt that he would be injured by this transaction, and tried to prove that the bargain had not actually been effected. A number of servants (*servientes*) are incidentally mentioned as belonging to the households of Walter and his children. Thus one of the witnesses who testified in the manor court in Roo's behalf and against Crane was a young woman, the 'servant' of Walter ; a second witness against Crane was 'arrested,' the next year, by two of Crane's 'servants.' A third 'servant' of Crane was charged with striking a woman 'servant' of Roo. Within a year or two Crane had died and the bailiff was ordered to seize all the lands that his widow held and provide a new tenant. A few months later an entry appears that suggests that serfs might be disseized of their lands on grounds that would not have sufficed had the tenants been of free status : ' Now on this account, because the daughters of Walter Bolitout are bondwomen of blood, it has been ordered by the lord's special command—certain considerations related and declared here in full court by the surveyor moving him thereto—to seize all the lands and tenements (of which Walter died seized).'

The fourth tenant, William, held at least 30 acres at his death in 1551. One of his sons died in 1538. His goods were valued at £4. 4s. 2d.[1] He left two infant sons, who never, apparently, became tenants of the manor. William's second son, a carpenter, held a messuage and three acres. In 1556 he and his descendants were manumitted.

Many members of this family dwelt outside the manor. Between 1400 and 1411 some four bondmen fled, whom the lord seems to have been unable to attach. During the fifteenth century seventeen bondmen paid chevage, and during the sixteenth century nineteen. In 1556 one of the chevage-paying serfs was manumitted, together with his descendants, some five or six of whom had paid chevage.

After 1556 the only chevage-paying serfs, and, so far as the court rolls show, the only serfs still connected with the manor, were of the family of Robert Bolitout. In 1575 Robert Bolitout and his children

[1] Appendix XIII. lxxxvii.–lxxxviii.

paid chevage for the last time. In that year serfdom came to an end in Forncett. This final disappearance of serfdom is to be attributed to the action of Queen Elizabeth, to whom the manor escheated after the execution of Lord Thomas Howard in 1572. In 1575 the Queen granted to Sir Henry Lee all the fines that he could get from 300 of her bondmen and bondwomen, not counting wives and children, for the manumission of themselves and their families[1]. From the document printed in Appendix XIV.[2] it appears that among these serfs were two bondmen of Forncett, Robert Bolitout and Thomas Lound. The document is undated, but since chevage payments suddenly stop in 1575 it is extremely probable that in that year Sir Henry Lee compelled the last serfs connected with Forncett Manor to purchase their freedom.

The Brakest Family. Between 1400 and 1406 three men and three women of this name dwelt outside the manor. In 1409 three more bondmen fled, 'relinquishing' their land. One relinquished eight acres, another five acres, and the third two and a half acres. In the following courts up to 1412 it was ordered to seize these fugitives. The rolls from 1412 to 1422 are missing, so that we cannot trace them further.

In 1428 William Brakest died, seized of one messuage and 14 acres. Richard, his brother and heir, took the land, but in the same court alienated it to a tenant of different family. This is the last entry in which a member of the Brakest family appears as holding land of Forncett manor. After alienating his newly inherited property Richard did not at once leave the vill, but although dwelling in Forncett he paid chevage because he was not a tenant of the manor. Two years later he paid 6d. for license to remain in Metfield, Suffolk. In 1432 he had fled from Metfield and paid no chevage. It was therefore ordered that he be attached. The next year the order was repeated, and this is the last entry in the Forncett records relating to the Brakest family. Apparently they had gained their freedom by flight from the manor, and to obtain their freedom some of them were willing to leave their land.

The Coliour Family. In 1404 Christina, daughter of Robert Coliour, paid a fine for license to marry. Apparently Robert had died before 1400. His land passed to his daughters.

The Dosy Family. A member of this family died in 1447, seized

---

[1] See *Notes and Queries*, 4th Ser., XI. 298, and 5th Ser., I. 118.
[2] The Decree and Order corresponding to this Bill and Answer has been sought in the Public Record Office, but without success.

of five messuages and 52 acres.   In 1487 his son died, seized of five messuages, two half-messuages, and 60 acres.   In 1500 there were three tenants of this name.   One died without descendants.   He held two messuages and 110 acres.   His money bequests amounted to between £9 and £10.   He left a legacy to a woman servant[1].

The second tenant held at his death one messuage and 5¼ acres.   His bequests in money came to 12s.[2]   His son seems to have been one of the chevage-paying serfs.

The third tenant was seized of seven messuages, two half-messuages, and 86 acres.   It was the oldest son of this tenant who, in 1556, was manumitted, together with his children[3].

Within the fifteenth century, so far as the records show, no member of this family withdrew from Forncett.   But in the sixteenth century there were two chevage-paying bondmen, who were probably sons of the tenants already mentioned.

The Forncett Family.   Just before his death in 1429 a tenant of this name 'surrendered' to his daughter one messuage and 15 acres.   In 1435 another tenant alienated 1½ acres.   This is the last occasion on which the family name of Forncett appears in the conveyances of land.   Apparently no one of the name paid chevage.

The Grey Family.   In 1412 William Grey died, seized of one messuage, two pightles and ten and a half acres.   His land was inherited by his daughter.

The Haughne Family.   One member of this family paid chevage in 1400 and 1401.   In the fifteenth century three tenants held small quantities of land.   In 1501 the last of these died, seized of 13½ acres, which passed to his daughter and heir.   He bequeathed 3s. 6d. to religious uses ; left to his wife a croft and 2½ acres, part of the barn, the west end of the hall with the chimney and the soler thereover, and half the fruit garden[4].

The Herberd Family.   Within the first half of the fifteenth century three tenants of this name held from 4½ to 13½ acres.   The branch of the family that remained on the manor seems to have failed in the male line by 1444 ; at any rate the land did not pass to male heirs.   In the early years of the fifteenth century three serfs paid chevage.   Of these one seems to have returned to the manor as a tenant, one fled, and the orders to 'attach' him seem never to have been executed.

---

[1] Appendix XIII. lxxix.   [2] Appendix XIII. lxxxi.
[3] Appendix XIII. lxxxiv–lxxxvi., xc–xci.   [4] Appendix XIII. lxxviii–lxxix.

The Hillyng Family. Members of one branch of this family held 13¼ acres in 1433, 18½ acres in 1469, 20¾ acres in 1493. The last male representative of this branch of the family died in 1506, holding land, as his will states, of five different manors[1]. He held 25 acres of Forncett. The second branch of this family was seized of smaller amounts of land—in 1471, 4 acres; in 1490, 5¼ acres; in 1501, 8¾ acres; in 1556, 9½ acres. In 1556 the members of this family were manumitted.

There is no evidence that any serfs of this name paid chevage before 1500. Later two men paid chevage, of whom one was freed by the manumission already referred to. The other died in 1536 without male heirs. From his will and the inventory of his goods it appears that he was a weaver. His goods were valued at £4. They included a mare, 5 kine, 9 sheep and lambs, 4 swine, a pair of looms, a mattress, blankets, two coverlets, pots and dishes, and sundry other articles[2].

The Hirnyng Family. There were three male tenants of this name, each of whom held at least 25 or 30 acres. The holding of the first of these tenants passed to his son, Peter; the greater part of the land held by Peter passed to his daughter. The third tenant 'surrendered' some 25 acres in 1461, and we cannot trace him further. Later four bondmen paid chevage. Of these one died in 1505, holding land, though not of Forncett manor. In his will he directed that 20s. be spent on his burial; his bequests in money amounted to about £2[3]. One son of this bondman ceased to pay chevage, 'because he had suddenly left the country'; another failed to pay 'on account of poverty.'

The Houlot Family. Robert Houlot, who died in 1401, is probably to be identified with the Robert Houlot who, in 1378, leased the manor of Williams and the demesne of Forncett manor. Shortly before his death he was seized of six messuages and 160 acres. After his death it was ordered to seize 236 acres that had passed through his hands, and were held by divers tenants whose title was not clear. His widow was fined £6. 13s. for having withdrawn the goods and chattels of Robert out of the lord's domain.

Houlot's property passed to his daughter and heir, Margaret. In 1408 Margaret and her husband 'surrendered' a small amount of land on condition that the incoming tenants should make cloth for them and their servant during their lives, or else pay 2s. yearly.

---

[1] Appendix XIII. lxxxii.   [2] Appendix XIII. lxxxiii–lxxxiv.   [3] Appendix XIII. lxxx.

The Hulle Family.   Representatives of the three generations of this family, living in the latter part of the fifteenth century, held respectively two messuages and 17½ acres, two messuages and 28 acres, and 25 acres.   In 1501 the son of the last of these tenants sold his land, remained in Forncett with the rector, and paid chevage till his death in 1503.

In the latter half of the fifteenth century two bondmen, and in the sixteenth century two or three bondmen, of whom one was poor, also paid chevage.

The Lound Family.   A tenant of this name died in 1447, seized of eight acres.   The land passed to his daughter, who was poor.

In 1401 it was ordered to attach a serf of this name who was in Norwich.

Between 1472 and 1556 five serfs paid chevage.   Of these one, who died in 1540, is said to have been very poor ; another, who died the following year, had chattels valued at 76s. 7d.

In 1555 Thomas Lound, dwelling in Martham, paid chevage for the last time.   However, it would appear that he, or possibly a descendant, was living in Martham twenty years later, for in 1575 Sir Henry Lee claimed Thomas Lound of Martham as a bondman, and doubtless compelled him to buy his freedom[1].

The Palle Family.   In 1404 account is rendered of the issue of one acre 'quam Robertus Palle recusavit tenere et reliquit in manus domini.'   In 1405 Robert Palle, *nativus,* surrendered two acres to the use of another tenant.   In a roll of 1432 it is recorded that one acre that had escheated upon the death of Robert Palle *nativus* without heir, had been let to farm.

The Pelet Family.   In the fifteenth century some six tenants of this name held small amounts of land—from four to eight acres. One tenant also leased 12½ acres, and afterwards his son leased the same.   Later 14 acres of demesne meadow were also leased by a father and son.   In 1500 but one member of this family held land of Forncett.   He was seized of four messuages and 24 acres.   Three of his sons were tenants, but two of them at least, and probably all three, alienated their land.   The last to hold land of Forncett 'surrendered' it in 1527, and soon thereafter 'fled' to Essex.   He paid no chevage, and we may perhaps assume that by his flight he freed himself from all the ties that had bound him to Forncett manor.

Between 1405 and 1527 nine or ten serfs paid chevage.

---

[1] See above, p. 92, and Appendix XIV.

From the foregoing accounts of the bond families several conclusions may be drawn. From 1400 to 1556 the number of bond
families holding land of Forncett manor steadily diminished, owing
to the withdrawal of serfs from the manor, to the lack of male heirs,
or possibly in some cases to the failure on the part of the heir
to enter upon his inheritance.

Withdrawal from the manor occurred under various conditions.
In many cases the serfs fled, and the manorial officers failed to attach
the fugitives. In other cases they paid chevage for license to remain
away, and the lord apparently failed to keep account of their
descendants or to exact any servile dues from them. After 1500
strict account seems to have been kept of the children of the serfs
who dwelt outside the manor, and some of them at least paid
chevage when they became of age. But, in the fifteenth century,
if a serf left the manor, he was fairly certain to win freedom for
his children, if not for himself.

Now, if the history of villeinage in Forncett is typical of its
history throughout England, sufficient importance has not been
assigned hitherto to the withdrawal of bondmen from the manor as
one of the causes of the disappearance of serfdom. Thus, in an
article in the *English Historical Review* for January, 1900 (p. 29),
we read: ' The fugitive villein appears as a regular character in the
literature and the local and national records. . . . Yet these can
have been only the restless spirits. All mediaeval influences tended
towards stability, not movement. . . . On the manor court rolls
the notices of departure are after all exceptional; the rolls rather
show a striking continuity of population. . . . Flight, like
voluntary manumissions, emancipated occasional persons, not a
whole class.'

But neither the Forncett nor the Moulton rolls show continuity in
the servile population, at least after 1350. The change comes slowly,
but gradually the old names of the bond families disappear. In
Forncett, by 1556, only three bond families were left as tenants
of the manor.

In that year these families were manumitted as well as the families
of two chevage-paying serfs.

After the granting of these manumissions, only two bond families,
and these non-tenants, appear to have been connected with the manor.
In 1563 a bondwoman purchased license to marry. In 1575, as has
been said, Sir Henry Lee sought out the representatives of these two
families and apparently exercised the power granted him by Queen

Elizabeth by compelling them to buy their freedom. Thus, in 1575, serfdom came to an end in Forncett.

Many of the serfs who left the manor went to neighbouring villages. From 1400 to 1575 serfs are named in the extant rolls as having withdrawn to 64 different places. Sixty-seven serfs dwelt in 36 places, which were all within a radius of 10 miles from Forncett ; 38 bondmen remained in 16 places, from 10 to 20 miles from Forncett ; and 21 were in 12 places, more than 20 miles distant.

Twenty-two serfs dwelt in Norwich—about 12 miles from Forncett ; and of the 21 who had travelled furthest, 14 remained in towns along the eastern coast—Martham, Yarmouth, Lowestoft, Somerton, Scratby, Hemesby, and Eccles.

The occupations followed by these fugitive serfs can be learned in only a few instances. One at least was a weaver ; four are described as tailors ; three as tanners ; a saddler, shoemaker, smith, and carpenter are also mentioned. In a number of cases there is evidence that they were servants or agricultural labourers ; and some who had ceased to be tenants of Forncett became tenants of other manors and cultivators of the soil.

How the serfs who left the manor prospered cannot be easily determined, though an occasional will, inventory, or valuation of their goods throws some light on this point. As for those who remained in Forncett, many certainly acquired holdings that were very large as compared with the tenements of their ancestors of the fifteenth century—amounting in a few cases to as much as a hundred acres. And their wills—all of which date from the fifteenth or from the sixteenth century—show that at this period some of the serfs were in comfortable circumstances[1].

---

[1] For an admirable study of the economic condition of serfs in the Tudor period, see A. Savine's 'Bondmen under the Tudors,' *Transactions of the Royal Historical Society*, N. S. xvii. 1903.

CHAPTER VIII.

POPULATION.

SOME forty years ago Dr Seebohm and Professor Thorold Rogers were in controversy regarding the total population of England shortly before the Black Death. Both agreed that in 1377 the population numbered about 2½ millions : but while Dr Seebohm held that before the Pestilence the population numbered five millions, Professor Rogers argued that the food supply available at that time was not sufficient to maintain more than 2½ millions, and that the population in 1346 and 1377 were the same.

Neither disputant presented entirely conclusive arguments. This at any rate seems to be the opinion of Dr Cunningham, who in his *Growth of English Industry and Commerce*[1] sums up the results of the controversy as follows :

'(1) The population was pretty nearly stationary at over two millions from 1377 till the Tudors.

'(2) Circumstances did not favour rapid increase of population between 1350 and 1377.

'(3) The country was not incapable of sustaining a much larger population in the earlier part of Edward III's reign than it could maintain in the time of Henry VII.'

From the negative character of two of these conclusions, it appears that further light is needed on the relative numbers of the population before the Black Death, and in the period from 1377 till the Tudors.

The question is important and difficult. In manor rolls, if anywhere, we might expect to find material for its solution. It is one of the purposes of this chapter to explain the methods that have been employed in attempting to solve the question with regard to Forncett manor. If the methods are sound and if they were applied in the case of a considerable number of other manors, we

---

[1] Vol. I. p. 332 n., 3rd edition.

might obtain a solid basis for generalizing with regard to England as a whole.

It must, however, be admitted at the outset that our method is not easy to apply, and that it leads past many pitfalls, all of which we may not have escaped. Yet as the several tests that we have used all point to one conclusion it seems reasonable to believe that that conclusion is correct.

Three matters will be discussed:

1. Evidence relating to the population of the manor in 1565.

2. Evidence showing a much larger population at an earlier date.

3. Evidence relating to changes in the numbers of the population between 1400 and 1565.

Our first argument is based upon the number of dwelling-houses, not directly upon the population. Yet this argument is probably valid, since it is unlikely that the dwellings of 1565 would have averaged a greater number of inhabitants than the dwellings before 1350.

Dwellings held by bond or copyhold tenure are first considered, for the history of these can be traced with most certainty, since, unlike the 'soiled' dwellings, they were from the first conveyed through the manor court; and their history can be traced with especial ease, since bond-dwellings are usually designated by the name of the 'tenement' of which they formed a part.

It is first necessary to examine the different terms used to denote dwellings or sites of dwellings.

1. *Messuagium.* This is commonly defined as a dwelling-house with the land belonging to it. But this does not appear to be the invariable significance of the term in these rolls. It seems sometimes to mean merely the vacant site. The distinction seems not always to be made between *messuagium* and *messuagium vacuum*. Thus in several instances the messuage of one conveyance is conveyed a few years later as *messuagium vacuum*; yet an examination of the rolls fails to disclose any evidence of the waste or decay of the messuage during the interval between the two conveyances. Again, in a court roll of 1564, 'three rods of land with the messuage of Selegrome tenement' were conveyed to M. N. But, according to the Survey of 1565, the messuage belonging to Selegrome tenement and held by M. N. was vacant.

The rolls give the impression that in the later period it was more usual than before to discriminate between *messuagia* on the one hand and *messuagia vacua* and *messuagia aedificata* on the other hand. Thus from 1499 to 1504 seven messuages were conveyed as *vacua* and seven as *aedificata,* all of which in the conveyances

next preceding had been described simply as *messuagia.* Yet not
a few *messuagia vacua* are mentioned in the early rolls.

But although it is not certain that '*messuagium*' invariably
signifies the existence of a dwelling-house, yet it appears to have
this meaning as a rule at least in 1565; and in attempting to
determine the approximate number of dwellings standing in Forncett
manor in 1565 we have counted each *messuagium* as a dwelling.

Messuagium aedificatum like *messuagium* may conceivably mean
a site upon which stands a barn or other out-building and no
dwelling. But all *messuagia aedificata* have been reckoned as
dwellings. The term is usually applied to those tenements that
have suffered waste and have been repaired.

Dimidium messuagium. Several 'half messuages' are mentioned
in the rolls. In estimating the number of dwellings should two
'half messuages' pertaining to the same bond tenement be reckoned
as one or as two houses? It is probable that in some cases the
division was ideal, indicating the shares held by two tenants in one
dwelling. Therefore when both halves of a messuage are described
in the same terms either as 'built' or as 'vacant' or simply as
messuagium it is considered that but one dwelling or one site is
described. On the other hand the division was sometimes real.
Thus, in Worthknot tenement there were two half messuages, one
built, the other vacant, separated by a ditch. In this case the tenement has been reckoned as built, since normally but one dwelling
belonged to a tenement. In case it were clear that the division was
real and that both halves were built, two dwellings would of course
be counted in calculating the number of dwellings in the manor.

Tenementum. This term is used not merely to denote the
entire holding, but also the mere dwelling or site. In this sense
it is used only a few times.

Messuagia vacua. Several phrases are used as practical equiva-
lents to this expression. Thus we read of *messuagia* and of *cotagia*
'quondam aedificata'; of tofts and of *pictella* 'quondam aedificata,'
and of *pictella* 'jam vacua.' Also we meet with the unqualified
terms 'tofts' and 'pightles,' and understand the former to mean
vacant dwelling sites, though we have not given this interpretation
to the latter term when unqualified.

The evidence regarding the number of dwellings and of vacant
sites found in the Court Rolls (1400–1565) and in the Survey is
presented in tabular form in Appendix IV.

In this table column 1 contains the names of the bond tenements
of the manor. The list has been compiled from two sources: first

from the list of 122 bond tenements given at the end of the Survey of 1565 ; second from the Court Rolls. But a comparison of the list in the Survey with the names of tenements that appear in the Court Rolls and in other parts of the Survey shows that the list (Nos. 1—122) is incomplete[1]. Making due allowance for the possibility that the same tenement may appear under more than one name, it seems safe to add to the surveyor's list the names of at least thirteen more tenements (Nos. 123—135). To this list of 135 bond tenements should be added three purprestures, two or three buildings on former demesne and one cottage 'recently built.'

Column 4 indicates the state of the *messuagia* in 1565—whether built or vacant—as described in the Survey. In a few cases information lacking in the Survey has been supplied from Court Rolls of about the same date.

Columns 5–10 record the dates of those extant Court Rolls in which the *messuagia* of the several tenements are conveyed for the first and last time respectively as *vacua, aedificata,* or simply as *messuagia*.

The information thus tabulated gives an approximate answer to our first question regarding the number of dwellings of bond tenure standing in 1565. These we count as 63, of which 57 formed part of the old servile tenements, while three were cottages (purprestures) near Westwood Green, and three or four buildings were erected comparatively late on former demesne and did not form part of any bond tenement[2].

Since there were some 135 bond tenements within the manor to each of which one messuage or dwelling would normally belong, then if only 57 houses pertaining to 57 bond tenements were standing in 1565 it is clear that at the same date the vacant bond dwelling sites must have numbered about 78. But as the table in Appendix IV. indicates, the vacant sites of only about 44 bond messuages are mentioned as such in conveyances or Survey. The messuages belonging to the 34 other bond tenements are nowhere clearly mentioned in the rolls. But we have reckoned these 34 messuages as vacant ; for the hypothesis that best explains the facts is that they had fallen into decay at an early date (1350–1400), and that

---

[1] For instance, the surveyor has failed to include the only tenement held of Forncett manor in Flordon vill and two out of the three Wymondham tenements.

[2] The three buildings referred to are a cottage built about 1500, near St Mary's Church, and two houses (it is not certain that they were dwellings) also near St Mary's Church and built on former demesne, one in the third and the other in the fourth quarter of the fifteenth century. These two houses are not described in the Survey and are not indicated on the Map. A third house on former demesne is shown on the Map near Cawdwell Common, St Mary's.

after 1400 the site of the former dwelling was conveyed as a ' croft' or ' pightle' or in some cases was not distinguished from arable land. The history of tenement Warde may probably be regarded as typical of the history of these 34 tenements. By 1376 this tenement had reverted to the lord, had been let by him at a money rent, and the tenemental services were no longer rendered. The tenemental name appears in the rolls from time to time in the lists of tenements annually chosen to fill the manorial offices[1]. It appears also in the surveyor's list of 122 tenements, but the lands of the tenement have not been identified by the surveyor, nor is the tenemental name mentioned in any conveyance in connection either with land or with messuage. The land of which the tenement was composed was doubtless conveyed merely as ' bond land[2].' The messuage, it seems probable, had already fallen into decay, and in the later conveyances it was either not distinguished from arable or was conveyed simply as a pightle or croft.

From all the obtainable evidence relative to dwellings held of Forncett manor by bond tenure, we conclude that some 57 were standing in 1565, while at the same date the vacant dwelling sites of this tenure numbered 78.

For information regarding messuages held by free tenure, the Survey of 1565 is practically the only source. According to the Survey, 36 *messuagia* and *messuagia aedificata* and eight *messuagia vacua* were held of Forncett manor freely in 1565; of soiled messuages, the surveyor described 12 as *messuagia* or *messuagia aedificata*, and only one as *vacuum*. But it is probable that these figures are not at all trustworthy as showing the actual proportion between ' built' and ' vacant' sites. The surveyor would certainly be much more likely to omit the recording of vacant sites as such, than of dwellings, and in the case of messuages held freely or by ' soiled' tenure there are not the means of checking his omissions that exist in the case of bond messuages. Very little weight, therefore, should be assigned to these numbers.

It is well known that the literature of the sixteenth century and the Rolls of Parliament contain many complaints relative to the

---

[1] Whenever in the fifteenth or sixteenth centuries this tenement was elected to some manorial office, it was said to be ' in the lord's hands,'—a phrase which in this connection appears to mean that the tenement, having reverted to the lord, and having been let by him at a new tenure, was no longer subject to the old obligations to fill the manorial offices.

[2] In this connection it must be explained that in both conveyances and Survey, a considerable total acreage is described simply as ' bond land' (*terra nativa*), *i.e.* it is not distinguished as pertaining to any tenement. This land is doubtless to be identified with the land of those tenements the names of which do not appear in the conveyances or in the descriptive portion of the Survey, although they are given in the list of tenements.

decay of houses and the diminution of the population, and that beginning with 1488, Parliament passed successive enactments against the pulling down of towns.

On the other hand, it is the opinion of some modern authorities that 'notwithstanding this general testimony to a general depopulation it is not at all certain that the total numbers were actually diminished—nothing is more delusive than popular estimates of population at any time.'[1]

It has been shown that, by 1565, a large number of houses held of Forncett manor had fallen into decay. In how far, if at all, is the decay to be assigned to the period between 1400 and 1565? How far was the number of houses maintained through the erection or repair of buildings? Does the evidence tend to show that the decline in population dates from before 1400 or from a later year?

In the period from 1400 to 1565 there was some rebuilding of houses that had fallen into decay. Thus in 1491 the messuage pertaining to tenement Aunfrey had fallen into decay, but was rebuilt between 1500 and 1542. In 1508 tenement Goodman was granted to a tenant on condition that he rebuild; and in 1565 this tenement was described as 'aedificatum.' In 1429 tenement Rugges was granted to tenants who were to build at their own cost; and in 1536–50 the tenement was 'aedificatum.' In 1496–1500 there was a 'pightle' apparently vacant, that in 1559 was 'aedificatum.' With regard to the rebuilding of old tenements the evidence of the rolls is incomplete, but it is to be observed that most of the instances clearly indicated in the rolls point to the earlier part of the sixteenth century as the period of the rebuilding of tenements.

With regard to the number of messuages newly built, and not forming part of any tenement, though held by bond tenure, the evidence of the rolls is nearly, if not quite, complete. As has already been stated there were at least three such buildings, of which one was erected in the third quarter of the fifteenth century, another in the last quarter of the same century, and the third about 1500.

The amount of evidence regarding the decay of dwellings is considerable; for, during a period beginning before the fifteenth century and continuing up to 1565, the rolls contain many presentments of waste, orders to repair or rebuild, and records of amercements for failure to repair or rebuild. Some of these entries are worded in general terms that, taken by themselves, give little definite

---

[1] Cheyney, *Social Changes in England in the Sixteenth Century*, 41, and Seebohm, *Fortnightly Review*, II. 149 ff., 268 ff.

information. For instance, this formula is sometimes used : ' M. N. vastum fecit in tenemento suo.' From an entry of this sort neither the degree of waste nor the kind of building wasted (dwelling or barn) can be learned. Such an entry also fails to give the name of the tenement, but this can often be supplied. Other entries give more definite information. Thus, in 1431, it was presented that ' W. B. fecit streppum in tenemento Cullyng in bondagio domini de ii domibus decasis et adnichillatis et maeremium inde proveniens abduxit et vendidit. Ideo in misericordia. Et praeceptum est reaedificare sub poena. Item quod R. K. eodem modo fecit in tenemento Willelmi Lound de i. domo capitali. Ideo in misericordia. Et praeceptum est reaedificare.' Many of the presentments fall somewhere between the examples cited as regards fulness of statement.

Starting from 1565, and tracing backwards through the rolls the history of each of the tenements that in 1565 was vacant, the following results are obtained : During the period between 1422–1565 from 6 to 10 tenements became vacant. The clearer cases of waste are :

1. 1426–31. The dwelling belonging to William Lound's tenement was carried off (abduxit). 2. 1431. Two houses (one dwelling?) pertaining to tenement Cullyng were 'annihilated' and the timber sold. In 1455 the 'messuagium' of this tenement was conveyed. This is the last recorded conveyance of the 'messuagium' which was 'vacant' in 1565. 3. 1497. Robert Wrong 'altogether devastated' the cottage pertaining to the tenement of Hugo Spires. From 1497–1565 the messuage of this tenement is described in the conveyances as vacant. 4. 1507–1527. Between these dates the messuage of tenement Hillhouse (*alias* Ratches) appears to have fallen into final decay. 5. 1524. The lord granted a license to let fall a messuage, formerly Pelet's. 6. 1548. License was granted not to rebuild the houses of tenement Brettons ' decayed and devastated divers years before.'

A few more cases of the total decay of dwellings may possibly be concealed among the more vaguely-worded presentments of waste. But a careful examination of the evidence points to the conclusion that at most not more than eight or ten dwellings, held by bond tenure, were totally devastated during the period 1422–1565. As three new buildings held by bond tenure were erected during this period, the conclusion is also reached that within this period there was no considerable diminution in the numbers of the population.

The great diminution in the numbers of dwellings and of population, which is indicated by the large number of 'vacant' messuages recorded in Court Rolls and Survey, must date back to a period before 1422. The materials for the years from 1350 to 1422 are scanty; but the Account Rolls of 1376–8 afford a basis for the belief that already the number of dwellings was much less than it had formerly been. For, in 1376–7, 232 acres of arable, formerly tenants' land, were let to farm. Now nearly all of this land had been held by bond tenure; and since, at an earlier period, the average area of bond land attached to a bond messuage was 7·5 acres, we should expect to find 31 messuages leased in connection with the 232 acres of bond land, provided that no 'decay' of messuages had occurred. That such decay had taken place is doubtless indicated by the fact that only seven messuages were let. There were also let one vacant cottage site, one curtilage, eight pightles, four crofts, and four closes.

For the period before 1350 few Court Rolls remain, but the series for the year 1332–3 is complete. Comparing the rolls of this year with those of the fifteenth century two facts are strikingly apparent; (1) the large number of persons' names and the large number of deaths of tenants recorded in the earlier as compared with the later rolls. Thus the rolls of 1332–3 contain 250 personal names, whereas the rolls of 1460–61 (a complete series chosen at random for comparison) contain only 126. In 1332–3 the deaths of twelve tenants are recorded; as large a number died in the year 1409–10, but, as a rule, the number of deaths entered in the rolls of any one year of the fifteenth century does not exceed three or four. It is of course obvious that the two facts just cited, when taken by themselves, are by no means to be considered as proofs of a greater population before 1350 than in the fifteenth century. But they are evidence of some slight confirmatory value.

All the evidence that has been gathered from the records points to the same conclusion, viz. that during the period 1376–1565 the population of the manor was only about half as great as it had been during the early part of the fourteenth century.

The evidence regarding Forncett vill also points to a similar decline in population. There were within the vill 1680 acres of arable exclusive of the demesne. If, as seems to have been the case, there was in the early fourteenth century one messuage to about eight acres of arable, the number of messuages at that period must have been about 210 or nearly twice the number standing within the vill in 1565.

TYPOGRAPHICAL DEVICES USED IN DOCUMENTS IN APPENDIX.

Doubtful extensions or words are printed within [ ].

Words that have been struck out are printed within { }.

Words that appear to have been added or interpolated are printed within ( ).

APPENDIX I.

MSS. RELATING TO FORNCETT MANOR.

THE following list consists mainly of the documents that have served as a basis for this book. It does not include documents relating chiefly to the feudal history of Forncett, or to the history of Forncett Honor. For a history of the Honor some material exists in a few rolls of the Honor Court or Knights' Court (curia militum, curia forinsec' tenentium) formerly owned by Mr A. C. Cole and now in the Cambridge University Library. The earliest roll dates from 1373. British Museum Additional Charters, 26, 598 contains a grant of the Knights' Court. Lists of knights' fees pertaining to the Honor are to be found in the British Museum, Additional MSS., 25, 293, Additional Charters, 19, 338, and in several Inquisitions post mortem in the Public Record Office, etc. Ministers' Accounts 935/8 (P. R. O.) contains an itemized statement of the receipt of scutages.

In the Public Record Office there are doubtless scores of documents that relate to the manor and its tenants and that are not referred to here. Many of these have been examined but have been omitted from this list because they have not proved serviceable. For further references consult *Norfolk Records* (*Norfolk and Norwich Archaeological Society*, 1886, 1892) and Walter Rye's *Index to Norfolk Topography, Index to Norfolk Pedigrees*, and *Index Rerum to Norfolk Antiquities*.

A. PUBLIC RECORD OFFICE.

    1. Ministers' Accounts :

935/2 (1270).	935/12 (1289–90).
935/3 (1272–3)[1].	935/13 (1292–3).
935/4 (1274–5).	935/14 (1299–1300).
935/5 (1277–8).	935/15 (1302–3).
935/6[2] (1278–9).	935/16 (1303–4).
935/8 (1279–80).	935/17 (1305–6).
935/9[3] (1281–2).	937/10 (1307).
935/10 (1283–4).	1121/1 (1307–8).
935/11 (1285–6).	1093/1 (1409–10).

    2. Inquisitions post mortem, 54 Hen. III. File 38, No. 17.
                         11 Hen. VI. No. 43.

    3. Escheators' Inquisitions.
        Series I. File 1185, Nos. 1 and 3. (1–2 Hen. IV.)
            ,, ,, File 1192, No. 6. (7–8 Hen. IV.)
            ,, ,, File 1215, No. 5. (11–12 Hen. VI.)

---

[1] Printed as Appendix VIII.   [2] 935/7 nearly duplicates 935/6.   [3] Mutilated.

4. Lay Subsidies, Norfolk. 149/7. (1 Ed. III. mostly illegible.)
   149/9. 67. (6 Ed. III.)[1]
5. Exchequer Special Commissions, Norfolk, No. 1602. (35 Elizabeth.)
6. Exchequer Depositions.
   37 Elizabeth, Easter, No. 4.
   37 Elizabeth, Trinity, No. 2.
7. Exchequer Q. R. Bills, Answers, etc. Elizabeth, Norfolk, Nos. 32[2], 161, 165, 196, 249.
8. Misc. Books. Exchequer Augm. Office, Vol. 502. Depwade, 33, 35.

B. BRITISH MUSEUM.

1. Egerton MSS., 2714, folio 204. Letter from Sir John Fortescue to the Steward of Forncett Manor, 1602.

C. CAMBRIDGE UNIVERSITY LIBRARY.

1. Account Rolls, 1376–8[3].
2. Court Rolls. 1332, 1333, 1342–1344, 1346–1348, 1358, 1373–1375, 1387, 1394, 1399, 1400[4]–1413, 1422–1451, 1454–1478, 1480–1509, 1523–65, and many rolls of later date.
3. Roll of Richmond rents pertaining to the Manor of Forncett, 2 and 3 Philip and Mary.
4. Survey, 1565[5].

D. HERALDS' COLLEGE.

1. Arundel MSS., No. 49, folio 24. Account Roll, 1527–8.

E. ARCHIVES OF THE DUKE OF NORFOLK.

1. Account Roll, 1605.
2. Court Roll, 1415.

F. OFFICE OF CLERK OF THE PEACE, SHIRE HALL, NORWICH.

1. Enclosure Award and Plan, 1813.

G. FORNCETT RECTORY.

1. Terriers, 1635 and later.
2. Tithe Apportionment and Map, S. Peter's, 1839 ; S. Mary's, 1841.

H. IN PRIVATE HANDS.

1. Court Rolls, temp. Ed. II. or Ed. III. (only a few abstracts examined).

I. PLACE OF DEPOSIT NOT KNOWN.

1. Inquisition post mortem, 35 Ed. I. No. 46, 'Fornesett maner' extent.' Catalogued in Public Record Office but apparently lost.
2. 'Accounts of the Manor and Honour of Forncet in the County of Norfolk, upon vellum. A roll 10 feet × 11 inches, 1395.' No. 675 in Puttick and Simpson's Catalogue of Sir John Fenn's Library, July 1866.
3. 'A Terrier of Moulton, Forncet, Wacton and Takelstone Hall in Norfolk ; a very valuable and ancient MS. on vellum, finely preserved.' No. 4695 in Messrs Booth and Berry's Catalogue of the Library of Mr Thomas Martin of Palgrave, reprinted in the *Norfolk Antiquarian Miscellany*, iii. 394 ff. Mr Martin's Library was dispersed about 1775.

---

[1] Printed as Appendix V.   [2] Printed as Appendix XIV.
[3] Printed as Appendix IX.   [4] A court roll of 1400 is printed as Appendix X.
[5] A partial abstract is printed as Appendix II.

APPENDIX II.

ABSTRACT OF PART OF THE SURVEY OF 1565.

THE portion of the Survey here given in abstract form relates to the first furlong of the fourth precinct of Forncett St Mary's. The strips are numbered from west to east ; unless otherwise stated, they were held of Forncett manor.

l. = terra libera ; n. = terra nativa ; s. = terra soliata ; ten. = tenement.

No. of piece	Area a. r.	Tenure	Tenant
1	3	l.	S. Buxton
2	3	n. ten. Eldred	,,
3	1½	glebe	Rector of Tacolneston
4	3	l.	H. Bexwell
5	2	n. ten. Baxter	J. Browne, sen.
6	2	s. (1 a.)	,,
7	2	l. of Tacolneston manor	W. Isbels
8	2	n. ten. Worthknot	,,
9	1 2	[n.] ten. Husbondes	Heirs of W. Wickes
10	2	l.	W. Kempe
11	3	n. ten Fitz Richard	J. Browne, sen.
12	2½	l. of Tacolneston manor	J. Browne at Style
13	1	—[1]	J. Browne, sen.
14	2	s.	T. Allexander
15	1½	l.	W. Kempe
16	2	n.	W. Isbels
17	2	l. of Tacolneston manor	S. Buxton
18	2	n.	W. Isbels
19	3	glebe	Rector of Tacolneston
20	2	l.	R. Browne
21	2	n. of Tacolneston manor	W. Isbels
22	1½	glebe	Rector of Tacolneston
23	3	l. of Tacolneston manor	Jno. Brown at Stile
24	2 2	glebe	Rector of Tacolneston
25	3	l.	Rob. Browne, sen.
26	3	l.	Jno. Browne, jun.
27	1½	l.	R. Browne, sen.
28	3	n. ten. R. Haughne	E. Davy
29	3	?	S. Buxton
30	3	l. of Tacolneston manor	T. Britief

[1] Tenure not stated.

No. of piece	Area a. r.	Tenure	Tenant
31	3	n.	E. Davy
32	1½	—	Rob. Browne, sen.
33	1	l. of Williams manor	R. Lincoln
34	1	—	T. Lincoln
35	2	n.	W. Kempe
36	2	s.	S. Browne
37	2	n. ten. Polpard	,,
38	2	n.	J. Britief
39	3	glebe	Rector of Tacolneston
40	2	l. of Tacolneston manor	W. Lincoln
41	2	glebe	Rector of Tacolneston
42	1	n. of Tacolneston manor	J. Britief
43	1½	s.	S. Buxton
44	3	n. (demesne)	W. Lincoln
45	1	l.	J. Brown at Stile
46	1	s.	J. Britief
47	2	ten. Eldredes	J. Brown at Stile
48	2	n. (demesne)	W. Lincoln
49	2	n.	W. Kempe
50	1	—	H. Britief
51	3	n.	W. Browne
52	1	glebe	Rector of Tacolneston
53	1½	—	Heirs of J. Britief
54	1½	n. ten. Polpard	R. Green
55	3	n. of Tacolneston manor	S. Browne
56	1½	l.	R. Browne
57	1½	n. of Tacolneston manor	S. Browne
58	1	l.	J. Britief
59	1	n.	R. Green
60	1	n.	S. Browne
61	3	n.	,,

APPENDIX III.

ENTRIES IN DOMESDAY BOOK RELATING TO THE VILL OF FORNCETT GROUPED ACCORDING TO HAMLETS.

TERRA ROGERI BIGOTI.

(ii. 180. b.) Fornesseta tenuit Colemanus liber homo sub Stigando. 1 carucata terrae. Tunc 1 villanus, post et modo 2. Et 1 ecclesia, 15 acr. Tunc 8 bordarii, post 10, modo 14. Semper 2 carucae in dominio et 2 carucae hominum. 12 acrae prati. Tunc 2 runcini, modo 5. Tunc 10 animalia, modo 12. Tunc 1 ovis, modo 80. Tunc 1 porcus, modo 18. Et 3 sochemanni, 27 acr. Tunc 1 caruca, modo dimidia. Et 1 bereuita Oslactuna....Et aliam bereuitam tenet Willelmus Tuanatunati....Tunc totum [i.e. Fornesseta, Oslactuna, Tuanatuna, Kekelingetuna, and Halas] valuit 60 solidos, modo 6 libras....Fornesseta habet 1 leugam in longitudine et dimidiam in latitudine et 6 d. et obol. de geldo.... (181. a.) In Fornesseta 30 acras tenuit Olfus T. R. E. Semper 1 villanus et 3 bordarii et 1 servus. Tunc et post 1 caruca in dominio, modo nil. Semper dimidia caruca hominum. 6 acrae prati. Silva 8 porcis. Tunc 1 runcinus. Tunc 3 animalia.......[a number of sokemen in neighbouring vills].......Tunc valuit totum 80 solidos modo 100 [solidos] et 10 denarios. Rex et Comes socam.

ISTI SUNT LIBERI HOMINES ROGERI BIGOT.

(189. a.) In Fornesseta 6 liberi homines commend[ati], 85 ac. Tunc 3 carucae, modo 2. 5 acrae prati.... (189. b.) In Fornesseta 1 liber homo, 2 ac.

TERRAE OSBERNI EPISCOPI.

(202. a.) In Foneseta 1 liber homo Stigandi, 30 ac. Semper 2 bordarii. Tunc et post 1 caruca, modo dimidia. 4 acrae prati. Tunc 2 molindina, post 1, modo 2. Et 2 liberi homines, 2 ac. Tunc valuit 20 solidos, post et modo 30[1].

INVASIONES IN NORDFULC.

(280. a.) In Forneseta tenuit Scula liber homo 13 acras de quo habuit antecessor Hermeri commendationem T. R. E. Modo est in manu regis. Valet 10 denarios. In hac terra erat domus T. R. E. quam Oschetel praepositus regis transtulit et ex hoc dedit vadem.

---

[1] A holding of 30 acres in Tasburgh is included in these values as well as the Forncett property.

Terra Rogeri Bigoti

(180. b.) Aliam bereuitam tenet Willelmus Tuanatunati, 40 ac. Semper 3 bordarii. Semper 1 caruca in dominio et dimidia caruca hominum. Et 4 acrae prati. Et 3 animalia. Et 1 sochemannus, 3 acr.... (181. a.) Et Tuanatuna 11 quarentinae in longitudine et 6 in latitudine et 10 perticae. Et 11 d. et obol. de gelto....In Tuanatuna 2 sochemanni, 6 acr.... (181. b.) In Tuanatuna 30 acras tenuit Hardekinc liber homo T. R. E. Semper 4 bordarii. Tunc 3 servi, modo 2. Semper 1 caruca in dominio et dimidia caruca hominum. Et 1 molendinum. Et 3 acrae prati. Et 11 liberi homines subse T. R. E. commend., 20 acr. Tunc 1 caruca et dimidia, modo 1. Tunc valuit 15 solidos, modo 23 et 7 denarios. Hoc reclamat de dono regis. Hoc tenet Walterus.

Isti sunt liberi homines Rogeri Bigot.

(189. b.) In Tuanestuna 12 liberi homines, 140 ac. Et 3 bordarii. Modo tenet Willelmus. Tunc 5 carucae, post 4, modo 3. Et 8 acrae prati. In eadem sub istis 4 liberi homines et dimidius, 6 ac. Et dimidia caruca....In Tuanatuna 1 liber homo Oslac, 30 acr. Tunc 5 bordarii, modo 10. Tunc 3 servi, modo 1. Semper 1 caruca in dominio et 1 caruca hominum. 4 acrae prati et 4 sochemanni, 6 ac. Et dimidia caruca. Et 1 ecclesia, 60 ac. de libera terra, elemosina plurimorum....In Tanatuna 3 liberi, 4 ac.

Terrae Alani Comitis.

(150. b.) In Tuanetuna 2 sochemanni, 7 ac. Et dimidia caruca.

Terrae Alani Comitis.

(150. b.) In Mildeltuna 1 liber homo et dimidius, 12 ac. et dim. Et dimidia caruca. Et 2 acrae prati. Hoc...est in pretio de Costeseia.

Terra Rogeri Bigoti.

(180. b.) In Kekelingetuna 2 sochemanni, 7 ac. Tunc dimidia caruca, modo 2 boves.... (181. a.) In Kekilingetuna 2 sochemanni, 6 ac.

Isti sunt liberi homines Rogeri Bigot.

(189. a.) In Kikelingatuna 3 liberi homines, 48 ac. Et 1 caruca. Et 3 acrae prati.... (189. b.) In Kikelingatuna 2 liberi homines, 2 ac.

Terrae Alani Comitis.

(150. b.) In Kekilinctuna 3 liberi homines, 73 ac. Et 3 bordarii. Tunc 2 carucae, post et modo 1 caruca et dimidia. Et 4 acrae prati.

APPENDIX IV.

BOND TENEMENTS OF FORNCETT MANOR, 1400-1565.

In column 3, M. = Moulton; K. = Keklington; Tac. = Tacolneston; F. M. = Forncett St Mary; W. = Wacton; F. P. = Forncett St Peter; T. = Twanton; C. = Carleton; S. = Stratton; Wy. = Wymondham; Tib. = Tibenham; B. = Bunwell; H. = Hapton; A. = Aslacton; Fun. = Fundenhall; Tas. = Tasburgh.

In column 4, m. = messuagium or cotagium; vac. = messuagium or cotagium vacuum; ed. = messuagium or cotagium edificatum.

	Name of tenement	Acreage	Location	Condition of homestead in 1565	Homestead first conveyed as 'messuag.'	Homestead last conveyed as 'messuag.'	Homestead first conveyed as 'vacuum'	Homestead last conveyed as 'vacuum'	Homestead first conveyed as 'edificatum'	Homestead last conveyed as 'edificatum'
1	Abbott	2 a. 2½ r.	M.	m.	1455	1564	—	—	—	—
2	Alverard or Alverde	5 a.	—	—	—	—	—	—	—	—
3	Aunfrey[1]	30 a. terrae 4 a. bosci 4 a. prati	K.	m.	1408	1494	—	—	1500	1542
4	Avelyn	5 a. terrae 1½ r. prati	Tac.	vac.	1463	1474	1499	1554	—	—
5	Aye	7 a. terrae	F. M.	vac.[2]	1406	1548	—	—	—	—
6	Backefenne	3 a. prati 12 a. terrae	F. M.	—	—	—	—	—	—	—
7	Baldwyn	3 r. prati 5 a. terrae 3 r. prati 2 r. turbariae	Tac.	m.	1422	1534	—	—	—	—
8	Barker	8 a.	W.	m.	1454	1558	—	—	—	—
9	Barnardes	10 a. terrae 3 r. prati	{ K. Tac.	—	—	—	—	—	—	—
10	Barron	8 a.	K.	m.	1426[3]	1536	1431[4]	1446[4]	—	—
11	Bartram	6 a. 2 r.	S.	vac.	—	—	—	—	—	—

[1] Seized in 1500 because of waste. The tenant 'per longum tempus antea et adhuc percussa est cum frennesia et aliis infirmitatibus non habens discressionem praedictum messuagium...occupare et manutenere prout decet.' Regranted to same tenant and heirs.
[2] *Sic*, in Survey.
[3] 1400, toft.
[4] Tofts, 'quondam edificat.'

D.

8

Name of tenement	Acreage	Location	Condition of homestead in 1565	Homestead first conveyed as 'messuag.'	Homestead last conveyed as 'messuag.'	Homestead first conveyed as 'vacuum'	Homestead last conveyed as 'vacuum'	Homestead first conveyed as 'edificatum'	Homestead last conveyed as 'edificatum'
12 Batalye	8 a. 2 r.	C.	(a) ed. (b) vac.	(a and b) 1400 or 1404	(a) 1493 (b) 1491	—	—	(a) 1525	(a) 1541
13 Beckehouse	5 a.	F. M.	vac.	1432	1464	1501	1501	—	—
14 Bigge	10 a.	{Tib. M.	—	—	—	—	—	—	—
15 Blomes	6 a. 1 r.	W.	ed. (?)	1408	—	—	—	—	—
16 Blunte	10 a. 1½ r.	M.	m.[1]	1402[2]	1565	—	—	—	—
17 Bolle	5 a.	—	—	—	—	—	—	—	—
18 Brakest	5 a.	M.	vac.	1428	1454	1504	1559	—	—
19 Brighouse[3]	6 a.	W.	—	—	—	—	—	—	—
20 Brixson	11 a. 1½ r.	Tac.	vac.	1464[4]	1464[4]	1477	1554	—	—
21 Broketothe	6 a. terrae / 1 a. prati / 2 r. bosci / 1 a. turbariae	F. P.	m.	1410[5]	1559[6]	—	—	—	—
22 Thos. Browne	2 a. 2 r.	{K. F. M.	m.	1469	1560	—	—	1429	1429
23 Browne voc. Bretons[7]	8 a.	K.	vac.	—	—	—	—	—	—
24 Bullitout	3 a.	M.	m.	—	—	—	—	—	—
25 Bullitout	5 a. 2 r.	M.	m.	—	—	—	—	—	—
26 J. Bullitout	4 a. 2 r.	M.	—	—	—	—	—	—	—
27 Burbills	18 a. terrae / 2 a. prati et turbariae / 3 r. feugar.	F. M.	vac.	1402	1447	1486[8]	1558[8]	—	—
28 Carpes	8 a. 3 r.	B.	(a) ed. (b) m.	(a) 1434 (b) 1559[9]	(a) 1470 (b) 1563	—	—	(a) 1477	(a) 1558
29 Ivo Charyers	3 a.	F. M.	vac.	1443	1443	—	—	—	—
30 Cleres	5 a.	T.	—	—	—	—	—	—	—

(a) 'Parcella unius messuagii cum quadam domo superedificata.' (b) 'Pictellum jam vac.'

1 Each of two tenants holds half of a messuage. 2 In 1401, a toft was conveyed; in 1402, one-fourth of a messuage. 6 One-third of messuage.

3 1412, pightle. 4 Half messuage. 5 Parcel of messuage.

7 Browne voc. Bretons. 8 In 1508, waste in Brettons tenement; in 1548 license not to re-build houses which had decayed 'many years before.'

8 Pightle. 9 The tenant holding in 1559 had taken the messuage in 9 Henry VIII.—a year for which the rolls are lost.

No.	Tenant	Acreage	Init.	Status						
31	Simon Cleres	2 a.	F. P.	vac.	—	—	—	—	—	—
32	Coll	2 a. 2 r.	—	—	1426	1440	1472	1560	—	—
33	Colman	9 a.	S.	vac.	—	—	—	—	—	—
34	Cooper	5 a.	F. M.	vac.	1412	1455	—	—	—	—
35	Cullyng	5 a.	F. M.	vac.	—	—	—	—	—	—
36	Culliour	7 a.	Tac., F. M.	vac.	1410[1]	1455[2]	1537	1537	1497[2]	1497[2]
37	Darlinges	5 a.	F. P.	(m.)[3]	1444	1444	—	—	—	—
38	Dewes	6 a.	S.	m.	1438	1464	—	—	—	—
39	Disse	7 a.	K.	m.	1464	1560	—	—	—	1561
40	Drill	5 a.	F. M.	ed.	1442	1442	—	—	1457	—
41	Benedict Drill[4]	2 a. 2 r.	F. M.	—	1436	1454	1500	1542	—	—
42	Edwardes[5]	11 a.	F. M.	vac.	1426	1439	—	—	1477	—
43	Elfleets	5 a.	F. P.	ed.	—	—	—	—	—	1561
44	Elswethes	7 a.	F. P.	vac.	—	—	1434[6]	(1538)[6]	—	—
45	Elvered or Eldrede	5 a. terrae, 2 r. prati, 1½ r. feugar.	F. M.	—	—	—	—	—	—	—
46	Fitz Galfrid	7 a.	M.	vac.	1412	1457	—	—	—	—
47	Galgrym	5 a.	F. M.	vac.	—	—	—	—	—	—
48	Gallard	2 a. 2 r.	F. P.	—	—	—	—	—	—	—
49	Hu. Gallard	5 a.	Tac.	vac.	1440	1530[7]	—	—	1447	1499
50	Gobigo	5 a.	C.	vac.[8]	1436	1493	—	—	—	—
51	Goldes	4 a.	—	—	—	—	—	—	—	—
52	Goodwyn Raven	2 a. 2 r.	M.	'modo'[9] edif.'	—	—	(1405)[9]	(1495)[9]	—	—
53	Michael Goose	—	M.	ed.	1400	1492	—	—	—	—
54	Grayes[10]	6 a. 2 r.	W.	vac.	—	—	—	—	1504	—
55	Harrold	14 a. 1 r.	M.	—	—	—	1543	1543[11]	—	1562
56	Haughne	11 a. 2 r. terrae, 1 a. prati, 2 r. turbariae	F. P., F. M.	vac.	—	—	1431	1561	—	—

[1] Part of messuage.　　[2] Half messuage.

[3] Survey, V. 5. 5.—'W. Botie tenet libere ut dicit parvam parcellam terrae cum parcella cotagii tenementi Darlinges.'

[4] 1541. 1 ac. = pightle.　　[5] 1376, Farm of 'cotag. non edific.'　　[6] Toft.　　[7] Half messuage.　　[8] 'Pictellum quondam edificatum.'

[9] Apparently vacant through fifteenth century, as the total acreage of this tenement was conveyed in 1405, 1435, 1447, 1467 and 1495, but without mention of a messuage.

[10] About 1527 two 'mess. edif.', of which one belonged to ten. Greye and the other to ten. Blomes, were seized for lack of repairs. Tenant was admitted on condition that he rebuild.

[11] There is reason to believe that this messuage was vacant at least as early as 1436.

Name of tenement	Acreage	Location	Condition of homestead in 1565	Homestead first conveyed as 'messuag.'	Homestead last conveyed as 'messuag.'	Homestead first conveyed as 'vacuum'	Homestead last conveyed as 'vacuum'	Homestead first conveyed as 'edificatum'	Homestead last conveyed as 'edificatum'
57 Ric. Haughne	5 a. terrae et prati	F. M.	ed.	1440	1470	—	—	1457	1561
58 W. Haughne	10 a.	F. M.	vac.	1438	1564	1501	1538	—	—
59 Haywardes	9 a. terrae; 1 a. 2 r. prati; 2 r. turbariae; 1 r. feugar.	F. M.	vac.	1443	1464	—	—	—	—
60 Reg. Herberd	10 a.	Tac.	ed.	1401	1444	—	—	1458	1559
61 Heveliche	11 a.	M.	vac.	1410	1410	1491	1563¾	1478	1478
62 Ric. Hill	18 a. terrae; 2 a. bosci; 2 a. prati; 2 a. turbariae	F.	m.	1401	1552	—	—	—	—
63 Roger Hill	18 a.	M.	ed.	1433	1536	—	—	—	—
64 Walter Hill alias Baxter	18 a. terrae; 2 a. 2 r. prati; 1 a. 2 r. turbariae	Tac., F. M.	ed.	—	—	—	—	1477	1565
65 Jno. Hirnyng	2 r. feugar.; 8 a.	A.	—	—	—	—	—	—	—
66 Walt. Hirnyng	8 a.	M.	—	—	—	—	—	—	—
67 Hoddings	5 a. terrae; 1½ r. turbariae	F. P., Tac.	vac.	1401	1477	1499	1554	—	—
68 Hors	2 a. 2 r.	F. P.	ed.[1]	—	—	1456	1541	—	—
69 Houlot	5 a.	F. P.	m.	—	1563¾	—	—	—	—
70 Hulle	18 a.	T.	m.	(a) 1423 (b) 1456	1557	—	—	—	—
71 Husbondes	24 a. terrae; 2 a. 2 r. prati; 2 a. bosci; 3 r. turbariae	F. M.	ed.	1425	1428	—	—	1456	1564
72 Rob. Ive	4 a.	K.	vac.[1]	1413	1499	1501	1535	—	—
73 Jordons	7 a. 2 r.	C.	—	1423	1495	1527	1565	1499	1538
74 Joye	7 a. 1 r.	C.	(a) vac. (b) ed.	1404	1446	—	—	1504	1540

[1] *Sic*, in Survey.

(a) (b) Half messuage.

No.	Name	Acreage	Initials	Status						
75	Kede	8 a. terrae; 2 r. prati	F. M.	—	—	—	—	—	—	—
76	Kemphead	11 a. 1 r. terrae; 1 r. prati	M.; A.	m.	1402	1558	—	—	—	—
77	Kinge	7 a.	F. P.	vac.	1405	1411	—	—	—	—
78	Leve	7 a.	F. M.	—	—	—	—	—	—	—
79	Ad. Long	5 a.	—	—	—	—	—	—	—	—
80	Ralph Lound[1]	7 a. terrae; 2 a. prati; 1 a. turbariae	F. M.	ed.	—	—	1447	1447	1457	1545
81	Roger Lound	7 a.	F. M.	(m.)	1437	1480	—	—	—	—
82	Wm. Lound	5 a.	F. M.	m.	1487	1548	—	—	—	—
83	Lumpes	2 a. 2 r.	S.	(vac.)[2]	—	—	—	—	—	—
84	Micklemowe	2 a.	M.	m.	1426	—	—	—	—	—
85	Ad. Miles	3 a.	K.	vac.	—	1536	1400[3]	1400[3]	—	—
86	Mones	5 a.	F. P.	ed.	1451	1458	1428[3]	1552[4]	—	—
87	Morehouse	18 a.	T.	vac.	—	—	—	—	1503	1560
88	Mowe	5 a.	M.	—	—	—	—	—	—	—
89	Oldestherst	5 a.	M.	—	—	—	(1405)	(1433)	—	—
90	Ordinges alias Osgottes	7 a. terrae prati et turbariae	Tas.	2 ed.[5]	—	—	—	—	(a) 1500; (b) 1497	(a) 1548; (b) 1504
91	Osburne	5 a.	Tib.	—	—	—	—	—	—	—
92	Osgoot	2 a. 3 r.	C.	—	—	—	—	—	1551	156½
93	Penninges	5 a.	C.	(a) ed.; (b) vac.	1433, 1423, 1457, 1463	1483, 156½, 1536	—	—	—	—
94	Penninges	5 a.	F.	(a) m.; (b) vac.	1403, 1426, 1446	—	1508	1560	—	—
95	Polpardes	7 a.	F.	vac.	—	1476, 1464	—	—	1501	1540
96	Pate	7 a.	W.	m.	—	156¾, 1488	—	—	—	—
97	Rafen	5 a.	K.	ed.	—	—	—	—	1505	1560
98	Simon Fitz Richard	18 a. terrae; 1 a. bosci; 3 a. prati	Tac.; F.	m.	1440	1561	1478	1478	—	—
99	Roweye	10 a. terrae; 1½ r. prati	F.	vac.	1411	1439	1476	1542	—	—

[1] Apparently vacant since the total acreage of the tenement was several times conveyed but always without mention of the messuage.
[2] In Survey tenant holds 'pightle containing two acres.'
[3] Toft.
[4] 'Cum parcella terrae quondam messuagio.'
[5] Apparently there were two 'messuagia edificata' connected with this tenement from 1500—1565.

Appendix IV.

	Name of tenement	Acreage	Location	Condition of homestead in 1565	Homestead first conveyed as 'messuag.'	Homestead last conveyed as 'messuag.'	Homestead first conveyed as 'vacuum'	Homestead last conveyed as 'vacuum'	Homestead first conveyed as 'edificatum'	Homestead last conveyed as 'edificatum'
100	Rugge	5 a.	F.	vac.	1446	1552	—	—	1536	1558
101	Rugge	3 a. 2 r.	M.	ed.	1473	1492	1429	1429	—	—
102	Rust voc. Baret	5 a.	H.	m.	1412	1461	—	—	—	—
103	Seiphire Preest	12 a. terrae / 2 r. prati / 1 a. turbariae	Fun.	vac.	1438	1438	1423[2]	1555	—	—
104	Selegroms	8 a.	T.	vac.	1546	156¾	—	—	—	—
105	Roger Smythe	2 a. 2 r.	F. P.	vac.	1412	1444	—	—	—	—
106	Sparhauke	13 a.	Wy.	vac.[1]	—	—	(1403)[2] 1457	1536	—	—
107	Spellers	5 a.	—	vac.	—	—	1497	1565	—	—
108	Hu. Spiers	7 a.	K.	vac.	1449	1491	—	—	—	—
109	Splitte	5 a.	K.	ed.	1446	1488	—	—	1505	1560
110	Tolie	16 a.	S.	ed.	1439	1468	—	—	1477	1552
111	Turner	7 a.	F. P.	ed.	1410	1447	—	—	1501	1546
112	Ukkes	19 a. 1½ r. terrae / 3 a. bosci / 1 a. prati / 1 a. pasturae / 2 a. turbariae	F.	m.	1410	1559	—	—	—	—
113	Wallenger	10 a. terrae / 3 r. prati	K.	ed.	—	—	1476[3]	1507[3]	1559	1559
114	Warde	5 a.	A. M.	—	—	—	—	—	—	—
115	White	5 a.	A.	m.	1440	1560	—	—	—	—
116	Whiting	8 a.	—	m.	(b) 1475	1540	—	—	(a) 1449 (b) 1461	(b) 1498 1469
117	Wisman	5 a.	—	—	—	—	—	—	—	—
118	Woodrowe	5 a.	—	—	—	—	—	—	—	—
119	Woodrowe	2 a. 2 r.	—	—	—	—	—	—	—	—
120	Worthknot	10 a.	Tac., F. M.	ed.	1446	1446	(b) 1461	1561	(a) 1461	(a) 1561
121	Wrong	2 a. 2 r.	K.	vac.	—	—	—	—	—	—
122	Yol or Zolle	15 a.	M.	m.	1405	1462	—	—	1530	1537

(a) (b) Half messuage. [1] Probably vacant. In 1432 the messuage was 'valde debile.' The tenant, however, was ordered to repair.
[2] Toft. [3] Pightle.

	Name									
123	Barfoot	—	Wy.	vac.	1413	1413	—	—	—	—
124	Crowes	—	F.	—	1449	1449	—	—	—	—
125	Flededes[1]	—	K.	—	1411	1411	—	—	—	—
126	Goodman	—	F.M.	ed.	1406	1563	1527	1563¾	1504	1507
127	Hillhouse	—	Wy.	vac.	1474	1474	1457	1536	—	—
128	Hippels	—	K.	vac.	—	—	1480	1557	—	—
129	Kelpons	—	F.P.	vac.	1450	1454	1457	1536	—	—
130	Mundes	—	K.	—	—	—	—	—	—	—
131	Nunnes	—	Flordon	—	—	—	—	—	—	—
132	Skirmishers	—	K.	ed.	1443	1464	—	—	1500	1538
133	Ulves	—	F.	vac.	1440	1440	—	—	—	—
134	Walshes	—	{Tac. K.	vac.	—	—	1411[2]	1559⅝	—	—
135	Yoles or Boles	—	M.	m.	1465	1537	—	—	—	—

[1] 1376, Farm of pightle.   [2] 1411, toft; 1478 and later, 'messuagium quondam edificatum.'

APPENDIX V.

LAY SUBSIDY, 149/9. 67. (1332).

VILLATA DE FORNESETE.

De Thoma Comite Norfolciae	xiiis.	iiiid.
De Rogero de Lound	iiis.	
De Ade de Lound		viiid.
De Johanne Herberd		viiid.
De Ricardo Kolet		viiid.
De Ricardo Haghne		viiid.
De Johanne Stevenes		xd.
De Ricardo Virly		xd.
De Willelmo Fayrman		xiid.
De Johanne Geyre		xd.
De Willelmo Dosy		viiid.
De Roberto Benselyn		viiid.
De Willelmo de Flordon		xd.
De Willelmo Aye		xd.
De Hugone Polpard		xd.
De Ricardo Dryl		xiid.
De Johanne de Lound		xiid.
De Ricardo Seriaunt		viiid.
De Waltero Edward		xiid.
De Ricardo Ulf		xiid.
De Roberto Geyre		xd.
De Willelmo Haghne		viiid.
De Roberto de Galgrym		viiid.
De Rogero Colyour		viiid
De Roberto Colyour		viiid.
De Rogero Baxtere		xviiid.
De Roberto Bek		xiid.
De Ade clerico		viiid.
De Johanne Elfred		viiid.
De Avelina le clerk		xiid.
De Willelmo Lewyn		xd.
De Waltero Gallard		viiid.
De Hugone Raven		viiid.
De Ricardo Gallard		xiid.
De Beatrice le Smyth		viiid.

De Rogero le Wayte		xiid.
De Johanne Baroun		viiid.
De Willelmo Gallard		xxd.
De Petro Lewyn		xd.
De Ricardo Hagne		viiid.
De Waltero Lewyn		viiid.
De Johanne le Clerk		xd.
De Johanne Shepird		xiid.
De Ricardo Gallard		xiid.
De Ricardo Aunfrey		xiid.
De Roberto de Hill		xviiid.
De Willelmo de Hill		viiid.
De Johanne Cupere		viiid.
De Rogero de Hill	iis.	iid.
De Johanne Seriaunt		viiid.
De Ricardo Bacoun		viiid.
De Thoma de Banham		viiid.
De Roberto le Suter		xd.
De Margareta Anastaz		xiiiid.
De Alicia Anastaz		xd.
De Johanne Belinle		xiid.
De Johanne Bustard		viiid.
De Rogero de Skeyton		xvid.
De Willelmo Bronston	vis.	
De Roberto Sariaunt		xiid.
De Johanne de Mor		viiid.
De Roberto Hulot		viiid.
De Johanne filio Ricardi		viiid.
De Ricardo Geyre		viiid.
De Waltero Bakefyn		xd.
De Ricardo Hulot		xiid.
De Ricardo Geyre		viiid.
De Henrico Hagghne		xiid.
De Rogero Oliver		viiid.
De Rogero Gallard		viiid.
De Thoma Benetout		viiid.

Summa iiiili. viid.
probatur.

APPENDIX VI.

LANDHOLDERS IN FORNCETT VILL AND TENANTS OF FORNCETT MANOR, 1565.

		In vill		In manor					In vill		In manor	
		A.	R.	A.	R.				A.	R.	A.	R.
1	Baxter, Thos.	164	1	131	2½	36	Bounde, Ric.		13		10	
2	Davy, Ed.	121	1	118		37	Browne, jun., Ric.		12	1	17	2½
3	Botie, Wm.	101	3	76		38	Bottomley, Rob.		10		10	
4	Whitefoote, Ric.	88	3	53	1	39	Buxton, Milo		9	3	9	3
5	Lincoln, Thos.	87	3	81	1	40	Baxter, Steph.		9	2	9	
6	Smith, Launcelot	68	3	68	3	41	Sad, Arthur		9	1	6	
7	Browne, jun., Jno.	65	1	81		42	Browne, sen., Jno.		8	2	22	½
8	Denne, Thos.	64	3	20		43	Lavyle, Ric.		8	2	26	2½
9	Browne, Steph.	64		63	3½	44	Botild, alias Hen-					
10	Britief, Jno.	62	2½	54	2½		nowe, Jno.		7	3	4	3
11	Hynde, Jno.	61		25	1	45	Goold, Jno.		7	1	7	1
12	Buxton, Stephen	57	2½	50	3	46	Browne, at Stile, Jno.		7		25	3½
13	Baxter, Jno.	56		24		47	Harte, Jno.		6	2½	6	2½
14	Ringer, Thos.	54		18	3	48	Browne, Wm.		4	½	32	1
15	Alexander, Ed.	52		47	1	49	Kettell, Johanna		3	2½	3	2½
16	Britief, Heirs of Jno.	49		52	1½	—	Deye, Leonard		3		—	
17	Baxter, Ric.	46		54	3½	—	Dowsing, Thos.		2	3	—	
18	Alexander, Kath.	45		38	½	50	Fuller, Humfridus		2	3	2	3
19	Greene, jur. ux., Rob.	41	1	41	1	51	Isbelles, Wm.		2	2	6	2
20	Lincoln, Wm.	41	1	35	3½	52	Wickes, Heirs of Wm.		2	2	2	2
21	Fawsett, Johanna	40	3	37	3	53	Sherman, Ric.		2	1	2	1
22	Clarke, Rob.	40		40		54	Bert, Jno.		2		7	
23	Cock, Rob.	38	2	40	2	55	Alman, —		2		2	
24	Alexander, Henry	34	2½	25	2½	56	Fulcher, Walter		2		2	
25	Botild alias Hen-					57	Cooke, Wm.		1	2	1	2
	nowe, Rob.	28	2	18	2	58	Thompson, Ed.		1	1	1	1
26	Kempe, Wm.	25	1½	28	½	59	Whitefoot, Geo.		1	1	1	1
27	Burgess, Jno.	25	1½	24	½	60	Parmenter, Eliz.		1		1	
28	Allen, Ed.	25	½	22	2½	61	Jacob, Ed.		1		1	
29	Gallard, Jno.	20	2	18	1	62	Newman, Thos.		1		1	
30	Lincoln, Rob.	20		26	3	63	Duncan, Wm.		1		1	
31	Browne, Rob.	18		24		64	Bexwell, Henry			3		3
32	Deye, Alice	16	3	14	3	65	Jacob, Thos.			3		3
33	Botie, Jno.	16	1	15	3	66	Britief, Thos.			3		2
34	Botie, Ric.	15	1	14	1	—	Outlawe, Thos.			3	—	
35	Tooke, Tho.	13	2½	13	2½	67	Sad, Jno.			2		2

	In vill		In manor	
	A.	R.	A.	R.
68 Cocke, Ric.	2		2	
— Clere, Armig., Ed.	1		—	
69 Ploughman, Roger	½		½	
— Hunter, Ric.	Purpresture		—	
Demesne in lord's hands	60		60	
Forncett glebe	48	½	48	½
Town of Forncett	4	3	4	3
Tacolneston glebe	11	1½	—	

In vill 2046 1½

	In manor	
	A.	R.
70 Sherman, Gent., Jno.	65	3½
71 Reve, Wm.	53	
72 Lanham, Rob.	38	
73 Moore, Thos.	36	2½
74 Wright, Jno.	34	
75 Talbot, Kt., Tenentes terrae nuper Galf.	30	
76 Horne, Jno.	27	3½
77 Banaster, Jno.	25	
78 Buxton, Jno.	21	1½
79 Brett, of Wacton, Jno.	17	2
80 Neve, Wm.	16	
81 Wilshere, Thos.	15	2
82 Swaine, Agnes	14	1½
83 Isbelles, Henry	13	1½
84 Wale, B.	13	½
85 Clement, jur. ux. Roger	13	
86 Knight, alias Kett, Jno.	12	3
87 Browne, jun. Rob.	12	
88 Heydon, Lady Anna	11	2
89 Cock, Ed.	11	1
90 Rixe, Jno.	11	
91 Kempe, Rob.	10	1½
92 Jex, Rob.	10	
93 Youngman, Thos.	10	
94 Hilling, Rob.	9	2
95 Revett, sen. Jno.	9	2
96 Rope, Jno.	9	1½
97 Revett, Andrew	9	
98 Legat, Johanna	8	2
99 Bocher, Wm.	8	
100 Duke, Armig., Ed.	8	
101 Alexander, Thos.	7	3½
102 Porter, Nich.	7	2
103 Dowe, Johanna	7	1½
104 Dawdrie, Geo.	7	½
105 Brett, of Tibenham, Jno.	7	
106 Browne, Heirs of Rob.	7	
107 Burgess, Agnes, late w. of Oliver	7	
108 Sherwin, Wm.	6	2
109 Harling, Jno.	6	

	In manor	
	A.	R.
110 Browne, Ric.	6	
111 Lincoln, Nich.	5	3½
112 Page, Wm.	5	3
113 Stephenson, Geo.	5	3
114 Browne, Marg.	5	1½
115 Reve, Gent., Thos.	5	½
116 Newman, Ed.	5	
117 Pudding, jur. ux. Thos.	5	
118 Seman, Rob.	5	
119 Stanton, Nich.	4	3
120 Jacobbes, —	4	3
121 Longe, Thos.	4	3
122 Armigeard, Jno.	4	1½
123 Toogood, Tenentes terr. Nich.	4	
124 Juby, Wm.	3	3½
125 Howling, —, late w. of Thos. Wade	3	3½
126 Rayner, Geo.	3	3
— Moulton, Vill of	3	2
127 Smith, Rob.	3	1
128 Machin, Thos.	3	
129 Hyrne, Wm.	3	
130 Lynforth, jur. ux. —	3	
131 Sendell, Jno.	2	3
132 Ariett, Jno.	2	2½
133 Taylor, Wm.	2	2
134 Partrike, Nich.	2	2
135 Dannok, Jno.	2	2
136 Knight, alias Kett, Agnes	2	2
137 Juby, Jno.	2	1½
138 Browne, Heirs of Peter	2	1
139 Fulwood, Rob.	2	1
140 Newman, Jno.	2	
141 Bullitout, Jno.	2	
142 Bullitout, Rob.	2	
143 Gooche, Jno., son of Nich.	2	
144 Paine, Wm.	1	2
145 Clement, Jno.	1	2
146 Hastings, Jno.	1	2
147 Kerison, Ric.	1	1½
148 Taylor, Peter	1	1
149 Barbour, Wm.	1	1
150 Lewuld, Wm.	1	1
151 Byrde, Rob.	1	1
152 Westgate, Jno.	1	1
153 Culling, Ric.	1	1
154 Togood, Rob.	1	1
155 Fuller, Simon	1	1
156 Gedge, Jno.	1	
157 Merten, Rob.	1	
158 Botild, Simon	1	
159 Sparrough, Thos.	1	
160 Clerk, Ric.	1	
161 Plante, Launcelot	1	

	In manor				In manor	
	A.	R.			A.	R.
162 Armigeard, jun. Jno.	1		171 Page, Jno.			3
163 Tyler, Rob.	1		172 Homyltoft, Heirs of Geo.			2
164 Porter, Ric.		3	173 Hamont, —			1
165 Boule, Wm.		3	174 Taylor, Jno.			1
166 Thrower, Widow of Rob.		3	175 Holland, Ric.			pightle
167 Fenne, Rob.		3	— Tenants not named			24
168 Seman, Wm.		3				
169 Turner, Alice		3	In manor		2664	2½
170 Jacob, Heirs of Wm.		3				

APPENDIX VII.

TABLE OF LEASES, 1401—1500.

m. = messuage. F = fee farm.

Date of Lease	Lessee	Area leased: Acres	Rods	Messuages, Crofts, etc. leased	Term of Years	Rent	Rent[1] per Acre
1401	R. Verdon	5			7	4s. 2d.	10d.
	R. Brown		2			2d.	
	C. Smyth	6		pightle	5	3s. 4d.	
	E. Broun	5		pasture	7	7s. 2d.	
1402	J. Davy	3			5	3s.	1s.
	H. Turnour	{ 2	1 } / {	1 [3] }		7	1s. 10d.	
	J. Kensy	{ 3	2 } / { 1 [4]	1 [4] }	garden	10	5s.	
1403	W. Stalun	2		toft	7	2s.	
	J. Wrighte	2 [5]			7	2s.	1s.
	M. Jebet	4	2		7	3s. 10d.	10¼d.
1404	A. Bonde and w.	3	3		10	3s. 2d.	10¼d.
1405	E. Gallard	4	½		10	2s. 6d.	7d.
	J. Wronge	8	3		7	8s.	11d.
	W. Sergeant	1	1	marsh	10	1s. 4d.	
	W. Hyrnyng	8			7	3s. 4d.	5d.
	R. Panel	5			7	3s. 4d.	8d.
1406	J. de Bekeswell	4		m.	5	4s.	
	N. Rynger	2			7	1s. 8d.	10d.
	R. Ropere and R. Koc	4			7	3s.	9d.
	R. Baxtere	120 [6]			7	30s.	(3d.)
	T. Hickes	2	1		7	2s.	10¾d.
1408	B. Kyng	3		meadow	7	2s. 8d.	
	J. de Hapton	4		curtilage	7	5s.	
	R. Dosy	4	1		7	3s. 6d.	10d.
	R. Verdon		3		7	8d.	10¾d.
	T. Hickes	{ 1	3 }		7	{ 1s. 5d. }[7]	
	T. Knygth	1			7	6d.	6d.
1409	W. Candeler	6			7	3s.	6d.
	T. Berd	9			3	8s.	10¾d.
	W. Dowe		1		10	3d.	1s.

[1] Reduced to the nearest farthing. Figures in parentheses indicate rent of pasture or meadow ; other figures, rent of arable.

[2] Purpresture 4 × 3 perches. [3] Meadow. [4] Meadow and pasture.

[5] Demesne. [6] Pasture called 'le Redynges.'

[7] Struck out 'quia conceditur per servicia.'

Date of Lease	Lessee	Area leased: Acres	Rods	Messuages, Crofts, etc. leased	Term of Years	Rent	Rent per Acre
1410	T. Ovedale	Manor of Williams in Tacolneston			1	£7	
	J. Wryghte	1	3	pightle	7	2s.	
	W. Dowe	3	1½	meadow	10	3s. 6d.	
	A. Hapton	3		vacant m.	7	2s. 4d.	
	N. Westhale	1	2		5	2	
1411	R. Wadeker	1			7	1s.	1s.
	R. Shepherde	3			7	1s. 8d.	6¾d.
	J. Cook		3		20	1s.	1s.
	A. Hacoun	1	2		10	1s. 2d.	9¼d.
	C. Smith and s.	6	1	pightle	10	2s. 8d.	
	R. Shepherde	7	1 ³ 1 ³ 1 ⁴	m.	10	5s.	
	J. Osberne	1	3		10	1s. 3d.	8½d
	R. Hawne	1 ⁵		close pightle turbary	10	4s. 2d.	
	J. Verdoun	120 ⁶			7	33s. 4d.	3¼d.
	R. Whitlok		3		10	8d.	10¾d.
	T. Ovedale	Manor of Williams			7	£8	
	R. Dosy	12	3 1 ³	pightle of pasture ¼ m.	10	12s. 4d.	
	J. Wronge	9	2 ⁷		20	8s.	10d.
	J. Drake	2	2	pightle	10	1s. 4d.	
1412	R. Hunne	3 1	2 1 ⁸ 1 ⁹	m.	10	6s.	
	R. Buk	12	2		20	13s. 6d.	1s. 1d.
	R. Gallard	1	2		7	1s. 3d.	10d.
	J. Pyllet	15 2 ³	½ ½		7	14s. 4d.	
	E. Gallard	4 ¹⁰ 3	½		7	5s. 2d.	8¼d.
	R. Racche	9		½ m.	7	4s. 6d.	
	J. Davy	18	2½		12	15s. 2d.	9¾d.
	R. Buk	12	2		20	14s. 2d.	1s. 2d.
	M. Broun	2	2	pasture	7	5s. 6d.	
	R. Doraunt	4 1 ¹⁰	1 ⁴		6	6s. 2d.	
	H. Herdelere	1	2 2 ³		9	3s.	
	J. Wryghte	2 7 ¹⁰	2	m.	6	7s. 11d.	
	A. Hobbes	3 ¹⁰	2 ¹⁰		7	2s. 4d.	8d.
	W. Floraunce	7			6	6s. 6d.	11¼d.
	R. Dosy	3 ¹¹ 5	1½		6	6s. 4d.	9d.
	R. and W. Rollston	1 ¹² 1	3 2 ¹²		10	4s. 4d.	1s. 4d.

¹ 'For so long as the manor of Forncete shall remain in the hands of Wm. Rees, Esq.'
² Blank in MS.   ³ Meadow.   ⁴ Pasture.
⁵ Meadow, 15 perches × 6 ft.   ⁶ Westwooderedyng.
⁷ Including 2 crofts and 1 toft, each containing 1 a. 2 r.   ⁸ Meadow and pasture.
⁹ Turbary.   ¹⁰ Demesne.   ¹¹ Length of term not stated.
¹² Enclosed.

Date of Lease	Lessee	Area leased: Acres	Rods	Messuages, Crofts, etc. leased	Term of Years	Rent	Rent per Acre
1413	H. Herdeler		3		8	6d.	8d.
	T. Hulle	3	2	m.		2s. 4d.	
1422	R. Shepherde	2	2		6	1s. 6d.	7¼d.
1423	J. Kirton	{ 1 / 1[1]	3 / 2 1 }		12	4s. 4d.	1s. 4d.
	R. Dosy	4			10	10d.	2½d.
	W. Broun	6			3	3s. 6d.	7d.
	J. Ryngere		1 [2]		10	3d.	1s.
	R. Buxton	1 [3]		close pightle turbary	10	4s. 6d.	
1424	J. Ryngere	3	1		10	2s. 10d.	10½d.
	R. Rede			pasture [1]	10	3s.	
	W. Florens	7			10	6s. 6d.	11¼d.
	R. Verdoun	15	2		7	10s. 4d.	8d.
	J. Ryngere, jun.	2			7	2s.	1s.
1425	T. Lyncolne	{ 9 /	3[4] / 1[5] }		12	6s.	7½d.
	T. Bonde	1	3		7	1s. 4d.	9¼d.
	T. Parmanter and J. Flete			herbage and pasture [6]	10	10s.	
	R. Balle	1			5	8d.	8d.
1426	J. Pekoc	2			7	1s. 4d.	8d.
	A. Whytfot	6[4]			20	2s.	4d.
	N. Baxtere	4[4]	2[4]		20	2s. 3d.	6d.
	W. Buntyng	6[4]			7	3s.	6d.
	J. Baxtere		3		20	6d.	8d.
	J. Bekiswell	2	2		10	1s. 8d.	8d.
	M. Mannyng	1			20	4d.	4d.
	R. Murdaunt	3	2	½ m.	40	2s. 3d.	
1427	J. Kock		2		20	3d.	6d.
	A. Page and s.	2	2		20	2s. 7d.	1s. ½d.
	R. Thorn	10	2½	m.	20	3s. 8d.	
	M. Mannyng	1	2		20	1s. 6d.	1s.
	W. Bolitout	1	3		7	10d.	5½d.
1428	E. Gallard	2	2		20	1s. 6d.	7¼d.
	W. Caston	3	2	toft	20	1s. 4d.	
	R. Verdon	4[4]			20	2s. 8d.	8d.
1429	J. Flete and w.	1	2		10	10d.	6¾d.
	W. Gegge and w.	3	2	vacant m.	F	2s. 8d.	
	T. Donne	3	2		10	2s. 3d.	7¾d.
1430	S. Hokir	5	2		7	3s. 2½d.	7d.
	R. Reede	2			10	1s. 8d.	10d.
	N. Baxtere	2	1		10	11¼d.	5d.
	R. Buxton	8	1		10	5s. 2d.	7½d.
	W. Buntyng and R. Verdon			warren	7	10s.	
1431	J. Pilet	{ 21 / 1[8]	/ 2[7] }		10	14s. 10½d. / 1s. 8d.	8½d. / 3s. 4d.
	T. Wulsy	{ 2[8] / 3[8] / 2	/ 2 }	m. pightle meadow	10	3s. 11½d.	10d.[9]
	R. Dosy		2		10	1s.	1s.
	W. Verdon	{ 1 / 1	/ 1 }		10	4d.	8d. / 9½d.
						1s.	

[1] Enclosed.   [2] In pightle.   [3] Meadow, 15 perches × 6 ft.
[4] Demesne.   [5] 'Cum le rones.'
[6] Of 'le Bromwode' called 'le Bares.'   [7] Meadow.
[8] In a croft.   [9] *Sic.*

Date of Lease	Lessee	Area leased: Acres	Rods	Messuages, Crofts, etc. leased	Term of Years	Rent	Rent per Acre
1431	J. Freman			meadow and pasture in close	5	14s.	
	J. Hapton			½ close called Redyng	7	17s. 2d.	
				close		1s. 2d.	
	G. Whityng	2	2		20	1s. 8d.)	8d.
		2				1s. 4d.)	
	T. Sweyn	11	1	2 tofts formerly built	10	3s. 9d.	
	T. Motte	6			F	8s.	1s. 4d.
	J. Wronge	25 [1]			10	8s. 7d.	
1432	J. Pelet			toft formerly built	20	1s.	
	T. Motte	24	2	m.	F	8s.	
	N. Hillyng		2		F	2d.	4d.
	W. Verdoun	8 [2]			10	5s.	7½d.
	S. Randolf	1			8	7d.	7d.
	R. Verdoun	2	2½		6	1s. 10d.	8½d.
	R. Reede	2			7	1s. 4d.	8d.
	R. Verdoun	7 [2]			7	4s. 1d.	7d.
	J. Drake	2	2	pightle	10	1s. 4d.	
1433	J. Ryngere		1 [3]		F	3d.	1s.
				divers pieces		11s. 3d.	
1434	R. Doosy	3	2		10	2s. 4d.	8d.
			3			8d.	10¾d.
		4				1s.	3d.
	W. Verdoun	1	3			6s. 8d.	
		1	2 [4]	m.			
	J. Southoo			meadow with marsh	7	15s.	
	J. Drake			close	10	1s. 2d.	
		2				1s. 4d.	
	J. Pelet and R. Verdon	21			10	14s. 10½d.	8½d.
			2 [5]			1s. 8d.	3s.
1435	W. Geygh		3 [6]		F	5d.	6¾d.
		1	1	close		10d.	8d.
	R. Buxton and s.	1 [3]		turbary	10	4s. 6d.	
		8	1	meadow		5s. 2d.	7½d.
	J. Bryghtgeve	9 [2]	3 [2]		12	5s. 9d.	7d.
	H. Buxton	4 [2]	2 [2]		10	3s.	8d.
	T. Hull	7			10	4s. 8d.	8d.
	R. Baxter	3	1		20	1s. 4d.	5d.
	W. Florens		2		10	3d.	6d.
	J. Waryn	1	3		12	11d.	6¼d.
1436	J. Buk	5 [2]			10	3s. 10d.	9¼d.
	R. Hykkes	8	2				
			3 [5]	toft	10	6s. 4d.	
		1 [6]	2 [6]				
1437	J. Drew		3	m. formerly built	10	3s. 11½d.	10d.[7]
		2	2	pightle			
	S. Broun		3 [8]		10	1s. 4d.	1s. 9¼d.
	J. Bekiswell	3			10	2s.	8d.
	J. Kyrton	6 [2]			7	3s.	6d.
	R. Sergeaunt		2 [9]		20	1s.	2s.
	E. Buk	1			10	8d.	8d.
	J. Davy and R. Dosy	19	3½		20	6s. 8d.	4d.

[1] Parcel of close called Westwood Redyng.   [2] Demesne.
[3] In a pightle.   [4] In a close.   [5] Meadow.
[6] In a croft.   [7] *Sic.*   [8] Demesne meadow.   [9] Pasture.

Date of Lease	Lessee	Area leased: Acres	Rods	Messuages, Crofts, etc. leased	Term of Years	Rent	Rent per Acre
1437	J. Hapton and J. Baxtere			½ close called "le Redyng"	7	17s. 2d.	
	J. Ryngere	2		toft	20	2s.	
1438	J. Gallard	1	1		20	10d.	8d.
	R. Reede	{ 2		pasture in close }	20	3s. / 1s. 8d.	10d.
	A. Osberne	1	•3		10	1s. 3d.	8½d.
	J. Suddon		2		20	4d.	8d.
	W. Denne	4		m.	10	2s. 8d.	
	T. Knyght	2			10	1s. 7d.	9½d.
	S. Coombys	1	2		7	1s. 2d.	9¼d.
		2	1			1s. 6d.	8d.
		2 [1]				1s. 4d.	8d.
	W. Fundenhale	{ 1 [1]	3 [1]		10	1s. 4d.	9¼d.
		2 [1]				1s. 4d.	8d.
		3 [1]	2 [1]			2s.	6¾d.
	R. Dosy		3		20	6d.	8d.
	R. Aunfrey	2	2½		10	2s. 2d.	10d.
	Parson of Tacolneston R. Dosy W. Verdon R. Reed			warren	7	10s.	
	R. Sherwynd	{ 2 [2]	2	m. }	10	2s. 5d.	
	J. Wrighte	2		m.	10	1s. 10d.	
	J. Gery	2			10	1s. 8d.	10d.
	J. Buk	3			10	2s. 6d.	10d.
	J. Patrik	{ 3 [1]	2 [1]		10	2s. 4d. / 10d. }	8d. / 8d.
		1	1				
	R. Broun	30 [3]			12	8s. 8d.	3½d.
	J. Wrighte	7 [1]			10	5s. 6d.	9½d.
	R. Gallard	3 [4]		pasture	10	11s.	
1439	J. Buk	4 [1]			10	2s. 4d.	7d.
	W. Hobbys	{ 2 [1]	2 [1]		10	1s. 6d. }	5¼d.
		1					
	I. Lambard		½ [5]		10	10d.	
	R. Bole	1			10	7d.	7d.
	J. Levyng	2			10	1s. 8d.	10d.
	R. Shepherde	8		m.	10	6s. 8d.	
1440	H. Jonneson	5	3	m.	10	3s. 8d.	
	J. Gallard		2½ [2]		10	4d.	6½d.
	J. Dosy and J. Pelet	3 [6]	2 [6]		7	6s. 8d.	(1s. 11d.)
	W. Buntyng	2 [6]			10	3s. 4d.	(1s. 8d.)
	R. Verdon	7 [1]			10	4s. 1d.	7d.
	J. Southawe	9 [1]			10	5s.	6¾d.
	R. Sylvestre	3	1½		7	2s. 4½d.	8½d.
1441	W. Stokkere and dau.		2 [8]		12	1s.	(2s.)
	R. Ingald	2			10	1s. 4d.	8d.
	J. Baxtere	5 [1]			10	2s. 6d.	6d.
	W. Mowere		3½ [1]		10	6d.	6¾d.
	G. Turpeys		1½ [8]		10	8d.	(1s. 9¼d.)
	N. Ryngere	2			10	1s. 8d.	10d.
	J. Man	3			20	2s.	8d.
	J. Buk	7			10	5s. 4d.	9½d.

[1] Demesne. [2] In croft. [3] Demesne, Westwoderedyng.
[4] Meadow. [5] In toft. [6] Demesne meadow.
[7] Term of years is illegible. [8] Pasture.

D.

Date of Lease	Lessee	Area leased: Acres	Rods	Messuages, Crofts, etc. leased	Term of Years	Rent	Rent per Acre
1442	R. Reede	2[1] / 2		pasture	20	6s.	
	W. Verdon	3[2]	2[2]		20	2s. 6d.	8½d.
	C. Davy and J. Sadde			¾ m.	20	2d.	
	J. Haghne	2[2]	1[2]	pightles meadow turbary	20	5s. 4d.	
	— Sybald A. Danyell W. Broune R. Hunne W. Hobbes R. Kensy			pasture[3]	10	10s.	
	R. and W. Hulle	10[2]	2[2]		F	7s.	8d.
	R. Stalon	1	1		20	10d.	8d.
	J. Wrong	25[4]			10	9s.	(4¼d.)
	W. Baxtere	13	1		10	6s. 7½d.	6d.
	J. Gery	1[5]			10	10d.	(10d.)
	T. Boole			"Land and closes called Williams"	20	£8. 6s. 8d.	
	J. Wacy	3			10	2s.	8d.
1443	J. Bolitout		1		F	1d.	4d.
	J. Gery	2[6]		m.	F	3s.	
	R. Hobbes	7			10	3s. 6d.	6d.
	E. Gallard	3			20	2s.	8d.
	W. Drake	2	2		20	1s. 4d.	6½d.
	M. Mannyng	2			20	1s. 4d.	8d.
	R. Randolf	3			20	2s.	8d.
	W. Funnale		3		20	6d.	8d.
	M. Mannyng and s.	2			F	1s. 4d.	8d.
1444	A. Mannyng	4			20	2s.	6d.
	R. Dosy	4[2]			10	2s. 4d.	7d.
1445	J. Rammesbury and J. Buk			½ close[7]	40	18s.	
	S. Brown		3[8]		12	1s. 4d.	(1s. 9¼d.)
	J. Davy	15	1 / 1½[8]		10	10s.	
	T. Chapman	3			10 F	1s.	4d.
	J. Buk			warren	10	10s.	
1446	J. Harneys	3	1		12	3s. 6d.	1s. 1¼d.
	J. Swene	12	1	2 tofts formerly built	10	4s. 1d.	
	J. Waryn		3		20	7d.	9¼d.
	A. Baxter and s.	12	1	m.	20	6s.	
	R. Dosy and s.	20		close meadow[9]	40	20s.	
	R. Hikkes	10[2]			20	8s. 4d.	10d.
	R. Bekyswell	2[2]			20	1s. 4d.	8d.
	J. Gallard	12	2		20	9s. 2d.	8¾d.
	T. Praty		2	2 m.	20	2s.	
	T. Gallard	2[2] / 1[8]	3[2]		20	1s. 4d.	5¾d.
	J. Buntyng		3[2]		16	1s. 4d.	

[1] Demesne land in croft.   [2] Demesne.
[3] Called 'les Bares in Bromwode.'   [4] Parcel of close called Westwoderedyng.
[5] Meadow and turbary.   [6] Land and turbary.   [7] le Redyng.
[8] Meadow.   [9] 32 perches and 3 rods of meadow.

Date of Lease	Lessee	Area leased: Acres	Rods	Messuages, Crofts, etc. leased	Term of Years	Rent	Rent per Acre
1447	J. Rynger	19	½[1]		F	12s.	
	R. Baxtere	2	2		10	1s. 4d.	6½d.
	R. Mannyng	6			[2]	3s. 2d.	6¼d.
	N. Rynger			meadow with marsh	20	15s.	
	J. Hastyng	1			10	8d.	8d.
	H. Buxton	2		m.	30	1s. 8d.	
	J. Gallard	1			20	10d.	10d.
1449	S. Osborn and w.	1	[2]		[2]	1s. 3d.	
	R. Verdon and w. and J. Curteys	7[3]			12	4s. 2d.	7¼d.
	N. Drake	2[4]		pightle	10	1s. 2d.	
1450	R. Bucke	6	3		16	5s.	9d.
	R. Buk, J. Pelet, E. Gallard			meadow[5]	10	46s. 8d.	
	J. Gallard		3[6]		16	11s.	
		2[7]	1[7]				
	W. Buntyng	2[8]			25	3s. 4d.	(1s. 8d.)
	J. Baxter and s.	1[9]	2[9]		20	9s.	
		9	2				
	T. Horn	2			20	1s. 4d.	8d.
	J. Wyoth, A. Aumfrey	2	2½		20	2s. 2d.	10d.
	J. Man	3			20	2s.	8d.
1451	W. Sadde	4[3]			F	2s. 4d.	7d.
	S. Hapton	8[4]		m.[4]	20	6s.	
	R. Broun	30[10]			20	8s. 8d.	3½d.
	A. Qwyghsette	6	2		20	2s. 4d.	4¼d.
	J. Kyrton	6[3]			12	3s.	6d.
1454	W. Clopton	2			20	8d.	4d.
	J Clement	1[9]	2[9]	m. formerly built	[11]	3s. 11½d.	10d.[14]
			3[9]				
		2	2	pightle			
	R. Godewyn	2[3]	3[3]		30	1s. 8d.	7d.
			½[13]				
	J. Clement	1			20	8d.	8d.
	N. Hynde	2[3]			20	1s. 6d.	9d.
	J. Brown		3½		20	6d.	6¾d.
	T. Gallard	1	3		20	1s. 4d.	9¼d.
	R. Bennok	1[3]	1[3]		12	1s.	9½d.
	J. Baxter	1[9]	2[9]		24	6s. 8d.[12]	
		10		m.			
	R. Davy	4[3]			F	2s. 4d.	7d.
	R. Bucke	1[3]	1[3]		12	9d.	7¼d.
	J. Serjaunt		2[3]		20	1s. 2d.	
			2[7]				
1455	T. Lyncoln	5	1		10	1s. 8d.	3¾d.
	J. Gallard		3½		40	6d.	6¾d.
	J. Buntyng	3			24	1s. 6d.	6d.
	J. Davy and sons	19	3½		20	6s. 10d.	4d.
	J. Wrong	25[13]			20	8s. 7d.	(4d.)
	J. Bucke, N. Drake, T. Drake, R. Bucke	1		warren	5	8s.	

[1] Demesne land and meadow. [2] Illegible. [3] Demesne. [4] Enclosed.
[5] Dam Meadow near St Mary's Church. [6] Meadow. [7] Pasture.
[8] Demesne meadow. [9] A croft. [10] Parcel of Westwoodredyng. [11] Blank in roll.
[12] Altered in roll to 9s. [13] Parcel of close called Westwoodredyng. [14] *Sic.*

Date of Lease	Lessee	Area leased: Acres Rods		Messuages, Crofts, etc. leased	Term of Years	Rent		Rent per Acre
1455	B. Ryder	3 1[1] 1[2]	2 1[1]	m.	12	2s.		
1456	T. Lyncoln	2 1[3]	1	meadow	3	2s.		
	W. Verdon			meadow and marsh[4]	20	10s.		
1457	W. Davy	14	3 1½[5]		20	10s.	8d.	
	J. Buntyng	3[4]			20	1s.	6d.	6d.
	S. Hapton	5		2 vacant m. m.	20	4s.		
	J. Doosy	11	1[6]		20	8s.	1d.	1s.
1458	J. Haughne	1[7] 1[4]	2[7] 1[4]		F	2s.	8d.	11¾d.
	J. Bukke and R. Davy			meadow[4]	20	6s.	8d.	
	J. Doosy and s.	1[5] 1[8]	1[5]		40	5s.	6d.	(2s. 5¼d.)
	J. Gallard	1[8] 1[5]	3[8]		40	5s.	6d.	(2s. 9d.)
1459	J. Haughne	1 1[9]	10		20	1s.	4d.	
	J. Buntyng	3[11] 3[4]	1[11]		40	2s.		
	R. Bucke and J. Pelet			meadow[12]	20	46s.	8d.	
	N. Rynger	2			F	1s.	8d.	10d.
	R. Whitforth	6[4]	2[4]		F	2s.	2d.	4d.
	R. Rede and J. Rede and s.	2			F	1s.	4d.	8d.
	J. Dosy, w. and s.		3		F		8d.	10¾d.
1460	R. Hotte and s.	3[4]			F	1s.		4d.
	R. Rede and Cecily Hapton and s.	5		2 vacant m. m.	40	4s.	10d.	
	R. Rede, s. and grands.	3[4]	1[4]	pasture[4]	F	5s.		
	R. atte Mere and s.	6			50	3s.		6d.
	J. Kyrton and R. Den	6[4]			20	3s.		6d.
1461	R. Brewster and w.	2	1		20	1s.	6d.	8d.
	J. Buntyng	3 1[1] 1[2] 2	2 1[1]		40	2s.	2d.	
	N. Davy and R. Verdon			warren	10	8s.		
	J. Clement	3[4]			40		7d.	9¼d.
1462	T. Boole and W. de Southagh			Lands and pasture of demesne called Williams	14	£8. 6s. 8d.		
	R. Brandon	5[4]	2[4]		F	3s.	8d.	8d.
	J. Pelet and s.	14[13]			20	£2. 6s. 8d.		(3s. 3½d.)

[1] Meadow and pasture.　　[2] Marsh.　　[3] Roll faded.　　[4] Demesne.
[5] Meadow.　　[6] And 32 perches.　　[7] Enclosed demesne.
[8] Demesne meadow.　　[9] Pightle of pasture containing 1 acre.　　[10] Meadow, 6 ft.
[11] Land and pasture.　　[12] Dam Meadow.
[13] Meadow and pasture of demesne called Dam Meadow.

Date of Lease	Lessee	Acres	Rods	Messuages, Crofts, etc. leased	Term of Years	Rent	Rent per Acre
1462	J. Fundnale	6[1]	2[1]		20	4s.	7½d.
	S. Broun		3[2]		F	1s. 4d.	(1s. 9¼d.)
	John Havne		3		F	6d.	8d.
1463	W. Gallard	12	2		F	9s. 2d.	8¾d.
	J. Brown	1	3		F	1s. 4d.	9¼d.
	C. Hapton and s.	1[1]	2[1]		F	1s.	8d.
	W. Kettes	2[1]			F	1s. 6d.	9d.
	R. Brandon and W. Pelet	4[1]	3[1]		F	3s. 4d.	8½d.
	J. Dosy and s.	2[1]			F	1s. 6d.	9d.
	T. Bolytowte	{ 2[1] / 1[2]	2[1] }		F	2s. 10d.	
	J. Randolff	1	2		F	1s.	8d.
	W. Davy	1[3]			F	3d.	3d.
1464	N. Mere	4		m.	10	2s. 8d.	
	W. Pelet	16[4]			F	10s. 8d.	8d.
	W. Buntyng / R. Redhed	2[5]			17	3s. 4d.	1s. 8d.
1465	T. Horn	1[5]	[6]		F	11d.	
	T. Lyncolne	5[1]	1[1]		20	2s.	4½d.
1466	J. Southagh and s.	9[1]			20	5s.	6¾d.
	T. Horn and w.	2			F	1s. 4d.	8d.
	N. atte Moore	6			F	2s. 8d.	5¼d.
1467	T. Collowe and w.	3	1	meadow	F	3s. 6d.	
	W. Gallard	{ 1[5] / 1[7]	3[5] }		F	5s. 6d.	
	W. Goldsmyth		2		F	5d.	10d.
	J. Buk			½ close[8]	F	9s.	
	W. Southaghe			½ close[8]	F	9s.	
1469	W. Verdon and s.	7			F	4s. 8d.	8d.
	R. Verdon			meadow and marsh[1]	F	10s.	
	H. Lyncoln	2	2	pightle	F	2s. 1d.	
	T. Lyncoln	1[1]	2[1]		10	1s.	8d.
1470	H. Buxton and s.	19	1	m.	F	13s. 4d.	
	W. Ryder and s.	{ 3 / 1[9]	1[9] }		F	2s.	
1471	R. Clere			warren	10	10s.	
	M. Lyngcoln	2[1]			7	10d.	5d.
	J. Gallard		3[1]		40	6d.	8d.
1472	J. Dosy	10			F	6s. 8d.	8d.
	W. Clopton		2		F	4½d.	9d.
						6s. 8d.	8d.
	R. Brandon and s.	{ 8[1] / 2[1]	}	pasture	F	8d.	
	E. Whyting		2		F	2d.	4d.
	E. Erle and w.		2		F	4d.	8d.
				close		1s. 2d.	
	T. Collowe and w.	{		pightle of underwood	F	6d.	
		2				1s. 4d.	8d.
	R. Verdon and s.	3	2	parcel of m.	F	2s. 4d.	
	W. Seman	9	1½	vacant m.	F	3s. 2d.	
	W. Sharforth	{ 3 / 2			} F	6d.	8d.
						2d.	4d.
1474	J. Randolf	2			F	1s. 4d.	8d.
	J. Gallard and s.	4	2		F	2s. 7d.	7d.

[1] Demesne. [2] Meadow. [3] Alderwood.
[4] Demesne and customary lands. [5] Demesne meadow.
[6] Meadow nine feet wide. [7] Meadow and pasture.
[8] Redyng, perhaps 30 acres. [9] Meadow and turbary.

Date of Lease	Lessee	Area leased: Acres	Rods	Messuages, Crofts, etc. leased	Term of Years	Rent	Rent per Acre
1474	R. Brown	30[1]			F	9*s.* 4*d.*	
1476	W. Davy and s.	14	3 1½[2]		F	10*s.* 8*d.*	
	J. Gallard and s.	4	1[3]	piece of land	F	3*s.* 2¼*d.* 7¾*d.*	9*d.*
	R. and W. Davy	18	1½		F	7*s.*	4½*d.*
	J. Alisaunder and w.	12	2½[4]		24	7*s.*	6½*d.*
1477	J. Gallard	4[5]			20	1*s.* 5*d.*	4¼*d.*
	T. Dannok and w.	2[6]	1[6]	m.[4]	F	1*s.* 10*d.*	
	J. Gallard	1	1		20	8*d.*	6½*d.*
	W. Drake		1½[5]		F	1½*d.*	4*d.*
	J. Dosy	2[7]			20	3*s.* 4*d.*	1*s.* 8*d.*
1478	S. Brown	20[8]			F	10*s.*	6*d.*
	S. Brown and s.	5[9]			F	2*s.* 6*d.*	6*d.*
	N. Sarays and s.	3	2	½ m.	F	2*s.* 3*d.*	
	R. Stevynson		1[10]		F		7*d.*[10]
1480	J. Brown		2		20	4*d.*	8*d.*
	R. Baxter and s.	1[11] 7	2[11] 2	vacant m.	F	9*s.* 2*d.*	
	W. Wadker and w.		2[12]		F	4*d.*	8*d.*
1481	W. Drake		1½		F	2*d.*	5¼*d.*
	J. Haughne	1					
	H. Wyard	1[13]			F	1*s.* 6*d.*	
1482	J. Langale	1[5]			F	4*d.*	4*d.*
	J. Dosy and s.	11	1		F	8*s.* 6*d.*	9*d.*
	R. Baxter and s.	8[14]	2[14]		F	5*s.* 8*d.*	
	W. Browne and w.	2			F	1*s.* 5*d.*	8½*d.*
1483	H. Bryce	2	1		F	1*s.* 6*d.*	8*d.*
1484	R. Chapman	3			20	1*s.*	4*d.*
1485	G. Burgeys		1½		F	2*d.*	5¼*d.*
	T. Drake and w.	3	1½	meadow	F	3*s.* 6*d.*	
1486	J. Newman	2			F	1*s.* 4*d.*	8*d.*
	C. and J. Hotte		2		F	2*d.*	4*d.*
	R. Hunte	3			F	3*s.* 1*d.*	1*s.* ¼*d.*
1487	T. Baxter	2[12]			F	11*d.*	5½*d.*
	R. Wrygth		3		F	6*d.*	8*d.*
1488	R. Clere			Manor called Williams	31	£8. 6*s.* 8*d.*	
1489	R. Stevynson	11[15]	3½[15]		F	6*s.* 5*d.*	
1490	R. Chamber	1			F	4*d.*	4*d.*
	H. Wyarde		2[5]		F	4*d.*	8*d.*
1491	T. Kette			The manor yard with one house	10	11*s.* 8*d.*	
	W. Bocher and s.	1	3	piece of land	F	1*s.* 2*d.* 4*d.*	8*d.*
	W. Grene and sons		2		F	4*d.*	8*d.*
	R. Botyld		2[5]		F	4*d.*	8*d.*
	W. Davy and s.	2[16]			F	1*s.* 4*d.*	6*d.*[17]
	J. Horn		2		F	6*d.*	1*s.*
1492	J. Alisaunder	3[5]	2[5]		F	2*s.* 2*d.*	7½*d.*

[1] Parcel of Westwoodredyng. [2] Meadow. [3] In a pightle.
[4] Formerly built upon. [5] Demesne. [6] In two crofts.
[7] Demesne meadow. [8] ¼ of a close called Redyng. [9] ⅕ of close called Redyng.
[10] Part of entry illegible. [11] In croft. [12] In close.
[13] In pightle. 6 ft. of meadow were also granted.
[14] And 27 swathes of meadow, all of demesne. [15] Land, meadow and pasture.
[16] Demesne, and a piece of demesne meadow 2 × 12 perches.
[17] Yearly rent of arable; rent of meadow, 4*d.* per acre.

Date of Lease	Lessee	Acres	Rods	Messuages, Crofts, etc. leased	Term of Years	Rent	Rent per Acre
1493	T. Kette	3[1]	2[1]		F	2s. $2\frac{3}{4}$d.	$7\frac{3}{4}$d.
		5[1]				3s. 4d.	$7\frac{3}{4}$d.
		7[1]				4s. 3d.	$7\frac{1}{4}$d.
1494	J. Verdon and w.	1[1]	1[1]		F	1s.	$9\frac{1}{2}$d.
		3[1]				2s.	8d.
			2[1]			4d.	8d.
1497	S. Denne and s.	6[1]			F	3s.	6d.
	W. Buxton and w.	2[1] 1[2]	1[1]		F	2s. 9d.	
	W. Gallard and s.	1[1]	2[1]		F	1s.	8d.
	W. Funhale and s.	6[1]	2[1]		F	4s.	$7\frac{1}{2}$d.
	W. Davy and s.	3[3]			F	6s. 8d.	2s. $2\frac{3}{4}$d.
1498	J. Brown		1[4]	garden	F	4d.	
	W. Southaughe and s.	10[1]	3[1]	meadow[5]	20	46s. 8d.	
						6s. 2d.	7d.
	W. Watker and s.	3[6] 3[7]	3[6]		F	2s. 2d.	
						Ancient services and customs	
1499	R. Gallarde	4[1]			F	1s. 8d.	5d.

[1] Demesne.   [2] Meadow.   [3] Demesne meadow.   [4] Pightle enclosed.
[5] Dam Meadow.   [6] Land and meadow.   [7] Turbary.

APPENDIX VIII.

ACCOUNT ROLL OF THE MANOR OF FORNCETT, 1272—3.

Fornesete. Anno regni Regis Edwardi primo.

Johannes le Graunt, serviens, Robertus Gallard, praepositus et collector, Walterus Disce, bedellus, reddunt finalia compota sua de receptis et expensis factis in manerio de Fornesete a crastino Sancti Michaelis anno regni Regis Henrici lvi. finiente usque ad festum Sancti Michaelis proxime sequens ultimo die computato anno regni Regis Edwardi primo per totum annum.

Arreragia. Idem respondent de ix*l.* vii*s.* iiii*d. ob. qa.* de arreragiis ultimi compoti.

Summa ix*l.* vii*s.* iiii*d. ob. qa.*

Redditus assisae. Idem respondent de ci*s.* ii*d. ob.* de redditu termini Sancti Andreae cum le custumpund. Et de x*s.* de scorfe ad Natale Domini de leta de Hadesco[1]. Et de xl*s.* de eodem de termino Natalis. Et de lxxi*s.* xi*d.* de redditu termini Paschae cum le staldinges. Et de xl*s.* de redditu de leta de Hadesco ad eundem terminum. Et de ii*s.* viii*d.* de redditu termini Pentechostes. Et de xvi*d.* de redditu de forthward[2] ad eundem. Et de ii*s.* viii*d.* de redditu ad Gulam Augusti qui dicitur saltpeny. Et de iiii*l.* xiii*s.* ix*d. qa.* de redditu termini Sancti Michaelis. Item i*d.* de incremento.

Summa xviii*l.* iii*s.* vii*d. ob. qa.*

Forum. Idem respondent de ii*s.* vi*d.* de firma fori de Strattone de quarta parte tolneti.

Summa ii*s.* vi*d.*

Chevagium. Idem respondent de viii*s.* vi*d.* de chevagiis de v^{xx} et ii. anlepimannorum reddentium chevagia.

Summa viii*s.* vi*d.*

Faldagium. Idem respondent de xxii*d.* de xiii. vaccis et xlv. bidentibus de faldagio, reddentes pro vacca i*d.* et pro v. bidentibus i*d.* Et de xxiii*d. ob.* de faldagio pro xxx. vaccis et pro iiii^{xx} et v. bidentibus, reddentes pro vacca *ob.* et pro x. bidentibus i*d.*

Summa iiii*s.* ix*d. ob.*

---

[1] 'Homagium quod vocatur Hadesco...valet per annum iiii*l.* x*s.*' Inq. p.m. 54 Hen. III. The tenants who paid 'skorfe' were 'in leta de Richemund' as appears from the 'Roll of Richmond rents pertaining to Forncett' and from *Rot. Hund.* i. 467, where some account is given of this feudal payment.   [2] Castle-guard at Norwich.

Arrurae. Idem respondent de iii*s.* ii*d.* de xii. arruris et dim. et i. bestia de sok[a] vendita de tempore seminationis frumenti, pretium arrurae iii*d.* Et de xi*s.* viii*d.* de xl. arruris venditis de tempore seminationis avenae, pretium arrurae iii*d. ob.* Et de xiiii*s.* iiii*d.* de xliii. arruris venditis de tempore seminationis ordei et rebinationis, pro arrura iiii*d.* Et de iii*d.* de iii. herciaturis venditis.

Summa xxixs. vd.

Opera iemalia, aestivalia et autumpnalia et cariagia. Idem respondent de xviii*d.* de liiii. operibus iemalibus per dimidiam diem venditis, pro iii. operibus i*d.* Et de xviii*d.* de xlv. operibus aestivalibus per diem integram venditis, pro v. operibus ii*d.* Et de xli*s.* viii*d.* de v^c. operibus autumpnalibus venditis, pro opere, i*d.* Et de v*s.* de vi^{xx} precariis autumpnalibus venditis hoc anno, pretium operis *ob.* et non plus quia[1]...Et de viii*d.* de viii. cariagiis autumpnalibus venditis.

Summa ls. iiiid.

Averagia. Idem respondent de xxix*s.* ix*d. ob. qa.* de xi^{xx} xviii. averagiis et dim. venditis, pretium averagii i*d. ob.*

Summa xxixs. ixd. ob. qa.

Factura brasei. Idem respondent de iii*s.* vi*d.* de factura brasei, scilicet de xxi. summis per custumarios.

Summa iiis. vid.

Herbagium. Idem respondent de iii*d.* de herbagio fossatorum circa Oldelondris. Et de viii*d.* de herbagio circa boscum de Nortle. Et de iiii*d.* de herbagio fossatorum circa campos de Hallecroft. Et de xvi*d.* de herbagio de Cronelesholm. Et de iii. *ob.* de herbagio fossatorum aput Therstonewde. Et de iiii*s.* xii*d.* de herbagio viiii. acrarum warecti in Buskescroft et de x. acris warecti in le Redinge, pretium acrae iii*d. ob. qa.* Et de iiii*s.* x*d.* de herbagio fossatorum circa campos de Bonewelleredinge. Et de viii*d.* de herbagio cujusdam viae in le Redinge vendito. Et de iii*s.* ix*d.* de scar[2] et pipes et junccis venditis, praeter le Herber qui falcabatur hoc anno et non vendebatur. Et de xx*d.* de xl. vaccis communicantibus in commuma de Langemor a Pentechoste usque ad Gulam, capientes pro vacca *ob.* Et de x*d.* de herbagio de x. equis communicantibus ibidem. Et de vii*d.* de vii. porcis communicantibus ibidem. Et de iii*d. ob.* de xxxvi. bidentibus communicantibus ibidem, capientes pro x. i*d.*

Summa xxs. iiiid.

Fenum. Idem respondent de lii*s.* xi*d.* de feno et foragio venditis.

Summa liis. xid.

Turbae et flaccae. Idem respondent de xvii*s.* vi*d. ob.* de flaccis venditis aput le Herber et turbae et aput Stubbi et subtus Lund et apud Kaldewelle et Serdesbusk.

Summa xviis. vid. ob.

Subboscus et alnetus. Idem respondent de xxv*s.* iii*d. ob.* de v. acris et dim. subbosci venditis in le Lund et in le Sunderwde venditis, pretium acrae iiii*s.* et pretium dim. acrae xix*d. ob.* Et de lxxi*s.* ii*d. ob.* de alneto vendito in Westwude per particulas. De escaeta de corticibus arborum prostratorum xii*s.* iiii*d.* Et de veteri porchia stabuli vendita, xvi*d.*

Summa vl. xs. iid.

Bladum frumenti. Idem respondent de lx*s.* de ix. summis frumenti venditis, pretium summae vi*s.* viii*d.* Et de xxxix*s.* vi*d.* de vi. summis frumenti venditis, pretium summae vi*s.* vii*d.* Et de vii*l.* xiii*s.* vi*d. ob. qa.* de xxiii. summis v. bu. frumenti venditis, pretium summae vi*s.* vi*d.* Et de vii*l.* v*s.* viii*d.* de xxiii. summis

---

[1] Hiatus in roll.   [2] *scara* = underwood.

frumenti venditis, pretium summae vi*s*. iiii*d*. Et de iiii*l*. v*s*. v*d*. de xii. summis dim. frumenti venditis, pretium summae vi*s*. x*d*. Et de {xviii*s*. viii*d*. *ob. qa.*} (xx*s*. xi*d*.) de iii. summis v. bu. curalli frumenti venditis, pretium summae v*s*. ii*d*. Et de iiii*s*. de i. summa secundi[1] curalli vendita. De i. summa frumenti vendita, vii*s*.

Summa frumenti, lxxix. summae vi. bu.
Summa xxv*l*. xv*s*. i*d*.

Ordium. Idem respondent de ix*l*. xix*s*. iiii*d*. de xlvi. summis ordei venditis, pretium summae iiii*s*. iiii*d*. De viii. summis ordei venditis xxxvi*s*., pretium summae iiii*s*. vi*d*. Et de xxxvii*s*. iiii*d*. de ix. summis ordei, pretium summae iiii*s*. iiii*d*. Et de xxxiiii*s*. de vi. summis ordei venditis, pretium summae v*s*. vi*d*. Et de x*s*. viii*d*. de ii. summis ordei venditis. Et de xiii*s*. ix*d*. de ii. summis dim. ordei venditis, pretium summae[2]...

Summa lxxiii. summae et dim.
Summa xvii*l*. xi*s*.

Pisae. Idem respondent de xx*s*. de v. summis pisarum venditis, pretium summae iiii*s*. Et de xli*s*. viii*d*. de x. summis pisarum venditis, pretium summae iiii*s*. ii*d*. Et de lxv*s*. de xv. summis pisarum venditis, pretium summae iiii*s*. iiii*d*. Et de ix*s*. iiii*d*. de i. summa vi. bu. pisarum venditis, pretium summae v*s*. iiii*d*.

Summa xxxi. summae vi. bu.
Summa vi*l*. xvi*s*.

Cicera. Idem respondent de xxi*s*. xi*d*. *qa.* de xvii^xx et xi. lagenis ciceris[3] venditis, pretium lagenae *ob. qa.*

Summa xxi*s*. xi*d*. *qa.*

De i. veteri stotto vendito, iiii*s*.

Staurum. Idem respondent de xii*s*. x*d*. de ii. vaccis venditis ad festum Sancti Martini ante fecundationem. Et de xvi*s*. iiii*d*. de ii. vaccis venditis ante fecundationem. Et de iiii*s*. ii*d*. de v. vitulis de exitu cardinae quia debilibus, pretium vituli x*d*. Et de ix*d*. de i. vitulo de exitu vendito pro debilitate. Et de xxvi*s*. viii*d*. de i. sue et vi. juvenis[3] porcis venditis. Et de iii*s*. vi*d*. de ii. porcellis venditis. Et de xv*s*. de ix^xx gallinis venditis, pretium gallinae i*d*. Et de xv*d*. de x. caponibus de redditu venditis. Et de xiiii*d*. de xxviii. pullis de exitu venditis. Et de iiii[3]*s*. vi*d*. *qa.* de xii^c et x. ovorum[3] venditis, pretium centenae iii*d*. *ob.* De dimidia centena ovorum vendita, iii*d*. *ob. qa.* Et de xii*s*. de xlviii. aucis venditis, pretium aucae iii*d*. Et de ii*d*. de coreo i. vituli masculi superannati vendito, mortui de morina. De melle et cera venditis[4], iii*d*.

Summa vi*l*. ii*s*. viii*d*.

Pesac'. Idem respondent de xvi*s*. de pesacio[3] vendito.

Summa xvi*s*.

Daieria. Idem respondent de iiii*l*. iii*s*. *ob. qa.* de caseo et butiro venditis de exitu xvi. vaccarum vitulantium et de iii. vaccis annuler.'

Summa iiii*l*. iii*s*. *ob. qa.*

Placita et perquisita. Idem respondent de {xiii*l*. xvi*s*. viii*d*.} (xiiii*l*.) et de placitis, perquisitis senescalli, et de finibus et releviis et aliis per totum annum.

Summa xiiii*l*. {xvi*s*. viii*d*.}

Misa. Idem respondent de {c*s*.} (vi*l*. xiii*s*. iiii*d*.) de auxilio vill[atae] hoc anno.

{Summa c*s*.} (vi*l*. xiii*s*. iiii*d*.)

---

[1] *Secundae* in roll.   [2] Blank in roll.   [3] Sic.   [4] *Emptis* in roll.

Forinseca. Idem respondent de servientibus feodi de firma de Burnham, xxvi*s*. vi*d*. Item xviii*s*. x*d*. *ob. qa.*

Summa xlv*s*. iiii*d. ob. qa.* Et de xii*l*. x*s*. ii*d. qa.* de blado vendito super compotum. Et de vi*d*. de gallinis et operibus super compotum.

Summa xii*l*. x*s*. viii*d. qa.*

Summa totius receptae cxxxix*l*. xv*s*. *qa.*

Expensae.

Redditus soluti et decasus. Computant in redditu soluto Hugoni filio Eustachii ad Pascham, ii*d*. Et Petro de Keleshal ad festum Sancti Andreae, ii*d*. Et Ricardo de Mora ad festum Sancti Michaelis, i*d*. Et ad waite ad castrum Norwici ad Pascham, xvi*d*. In allocatione redditus Thomae Broketotht ad iii. terminos, ix*d*. In allocatione redditus Walteri Broketotht ad tres terminos, ii*d. ob.* In decasu redditus i. viae in le Redinge quae fuit purprestura per annum, iiii*d*. In allocatione redditus Johannis de Curzun, *ob.* In allocatione redditus Widonis Toward ad festum Sancti Michaelis, iii. *ob.*

Summa iii*s*. ii*d. ob.*

Custus ii *carucarum.* In v. garbis dim. et x. sperdutis aceri emptis, iii*s*. x*d. ob.*, pretium garbae viii*d*. In fabricatione ejusdem aceri, iii*s*. viii*d. qa.*, pro garba vii*d. ob.* In iii. vomeribus emptis, ix*d*. In vii. majoribus clutis et in aliis clutis emptis, ii*s*. i*d*. In carucis noviter faciendis et in aliis assidendis et in maeremio scapulando ad carucas et ad hercias, x*d. ob.* In ii. paribus rotarum emptis ad carucas emptas, vi*d*. In ferura x. stottorum per annum, vii*s*. ix*d. ob.* Datum carucariis ad primum exitum carucarum post Natale, iiii*d*. de consuetudine. In potura xx. carucariorum de precariis tempore seminationis ordei, iii*s*. iiii*d*. In stipendio iiii. carucariorum per totum annum, xii*s*. In stipendio i. herciatoris ad Pentechosten, iiii*d*. In i. stotto empto ad carucam, viii*s*. x*d*.

Summa xliiii*s*. iiii*d. ob. qa.*

Custus carectarum. Computant in factura i. corporis carectae, vi*d*. In i. tumberello faciendo de novo cum tymonibus cum i. homine per i. diem, ii*d*. In carpentaria i. corporis carectae ad autumpnum de novo, vi*d*. In stipendio i. carpentarii per iiii. dies scapulando maeremium ad rotas et ad carectas, viii*d*. In i. pare rotarum de novo faciendo, x*d*. In ii. paribus rotarum veterum circulandis, x*d*. In carectis reficiendis et emendendis contra autumpnum, vi*d*. In strakes rotarum ferratarum refabricandis cum ligamine et clavis, vii*d. qa.* cum impositione. In vi. hurthirnes emptis, ii*d. ob.* In i. cerculo empto ad muellam emptam, i*d*. In xx. carteclutis emptis, xiiii*d*. In i. sella cum baz[1] empta, iiii*d. ob.* In ii. colariis de coreo emptis, viii*d*. In colariis veteribus emendendis et in veteribus bazis emendendis, ii*d*. In iii. paribus tractuum emptis ad carectas, ix*d. ob.* In ii. cordis emptis ad carectas emptas, x*d*. In x. libris unctus et sepi emptis ad carectas, xiii*d. ob.* In stipendio i. carectarii per annum, iii*s*.

Summa xii*s*. xi*d. qa.*

Custus molendini. In stipendio i. molendinarii per annum, ii*s*. In i. mola empta, xxvii*s*.

Summa xxix*s*.

Custus domorum necessariarum. In recarpentaria grangiae quae fere cadebat, xiii*s*. iiii*d*. In daubura parietis ejusdem, v*s*. In stipendio i. coopertoris per x. dies recooperantis super eandem, xx*d*. In v[c]. de lattenail emptis ad eandem, iiii*d. ob.* In parietibus boveriae recarpentandis quae fractae fuerunt de posticulis resuis[2] et

---

[1] *baz* = bag of calfskin or sheepskin.
[2] *reswes* occurs in roll of 1378, p. lvi.

splentandis cum i. carpentario per i. diem et dim., ii*d. ob.* In daubura ejusdem cum ii. hominibus per ii. dies, viii*d.* In [stipendio] i. hominis per iiii. dies recooperiantis super turallum, viii*d.*

Summa xxi*s.* x*d.*

Custus murorum et pinfaldae. In stipendio i. hominis per xvii. dies facientis super muros pinfaldae praeter auxiliis operum totaliter de novo et facientis i. murum[1] ante curiam boveriae ex longitudine[2] perticarum et facientis i. peciam muri[3] ante gardinum ex longitudine[2], ii*s.* x*d.* In stipendio i. hominis per xii. dies cooperiantis super praedictos muros et super alios muros in parte circa curiam, ii*s.* In stipendio i. hominis crescantis praedictos muros et gallinarium et super alios muros circa curiam per xiii. dies, ii*s.* ii*d.*

Summa vii*s.*

Minutae necessariae. In {ix.} (iiii.) saccis emptis {ii*s.* ix*d.*} (xvi*d. ob.*). In i. panno empto ad desuper ventilandum, xvi*d.* In i. civera empta, iiii*d.* In factura vi. capistrorum et i terae[4] de pilo stottorum, i*d.* In i. estrilio empto ad stottos, i*d.* {In iii. capistris emptis ad stottos iii. *ob.*} In i. trubulo[5] cum ferro empto, ii*d.* In i. cribo[6] ad bladum mundandum empto, iii. *ob.* In refabricatione i. falcae, *ob.* In refabricatione i. pikosiae[7], *ob.* In astra grangiae exaltanda et aequenda et rameanda et facienda, x*d.* In stipendio i. hominis per vi. dies recooperiantis super tassos feni et foragii, xii*d.* {In i. ligno carpentando ad ponendum ultra pontem i*d.*} In arundine metendo in stagno, xiiii*d.* In i. clave empto ad ostium grangiae, i*d.* In emendatione presurae ad pomos de carpentaria, i*d.* In unctu et cepo ad eundem, i. *ob. qa.* Dati pro decima porcellorum, iiii*d.*

Summa {viii*s.* ix*d. ob. qa.*}
(vii*s.* ii*d. ob. qa.*).

Daieria. In iiii. bu. salis emptis ad sustentationem famulorum et ad daieriam in parte, xiiii*d.* In i. bu. albi salis ad daieriam, vi*d.* In panniculis emptis ad daieriam, {v*d. ob.*} (iiii*d.*). In ollis et patellis emptis ad daieriam, ii*d. ob. qa.* In bukatis emendendis ad daieriam, iii. *ob.* In stipendio i. daiae per annum, xii*d.* In stipendio i. vaccarii per annum, xii*d.*

Summa iiii*s.* {v.} (iii)*d.* {*ob.*} *qa.*

Custus porcorum. In vii. summis drachei emptis in ieme ad vii. porcos sustinendos, ii*s.* iiii*d.*

Summa ii*s.* iiii*d.*

Trituratio. In trituratione lxiiii. summarum ii. bu. frumenti, {xvi*s. ob. qa.*} (xiii*s.* iii*d. ob.*), pro summa {iii*d.*} (ii*d. ob.*). In trituratione iiii[xx]. summarum et viii summarum ordei, xi*s.*, pro summa i*d. ob.* In trituratione xxviii. summarum pisarum iiii*s.* viii*d.*, pro summa ii*d.* In trituratione lx. summarum avenae, iii*s.* ix*d.*, pro summa *ob. qa.* In liberatione i. hominis existentis ultra triturationem bladorum per xxxiii. dies, {iiii*s.* i*d. ob.*} (ii*s.* ix*d.*).

Summa {xxxix*s.* vii*d. qa.*}
(xxxv*s.* v*d. ob.*).

Pratorum custus[8] *et autumpnalii.* In datione custumariorum pro pratis falcandis de consuetudine, xiii*d.* Dati famulis die Ad Vinculam ad lamessilver qui habent de consuetudine, iii*d.*

Summa xvi*d.*

---

[1] *murem* in roll.   [2] Hiatus in roll.   [3] *mure* in roll.
[4] Headstall or tether. *Durham Account Rolls*, iii. glossary, Surtees Soc. vol. 103.
[5] *tribulum* = shovel. [6] Same as *cribra*, sieve? [7] pickaxe. [8] *custa* in roll.

Staurum emptum. In i. vacca empta ante fecundationem ad festum Sancti Martini, viii*s*. vi*d*. In i. vacca empta ante fecundationem, viii*s*. i*d*.

Summa xvi*s*. vii*d*.

Serviens. In liberatione servientis hic per xxvi. septimanas, xxxix*s*.

Summa xxxix*s*.

Senescallus. In expensis senescalli per suos adventus per totum annum, {xxvi*s*. v*d*. *ob*.} (xxiiii*s*. vi*d*. *ob*.).

Summa {xxvi*s*. v*d*. *ob*.}
(xxiiii*s*. vi*d*. *ob*.).

In liberatione i. garcionis senescalli perhendinantis cum i. equo senescalli a die Mercurii proxima ante festum Sancti Gregorii per xviii. dies sequentes, ii*s*. iii*d*. per diem iii. *ob*.

Summa ii*s*. iii*d*.

{Summa denariorum in resumptione manerii, xiii*l*. viii*d*. *ob*. *qa*.}

Custus domorum non necessariarum. In camera militum recarpentanda fere de novo de netherwalses et impositione de stuthes et resues et faciendis fenestras et aliis emendendis fere de novo et in lattura ejusdem, i*is*. ii*d*. *ob*. In M. et c. de lattenail emptis, viii*d*. *ob*. In daubura ejusdem de parietibus, x*d*. In plaustrura de le walses postea, vi*d*. In cooperatione dictae camerae militum et in cooperatione solaris ibidem ad caput ad taskam, iiii*s*. iiii*d*. In crescura ejusdem camerae et solaris, iiii*d*. In cooperatione camerae comitis cum i. homine per v. dies, x*d*.

Summa ix*s*. ix*d*.

In longo stabulo comitis recarpentando fere de novo ad taskam, scilicet erigendo de novis walsis et parietibus noviter recarpentandis et postea impenendis[1], vi*s*. iiii*d*. In daubura ejusdem totum fere de novo, iii*s*. iiii*d*. In cooperatione ejusdem stabulae fere de novo, iii*s*. iii*d*. In v°. de lattenail emptis, iiii*d*. *ob*. In stipendiis ii. carpentariorum per ii. dies et dim. facientium manguras et crechias de novo ibidem, xv*d*. In stipendiis ii. carpentariorum per i. diem et dim. carpentando manguros[1] et crechios[1] in parvo stabulo comitis infra curiam, viii*d*. In lx. de splentenail emptis, i*d*. In stipendio i. hominis redaubantis parietes salsarii et lardarii quae fractae fuerunt in parte per iii. dies dim., vii*d*. In stipendio i. hominis per vi. dies recooperiantis super aulam de arundine et in i. stipendio i. hominis sui[2] per idem tempus et qui crescaverunt aulam per illos dies, ii*s*. vi*d*.

Summa xviii*s*. iii*d*. *ob*.

Avena empta ad praebendam. In i. summa dim. avenae empta ad praebendam equorum comitis et comitissae, iii*s*. ix*d*. In iiii. summis avenae emptis, xi*s*. iiii*d*., pretium summae ii*s*. x*d*. In iii. summis vi. bu. avenae emptis, x*s*., pretium summae ii*s*. viii*d*. In ii. summis i. bu. dim. avenae emptis aput Keninghale rubeae avenae, v*s*. i*d*. *qa*. In iii. summis avenae emptis, ix*s*., alibi de alia avena. In iii. summis iii. bu. avenae emptis, x*s*. i*d*. *ob*., pretium summae iiii*s*. In iiii. summis et dim. bu. avenae emptis, xi*s*. ix*d*. *ob*., pretium summae[3]. In i. summa vi. bu. avenae emptis, v*s*. iii*d*. In ii. bu. avenae emptis, ix*d*.

xxiii. summae vii. bu.   Summa lxvii*s*. i*d*. *qa*.

Frumentum emptum. In vi. summis frumenti emptis post festum Exaltationis Sanctae Crucis in autumpno ad seminandum in anno futuro, xlv*s*., pretium summae vii*s*. vi*d*. In i. summa frumenti empta, vii*s*. viii*d*. In v. summis ii. bu. frumenti emptis tunc, xl*s*. iii*d*., pretium summae vii*s*. viii*d*.

Summa xij. summae ii. bu.   Summa iiii*l*. xii*s*. xi*d*.

---

[1] sic.   [2] In roll, *homine suo*.   [3] Hiatus in roll.

Vasa custa. In stipendio i. cuperii per iiii. dies reficientis vasa et cuva et stoppes circulandas et reficiendas, viii*d.*

Summa viiid.

Perhendatio. {In liberationibus ad vadia[1] garcionum comitis et comitissae et Magistri Johannis ferratoris ad acquietandum et in feno et foragio ad dictos equos et in reynes et cengulis ad dextrarium perhendinantem a die Sabbati proxima ante festum Sancti Valentini usque in Dominicam proximam post Pascham per ix. septimanas, ix*l.* ii*s.* vi*d. ob.* In feno empto ad dictos equos, xii*d.*

Summa ixl. iiis. vid. ob.}

In expensis Domini Abbatis[2] ad festum Circumcisionis quando audivit compotum, xv*s.* iii*d.* Item in expensis Domini Andreae et Domini Radulphi monachorum[3] Abbatis ad festum apostolorum Petri et Pauli ad visum capiendum, ii*s.* v*d. ob.* In expensis Rogeri de Bikerwik per ii. vices ad visum recipiendum, iii*s.*

Summa xxs. viiid. ob.

Pacati Willelmo ballivo hundredi praecepto senescalli pro i. summa frumenti quam ei dedit, {viii*s.*} (dimidia marca).

Summa {viiis.} (vis. viiid.).

Liberati Domino Roberto capellano receptori comitis, lxxiiii*l.* xx*d. qa.* per vii. tallias. Item eidem, xiii*l.* per i. talliam.

Summa iiii^{xx}. viil. xxd. qa.

{In suspenso per Dominum Abbatem prout patet in praecedente compoto de denariis quos homines Domini Comitis expenderunt aput Felmingham praecepto senescalli et quia dictus senescallus non habuit breve comitis ex praecepto inde xx*s.*

Summa xx. s.}

Summa omnium expensarum tam in resumptione manerii quam in commoditatibus et liberationibus[4].

Summa omnium expensarum et liberationum, cxl*l.* ix*s.* ii*d.* Et sic debet xxix*l.* v*s.* x*d. qa.*

De quibus in suspenso de vadiis garcionum comitis et comitissae[5], ix*l.* iii*s.* vi*d. ob.* Et x*l.* xvi*s.* xi*d. qa.* de lxxii. qr. ii. bu. et dim. avenae in praebenda equorum suorum. Et xx*s.* de nundino de Felmingham (allocantur per breve comitis). Et (in respectu) vii*s.* i*d. ob.* de avena ii. qr. iii. bu. avenae in praebenda senescalli non allocatae pro defectu talliarum et ii*s.* i*d.* in denariis. Et sic debet de claro vii*l.* xvi*s.* ii*d.*

Et in respectu de misa xxxiii*s.* iiii*d.*

Et sic debet vi*l.* ii*s.* x*d.*

[6]GRANGIA DE FORNESETE ANNO REGNI REGIS EDWARDI PRIMO.

Frumentum. Idem respondent de lxxiiii. summis de exitu frumenti et i. bu. Et de curallo ejusdem exitus, iii. summae v. bu. Et i. summa debilis curalli. Et de xv. summis receptis de praeposito de Multone, de Elbald. Item de emptione circa festum Exaltationis Sanctae Crucis in autumpno ad seminandum in anno futuro, xii. summae ii. bu.

Summa c. et vi. summae.

---

[1] *vadiis* in roll.
[2] In the account roll of 1290 (935/12) the Abbot of Tintern is mentioned as an accountant.
[3] *monachi* in roll.   [4] The sum is erased.   [5] *et* is written here in the roll.
[6] The remainder of the account is on the dorse of the roll.

Inde. In semine super xlix. acras iii. rodas, xiiii. summae. In venditione, lxxix. summae vi. bu. Summa iiii^{xx}. xiii. summae vi. bu. Et remanent ad seminandum in anno futuro, xii. summae ii. bu.

Ordium. Idem respondent de c. et xviii. summis et dim. bu. de exitu ordei. Et de ii. summis iiii. bu. dim. curalli ejusdem exitus. Et de xxviii. summis de exitu molendini in toto sine decima, et lib[eratione] mol[endinarii].

Summa vii^{xx}. viii. summae v. bu.

Inde. In semine super lxxiii. acras, xli. summae ii. bu. In liberatione iiii. carucariorum et i. carectarii {et i. daiae} per annum, in toto {xxvi. summae} (xxi. summae iiii. bu. et dim.) qui ceperunt summam per xii. septimanas. In liberatione i. vaccarii per totum annum, iii. summae v. bu. et dim. qui cepit summam per xiiii. septimanas. In liberatione i. herciatoris a Purificatione usque ad festum Sancti Augustini per xvi. septimanas, i. summa {ii. bu. dim.}. In praebenda stottorum mixtata cum avena, i. summa vii. bu. curalli. In porcis et porcellis, aucis, gallinis sustinendis, iiii. bu. de curallo. Dati custumariis pro eorum repesof, quam habent de consuetudine, iiii. bu. In venditione, lxxiii. summae et dim.

In liberatione i. daiae per annum, iii. summae v. bu. dim. In venditione super compotum, i. summa et dim. bu.

Summa vii^{xx}. et viii. summae v. bu.

Pisae. Idem respondent de xlii. summis ii. bu. de exitu pisarum.

Summa xlii. summae ii. bu.

Inde. In semine super xxxvii. acras i. rodam et dim., x. summae et dim. In venditione, xxxi. summae vi. bu.

Summa xlii. summae ii. bu.

Avena. Idem respondent de v. summis avenae de remanenti. Et de iiii^{xx}. xv. summis ii. bu. de exitu. Et de x. summis per aestimationem in garbis ad boves et ad vaccas. Et de {xxii.} xliii. summis dim. de reddito villae {hoc anno et residuum in anno praeterito}. Et de xxiii. summis vii. bu. de emptione ut supra.

Summa clxxvii. qr. v. bu.

Summa {viii^{xx}. xvi. summae v. bu.}.

Inde. In semine super xlv. acras et dim., xxiiii. summae ii. bu. In potagio famulorum, i. summa et dim. In praebenda xi. stottorum a festo Sancti Lucae Evangelistae usque ad festum Sancti Dunstani per xxxii. septimanas, xxi. summae et dim. et ideo majus quia nichil habuerunt de pisis nec de foragio (mixtato) quia equites comitis et comitissae totum expenderunt. In praebenda ii. carectariorum tempore venditionis bladorum comitis cariantium usque Norwicum et alibi, i. summa et dim.

In potura bovum per aestimationem in garbis, ix. summae. In vaccis et vitulis sustinendis, i. summa in garbis. In praebenda equorum servientis, x. summae. In praebenda equorum senescalli per suos adventus, {iiii. summae} (ii. qr. iii. bu. et dim.). In praebenda equorum Domini Abbatis et computatorum, ii. summae i. bu. et dim. per ii. tallias. In praebenda equorum Rogeri de Bikerwic per ii. adventus, ii. bu. et dim. {In praebenda equorum comitis et comitissae perhendinantium per ix. septimanas, lxxii. summae ii. bu. et dim.} In praebenda i. equi senescalli perhendinantis per xviii. noctes, i. summa i. bu.

{Summa vii^{xx}. et xiii. summae ii. bu. et dim. Et remanent iii. summae ii. bu. et dim.}

In expensis Domini Regis aput Lopham in anno praeterito xxi. summae. In venditione super compotum iiii^{xx}. qr. et i. qr. vi. bu. et dim.

Et nichil remanet.

STAURUM.

Stotti. Idem respondent de x. stottis de remanentibus. Et de i. de emptione.

Summa xi.

Inde. In venditione i. Et remanent x.

Boves. Idem respondent de viii. bobus[1] de remanentibus. Et de iii. de adjunctis[2] qui fuerunt bovetti in anno praeterito.

Summa xi. Et remanent omnes.

Vaccae. Idem respondent de xvii. vaccis de remanentibus. Et de i. de adjuncto quae fuit juvenca in anno praeterito. Et de ii. de emptione ante fecundationem. Et de iii. vaccis receptis de Multone de praeposito ante fecundationem.

Summa xxiii.

Inde. In venditione ut supra ante fecundationem, iiii.

Summa iiii. Et remanent xix quarum iii. annuler' et steriles.

Bovetti. Idem respondent de iiii. boviculis[2] de remanentibus qui modo sunt bovetti hoc anno.

Summa iiii. Et remanent bovetti.

Juvenculae. Idem respondent de iii. juvenculis de remanentibus quae modo sunt juvencae hoc anno.

Summa iii. Et remanent juvencae.

Vituli superannati. Idem respondent de iii. vitulis masculis de remanentibus qui modo sunt boviculi. In morina[3] i. Et remanent ii. boviculi.

Idem respondent de iiii. vitulis femellis de remanentibus quae modo sunt juvenculae. Et remanent juvenculae.

Vituli de exitu. Idem respondent de xvi. vitulis de exitu.

Summa xvi.

Inde. In decima i. In venditione vi.

Summa vii. Et remanent ix., quorum iii. masculi.

Porci. Idem respondent de vi. porcellis de remanentibus qui modo sunt porci. Et venduntur ut supra et nichil remanet.

Sus. Idem respondent de i. sue de remanenti. Et venditur ut supra. Et nichil remanet.

Porcelli. Idem respondent de ii. porcellis de exitu. Et venduntur ut supra. Et nichil remanet.

Aucae. Idem respondent de xi. aucis de remanentibus. Et de liii. de exitu.

Summa lxiiii.

Inde. In decima, v. In venditione, xlviii.

Summa liii. Et remanent xi.

Capones. Idem respondent de x. caponibus de redditu. Et venduntur ut supra.

Gallinae. Idem respondent de xxii. gallinis de remanentibus. Et de v^{xx}. et x. de redditu. Et de lok, lx. Et de xxxi. pullis de exitu.

Summa xi^{xx}. et iii.

---

[1] *boves* in roll.   [2] *bowuculis* in roll.   [3] *orina* in roll.

Inde. In {decima pro puzinis[1], iii.}. In venditione ut supra, ix^{xx} Item in venditione de pullis, xxviii. In venditione super compotum, iiii.

Summa x^{xx}. et xi. et remanent {xii.} xi.

Ova. Idem respondent de iii^{cc}. et dim. de exitu. Et de ix^{cc}. et x. de redditu.

Summa xii^{cc}. lxx.

Inde. In venditione ut supra, xii^{cc}. et lxx.

Acerum. Idem respondent de v. garbis et dim. et x. sperdutis aceri superius emptis.

Inde. In carucis expenduntur omnes.

Compotus de serviciis et consuetudinibus.

Arrurae. Idem respondent de lxiiii. arruris custumariorum hoc anno a festo Purificationis usque ad Pentechosten per xvi. diebus Lunae infra idem tempus et non amplius quia inter omnes custumarios non jungunt nisi cum iiii^{or}. carucis integris qualibet caruca faciente i. arruram qualibet die Lunae. Et de lxiii. arruris soknae de soknemen de omnibus hoc anno secundum quod jungunt cum xxi. carucis integris inter omnes qualibet caruca faciente iii. arruras. Et de xli. arruris de precariis hoc anno et dim. de tota soka. Et de vii. arruris pro pratis de certo.

Summa viii^{xx}. xv.

Inde. In arrurando xi. acras et dim. tempore seminationis frumenti, xvii. arrurae. In arrurando xxvi. acras et dim. tempore seminationis avenae et re-binationis ad ordeum, xxxvii. et dim. In arrurando xix. acras tempore seminationis ordei, xxiiii. et dim. In venditione, iiii^{xx}. et xvi.

Summa viii^{xx}. et xv.

Herciaturae. Idem respondent de iii. herciaturis de consuetudine. Et venduntur ut supra.

Opera manualia. Idem respondent de M. et D. et v. operibus manualibus a festo Sancti Michaelis usque ad festum Apostolorum Petri et Pauli per dimidiam diem et per minus[2] centum. Et valent iii. opera i*d.*

Summa M. D. et v.

Inde. In allocatione facta custumariis pro cariatione fimorum, xliii. In allocatione facta xi. custumariis pro lxiiii. arruris ipsorum quam habent de consuetudine, viii^{xx}. et xvi. In trituratione xi. summarum frumenti, lxvi. opera. In trituratione· xxii. summarum ordei, lv. opera. In trituratione xi. summarum pisarum, lv. opera. In trituratione xxv. summarum avenae, l. opera. In mundatione de xiii^{xx}. summis bladorum, viii^{xx}. vi. In carucis fugandis tam tempore seminationis frumenti quam avenae quam ordei, xxii. In euntibus ad herciam tempore avenae et ordei, xxxi. In blestis frangendis et in pikking tempore seminationis ordei, xxii. In fossatis erigendis at Kalfpictel ad defensionem bladi comitis, ix. In fossatis erigendis aput Smalebusk ad defensionem bladi comitis, ix. In fossatis aput portam Ricardi Hane et ante Caldewellewong, ix. In fossatis erigendis ad portam Simonis Hane ubique ibidem, xx. In fossatis erigendis aput Hallecroft circa campos ubique ibidem, xvi. In fossatura ante pratum comitis, iiii. In daubura parietis boveriae ex parte australi, xii. cum arzilio fodiendo et temperando. In daubura parietis ejusdem ex parte aquilonari cum arzilio fodiendo et temperando, vi. (In astra grangiae exaltanda et ramehanda de novo, xxiii.) In auxiliis ad daubandum parietem grangiae cum arzilio fodiendo et temperando,

---

[1] *pulcini*=chickens. *Durham Account Rolls*, iii., glossary.   [2] In roll, *minorem.*

xxvii. In daubura parietum turalli cum arzilio fodiendo et temperando, iiii. In cooperimento tractando ad grangiam, xxviii. In coopertura tractanda ad turallum, iiii. In cooperimento tractando ad cameram servientis, v. In cooperimento tractando ad muros circa curiam et infra curiam et in crescura murorum et daubura et emendatione eorundem, lxxi. In auxiliis ad faciendum muros pinfaldae de novo totaliter cum arzilio fodiendo et temperando et in portatione straminis et in cooperimento tractando ad cooperiandum et in crescura eorundem, exceptis denariis custumariis, lviii. In discooperatione camerae militum et solaris ibidem, xix. In dicto veteri cooperimento tractando et mixtando cum alio stramine et stupula, xxviii. In cooperimento tractando ad cooperiandum eandem de novo cum portatione cooperturae et cum aqua portanda (et in crescura ejusdem) et brochiis faciendis, xlii. In veteribus parietibus prosternendis et in arzilio fodiendo et temperando cum remotione veteris[1] arzilii et in daubura earundem, xxviii. In viii. acris stupulae stupulandis ad cooperimentum, xxvi. In cooperimento tractando ad cameram {militum} comitis, iiii. In auxiliis ad temperandum arzilium ad crescandam aulam, vi. In auxiliis ad daubandum longum stabulum fere de novo, xviii. In cooperimento tractando ad eundem, xix. In daubura parietum lardarii et in cooperatione ejusdem tractanda, xi. In daubura parietum salsarii, iiii. In emendatione parietum koquinae, iii. In auxiliis ad daubandum manguras in stabulo comitis cum arzilio fodiendo, xii. In tasso straminis faciendo cum portatione et tassatione, xxxiii. In cooperatione tractanda ejusdem, iii. In i. portione veteris tassi foragii portando usque in horeum[2] ad salvandum ad bestias, vi. In i. tasso pisarum frangendo et portando usque ad aulam et usque in grangiam ad triturandum, lxvii. In sarclatione xlvi. acrarum frumenti, lxxvi. In walewrt et in hamerokes et dokkes abradicandis extra frumentum, xxvii. {In curtino reparando, vi.} In fossatis[3] erigendis circa boscum de Oldelondris, x. In fossatis erigendis circa campos de Bonewelleriding, xii. In venditione, liiii. In venditione super compotum, vi.

Summa M. D. et v.

Adhuc opera aestivalia. Idem respondent de ccxlv. operibus aestivalibus a festo Apostolorum Petri et Pauli usque in diem Ad Vinculam per diem integrum et per minus centum.

Inde. In allocatione facta custumariis pro pratis falcandis, xliii. In i. tasso foragii et feni faciendo et mixtando cum portatione straminis extra grangiam, xxxi. In eodem cooperando, iii. In lxiii. acris ordei sarclandis, lv. In xlii. acris avenae sarclandis, xxxviii. In pomis frissandis et conculcandis ad ciceram faciendam, xxx. In venditione, xlv.

Summa talis.

Opera autumpnalia. Idem respondent de M. cc. et xxiii. operibus autumpnalibus per minus centum. Et de vi[xx]. precariis de soknae et non plus quia alii sunt liberi omnes et nichil dabunt.

Summa Mccc. xliii.

Inde. In allocatione facta praeposito, xxiiii. In allocatione facta ii. bedellis, vi. In allocatione facta de le carte reve et le repe reve, vi. In messione, ligatione et adunatione ccv. acrarum dim. et dim. rodae, vi[c]. et lv. In blado cariando cum carectis comitis prout necesse fuit, xx. In blado tassando in horeo, xii. In venditione, v[c]. Item in venditione, vi[xx]. precariae.

Summa talis.

---

[1] *veteri* in roll.　　　[2] *horeo* in roll.　　　[3] *fossandis* in roll.

Cariagia autumpnalia. Idem respondent de xliii. cariagiis autumpnalibus ad bladum comitis cariandum.

Inde. In blado comitis cariando, xxxv. In venditione, viii.

Factura brasei. Idem respondent de factura de xxi. summis brasei de ordeo comitis per custumarios.

Et venduntur ut supra.

Cariagia fimorum. Idem respondent de xliii. carectis custumariorum cariantibus fimum quousque totum carietur. In fimis cariandis, omnes.

Averagia. Idem respondent de xvii^{xx}. et i. averagiis de tota soka per annum.

Inde. In allocatione facta praeposito, iii. In allocatione bedello, iii. In allocatione i. alii bedello, i. et dim. In xviii. summis frumenti cariandis usque Norwicum ad vendendum, xxxvi. In xvi. summis pisarum cariandis eodem modo ad vendendum, xxxii. In viii. summis ordei cariandis usque Norwicum ad vendendum, xvi. In mensa senescalli de Norwico ducendo, iii. In literis senescalli portandis usque Kenet ad nunciandum servienti de arreragiis, i. In literis senescalli ibidem portandis pro denariis levandis, praecepto Rogeri de Bik[erwik], i. In literis senescalli ibidem portandis pro venditione de konines, i. In literis senescalli portandis usque Okele ad levandum arreragia, i. In literis senescalli portandis ibidem ad faciendum distringere Dominum Willelmum de Monchensi pro transgressione facta, i. In literis senescalli portandis usque Hanewrthe ad levanda arreragia, i. In literis senescalli portandis ibidem ad nunciandum de i. curia, i. In literis senescalli portandis usque Blakeshal ad Dominum T. Welond, i. In venditione, xi^{xx}. xviii. et dim.

Summa talis.

Factura brasei. Idem respondent de xxi. summis brasei faciendis. Et venduntur ut supra.

Cariacio fimorum. Idem respondent de xliii. carectis custumariorum ad fimos[1] cariandos.

Inde. In fimis cariandis, omnes.

[1] *fimes* in roll.

APPENDIX IX.

ACCOUNT ROLLS OF THE MANOR OF FORNCETT, 1376–8[1].

Fornecete. Compotus Willelmi Hernynge praepositi[2] ibidem a festo Sancti Michaelis Archangeli anno regni Regis Edwardi Tertii post Conquestum quinquagesimo[3] usque idem festum Sancti Michaelis proxime sequens anno regni Regis Ricardi Secundi post Conquestum primo[4].

Arreragia. De arreragiis compoti ultimi anni praecedentis, xx*l.* xvii*s.* viii*d. ob. di. q*ᵃ.[5].

Summa xx*l.* xvii*s.* viii*d. ob. di. q*ᵃ.

Redditus assisae. Et de ciiii*s.* viii*d.* de redditu ibidem termino Sancti Andreae Apostoli. Et de li*s.* iii*d. ob.* de redditu ibidem termino Natalis Domini. Et de cxvii*s.* vii*d. ob.* de redditu ibidem termino Paschae. Et de ii*s.* viii*d.* de redditu ibidem termino Pentecostes. Et de xvi*d.* de forwardsylver ad eundem terminum. Et de ii*s.* viii*d.* de saltpeny ad Gulam Augusti. Et de cxs. ii*d. ob. q*ᵃ. de redditu ibidem ad terminum Sancti Michaelis. Et de ii*s.* vi*d.* de novo redditu Simonis Spellere pro i. messuagio i. curtilagio quondam Rogeri Spellere et nuper Abel per annum terminis Sancti Andreae Apostoli et Sancti Michaelis. Et de obolo de incremento redditus Rogeri Bole pro i. cotagio in Aslactone. Et de *id.* de incremento redditus Johannis Bolytoute pro i. acra dim. terrae in Multone quondam Johannis Madame per annum terminis Paschae et Sancti Michaelis. Et de *id.* de incremento redditus Radulphi Brakest pro medietate unius pightelli et ii. acrarum unius rodae terrae in Multone. Et de *id.* de incremento redditus Walteri Bolytoute pro i. acra terrae in Multone adquisita de Alicia Glise per annum. Et de *id.* de incremento redditus Aliciae Rugge pro ii. acris terrae adquisitis de Hugone Solfa in Waketone. Et de *id.* de incremento redditus Johannis Bolytoute junioris pro i. {placia} (pecia) terrae continente iiii. acras. Et de *ob.* de incremento redditus Walteri Bolytoute pro i. acra terrae in Aslactone adquisita de Johanne Fornecete. Et de *q*ᵃ. de incremento redditus Ricardi Galgrim pro i. roda terrae quam perquisivit de Roberto Elham termino Sancti Michaelis. Et de *ob.* de incremento redditus percipiendo per annum de ii. acris dim. terrae liberae quas Johannes Bolytoute et Sarra filia ejus nativi dominae

---

[1] The account roll of 1376–7 is printed in full. New matter and the more important variant forms occurring in the roll of 1377–8 are given in the footnotes.

[2] 1378. Compotus Johannis ate Lound, praepositi.

[3] 1378. Anno regni Regis Ricardi Secundi post conquestum primo.

[4] 1378. Anno regni ejusdem Regis Ricardi Secundo.

[5] 1378. Arrears amounted to £9. 14*s.* 1*d. ob. q*ᵃ. besides arrears of the knights' courts. Part of the entry is illegible.

perquisiverunt libere per cartam in Multone ut patet per rotulum curiae, hoc anno xv°. Et de ii*s.* de novo redditu Johannis Kyng, ut exonerentur[1] de tenura v. acrarum terrae quondam Hippelle ut patet per rotulum curiae solvendis ad terminum vitae dicti Johannis per annum terminis usualibus. Et de {iii*d.*} (xii*d.*) de novo redditu Johannis Elred (pro termino Sancti Andreae Apostoli in partem xii*d.* per annum) ut exonerentur[1] de tenura v. acrarum terrae ad terminum vitae suae ad terminos usuales et non plus hoc anno (nec de caetero quia idem Johannes moriebatur hoc anno prima septimana Quadragesimae). Et de xviii*d.* de novo redditu Johannis Rougheye nativi dominae manentis in Ryveshalle pro licentia manendi extra dominium dominae ad terminum vitae suae per annum terminis usualibus. Et de xviii*d.* de novo redditu Ricardi Galgrim pro ii. acris i. roda terrae quas nuper Johannes Sunwyne perquisivit sibi et haeredibus suis ad voluntatem dominae, ultra iiii*d.* per annum de certo redditu inde prius debito, hoc anno xii°., per annum terminis usualibus. Et de xv*s.* de novo redditu uxoris Thomae Southawe pro omnibus operibus et custumis omnium terrarum et tenementorum suorum eidem relaxatis per dominum Walterum Manny nuper dominum istius manerii ex gratia sua speciali ad terminum vitae dictae uxoris per annum terminis usualibus. Et de *q*ᵃ. de incremento redditus Johannis Bolytoute, Aliciae et Margaretae filiarum ejusdem Johannis nativorum dominae pro i. messuagio iiii. acris dim. terrae perquisitis libere per cartam sibi et haeredibus suis per annum termino Sancti Michaelis, hoc anno xi°. Et de *ob.* de incremento redditus Johannis Rougheye et Agnetis uxoris ejus pro ii. placiis cum i. domo superaedificata in Ryveshalle perquisitis libere per cartam sibi et haeredibus suis per annum termino Sancti Michaelis, hoc anno xi°. Et de *q*ᵃ. de incremento Roberti Coyllour junioris pro omnibus terris et tenementis suis quae prius captae fuerunt in manus dominae ex certa causa ad festum Paschae, hoc anno x°². Et de *q*ᵃ. de incremento Walteri Dryl pro i. messuagio libere perquisito sibi et haeredibus suis ad festum Sancti Michaelis. Et [de] *id.* de incremento Walteri Bolytoute senioris pro i. {placia} (pecia) terrae continente v. acras libere perquisita per cartam ad festum Sancti Michaelis per annum, hoc anno x°. Et de *q*ᵃ. de incremento redditus Walteri Bolytoute junioris et Willelmi Hernynge nativorum dominae pro i. messuagio continente dim. rodam terrae perquisito de Roberto Fot libere sibi et haeredibus suis per annum termino Sancti Michaelis, hoc anno ix°. Et de ii*d.* de incremento redditus Walteri Bolytoute junioris et Johannis filii ejus nativorum dominae pro x. acris terrae cum i. messuagio in Aslaktone perquisitis libere sibi et haeredibus suis termino Sancti Michaelis, hoc anno viii°. Et de *id. ob.* de incremento Ricardi filii Willelmi Baxtere nativi dominae pro i. messuagio et vi. acris dim. terrae perquisitis libere in Multone sibi et haeredibus per annum termino Sancti Michaelis, hoc anno viii°. Et de *q*ᵃ. de incremento Walteri Bolytoute nativi dominae pro ii. acris terrae liberae in Aslaktone quas perquisivit de Edwardo de Castone sibi et haeredibus suis per annum termino Sancti Michaelis, hoc anno v*to*. Et de *id.* de incremento redditus Walteri Bolytoute junioris, Ricardi filii ejus pro medietate unius messuagii cum medietate unius peciae terrae in crofto ejusdem messuagii adjacente in Aslaktone et pro i. messuagio et ii. acris terrae jacentibus in crofto ejusdem messuagii et pro vi. peciis terrae et prati quas perquisiverunt de Thoma Hardegrey et Amabilla uxore sua ut patet per rotulum curiae, hoc anno iiii*to*. termino Sancti Michaelis. Et de *ob.* de incremento redditus unius messuagii in Longestrattone quondam Willelmi Schaundeler quod Robertus Dosi de Fornecete nativus dominae et Alicia filia ejus perquisiverunt de Galfrido Hardegrey de Mor[n]yngthorpe Johanne ate

---

[1] *Sic.* 1378. exoneretur.   [2] 1378. x°.

Hyl[1] capellano et Johanne Buke solvendo ad festum Sancti Michaelis, hoc anno iii[tio]. Et de i*d*. de incremento redditus ejusdem Roberti Dosi pro i. messuagio quondam Roberti Jebat quod perquisivit de Waltero Fairman et Martino Mariot capellano in Fornecete ad festum Sancti Michaelis, hoc anno iii[tio]. Et de (i*d*.) *ob*. de incremento Ricardi Coliour et Nicholai filii sui pro iii. acris terrae jacentibus in quatuor peciis quas perquisiverunt de Nicholao Welham, hoc anno primo. Et de *ob*. de Waltero Bolytoute et Ricardo filio suo pro i. messuagio et iii. peciis terrae cum i. pygthelo in Multone quas perquisiverunt de Ricardo Horn et Roberto Hernyng, hoc anno primo. Et de *ob*. de praedicto[2] Waltero et Ricardo pro ii. acris terrae in Multone quas perquisiverunt de Johanne Madame, hoc anno primo. Et de *q^a*. de Roberto Dosy pro i. pecia terrae jacente apud Kykelyng-tounesende quam perquisivit de Johanne Gallard, hoc anno primo. Et de *q^a*. de Roberto Dosy Alicia uxore ejus et Johanne filio eorundem pro i. acra dim. terrae quam perquisiverunt de Ricardo Curlenache de Thrandestone et Katerina uxore ejus, hoc anno primo[3].

Summa xx*l*. {xiiii*s*. ix*d*. *q^a*.} (xv*s*. vi*d*. *q^a*.)[4].

Firmae terrarum. Et de vi*s*. viii*d*. de firma quartae partis fori de Strattone dimissae Willelmo Hernynge hoc anno. Et de viii*l*. de firma terrarum et tenementorum vocatorum Wylliamesthyng in Thakelestone[5] dimissorum Roberto Houghlot et Willelmo Hernynge hoc anno, solvendis ad festum Sancti Michaelis. Et de x*d*. de firma iiii. acrarum terrae apud Wathlefelde[6] dimissarum Johanni Panel solvendis ad festa Paschae et Sancti Michaelis. Et de iiii*s*. viii*d*. de firma ii. acrarum terrae cum i. crofto juxta domum Henrici Hagne[7] quondam Charer dimissarum Johanni ate Lound ad terminum vii. annorum, hoc anno primo. Et de xiii*d*. de firma ii. acrarum terrae nuper dimissarum Rogero Petyfer et i. inclausi vocati Mekele Crofte dimissi Ricardo Ode ad terminum v. annorum, hoc anno ultimo, solvendis ad terminum Sancti Michaelis[8]. Et de xvi*d*. de i. acra dim. terrae cum i. pygthello quondam Flededes dimissis Simoni Hyckes hoc anno. Et de xvi*d*. de firma iiii. acrarum terrae quondam David Toward dimissarum Roberto Hughlot hoc anno. Et de v*s*. de firma i[us]. messuagii et ii. acrarum terrae quondam Hippele et i. messuagii et i[us]. acrae dim. terrae quondam Johannis de Fornecete vocatorum Mundes dimissorum Johanni Gallarde ate Grene ad terminum vii. annorum, hoc anno iiii[to]. Et de xx*d*. de firma i. acrae dim. terrae de tenemento quondam Hyppele de Fornecete et i. acrae terrae quondam Wardes dimissarum Roberto Seriante ad terminum vii. annorum, hoc anno iiii[to]. terminis Paschae et Sancti Michaelis. Et de xviii*d*. de firma ii. acrarum i. rodae terrae de tenementis Kelpone Hippele et Gallard dimissarum Johanni Gallard ad terminum v. annorum, hoc anno iiii[to]., per annum, dicto termino. Et de {iii*d*.} (iiii*d*. *ob*.) de firma i. rodae dim. terrae de tenemento Fornecete nuper dimissarum Roberto Sterre[9]. Et de {vi*d*.} (xii*d*.) de firma i. acrae terrae de tenemento Fornecete dimissae Johanni Hyllyng hoc anno. Et de viii*d*. de Willelmo Wayte pro firma de tenemento Hippele Fornecete (iii. rodis terrae) vocato Mundes sic dimisso hoc anno. Et de

---

[1] 1378. ate Hull.   [2] *Sic.*   [3] In margin: Summa xx*l*. xiiii*s*. ix*d*. *q^a*.

[4] 1378. Nearly half of this entry is missing, several inches of parchment having been torn from one side of the roll. The entry seems to have corresponded closely to that of 1377. The sum total amounts to xx*l*. xiiii*s*. vi[*d*.].

[5] The manor of Williams in Tacolneston.

[6] 1378. Watlesfeld.   [7] 1378. Haughne.

[8] Et de xiii*d*. de Radulpho Treye pro ii. acris terrae nuper dimissis Radulpho (*sic*) Petifer in i. inclauso......anno primo per rotulum curiae solvendis ad festa Paschae et Sancti Michaelis.

[9] 1378. Nuper dimissarum Roberto Sterre (dimittuntur Ricardo Sterre).

viii*d*. de firma i. acrae terrae de tenemento quondam Hippyl Fornecete dimissae Roberto Bole hoc anno. Et de iii*s*. iiii*d*. de firma v. acrarum cum i. messuagio quondam Tedgor dimissarum Johanni Panel hoc anno. Et de v*s*. de Johanne Kensy pro firma iii. acrarum terrae tenementi Bert vocati Ruste hoc anno. Et de xx*d*. de firma ii. acrarum terrae ejusdem tenementi dimissarum {Johanni} (Nicholao) Everard ad terminum v. annorum, hoc anno secundo. Et de iiii*s*. vi*d*. de firma v. acrarum terrae quondam Elred dimissarum Waltero Davy ad terminum vii. annorum, hoc anno {primo} (secundo). Et de ii*s*. viii*d*. de firma ii. acrarum dim. terrae quondam Lestan dimissarum Roberto Herberd ad terminum vii. annorum, hoc anno iiiiᵗᵒ., per annum, dicto termino. Et de vi*s*. de firma v. acrarum terrae quondam Johannis Wlsy vocatarum Knygthes et iii. rodarum terrae de tenemento Hippele dimissarum Johanni Baxtere ad terminum vii. annorum, hoc anno iiiiᵗᵒ. Et de iii*s*. viii*d*. de firma i. messuagii cum crofto continentis i. acram dim. quondam Johannis Jebat vocati Kelpone dimissi Andreae Bonde ad terminum vii. annorum, hoc anno iiiiᵗᵒ. Et de ii*s*. i*d*. de firma ii. acrarum dim. terrae quondam dicti Kelpone dimissarum Matildae Ropere hoc anno. Et de ii*s*. vi*d*. de firma ii. acrarum terrae quondam Johannis Kynge dimissarum Thomae Barfot hoc anno. Et de x*d*. de firma iii. rodarum terrae quondam dicti Kynge dimissarum Roberto Seriant hoc anno. Et de viii*d*. de firma iii. rodarum terrae quondam praedicti Roberti Kynge dimissarum Rogero Gallard hoc anno. Et de xx*d*. de firma i. acrae dim. terrae quondam dicti Kynge dimissarum Roberto Hagne ad terminum vii. annorum, hoc anno iiiiᵗᵒ. Et de viii*d*. de firma iii. rodarum dim. terrae de tenemento Galfridi capellani dimissarum Ricardo Sawere hoc anno. Et de iiii*s*. vi*d*. de firma v. acrarum terrae quondam Elflede vocatarum Wrong dimissarum Johanni Buke hoc anno. Et de vii*d*. *ob.* de firma iii. rodarum terrae quondam Wardes dimissarum Ricardo Davy. Et de vi*d*. de pastura iii. rodarum terrae ejusdem tenementi vendita Johanni Lound hoc anno. Et de viii*d*. de firma i. rodae dim. terrae quondam Wardes dimissarum Waltero Davy hoc anno. De firma iii. rodarum terrae ejusdem tenementi quondam dimissarum Johanni Dosy pro x*d*. per annum {nihil hoc anno quia jacebant friscae et non poterant dimitti} (x*d*.)¹. De firma iii. rodarum terrae ejusdem tenementi computatarum dimissarum eidem Johanni in anno ultimo praecedente, nihil hic nec de caetero quia firma praedictarum iii. rodarum terrae bis onerata fuit eodem anno². Et de vi*d*. de i. acra terrae ejusdem tenementi dimissa Johanni Gallard. Et de ix*d*. de firma ii. rodarum dim. terrae ejusdem tenementi dimissarum Ricardo Davy ad terminum vii. annorum, hoc anno ultimo³. Et de ii*s*. vi*d*. de firma i. acrae dim. terrae quondam Floraunce dimissarum Thomae Parmunter hoc anno. Et de viii*d*. de firma dimidiae acrae terrae dicti Florance dimissae Johanni Prati hoc anno. Et de xii*d*. de firma i. acrae i. rodae terrae quondam Floraunce vocatarum Elfled dimissarum eidem Johanni ad terminum vii. annorum, hoc anno ultimo⁴. Et de xix*d*. de i. acra i. roda terrae cum i. crofto quondam Bretone dimissis Stephano Prati capellano hoc anno⁵. Et de iiii*d*. de i. roda terrae quondam Roberti Yve

---

¹ 1378. Et de......firma iii. rodarum terrae ejusdem tenementi dimissarum Waltero Davy hoc anno.
² 1378. This sentence is omitted.
³ 1378. Et de ix*d*. de firma ii. rodarum dim. terrae ejusdem tenementi dimissarum Willelmo Pelet hoc anno.
⁴ 1378. Et de {viii*d*.} (xii*d*. ut anno praecedente) de firma i. acrae i. rodae terrae quondam Florance vocatarum Elfled dimissarum eidem Johanni per rotulum curiae ad terminum vii. annorum, hoc anno primo.
⁵ 1378. De firma i. acrae i. rodae terrae cum i. crofto quondam Bretone nuper dimissarum Stephano Prati pro xix*d*. nichil hic quia dimittuntur Willelmo Schepherde per rotulum curiae pro xiiii*d*. inferius.

dimissa Willelmo Jebat. Et de iii*s.* de firma i. acrae dim. terrae cum crofto quondam Margaretae Raven dimissarum Matilli Ropere hoc anno. Et de ii*d.* de i. roda terrae ejusdem tenementi dimissa Ricardo Wadeker. Et de xvi*d.* de firma ii. acrarum dim.[1] terrae de tenemento Mones quondam Haggechese dimissarum Willelmo Seriante ad terminum vii. annorum, hoc iiii*to.* Et de {v*s.*} (vi*s.* viii*d.*) et non plus quia per rotulum curiae pro firma v. acrarum terrae quondam Ricardi Galgrim dimissarum Johanni Lyncolne ad terminum vi. annorum, hoc anno iii*o.* Et de ii*s.* iiii*d.* pro firma i. inclausi ii. acrarum terrae dim. quondam Simonis Spellere dimissorum Rogero Gallard ad terminum v. annorum, hoc anno iiii*to.* Et de xx*d.* de firma ii. acrarum terrae quondam dicti Simonis dimissarum Nicholao Wylyard ad terminum v. annorum, hoc anno iiii*to.* Et de iii*d.* de firma i. acrae terrae dicti tenementi dimissae Johanni Lound. Et de viii*d.* de firma i. rodae terrae cum quadam parva pecia pasturae vocata Haseholt quondam Walteri Bakfens dimissa Hugoni Gallard hoc anno. Et de {xii*d.*} (xx*d.*) pro i. acra terrae et i. acra prati quondam Davy Tooward dimissis Simoni Baxtere per rotulum curiae ad terminum vii. annorum, hoc anno iii*o.* Et de ii*s.* iii*d.* de pastura v. acrarum dim. terrae quondam dicti Davy et dim. acrae terrae quondam Ordynge dimissa Thomae Colman ad terminum v. annorum, hoc anno iiii*to.* Et de ii*s.* de Beatrice uxore quondam Willelmi Pote pro medietate vii. acrarum terrae quondam dicti Willelmi eidem dimissa hoc anno et altera medietas dimittitur pro antiqua consuetudine[2]. Et de xvi*d.* pro firma iii. rodarum terrae quondam Hugonis Baroun dimissarum Willelmo Wayte ad terminum vii. annorum, hoc anno vi*to.* Et de xx*d.* de firma i. acrae dim. terrae cum i. inclauso quondam dicti Hugonis de tenemento quondam Rogeri Smyth dimissarum Roberto Spyr ad terminum vii. annorum, hoc anno v*to.* Et de vi*d.* pro iii. rodis terrae quondam dicti Hugonis dimissis eidem Roberto hoc anno. Et de xii*d.* de firma iii. rodarum dim. terrae dicti Hugonis dimissarum Roberto Lewyn. Et de vi*d.* de i. roda dim. terrae quondam dicti Hugonis dimissis Willelmo Jebat hoc anno. Et de x*d.* pro iii. rodis terrae quondam dicti Hugonis dimissis Roberto Lewyn hoc anno. Et de vi*d.* de firma dimidiae acrae terrae quondam dicti Hugonis dimissae Johanni Gallard hoc anno. Et de xx*d.* de firma i. acrae iii. rodarum terrae quondam Rougheye[3] Rogeri Smyth et Hippelle quas dictus Hugo tenuit dimissarum Roberto Spyr ad terminum vii. annorum, hoc anno vi*to.* Et de v*d.* de firma i. acrae terrae quondam dicti Hugonis dimissae Johanni Skylman ad terminum vii. annorum, hoc anno ultimo[4]. Et de vii*d.* pro i. cotagio non aedificato quondam Edwardes dimisso Waltero Lacchelos hoc anno. Et de vi*d.* de i. roda terrae quondam dicti Edwardes dimissa eidem Waltero. Et de x*s.* de firma medietatis omnium terrarum et tenementorum in Redelyngfelde quae devenerunt in manus dominae post mortem Radulphi Toly dimissae Roberto Cyne et Willelmo Hernyng ad terminum v. annorum, hoc anno iiii*to.* Et altera medietas liberatur viduae per rotulum curiae hoc anno (ut patet in curia tenta ad festum Conversionis Sancti Pauli)[5]. Et de {xii*d.*} (xiiii*d.*) de i. acra prati quondam Ricardi Galgrim dimissa

[1] 1378. dim. omitted.   [2] 1378. pro antiquo servitio.
[3] 1378. Rougheyne.
[4] 1378. Et de v*d.* de firma i. acrae terrae quondam dicti Hugonis dimissae Johanni Skylman hoc anno.
[5] 1378. [In marg.] Memorandum quod quidam homo optulit dominae de fine pro tenemento Toly sibi et haeredibus suis habendo c*s.* et hoc anno per favorem ministrorum dominae Robertus Toly cepit dictum tenementum per finem xxiiii*s.* in praejudicium dominae ut patet in curia etc. Ideo praeceptum est etc.
1378. {Et de v*s.* de firma medietatis omnium terrarum et tenementorum in Redelyngfeld quae devenerunt in manus dominae post mortem Radulphi Tooly a festo Sancti Michaelis usque festum Sancti Dunstani in partem x*s.* per annum et non plus de caetero quia Robertus

Petro de Westhale hoc anno. Et de vs. de firma quartae partis terrarum et tenementorum quondam Clerke dimissae diversis hominibus hoc anno. Et de iiii*s*. iiii*d*. pro firma iii. acrarum dim. terrae quondam Geyres et Broketothe unde i. acra quondam Broketothe dimittitur Rogero Wylard hoc anno. Et de iiii*d*. de Johanne Bustard pro dimidia acra terrae quondam Hugonis ate Hil sic sibi dimissa hoc anno. Et de viii*d*. pro i. acra i. roda terrae quondam Simonis Spellere dimissis Johannae Schilman ad terminum vii. annorum, hoc anno ultimo[1]. Et de ii*s*. ii*d*. de firma ii. acrarum dim. terrae quondam Durrant dimissarum Roberto Thaxtere ad terminum vii. annorum, hoc anno ultimo[2]. Et de xii*d*. de firma j. acrae terrae quondam Aliciae Baldewyne dimissae Willelmo Herberd. Et de xii*d*. de firma iii. acrarum terrae in Multone quondam Willelmi Carletone dimissarum Ricardo Heued ad terminum viii. annorum, hoc anno vii°. Et de ii*d*. pro dimidia acra terrae in Haptone quondam Unewyne dimissa Johanni Herward ad terminum x. annorum, hoc anno vii°., solvendis ad terminum Sancti Michaelis. Et de iii*d*. de i. roda dim. terrae de tenemento Hippelle et Mundes dimissis Johanni Schilman ad terminum vii. annorum, hoc anno vi^to. Et de iiii*d*. de dimidia acra terrae in Waktone quondam Willelmi Grey dimissa Alano Elmeswelle hoc anno. Et de vi*d*. pro firma ii. acrarum terrae cum i. parcella i^us. pigthelli in Tybenham quondam Thomae Avelyne dimissarum Thomae Baroun ad terminum vii. annorum, hoc anno ultimo[3]. Et de ix*d*. pro iii. rodis terrae quondam Lythfot dimissis Willelmo Pelet ad terminum vii. annorum, hoc anno ultimo[4]. Et de viii*d*. de iii. rodis terrae jacentibus in ii. peciis de tenemento quondam Rogeri Smyth de tenemento Hugonis Baroun videlicet super Northcroft et Halleyerd dimissis Willelmo Jebat hoc anno. Et de xviii*d*. de firma i. acrae terrae de tenemento Clyre quondam Simonis Spellere et dimidiae acrae terrae quondam Hugonis Baroun apud Haggechese dimissarum Johanni Hyllyng ad terminum vii. annorum, hoc anno primo. Et de ii*d*. pro iii. rodis terrae quondam Willelmi Grey dimissis Johanni Donyngtone. Et de ii*d*. de iii. rodis terrae quondam Roberti de Wode dimissis eidem Roberto. Et de xviii*d*. de i. messuagio i. acra dim. terrae quondam Willelmi Scrape dimissis Johanni Praty. Et de xii*d*. de iii. rodis terrae quondam Scrapes dimissis Matilli Ropere. Et de {viis.} (xis. ix*d*.) de firma ix. acrarum i. rodae terrae et i. acrae i. rodae prati quae devenerunt in manus dominae post mortem Roberti Houlot[5] senioris et uxoris ejus dimissarum diversis hominibus hoc anno, ultra i. acram i. rodam dim. ejusdem tenementi dimissas Roberto Lewyn ut patet inferius. Et de xii*d*. de firma ii. acrarum dim. terrae tenementi quondam Gooses et i. acrae dim. terrae tenementi quondam Bygges quae devenerunt in manus dominae post mortem Mathiae Hernynge dimissarum Ricardo Heued et Roberto Heued ad terminum viii. annorum, hoc anno iiii^to. Et de xii*d*. de firma ii. peciarum pasturae et i. pygthelli in Morgate quondam praedicti Roberti quae devenerunt in manus dominae modo praedicto dimissarum Ricardo Mor ad terminum vii. annorum, hoc anno iiii^to. Et de xs. de firma x. acrarum i. rodae terrae et dimidiae acrae prati in Trystone[6] quondam Roberti Bacoun dimissarum Henrico Rynggere ad terminum viii. annorum, hoc anno iiii^to. Et de ix*d*. de firma dimidiae acrae terrae et i. rodae prati cum quodam messuagio quondam Ricardi Davy[7] ut patet per rotulum curiae et dimittuntur Willelmo Pelet ultra servitia

Tooly filius praedicti Radulphi recepit dicta terras et tenementa de domina per finem ut patet in curia tenta die Lunae proxima ante festum Sancti Dunstani per antiquam consuetudinem.} (Quia dicta concessio fuit in praejudicium dominae et sine warranto.)

[1] 1378. dimissis Johannae Schilman hoc anno.
[2] 1378. dimissarum Roberto Thaxtere hoc anno.
[3] 1378. dimissarum Thomae Baroun hoc anno.
[4] 1378. dimissis Willelmo Pelet hoc anno.
[5] 1378. Houghlot.   [6] Tharston.   [7] 1378. Doosy.

et consuetudines. Et de iii*d.* de firma iii. rodarum terrae quondam Christianae de Bynham quae devenerunt in manum dominae post mortem dictae Christianae dimissarum Margaretae Lound per annum. Et de iii*s.* de firma xi. acrarum {pasturae} (terrae) vocatarum Wronglond quondam Roberti Bakoun superius nominati dimissarum Willelmo Schuldre ad terminum vii. annorum, hoc anno primo (secundo). Et de xx*d.* de firma iiii. acrarum terrae ejusdem tenurae dimissarum Adae Gallard. Et de ii*s.* vi*d.* de firma viii. acrarum terrae et unius pygthelli quondam dicti Roberti dimissarum Johanni Bustard ad terminum v. annorum, hoc anno [iiii^to.]. Et de ii*d.* *ob.* de firma i. rodae dim. terrae de tenemento Clerke in Takelestone dimissae Stephano Praty capellano ad terminum vii. annorum, hoc anno iiii^to. Et de ii*s.* de firma ii. acrarum terrae dim. de tenemento Pennynge dimissarum Willelmo Jebat ad terminum vii. annorum, hoc anno iiii^to. Et de xii*d.* de firma i. acrae i. rodae de tenemento Davyd dimissarum Emmae Cooke ad terminum vii. annorum, hoc anno iiii^to. Et de [x]*d.* de firma i. acrae i. rodae (terrae) et dimidiae rodae prati quondam Roberti Houlot senioris dimissarum Roberto Lewyn ad terminum viii. annorum, hoc anno iiii^to. Et de v*s.* de firma v. acrarum terrae tenementi Crowes quondam Herberd dimissarum diversis hominibus hoc anno. Et de iiii*s.* vi*d.* de firma v. acrarum terrae weyvatarum per Johannem Colman mense Julii[1], hoc anno iii°. dimissarum Willelmo Schepherde ad terminum vii. annorum, hoc anno primo. Et de iii*d.* de firma dimidiae acrae terrae in manu dominae post mortem Walteri Gallard, hoc anno iii°. Et de xiiii*d.* de firma i. acrae i. rodae terrae cum i. crofto quondam Bretone nuper dimissarum Stephano Prati capellano dimissarum Willelmo Schepherde ad terminum vii. annorum, hoc anno primo[2]. Et de iiii*s.* ii*d.* de Waltero Davy pro firma iiii. acrarum dim. terrae de tenemento Longes eidem dimissarum ad terminum vii. annorum, hoc anno secundo. Et de iiii*d.* de Alicia Hagne pro firma i. rodae dim. terrae ejusdem tenementi eidem dimissarum ad eundem terminum. Et de viii*d.* de {Roberto} (Willelmo) Seriaunt pro firma i. acrae terrae de tenemento Hors in manu dominae existentis post mortem Johannis Lythfot eidem dimissae ad terminum vii. annorum, hoc anno secundo. Et de viii*d.* de Ricardo Potekyn pro firma iii. rodarum terrae ejusdem tenementi eidem dimissarum ad terminum vii. annorum, hoc anno secundo. Et de iiii*d.* de Petro de Westhale pro iii. rodis terrae ejusdem tenementi eidem dimissis hoc anno. Et de {iiii*s.*} (v*s.* ut in anno praecedente) de Rogero Gallard pro firma i^us. messuagii

Praeceptum est.   {iii.} (i^us.) acrae {i. rodae} (dim.) terrae (praeceptum est inquirere de residuo) in manu dominae existentium post decessum Johannis Bynorth tanquam escaeta quae tenebatur[3] de domina per servitium i*d.* *ob.* de redditu per annum[4]. De firma i. cotagii in Bonewelle quondam Willelmi Chapeleyn nihil hic quia conceditur Roberto Skynkyl tenendum sibi et haeredibus suis per antiqua servitia et consuetudines (per rotulum curiae hoc anno)[5]. Et de

---

[1] 1378. Junii.

[2] 1378. Et de {xiiii*d.*} (xix*d.*) de firma i. acrae i. rodae terrae cum i. crofto quondam Bretoun nuper dimissarum Stephano Praty capellano pro xix*d.* ut patet supra dimissarum Willelmo Schepherde ad terminum vii. annorum per rotulum curiae, hoc anno secundo.

[3] *Sic.*

[4] 1378. Et de v*s.* de firma unius messuagii i. acrae dim. terrae in manu dominae Praeceptum   existentium post decessum Johannis Benorthyn tanquam eschaeta quae te-
est inquirere   nebatur [sic] de domina per servitium {i*d.* *ob.*} (ii*d.*) de redditu per annum
de residuo   dimissarum Rogero filio Walteri Gallard per rotulum curiae ad terminum
terrae dicti   quinque annorum, hoc anno primo.
Johannis
Benorthe

[5] 1378. Conceditur Roberto Skynkyl tenendum sibi et haeredibus suis per rotulum curiae hoc anno secundo per antiqua servitia et consuetudines.

viii*d*. de Johanne ate Lound pro firma i. acrae iii. rodarum dim. terrae in manu dominae existentium per mortem Johannae uxoris Willelmi Sot eidem dimissarum ad terminum viii. annorum per annum, hoc anno primo.

Summa xviii*l*. {ii*s*. x*d*. *ob*.} (iii*s*. vi*d*. *ob*.).

[1]Et de iii*d*. de Henrico Chaundeler pro firma i^{us}. gardini in Strattone quondam David Toward sibi dimissi ad terminum vii. annorum, hoc anno primo. Et de ii*s*. ii*d*. de Johanne Baxtere pro iii. rodis terrae cum i. curtilagio de tenemento Pennynge, iii. rodis terrae tenementi Ravons et i. acra i. roda terrae tenementi Mundes eidem dimissis ad terminum annorum, hoc anno primo. Et de x*d*. de Johanne Aye pro i. acra i. roda terrae tenementi Smythes eidem dimissis ad eundem terminum, hoc anno primo. {Et de xv*s*. de Ricardo Longlys pro firma x. acrarum terrae tenementi quondam Southawe eidem dimissarum per rotulum curiae hoc anno} (quia oneratur supra in titulo de reddit u assisae)[2]. Et de iiii*d*. de Ricardo Keede pro dimidia acra terrae eidem dimissa ad terminum x. annorum, hoc anno primo. Et de viii*d*. de Willelmo Pelet pro i. acra terrae tenementi Kelmond eidem dimissa hoc anno et per vi. annos sequentes per rotulum curiae[3].

Firmae terrarum dominicalium manerii. Et de viii*l*. vi*s*. vi*d*. de Roberto Herberd et Roberto Houlot pro firma omnium terrarum dominicalium arrabilium pertinentium huic manerio excepto le {Redynge} (Westwoderedynge) quae continent clxvi. acras et dim. videlicet pro acra xii*d*. dimissarum eisdem ad terminum vii. annorum, hoc anno iiii^{to}., solvendis ad festa Paschae et Sancti Michaelis. Et de iiii*l*. vii*s*. i*d*. de eisdem Roberto et Roberto pro firma xxvi. acrarum dim. rodae prati dominicalis manerii ultra iiii. acras in Mekelemedwe quae remanent in manu dominae eisdem dimissarum ad eundem terminum solvendis ad terminos praedictos videlicet pro acra iii*s*. iiii*d*. Et de x*s*. de consuetudine falcationis pratorum dominae exeunte de tenentibus dominae ibidem dimissa Roberto et Roberto praedictis ad terminum supradictum, hoc anno iiii^{to}.,

---

[1] Written on a strip of parchment sewn to the edge of the roll.

[2] 1378. De firma i. messuagii et x. acrarum terrae quondam Thomae Southagwe dimissarum Rogero Wrygthe pro xiiii*s*. per rotulum curiae hoc anno nichil hic quia oneratur in reddit u assisae ad xv*s*. supra.

Praeceptum est inquirere si sit illud messuagium quod oneratur in reddit u assisae supra.

[3] 1378. Et de viii*d*. de Willelmo Pelet pro i. acra terrae tenementi Kelmond eidem dimissa ad terminum vi. annorum, hoc anno primo. Et de ii*d*. de firma i. rodae terrae tenementi Husbonde dimissae Johanni ate Hull ad terminum x. annorum per rotulum curiae, hoc anno primo. Et de x*d*. de i. acra dim. terrae tenementi Splyttes, in manu dominae hoc anno primo ut patet extra, dimissis Roberto Mullere hoc anno. Et de vi*d*. de iii. rodis ejusdem tenementi dimissis Thomae Thatchere hoc anno. Et de ii*d*. de i. roda terrae ejusdem tenementi dimissa Johanni Dozi hoc anno. Et de iiii*d*. de i. pigthello ejusdem tenementi dimisso Willelmo Jebat per rotulum curiae ad terminum x. annorum, hoc anno primo. Et de xviii*d*. de i. acra dim. terrae ejusdem tenementi dimissis Johanni Praty hoc anno. Et de viii*d*. de i. acra terrae ejusdem tenementi dimissa Agneti Splitte hoc anno. Et de v*s*. iiii*d*. de firma v. acrarum iii. rodarum terrae tenementi Spyr in manu dominae, hoc anno primo, dimissarum Johanni Praty hoc anno. Et de ii*s*. de firma i. pigthelli iii. acrarum terrae tenementi Rogeri Hulle in manu dominae hoc anno primo ut patet per rotulum curiae, dimissarum Rogero Wyllard hoc anno. Et de ii*s*. de firma ii. acrarum dim. terrae cum i. pigthello de tenemento in Fornecete quod Rogerus Gallard weyvavit, in manus dominae hoc anno primo, dimissarum Roberto Dosy per rotulum curiae ad terminum vii. annorum, hoc anno primo.

Summa xviii*l*. x*s*. viii*d*. *ob*. Item viii*s*. iiii*d*.

solvendis ad terminos praedictos. {De firma i. domus bercarii infra manerium nihil hic quia prostrata fuit in anno ultimo elapso per magnum ventum accidens ad festum Sancti Martini.} {Et de vi*s*. viii*d*.} {Quia inferius de Johanne ate Lound et Waltero Bolytoute pro firma i^{us}. domus bercarii simul cum cursu i. faldae sibi dimissae hoc anno quod Robertus Houlot solebat habere.} (Quia oneratur super Robertum Houglot ex antiqua consuetudine.) {Et de iii*s*. vi*d*. de firma i^{us}. inclausi vocati le Orchyerd et i^{us}. domus infra manerium vocatae le Stottestable dimissorum Willelmo Pelet ad eundem terminum, hoc anno iiii^{to}.[1], solvendis ad festum Sancti Michaelis.} (Quia oneratur in billa huic annexata.) {Et de ii*s*. ii*d*. de firma i. in-clausi vocati Cornescroft dimissi Roberto Hagne ad terminum vii. annorum, hoc anno iiii^{to}., solvendis ad festa Paschae et Sancti Michaelis.} (Quia oneratur in billa huic annexata.) {Et de xii*d*.} (ii*s*. iiii*d*.) de firma i. camerae juxta portam manerii ex parte occidentali dimissae Johanni de Lound hoc anno.} (Quia oneratur in billa huic annexata.) {Et de iiii*s*. de firma pasturae et fructus gardini manerii dimissorum Johanni Lound et sociis suis hoc anno.} (Quia oneratur in billa huic annexata.) {De firma domus boverii in manerio nihil hoc anno quia totum prostratur et de novo aedificatur ut patet inferius.} (Quia oneratur in billa huic annexata.) {Et de x*d*. de firma i. camerae juxta portam manerii ex parte orientali dimissae Roberto Ropere hoc anno.} (Quia oneratur in billa huic annexata.) (Et de iiii*d*. de quadam domo vocata le Gatehous[2] dimissa Roberto Hagne hoc anno.) (Quia oneratur in billa huic annexata.) {Et de vi*s*. viii*d*. de Johanne ate Lound et Waltero Bolytoute pro firma i^{us}. domus bercarii infra manerium simul cum cursu i. faldae supra dimissae hoc anno quod Robertus Houlot solebat habere.} {Et de iii*s*. iiii*d*. de firma i^{us}. grangiae manerii dimissae Johanni Lound hoc anno.} (Quia oneratur in billa huic [annexata].)

Summa xiiii*l*. {vi*s*. ix*d*.} (vii*s*. xi*d*.).

[3]Et de vi*s*. viii*d*. de Roberto Houglot pro firma unius domus bercarii infra manerium cum libero introitu et exitu cum cursu i^{us}. faldae eidem dimissae ad eundem terminum hoc anno iiii^{to}.[4] Et de iii*s*. vi*d*. de firma unius inclausi vocati le Orchyerd et i^{us}. domus infra manerium vocatae le Stottesstable dimissorum Willelmo Pelet ad eundem terminum, hoc anno v^{to}., solvendis ad festum Sancti Michaelis. Et de ii*s*. ii*d*. de firma i^{us}. inclausi vocati Cornescroft dimissi Roberto Haugne ad terminum vii. annorum, hoc anno iiii^{to}., solvendis ad festa Paschae et Sancti Michaelis. Et de ii*s*. iiii*d*. de firma i^{us}. camerae juxta portam manerii ex parte occidentali dimissae Johanni de Lound hoc anno[5]. Et de iiii*s*. de firma pasturae et fructus gardini manerii et herbagii de Pondyerd et Kecheneyerd dimissorum Waltero Lacchelos ad terminum v. annorum, hoc anno iiii^{to}. Et de iii*s*. iiii*d*. de firma i^{us}. grangiae manerii nuper dimissae Roberto Wylyard, modo dimissae Johanni Lound hoc anno. De firma domus boverii in manerio nuper dimissae Johanni Westhale pro x*d*. nihil hoc anno quia totum prostratur et de novo aedifi-catur ut patet inferius. Et de {x*d*.} (ii*s*. oneratur ut in anno praecedente) de firma i^{us}. camerae juxta portam manerii ex parte orientali nuper dimissae Johanni Seriant

---

[1] 1378. vi^{to}.

[2] *Sic.* Elsewhere Cartehous.

[3] The following paragraph is written on a strip of parchment sewn to the margin of the roll.

[4] 1378. De firma unius domus bercarii infra manerium cum cursu faldae nuper venditae Roberto Houglot pro vi*s*. viii*d*. nihil quia dicta domus prostratur et falda occupatur cum bidentibus dominae praecepto Willelmi Gunnyld (vi*s*. viii*d*. ut in anno praecedente).

[5] 1378. De firma i. camerae juxta portam manerii ex parte occidentali nuper dimissae Johanni ate Lound pro ii*s*. iiii*d*. nihil hoc anno quia ocupatur cum bidentibus dominae praecepto ejusdem Willelmi (ii*s*. iiii*d*. ut in anno praecedente).

pro ii*s.* supra dimissae Roberto Ropere hoc anno[1]. Et de iiii*d.* de quadam domo vocata le Cartehous dimissa Roberto Haugne hoc anno[2].

Redditus mobiles cum operibus venditis. Et de xii*d.* de iiii. libris cymini de redditu termino Sancti Michaelis venditis. Et de v*s.* iiii*d.* de xvi. caponibus de redditu venditis, pretium capitis iiii*d.* Et de xxiii*s.* de cxxxviii. gallinis de redditu venditis, pretium capitis ii*d.* Et de iii*s.* vii*d.* de Dccclx. ovis de redditu venditis, pretium centenae v*d.* Et de x*s.* x*d.* de ccciiii*xx*x. operibus yemalibus venditis, pretium iii. operum i*d.* Et de xi*s.* iiii*d.* de cccxl. operibus aestivalibus venditis, pretium v. operum ii*d.* Et de ii*s.* iiii*d.* de ix. arruris vocatis Medwerthes venditis, pretium arrurae iiii*d.* Et de vii*d.* de ii. arruris Quadragesimae venditis, pretium arrurae iiii*d. ob.* Et de viii*d.* de ii. arruris ad ordium venditis, pretium arrurae iiii*d.* Et de viii*d.* de ii. arruris de precariis venditis, pretium operis iiii*d.* Et de xxxii*s.* iii*d. ob. q*^{a}. de cclviii. averagiis dim. venditis, pretium averagii i*d. ob.* Et de xvii*d.* de factura viii. quarteriorum iiii. bussellorum brasei vendita, pretium quarterii ii*d.* Et de lxviii*s.* ii*d. ob.* de Dcccxviii operibus autumpnalibus dim. venditis, pretium cujuslibet operis i*d.* Et de vi*s.* viii*d.* de plus in toto pro xl. operibus venditis Roberto Herberd pro opere iiii*d.* ut patet in compoto anni xlviii^o. Et de iii*s.* iiii*d.* de xxxix. cariagiis autumpnalibus venditis, pretium cariagii i*d.*

Summa viii*l.* {iiii*s.* v*d. q*^{a}.} (xii*s. id. q*^{a}.)[3].

Officium praepositi. Et de xl*s.* de tenemento Willelmi Hernynge ut exoneretur de officio praepositi hoc anno de consuetudine.

Summa xl*s.*[4]

Venditio pasturae. Et de iii*s.* vi*d.* de Edmundo ate Grene de Habetone de pastura yemali et aestivali in Bromwode. Et de {ii*s.*} (iii*s.* vi*d.*) de pastura dil Cliff dimissa eidem Edmundo. Et de viii*d.* de pastura de Beywynesmede vendita Margaretae Lound. Et de x*d.* de agistamento xx. bestiarum euntium in communa de Langemor in aestate pro capite *ob.* (onus messoris). Et de iiii*d.* de herbagio de Wadeker vendito hoc anno. Et de xv*d.* de pastura vii. acrarum terrae friscae subtus boscum de Tristone de tenemento existente in manu dominae pro defectu tenentium vendita Roberto Houlot. Et de xiiii*s.* de pastura {c.} (clxvi.) acrarum dim. terrae apud Westwoderedynge vendita {Roberto} (Ricardo) Kede ad terminum vii. annorum hoc anno iii^o. Et de iii*s.* ii*d.* de herbagio de Homemede

---

[1] 1378. De i. camera ex parte orientali nuper dimissa Roberto Ropere pro x*d.* nihil hoc anno pro eo quod nullae bestiae essent infra manerium praeter bestias dominae praecepto Willelmi Gunnyld (x*d.* oneratur).

[2] 1378. De firma i. domus vocatae le Cartehous nuper dimissae Roberto Hagne pro iiii*d.* nihil pro eodem (iiii*d.* oneratur ut in anno [praecedente]).

Summa xiiii*l.* vi*s.* ix*d.*

[3] 1378. Et de xii*d.* de iiii. libris cymini de redditu termino Sancti Michaelis venditis Et de v*s.* iiii*d.* de xvi. caponibus de redditu venditis ut patet extra, pretium capitis iiii*d.* Et de xi*s.* x*d.* de lxxi. gallinis de redditu venditis, pretium capitis ii*d.* Et de iii*s.* iiii*d. q*^{a}. de Dcciiii^{xx}. v. ovis de redditu venditis, pretium centenae v*d.* Et de ii*s.* xi*d. q*^{a}. et tertia parte *q*^{a}. de Cvi. operibus yemalibus venditis, pretium iii. operum i*d.* Et de x*s.* vi*d. q*^{a}. de cccxv. operibus aestivalibus venditis ut extra, pretium v. operum ii*d.* Et de ii*s.* de viii. arruris vocatis Medwerthes venditis ut extra, pretium arrurae iiii*d.* Et de xxix*s.* ii*d. q*^{a}. de ccxxxiii. averagiis dim. venditis ut extra, pretium averagii i*d. ob.* Et de xi*d.* de factura v. qr. iiii. bu. brasei vendita, pretium quarterii ii*d.* Et de lxi*s.* iii*d. ob.* de vii^c. xxxv. operibus autumpnalibus dim. venditis, pretium operis i*d.* Et de vi*s.* viii*d.* de plus in toto pro xl. operibus venditis Roberto Herberd pro opere iiii*d.* ut patet in compoto de anno xlviii. Et de ii*s.* x*d.* de xxxiiii. cariagiis autumpnalibus venditis ut extra, pretium cariagii i*d.* (per conventionem factam cum Domino Nicholao de Hortone tunc capitali senescallo).

Summa vii*l.* xvii*s.* ix*d. ob.* tertia pars *q*^{a}.

[4] 1378. Et de xl*s.* de tenemento Jurdon ut exoneretur de officio praepositi hoc anno de consuetudine.

Summa xl*s.*

vendito Thomae Barfot hoc anno. Et de iii*s.* iiii*d.* de herbagio de cap[itali] prato de Dammedwe vendito Aliciae Hagne et Roberto Dosy. Et de iiii*d.*[1] de agistamento viii. bestiarum euntium in le Lound hoc anno pro capite *ob.* Et de {ii*s.*} (iii*s.* iiii*d.*) de parte pasturae de Heyker vendita Thomae Barfot ad terminum vii. annorum, hoc anno iii°. et altera pars dimittitur inter firmarios dominicalis manerii supra. Et de viii*d.* de pastura apud Hallebrygge vendita Aliciae Hagne. De pastura circa boscum dominae vocatum Northlee nihil in defectu emptorum tamen solebat vendi pro v*d.* Et de iii*s.* x*d.* de feno vendito Roberto Dosy et Beatrici Elred.

Summa xxxviii*s.* ix*d.*[2]

Venditio subbosci. Et de iii*s.* de subbosco dominii et alneto apud Habtonebeke venditis Willelmo Everard. Et de xx*d.* de dimidia acra subbosci in Gyldreswode vendita Johanni Baxtere. Et de x*d.* de i. roda subbosci in Gyldreswode vendita Roberto Lewyn. Et de x*d.* de i. roda subbosci ibidem vendita Ricardo Sterre.

Summa vi*s.* iiii*d.*[3]

Venditio bladi. Et de {xxxii*s.* vi*d.*} (xliii*s.* iiii*d.*) de xiii. quarteriis avenae de redditu venditis, pretium busselli {iiii*d.* *ob.* *q*ᵃ.} (v*d.*). Et de {xxiii*s.* iiii*d.*} (xxviii*s.*) de vii. quarteriis multurae molendini venditis, pretium busselli vi*d.* Et de {xii*s.*} (xv*s.*) de iiii. quarteriis iiii. busellis multurae de firma molendini venditis, pretium busselli {iiii*d.*} (v*d.*).

Summa {lxvii*s.* x*d.*} (iiii*il.* vi*s.* iiii*d.*[4]).

Perquisita curiae. Et de xliii*s.* ii*d.* de curia tenta die Jovis proxima ante festum Sancti Lucae Evangelistae. Et de lxvii*s.* ix*d.* de curia tenta die Jovis proxima ante festum Conversionis Sancti Pauli. Et de lii*s.* x*d.* de curia tenta die Jovis proxima ante festum Sancti Marci Evangelistae. Et de iiii*l.* v*s.* i*d.* de curia tenta die Martis proxima post festum Sanctorum Petri et Pauli. Et de ix*l.* ii*s.* viii*d.* de curia tenta die Sabbati in festo Sancti Petri ad Vincula. De forinceca curia militum nihil hic quia rotulae dificiunt super compotum.

Summa xxii*l.* xi*s.* vi*d.*[5]

Marginal note: Praeceptum est ballivo quod non permittat clericum curiae abducere rotulos curiae extra manerium sub poena xl*s.*

---

[1] 1378. (onus messoris.)

[2] 1378. De feno nihil vendebatur hoc anno pro salvacione agnorum dominae.
Summa xxxiiii*s.* xi*d.*

1378. [Marginal note opposite entries relating to agistment in the Lound and Heyker pasture] Praeceptum est onerare pretium secundum exstentam de cariagio fymi exeunte de omnibus custumariis manerii etc.

[3] 1378. Et de xvi*d.* de Ricardo Benselyn pro subbosco et spinis unius fossati ex parte occidentali de Gyldrycheswode. Et de x*d.* de Simone Hyckes pro spinis i. fossati ex parte orientali ejusdem bosci. Et de xvi*d.* de Roberto Dosy pro i. portione subbosci in Bromwode sibi vendita.
Summa iiii*s.* vi*d.*

[4] 1378. *Venditio bladi et stauri.* Et de xvi*s.* ix*d.* *ob.* de vii. qr. vi. bu. avenae de redditu ut extra venditis, pretium qr. ii*s.* ii*d.* Et de {xiiii*s.* ix*d.* *q*ᵃ.} (xviii*s.* ii*d.*) de vi. qr. vi. bu. dim. multurae de firma molendini venditis ut extra, pretium buselli {iiii*d.* *q*ᵃ.} (iiii*d.*). Et de viii*d.* de xvi. pelliculis agnorum venditis ut extra, pretium cujusque *ob.*
Summa xxxv*s.* vii*d.* *ob.*

[5] 1378. Et de ciii*s.* iiii*d.* de curia generali tenta die Lunae proxima post festum Sancti Lucae Evangelistae (cum ix*s.* de exitu tenementi Spir). Et de xii*s.* v*d.* de curia tenta die Lunae proxima post festum Sanctae Luciae Virginis. Et de xiii*s.* vi*d.* de curia tenta die Martis proxima post festum Sancti Gregorii Papae. Et de xlviii*s.* v*d.* de curia tenta die Lunae proxima ante festum Sancti Dunstani praeter ii. pullis feminis de extrahura, pretium iiii*s.* Et de lvi*s.* ii*d.* de curia tenta die Veneris proxima post festum Translationis Sancti Thomae Martiris. Et de xxxs. viii*d.* de curia tenta die Lunae proxima ante festum Nativitatis Beatae Mariae.
Summa xiii*l.* iiii*s.* v*d.*

Marginal notes: rotulus deficit. [xii]i*l.* iiii*s.* v*d.*

Venditio super compotum. De diversis venditis super compotum v*s.* i*d. ob.*

Summa v*s.* i*d. ob.*[1]

Summa totalis receptae cum arreragiis cxiii*l.* iiii*s.* x*d. di. q*ᵃ.[2]

Decimae solutae. In decima soluta pro herbagio superius vendito ii*s.* x*d. ob. q*ᵃ. Item pro subbosco superius vendito et non decimato vii*d. ob.*

Summa iii*s.* vi*d. q*ᵃ.[3]

Resolutio et defectus redditus. In redditu resoluto ad Castrum Norwyci per annum terminis Paschae et Sancti Michaelis xvi*d.* Item in defectu reddituum diversorum terrarum et tenementorum in manu dominae existentium et ad firmam supra videlicet dimidiae acrae terrae quondam Stalon per annum xii*d.* Et tenementi quondam Ivonis Charer iii*s.* viii*d. ob. q*ᵃ. tenementi Johannis Hors ii*d. ob. q*ᵃ. tenementi Ricardi Fledede ix*d. q*ᵃ. tenementi Ricardi Agas iiii*d.* Et de iiii. acris quondam David Tooward quas dominus Willelmus Germyn weyvavit xii*d.* tenemento Margaretae Hippelle vi*d. ob.* tenemento Tedgor x*d.* {Item tenemento Hippelle pro cariando fymum vi*d.*}[4] tenemento Tedgor pro eodem vi*d.*[5] Item tenementis Tedgor et Hippelle pro eorum saltpeny ii*d. q*ᵃ. Item ii. acris terrae quondam Rogeri Petyfer iiii*d.* tenemento Rust vocato Bert vii*d. ob.* tenemento Elred de redditu vi*d. ob.* de cariando [fimum] vi*d.*[4, 6] et de saltpeny i*d. di. q*ᵃ. (Tenemento Lestan ii*d. ob. q*ᵃ.) Et iii. rodis terrae existentibus in manu dominae post mortem Johannis Asshwelle quas Johannes Comay intrusit sine licentia videlicet de redditu ii*d.* Et de aliis consuetudinibus i*d. ob.* et iiii^{or}. tenementis v. acrarum tenurae videlicet Johannis Kyng, Roberti Jebat, Johannis Vlsi et Johannis de Fornecete videlicet de redditu ii*s.* ii*d.* pro quolibet tenemento vi*d. ob.* Et pro cariando fymum ii*s.* pro quolibet tenemento vi*d.*[4] et pro saltpeny iiii*d. ob.* pro quolibet tenemento i*d. di. q*ᵃ. [Et] tenemento vocato Wronge xi*d. q*ᵃ. Tenemento Warde v. acrarum tenurae weyvato per Ricardum Coillour videlicet de redditu vi*d. ob.* de cariando fymum vi*d.*[4] Et de saltpeni i*d. di. q*ᵃ. Tenemento Thomae Southawe de redditu vi*d. ob.* de cariando fymum xii*d.*[7] et de saltpeny i*d. di. q*ᵃ. In defectu consuetudinum in. rodarum terrae quae fuerunt Nicholai Bagfens quia in manu dominae et ad firmam iiii*d.* pro omnibus servitiis. Et unius acrae terrae quondam Dewy et nuper Toly pro omnibus servitiis ii*d.* Et v. acrarum terrae quondam Ricardi Galgrim de redditu vi*d. ob.* de cariando fymum vi*d.*[8] et de saltpeny i*d. di. q*ᵃ. Et v. acrarum terrae quondam Simonis Spellere de redditu vi*d. ob.* de cariando fymum vi*d.*[8] et de saltpeny i*d. di. q*ᵃ. Tenementi Johannis Gallard nuper Maddy Raven per annum vi*d. ob.* Tenementi

---

[1] 1378. *Forinseca recepta.* Et de xv*l.* xix*s.* viii*d.* receptis de cclxxiiii. bidentibus venditis apud Framlingham per manus Willelmi Gunnyld. Et de xxii*s.* receptis de Roberto Rokel collectore perquisitorum curiae militum per i. talliam ut extra.

Summa xvii*l.* xx*d.*

1378. In diversis rebus venditis super compotum. ii*s.* xi*d.*

Summa ii*s.* xi*d.*

[2] 1378. cvi*l.* xv*s.* iii*d. ob.* tertia pars *q*ᵃ. [The sum is repeated in margin and followed by the word *probatur.*]

[3] 1378. Inde in decima soluta pro herbagio superius vendito iii*s.* iiii*d. ob.* Item pro subbosco superius vendito et non decimato iiii*d. q*ᵃ.

Summa iii*s.* viii*d. ob. q*ᵃ.

[4] 1378. This and all the following sentences that relate to the carriage of manure are struck out. Above the cancelled sentence is written : quia cariagium fymi non oneratur extra.

[5] 1378. Above the cancelled sentence are the words : eadem causa.

[6] 1378. In the margin opposite this entry are the words : Praeceptum est onerare in proximo compoto denarios de cariando fymum omissos per plures annos.

[7] 1378. Sentence struck out.

[8] 1378. De cariando fymum, etc., is struck out.

Willelmi Florance per annum vi*d. ob.* Tenementi Bretone per annum vi*d.* Et
v. acrarum terrae quondam Willelmi Pote per annum xiiii*d.* Item v. acrarum
terrae quondam Hugonis Baroun de ii. tenementis per annum de redditu vi*d. ob.*
de cariando fymum vi*d.*[1] et de saltpeny i*d. di. q*ᵃ. Item xxv. acrarum terrae in
Redelyngfeld quae devenerunt in manus dominae post mortem Ranulphi Toly
et ad firmam supra per annum {xii*d.*} (vi*d.* et non plus quia medietas liberatur
viduae)[2]. Et iii. acrarum dim. terrae tenementi Geyres per annum vi*d. ob. q*ᵃ
Tenementi Elfled ii*d. ob. q*ᵃ. In defectu redditus et consuetudinum quartae partis
tenementi quondam Clerke quia in manu dominae et ad firmam supra per annum
de redditu x*d. ob.* et operibus extra non computatis ix*d.* Et unius acrae terrae
quondam Aliciae Baldewyne quia in manu dominae et ad firmam supra Willelmo
Herberd i*d. ob.* Et ii. acrarum dim. terrae quondam Durraunt quia in manu
dominae et ad firmam supra Roberto Thaxtere de redditu iii*d. q*ᵃ. et de cariando
fymum iii*d.*[1] Et iiii. acrarum terrae in Multone quondam Willelmi Carletone de
redditu per annum xii*d.* et de aliis operibus extra non computatis v*d. q*ᵃ. et *di. q*ᵃ.
Et dimidiae acrae terrae in Haptone quondam Unewyne per annum i*d.* Et i. acrae
i. rodae terrae in Waketone quondam Willelmi Grey per annum de redditu vi*d. q*ᵃ.
et aliis consuetudinibus extra non computatis ii*d.* Et ii. acrarum terrae in Tybenham cum i. parcella unius pygthelli quondam Thomae Avelyn per annum de
redditu vi*d.* Et iii. rodarum quondam Lythfot per annum de redditu i*d. ob.* de
cariando fymum *ob.*[3] et pro aliis consuetudinibus extra non computatis iiii*d. q*ᵃ.
Et i. acrae terrae quondam Clyre per annum de redditu iii*d. ob.* de cariando
fymo i*d. q*ᵃ. et pro aliis consuetudinibus extra non computatis vii*d.* Et i. acrae
iii. rodarum terrae quondam Simonis Spellere vocatarum Sokenelond per annum
de redditu iiii*d.* de cariando fymum i*d.*[3] et pro aliis operibus extra non computatis ix*d. q*ᵃ. Et iii. rodarum terrae quondam Roberti de Wode per annum de
redditu iiii*d.* de cariando fymo i*d.*[3] et pro aliis consuetudinibus[4] extra non computatis iiii*d. q*ᵃ. Et de ii. acris dim. terrae weyvatis per Willelmum Scrape et ad
firmam supra de redditu ii*d. ob. q*ᵃ. et pro cariando fymum iii*d.*[3]. Et medietate[5]
ix. acrarum i. rodae[6] et i. acrae i. rodae prati quondam Roberti Houlot senioris unde
respondit supra de firma de redditu ii*s.* ii*d.* et pro cariando fymum i*d.*[3] et pro aliis
operibus extra non computatis viii*d. ob.* {Et altera medietas dictae terrae et pratorum
dimittitur uxori dicti Roberti pro servitiis et consuetudinibus} (quia dimittitur ad
firmam supra)[7]. Et dimidia acra terrae quondam Aliciae Baldewyne quia in manu
dominae et ad firmam supra de redditu i*d. ob.* et pro consuetudinibus[4] extra non
computatis i*d.* Et ii. acris dim. terrae quondam Gosses de redditu vi*d. q*ᵃ. de
cariando fymum i*d. ob.*[1]. Et ii.[8] acris dim. terrae tenementi Bygges de redditu
iiii*d. ob.* de cariando fymum i*d.* Item in defectu reddituum diversarum terrarum
quondam Roberti Bacoun praenominati quae sunt in manu dominae per escaetam
et ad firmam supra v*s.* iii*d. q*ᵃ. In defectu redditus tenementi Rogeri Herberd
v. acrarum tenurae vi*d. ob. q*ᵃ.[9] de cariando fymum vi*d.* In defectu redditus tenementi Walteri Gallard v. acrarum tenurae iiii*d.* et pro cariando fymum iii*d.* Item
in decasu redditus i. acrae iii. rodarum dim. terrae in manu dominae existentium
post mortem Johannae uxoris Willelmi Sot et superius ad firmam Johanni ate

---

[1] 1378. De cariando fymum, etc., is struck out.
[2] 1378. Et non plus quia supra.
[3] 1378. De [pro] cariando fymum, struck out.
[4] 1378. operibus. [5] medietate, erased.
[6] 1378. terrae. [7] 1378. Et altera medietate...supra, omitted.
[8] 1378. i. acra.
[9] 1378. Item tenementi Crowes quod Rogerus Herberd nuper tenuit v. acrarum tenurae
in manus dominae de redditu vi*d. ob. di. q*ᵃ.

Lound v*d*. et pro i. quarterio unius gallinae *ob*. et pro dimidio averagio extra non allocato *ob*. *q*ᵃ. et pro dimidio opere autumpnali extra non allocato *ob*.[1]

Summa l*s*. {vii*d*.} (iiii*d*.) *q*ᵃ. et di *q*ᵃ.

Custus molendini. In conventione carpentario pro uno countrebas et i. trabe[2] construendis et ponendis in molendino et pro parietibus ventricei et aliis defectis super molendinum emendandis, xx*s*. ex conventione. Item in expensis hominum auxiliantium pro praedictis countrebas et trabe ponendis in molendino, xi*d*. *ob*. Item in expensis viii. hominum cum ii. carectis et xvi. equis usque Wynneferth pro maeremio ad idem ibidem quaerendo; in pane, cervisia et pisce emptis, xvi*d*. Item soluti pro emendatione de le pannyren, iiii*d*. Item in i. ryne[3] de novo faciendo pro molendino et pro faucibus superiorum fusillorum[4] et inferiorum fusillorum[4] de novo faciendis cum ferro ad idem empto, v*s*. vi*d*. ex conventione. In lx. clavis emptis pro tabulis super molendinum reclavandis, iiii*d*. In xvi. clavis emptis pro rota molendini reclavanda, i*d*.

Summa xxviii*s*. v*d*. *ob*.[5]

Novum aedificium. In conventione carpentario facta per Willelmum Gunnyld pro una domo pro stabulo et vaccaria habendis in parte australi manerii de novo fabricanda de carpenteria continente in longitudine iiiiˣˣ. iiii. pedes, xxx*s*. In iiiiˣˣ. viii. tignis[6] ad idem emptis in bosco de Thorpe, xi*s*., pretium cujusque i*d*. *ob*. In expensis hominum cum iii. carectis pro dictis tignis ibidem quaerendis, vi*d*. In cclx. clavis de spikynges[7] emptis pro tignis et waterbordes, xiii*d*. Item in expensis diversorum hominum amputantium et colligentium Dcc. splyntes in bosco vocato Westwode simul cum expensis factis pro eisdem quaerendis ad manerium, vi*d*. Item in v. operariis conductis per x. dies dalburandis[8] ad plenum et emendandis unam panellam parietis grangiae et faciendis unum parvum murum prope portas manerii, xvi*s*. viii*d*. capiens quilibet per diem iiii*d*. In Mˡ. Mˡ. latthes quaerenda de Wynnef[erthing] pro coopertura dictae domus vii*d*. In viii. Mˡ. latthenayl ad idem (et pro alia domo) emptis, viii*s*., pretium Mˡ. xii*d*. In i. coopertore conducto quasi per xxxvi. dies pro dicta domo de novo cooperienda, xii*s*. capiente per diem iiii*d*. In i. servitore suo per xvi. dies iiii*s*. capiente per diem iiii*d*. Item in uno alio servitore auxilianti eidem per iiii. dies per vices pro stramine spargando et aquando, xii*d*. capiente ut supra. (Et residuum per opera custumariorum.) In xiiii. carectatis[9] straminis emptis pro coopertura ejusdem viii*s*. In expensis diversorum hominum cum xiiii. carectis suis auxiliantibus pro dicto stramine quaerendo de rectoria de Fornnecete, xxi*d*. Item in stramine empto de diversis hominibus pro coopertura et dalbura dictae domus cum expensis circa cariagium, x*s*. x*d*. Item in conventione carpentario facta per Willelmum Gunnyld pro una camera de novo fabricanda de quadam veteri domo vocata le Heyhous

---

[1] 1378. Item in allocatione redditus tenementi Splyttes v. acrarum tenurae in manu dominae et superius ad firmam diversis hominibus vi*d*. *ob*. di. *q*ᵃ. {de cariando fymum vi*d*.}. Item tenementi Spyr v. acrarum tenurae in manu dominae et superius ad firmam Johanni Prati de redditu iiii*d*. Item tenementi Rogeri Hulle iii. ac. [tenurae] in manu dominae et superius ad firmam Rogero Wyllard iiii*d*. Item tenementi ii. acrarum dim. tenurae quod Rogerus Gallard weyvavit in manus dominae et ad firmam supra Roberto Dosy ii*d*. *ob*. *q*ᵃ. {et de cariando fymum iii*d*.}.

Summa xlii*s*. iiii*d*. *q*ᵃ. di. *q*ᵃ.

[2] Beam or rafter.
[3] The rynd is a piece of iron inserted in the centre of the upper mill stone; see glossary, *Charters of Priory of Finchale*, Surtees Society, vol. 6.
[4] In roll, fusil². Fusillus = the spindle of a mill; glossary, *Durham Account Rolls*, iii., Surtees Society, vol. 103.
[5] 1378. In i. panyren de novo faciendo de veteri panyren et ferro ad idem empto, xix*d*.

Summa xix*d*.

[6] Spars, rafters, or laths.
[7] Spike nails; glossary, *Durham Account Rolls*, iii.
[8] Dalbura = plastering.
[9] Cartloads.

pro camera senescalli, x*s*. in grosso. Item in conventione cum operariis pro dicta camera daubanda, vi*s*. viii*d*.

Summa vi*l*, ii*s*. vii*d*.

Custus domus et portarum. In i. coopertore conducto per xii. dies dim. pro aula manerii de coopertura emendanda in omnibus partibus ubi magis necesse fuerat, iiii*s*. ii*d*. capiente per diem iiii*d*. In servitore suo per opera custumaria. Item in conventione carpentario facta per W. Gunnyld pro magna porta ad exitum manerii de novo dirigenda et facienda et pro valvis[1] apponendis et faciendis et pro parva porta ibidem annexata totum de novo facienda et pendenda et pro summitate dictarum portarum de novo facienda de carpenteria, vii*s*. in grosso. In iiii^xx. clavis emptis pro parva porta, iiii*d*. In i. plate et i. gowun[2] ad idem emptis, i*d*. *ob.* In ccc. latthenayl emptis pro coopertura ejusdem, iii*d*. *ob.* In coopertura dictarum portarum, nihil hic quia per operarios conductos inter novum aedificium[3].

Summa xi*s*. xi*d*.

[1] In roll, vīm. valvae = folding doors.
[2] Gudgeon, goioun, an iron pivot; glossary, *Hatfield's Survey*, Surtees Society, vol. 32.
[3] 1378. *Custus domus.* In i. coopertore conducto per xxi. dies pro camera vocata le Heyhous de novo facta de carpenteria in compoto praecedente cooperienda...de novo, vii*s*. capiente per diem iiii*d*. {In servitore suo per idem tempus, iiii*s*. iiii*d*. *ob.* capiente per diem ii*d*. *ob.*} (quia per opera custumaria extra). In stramine empto ad idem de parochia de Fo[rnecete], viii*s*. Item de Roberto Dosy, ii*s*. Item de Roberto Dryl, iiii*s*. iiii*d*. Item de Rogero Coke, xviii*d*. Item in c. [clavis]......emptis pro le waterbord et i. wyndspelt ejusdem domus clavandis, v*d*. Item in expensis xx. hominum cum x. carectis de......pro stramine praeempto cariando in manerium, xx*d*. Item in conventione cum Ricardo Potekyn carpentario pro domo vocata le Stywardesen......facienda in latere aquilonari de tignis vocatis walsshez et dicta (*sic*) latere de novo stodando, ii*s*. In cc. latthenayl emptis......iiii*d*. Item in c. clavis pro reswes et waterbord, v*d*. Item in stramine empto pro dicta domo cooperienda de St[ephano]......Praty, ix*s*. Item de Johanne Eaye pro dicta domo et domo vocata le Deyehous, iiii*s*. vi*d*. Item in expensis hominum......de amore cum carectis pro dicto stramine cariando in manerium, vi*d*. Item soluti Roberto Thaxtere conducto per xiii. dies cooperienti super dictam domum et le Deyehous, iiii*s*. 'iiii*d*. In servitoribus suis per opera custumaria. Item in ii. operariis conductis per v. dies pro pariete dictae domus vocatae le Stywardasen dalbanda et spargettand, iiii*s*. iiii*d*. utroque per diem iiii*d*. In ii. carpentariis conductis per i. diem pro defectu tecti domus stabuli bovum reficiendo et dirigendo, viii*d*. In c. latthenayl emptis ad idem, i*d*. *ob.* In clavis emptis pro waterbord ad idem, v*d*. Item in stramine empto de parochia de Fornecete pro coopertura dictae domus, x*s*. Item in stramine empto de Rogero Wylyard pro eodem, iiii*s*. vi*d*. Item in expensis pro dicto stramine cariando in manerium, xv*d*. In conventione cum Roberto Thaxtere pro dicta domo totum de novo cooperienda in grosso, x*s*. Item in conventione facta cum eodem Roberto per Willelmum Gunnyld pro domo vocata le Stywardesen, le Heyhous, stabulis stottorum et bovum, et le Gatehous de novo crescandis in grosso, viii*s*. vi*d*. In ii. carpentariis conductis per i. diem pro i. camera vocata Warderop capienda de aula et ponenda juxta le Stywardesen praecepto Willelmi Gunnyld, viii*d*. Item in ii. operariis conductis per iiii. dies pro dicto Warderop dalbando simul cum i. panella aulae et i. panella parietis inter coquinam et stabulum {ii*s*. viii*d*.} (ii*s*.) uterque per [diem] {iiii*d*.} (iii*d*.). Item in xx. bordes de estrych emptis apud Norwycum pro hostiis fenestrarum i^us. domus vocatae le Heyhous...pro uno fumberell de le Stywardeschambre, iiii*s*. ii*d*. pretium cujusque ii*d*. *ob.* In eisdem cariandis de Norw[ico]...In c. clavis emptis pro dictis hostiis et fumberell, v*d*. In ii. vertinellis et ii. hoockes ferri emptis ad idem...In cc. clavis emptis pro fenestris vi*d*.

Summa iiii*l*. xiii*s*. i*d*. *ob.*

1378. *Custus murorum.* In conventione facta cum Johanne Benselyn et Rogero Paneys pro i. muro de novo faciendo ex parte occidentali ma[nerii] juxta portam, continente in latitudine vii. perticas, x*s*. vi*d*. pro pertica xviii*d*. Item in stramine empto pro dalbura et coopertura ejusdem muri, iiii*s*. iiii*d*. In ii. coopertoribus conductis per iiii. dies pro dicto muro cooperiendo, ii*s*. viii*d*., uterque capiens per diem iiii*d*. In servitoribus suis per opera custumaria ut extra.

Summa xvi*s*. vi*d*.

1378. *Custus faldae et bidentium.* In xlviii. clatibus emptis pro falda pro bidentibus

Expensae necessariae et forinsecae. In percameno empto pro rotulo curiae extracto et pro isto compoto ii*s.* Item in expensis diversorum hominum auxiliantium pro chacia de Karletonemor facienda hoc anno, ii*s.* x*d.* Et tantum quia bis fiebat hoc anno.ı Item pro chacia apud Westwode, xii*d.* Item pro chacia apud Waketone, x*d.* et tantum quia bis fiebat hoc anno. In i. baga de coreo empta pro rotulo curiae imponendo iiii*d.* Item soluti cuidam bercario manerii de Lopham fuganti bidentes crones[1] de Lopham usque Framyngham, v*d.* praecepto Willelmi Gunnyld. Item soluti pro pastura aestivali pro ii. pullanis feminis provenientibus de extrahura hoc anno, xviii*d.*

Summa ix*s.*

Stipendia. In stipendio Willelmi Hernynge praepositi pro officio suo hoc anno xl*s.* superius recepti de officio praepositurae[2].

Summa xl*s.*

dominae, v*s.*, pretium cujusque i*d.* *q^u.* In v. lagenis et i. qr....emptis ad idem, iii*s.* vi*d.*, pretium lagenae viii*d.* In uncto empto ad idem, xvi*d.* In iii. caractatis...emptis pro bidentibus dominae sternendis, iiii*s.* In i. carectata dim. feni emptis pro bidentibus et agnis dominae sustinen[dis]...yeme vii*s.* Item in ciiii^xx. garbis avenae emptis pro sustentatione eorundem, iii*s.* In candelis [emptis pro] {vigilando} in yeme (supervidendo et custodiendo), i*d. ob.* Item in rubia petra empta pro bidentibus et agnis dominae signandis, iiii*d.* In ferro empto pro falda dominae ponenda in aestate, viii*d.* Item in stipendio bercarii per annum, vi*s.* viii*d.*...oblationibus suis pro diebus Natalis Domini et Paschae, ii*d.*...

Summa xxxi*s.* ix*d. ob.*

1378. *Expensae necessariae.* In percameno empto pro rotulo curiae extracto et pro isto compoto, ii*s.* In ii. cordis emptis pro agnis pascendis, iiii*d.* In iiii. rackes faciendis de maeremio dominae pro agnis dominae longitudinis quilibet xxviii. pedum, xvi*d.* pro quolibet iiii*d.* In iii. rackes faciendis pro bidentibus dominae longitudinis quilibet xxiii. pedum, ix*d.* pro quolibet iiii*d.* Item in v. hominibus conductis per vi. dies pro i. fossato ex parte australi manerii de novo faciendo et cum spinis ponendis, {x*s.*} capiens (vii*s.* vi*d.*) quilibet eorum per diem iiii*d.* (iii*d.*). In spinis ad idem tractandis per opera custumaria ut extra. In i. serura cum clavis et i. stapil ferri ad idem emptis pro hostio bercariae, v*d. ob.* Item in i. serura cum clavis et i. stapil ferri emptis...idem pro hostio domus vocatae le Heyhous v*d.*

Summa xii*s.* ix*d. ob.*

[In marg.] 1378. Memorandum de terra arata ad opus dominae videlicet ix. ac.
[1] Old ewes.
[2] 1378. *Stipendia.* In stipendio Johannis ate Lound praepositi pro officio suo hoc anno, xl*s.* superius recepti de officio praepositurae. Item [pro] roba sua {aretro per conventionem Willelmi Gunnyld hoc anno, x*s.*}. Item in stipendio Johannis Dosy mes[soris] hoc anno {xxx*s.*} (v*s.* iii*d.* prout tenementum dimittitur supra) pro eo quod tenementum Spir gerens officium messoris est in manu dominae ut patet per rotulum curiae hoc a[nno] et dimissum ad firmam superius.

Summa xlv*s.* iii*d.*

1378. *Expensae senescalli.* In expensis senescalli per suos adventus pro vi. curiis tenendis hoc anno, xxiiii*s.* v*d. ob.* per vi. billas. Item in expensis...clericorum domini Walteri Amyas ibidem existentium per iii. dies mense Januarii pro finali compoto faciendo, xviii*d.* Item in expensis domini Walteri Amyas, Willelmi Gunnyld, et aliorum existentium ibidem per ii. vices pro visu compoti capiendo ad clausum Paschae et finali compoto capiendo ad festum Sancti Michaelis per i. billam, viii*s.* non s[oluti].

Summa xxv*s.* xi*d. ob.* Item viii*s.*

1378. *Expensae forincecae.* In expensis pro chacia de Karletonemor faciendo nihil quia fiebat per ballivum de Wynnef(erthing) hoc anno. In expensis...auxil' pro chacia de Westwode facienda hoc anno, xiii*d.* Item pro chacia de Waketone, ix*d.* Item soluti... domino Regi {concess' hoc anno praecepto Willelmi Gunnyld, xx*s.*}. Item in expensis Johannis ate Lound cum iii....viii. equ[is] laborantis usque Asshlee in adjutorio messorum dominae ibidem {praecepto Willelmi Gunnyld. In denariis comput', x.}. Item in xii. caponibus emptis pro expensis consilii dominae existentis apud Thefford in negotio dominae, iii*s.* pro capite iiii*d.* I[n] pulcinis emptis pro eodem, {xv*d.*} (xii*d.*). {In xii. caponibus emptis pro expensis hospitii dominae existentis apud Lopham mense Augusti et in.... In xii. pulcinis emptis pro eodem, xv*d.*} (Quia warr' deficit.)

Summa v*s.* x*d.*

Expensae senescalli et supervenientium cum feodis. In expensis Edwardi de Clypesby senescalli curiae dominae ad v. curias tenendas ut supra, xxiis. id. per v. billas. Item soluti eidem pro feodo suo aretro existente de anno elapso, lxvis. viiid. praecepto Domini Waltero Amyas. Item in expensis Domini Walteri Amyas et Willelmi Gunnyld existentium ibidem per i. noctem in eundo versus Norwycum ad loquendum cum Episcopo ibidem super negotio dominae, ixd. ob. per billam.

Summa iiiil. ixs. vid. ob.

Liberatio denariorum. Computat liberatos Dominae Comitissae Norfolciae per manum Hugonis Fastolf de perquisitis curiae per i. talliam contra Willelmum Gunnyld et per litteram Dominae de Warr[enna,] lvis.

Item liberatos domino Henrico de Glastone receptori denariorum Dominae Comitissae de perquisitis curiae per i. talliam, lxxiis.

Item liberatos eidem Henrico de arreragiis Johannis ate Lound praepositi anni praecedentis per i. talliam, xiiiil. xs.

Item liberatos eidem Henrico de redditu termino Sancti Andreae Apostoli per i. talliam, cs. ixd.

Item liberatos eidem de perquisitis curiae per i. talliam, lis. iiid. ob.

Item liberatos eidem Henrico de redditibus et firmis de termino Paschae per i. talliam, xvil. vs. vid. ob.

Item liberatos eidem Henrico de perquisitis curiae per i. talliam, xlviiis. vd.

{Item liberatos eidem Henrico de aliis exitibus manerii per i. talliam, lis. iiiid.} (quia non exhibet talliam).

Item liberatos eidem Henrico de redditu, et firmis termino Sancti Michaelis per i. talliam, xxil. praeter lxiiiis. vid. ob. allocatos per talliam in pede.

Item liberatos eidem Henrico de perquisitis curiae per eandem talliam, viiil.

Forincec' Item liberatos Johanni Rycher ballivo de Lopham per manum Willelmi Gonnyld pro novo aedificio ibidem per i. talliam, xls.

Summa lxxviil. xiiiis.

Summa omnium expensarum et liberationum, iiiixx. xvl. ixs. vd. di. qᵃ.

Et [debet] xviil. xvs. vd. De quibus allocantur de amerciamento Johannis Herlyng, iiiil. condonati per Dominam apud London' ut testatur per Dominum Walterum Amyas.

Et sic debet domino ulterius xiiil. xvs. vd. unde super Willelmum Schuldre messorem iiiil. vis. viiid. ob. qᵃ. super Willelmum Hernynge praepositum viil. xviiis. viiid. qᵃ.

Postea allocantur eidem de quodam amerciamento Willelmi Hoore de chacia super Carletonemor iis. in partem lxiis. condonati secundum considerationem ministrorum dominae videlicet de onere messoris[1].

---

[1] 1378. *Liberatio denariorum.* Computat liberatos domino Henrico de Glastone Receptori denariorum dominae Comitissae Norfolciae de perquisitis curiae post festum Sancti Michaelis per i. talliam, ciis. viiid.

Item eidem domino Henrico de redditu termini Sancti Andreae Apostoli per i. talliam, cs. ixd.

Item eidem de perquisitis curiae ad festum Sanctae Luciae Virginis per i. talliam, ixs.

Item eidem de redditu termini Natalis Domini per i. (eandem) talliam, lis. iiid. ob.

Item eidem de perquisitis curiae termini Sancti Gregorii Papae, ixs.

Item eidem domino Henrico de redditu termini Paschae per i. talliam, xl.

Item eidem domino Henrico de firma termini Paschae per i. talliam, vil. vs. v....

Item eidem domino Henrico de perquisitis curiae termini Paschae per i. talliam, xlii....

Item eidem domino Henrico de perquisitis curiae termini Sancti Thomae Martiris per i. talliam, xxv....

Item eidem domino Henrico de curia termini Nativitatis Beatae Mariae per i. talliam, xv.

De perquisitis curiae militum. Item allocantur eidem de expensis Domini Walteri Amyas simul cum expensis suis extra manerium tam apud Norwycum quam apud Jernemuth in negotio Dominae xiiii*s*. viii*d*. *ob. q*ᵃ. in partem videlicet de onere messoris.

Et sic debet Dominae ulterius xii*l*. xviii*s*. viii*d*. *q*ᵃ. unde super Willelmum Hernynge praepositum computatos per se viii*l*. xviii*s*. viii*d*. *q*ᵃ. et super Willelmum Schuldre messorem iiii*l*. vi*s*. viii*d*. *ob. q*ᵃ.

Postea allocantur [eidem] xiiii*s*. vi*d*. *ob.* liberatos Domino Henrico de Glastone Receptori per i. talliam ut de onere Willelmi Hernynge. Et sic debet ulterius ix*l*. xiiii*s*. i*d*. *ob. q*ᵃ. unde......[1] comp' cxiiii*s*. i*d*. *ob. q*ᵃ. et super Willelmum Schuldre messorem ut supra iiii*l*.

[2][*Avenae.*] De remanentibus xviii. qr. avenae de redditu in manibus tenentium dominae. Et de xliii. qr. iiii. bu. avenae de redditu custumariorum manerii per annum ad festum Sancti Michaelis.

Summa lxi. qr. iiii. bu.

Inde in defectu redditus diversorum terrarum et tenementorum in manu dominae existentium et ad firmam infra videlicet tenementi Johannis Hors, vi. bu. tenementi Tedgor, i. qr. iiii. bu. tenementi Margaretae Hyppelle, i. qr. iiii. bu. tenementi Lestan, vi. bu. tenementi Bottes, i. qr. iiii. bu. Et tenementorum v. acrarum tenurae videlicet tenementi Johannis de Fornecete Johannis Kynge Roberti Jebat et Johannis Wlsi vi. qr. videlicet pro quolibet tenemento i. qr. iiii. bu. Et de v. acris terrae de tenemento Wardes weyvatis per Ricardum

Item eidem domino Henrico de redditu termini Sancti Michaelis per i. talliam, xxiiii*l*. iiii*s*.

{Item eidem domino Henrico de arreragiis Willelmi Hernynge praepositi anni praecedentis per i. talliam, lxiiii*s*. vi*d*.} (quia dicti denarii allocantur in pede compoti anni praecedentis per talliam remanentem).

Forinsec' Item liberatos Willelmo Gunnyld de arreragiis Willelmi Schuldre messoris (per manus Johannis ate Lound) pro novo aedificio apud Lop[ham]...xv....[1]

Item liberatos Willelmo Hernynge ballivo de Wynnef(erthing) de arreragiis suis propriis ballivi anni praecedentis.

Item liberatos Willelmo Gunnyld secundum talliam de arreragiis Willelmi Schuldre per manus Willelmi Boole.

Item liberatos pro novo aedificio infra manerium de Lopham (de onere Dozy messoris) per i. indenturam remanentem per manus Thomae Banham, iiii*l*.

Item liberatos pro eodem aedificio infra manerium de Lopham de arreragiis Willelmi Schuldre per manus ejusdem T(homae) Banham per indenturam, xxii*s*.

Item liberatos pro novo aedificio infra manerium de Lopham de onere Johannis Dozy messoris per manus T(homae) Banham per indenturam, xx*s*.

Summa lxxiii*l*. ii*s*. v*d*. *ob. q*ᵃ.

1378. *Emptio Stauri.* In i. hurtardo iiii. multonibus et ciiii^xxvi. ovibus matricibus emptis ut extra per Willelmum [Gunnyld]....[1] in principio anni, xiiii*l*. vi*s*. vi*d*., pretium capitis xviii*d*.

Summa xiiii*l*. vi*s*. vi*d*.

1378. Memorandum quod Alicia Toly uxor Radulphi Toly fecit vastum in bondagio dominae in Retelyngf(eld). Ideo praeceptum est ballivo attachiare dictam Aliciam pro vasto reparando sub poena c*s*.

Summa omnium expensarum et liberationum, ci*l*. xv...[1]

Et debet iiii*l*. xix*s*. v*d*. *ob.* di. *q*ᵃ. tertia pars...[1]

De quibus allocantur eidem de diversis rebus additis et retractis super c[ompotum]...[1]

audit xxvii...[1]

et tertia pars qa...[1]

tertia pars Willelm[us]...[1]

pell' remanen' in manus...[1]

xxvii*s*. x*d*. *q*ᵃ. et di....[1]

[1] The roll is torn away. [2] The remainder of the account is on the dorse of the roll.

Coyllour anno x⁰. i. qr. iiii. bu. Et tenementi Thomae Southauwe eo quod uxor
ejus tenet dictum tenementum per exstentam pro certis denariis ut infra ad
terminum vitae suae ex concessione domini Walteri de Manny nuper dominus[1]
istius manerii iii. qr. Et v. acrarum terrae quondam Ricardi Galgrim quia in
manu dominae et ad firmam ut infra i. qr. iiii. bu. Et v. acrarum terrae quondam
Simonis Spellere eadem causa i. qr. iiii. bu. Et ii. acrarum dim. terrae quondam
Florance eadem causa vi. bu. Et de ii. acris dim. terrae weyvatis per Johannem
Schacheloke eadem causa vi. bu. Et de v. acris terrae quondam Hugonis Baroun,
existentibus in manu dominae post mortem dicti Hugonis i. qr. iiii. bu. Et ii. acris
dim. terrae quondam Dorrant existentibus in manu dominae pro defectu tenentium
hoc anno vii⁰. vi. bu. Et de ii. acris dim. terrae weyvatis per Willelmum Scrape
existentibus in manu dominae hoc anno vi⁰. vi. bu. Et v. acris terrae quondam
Causa defec- Rogeri Herberd[2] existentibus in manu dominae[3] i. qr. iiii. bu. Item
tus avenae liberantur Johanni Sparwe ballivo ad Wynneferthynge v. qr. per i.
xxv. qr. iiii. bu. talliam. Item in venditione ut infra xiii. qr.

Summa xliii. qr. iiii. bu.[4]. Et remanent xviii. qr. avenae de redditu in manibus
tenentium dominae.

Multura molendini. Respondet de {xiii. qr. iiii. bu.} (xiiii. qr. iiii. bu. ut in
compoto praecedente) multurae de firma unius molendini ventritici ultra decimas
per annum.

Summa xiiii qr. iiii. bu.[5].

Inde in liberatione Roberti Houlot custodis warrennae dominae ibidem i. qr.
iiii. bu.[6] (Item in allocatione molendinarii pro ix. diebus dum stetit in reparando
ut patet infra iiii. bu. Item in venditione ut infra xi. qr. iiii. bu. Et aequae.)
iii*s.* iiii*d.* Et in venditione super compotum i. qr. pro termino Sancti Michaelis.

Cyminum. Et de iiii. libris cymini de redditu termino Michaelis.

Summa iiii. librae. Et venduntur ut infra. Et aequae.

Capones. Et de xiiii. caponibus de redditu custumariorum manerii termino
Paschae. Et de i. capone de redditu Johannis Stodere eodem termino. Et de
vi. caponibus de redditu Agnetis Lavender dicto termino. Et de ii. caponibus de
redditu Johannis Kynge pro tenemento quondam Hippelle ad terminum vitae suae
per annum dicto termino. {De i. capone de} (Et de i. capone incrementi) redditus
Johannis Elred {ad terminum vitae suae} (quia reddit de incremento). {(Nihil hic
nec de caetero quia idem Johannes moriebatur hoc anno in prima septimana
Quadragesimae.)} Et de vi. caponibus de chevagio Rogeri Nunne nativi dominae
pro licentia habenda manendi ubicunque voluerit per annum dicto termino. Et
de i. capone de Waltero Dryl pro firma unius messuagii quondam Simonis Spellere

---

[1] *Sic.*   [2] 1378 (tenementi Crowes).
[3] 1378. Entry continues : Item in allocatione tenementi Splyttes continentis... v. acr'
terrae in manu dominae ut patet per rotulum curiae hoc anno primo et ad firmam ut infra
i. qr. iiii. bu. avenae. Item tenementi... vii. acr' in manu dominae eodem modo nihil. Item
i. tenementi quod Rogerus Gallard weyvavit continentis ii acras terrae dim... in manus
dominae eodem modo vi. bu. avenae. Item in liberatione Willelmi Pelot bercarii custodientis
bidentes.. i. bu. (farina potagii sui) Item liberantur Willelmo Bole ballivo de Lopham x. qr.
avenae. Item in venditione ut infra.
[4] 1378. xlv. qr. vi. bu.   [5] 1378. xv. qr. 6 bu.
[6] 1378. Item in liberatione Willelmi Pelet bercarii custodientis oves...per annum,
v. qr. i. bu. dim. capientis per x. septimanas i. qr. Item in liberatione i. garcionis
auxiliantis...tempore agnellationis...Gunnyld, i. qr. Item in venditione ut infra, vi. qr.
vi. bu. dim.

Summa quae supra. Et aequae.

dicto termino. Et de iii. caponibus de novo redditu Johannis Lythfol quondam Johannis Hors dicto termino.

Summa xxxiiii[1].

Inde in defectu tenementi retro stabilum[1] et porcarium quia in manu dominae in defectu tenentium viii. capones. Item in defectu redditus tenementi quondam Agnetis Lavender vi. capones. In defectu redditus tenementi quondam Hors quia in manu {dominae post decessum Johannis Lythfol iii. capones}. (Quia non in compoto praecedente.) Item in venditione ut infra. xvi.[1]

Summa quae supra. Et aequae.
Et in venditione super compotum iiii.[2] pro[3].

Gallinae. Et de clxxvi. gallinis de redditu custumariorum manerii per annum termino Natalis Domini.

Summa clxxvi.

De quibus in allocatione redditus tenementi Willelmi Hernynge pro officio praepositurae hoc anno nihil[4]. In defectu[5] redditus diversorum terrarum et tenementorum in manu dominae existentium et ad firmam ut infra videlicet tenementi Fledede dim. gallina tenementi Sunwyne vocati Stalon i. gallina tenementi Ricardi Agas i. gallina tenementi Elred i. gallina tenementi Hors quia liber[i] per cartam Comitis Mareschalli i. gallina tenementi Hyppelle i. gallina tenementi Tedgor i. gallina tenementi Lestan i. gallina tenementi Bret i. gallina. Et iiii[or]. tenementorum v. acrarum tenurae videlicet tenementi Johannis de Fornecete Johannis Kynge Roberti Jebet et Johannis Wlsy iiii. gallinae pro quolibet tenemento i. gallina tenementi Elfied weyvati per Johannem Smyth iii. gallinae tenementi Wardes v. acrarum tenurae weyvati per Ricardum Coillour i. gallina tenementi quondam Thomae Southawe quia relaxatur per dominum Walterum de Manny pro certis denariis ut infra i. gallina. Tenementi Bretone i. gallina tenementi Mones ii. gallinae dim. tenementi David Toward i. gallina. Et v. acrarum terrae quondam Ricardi Galgrim i. gallina. Et v. acrarum terrae quondam Simonis Spellere i. gallina. Et ii. acrarum terrae quondam Florance i. gallina. Et ii. acrarum dim. terrae weyvatarum per Johannem Schakeloc i. gallina. Et super medietate vii. acrarum terrae quae devenerunt in manus dominae post mortem Willelmi Pote in Waketone iii. gallinae et altera medietas manuoperatur per haeredes. Et unius messuagii quondam Edwardes i. gallina. Item v. acrarum terrae quondam Hugonis Baroun i. gallina. Item ii. acrarum dim. terrae de tenemento Geyres quod Helfied nuper tenuit et est in manu dominae i. gallina dim. Item medietatis unius messuagii quondam Broketothe eadem causa dimidia gallina. Et ii. acrarum dim. terrae quondam Durrant existentium in manu dominae ut infra i. gallina. Item unius messuagii et ii. acrarum terrae weyvatorum per Willelmum Scrape in manu dominae et ad firmam ut infra i. gallina. Item ii. acrarum dim. terrae quondam Gooses quod Mathaeus Hernynge nuper tenuit quia mortuus est ut patet per rotulum curiae et est in manu dominae et ad firmam ut infra i. gallina dim. Et i. messuagii i. acrae dim. tenementi quondam Bygges eodem modo i. gallina dim. unde pro messuagio i. gallina. Item in venditione ut infra cxxxviii. gallinae[6].

Summa quae supra. Et equae.

---

[1] *Sic.*   [2] 1378. iii.   [3] Hiatus in roll. 1378. xxxiii.
[4] 1378. tenementi Jurdon pro officio praepositurae hoc anno i. gallina (Item pro officio messoris i. gallina).   [5] 1378. allocatione.
[6] 1378. Two or three inches are torn away from the margin of the roll through this entry, but the remaining fragment corresponds to the entry of 1377 so far as that entry

Decasus et allocationes xxxviii. gallinae.

Memorandum pro compoto sequenti Ballivus manerii fecit cariari usque Lopham x. perdices quae computantur in morina[1] eodem die pro defectu custodiae dicti ballivi videlicet in vigilia Sancti Martini.

Ova. Et de M¹x. ovis de redditu custumariorum manerii ibidem per annum termino Paschae.

Summa M¹x. ova.

[2]De quibus in allocatione redditus tenementi Willelmi Hernynge pro officio praepositi nihil. Item in decasu diversorum terrarum et tenementorum in manu dominae existentium pro xxxviii. gallinis allocatis supra in defectu {clxx.} (ciiii^{xx}x.) ova pro qualibet gallina v. ova. Item in venditione ut infra viii^{c}lx. ova.

Summa quae supra.   Supra exitus xl.   Et sic exitus.

Opera yemalia. Respondet de M¹D^{c}v. operibus yemalibus de exitu custumariorum manerii inter festum Sancti Michaelis et festum Apostolorum Petri et Pauli pretium iii. operum i*d.*

Summa M¹D^{c}v. opera.

De quibus in defectu et allocatione[3] operum diversorum terrarum et tenementorum in manu dominae existentium videlicet tenementi Johannis Hors xxxv. opera. Tenementi Lestan xxxv. opera. Tenementi Margaretae Hyppelle lxx. opera. Tenementi Elred vocati Longere lxx. opera. Et iiii^{or}. tenementorum v. acrarum tenurae videlicet tenementorum Johannis Fornecete Johannis Kynge Roberti Jebat et Johannis Wlsi quia sunt in manu dominae cciiii^{xx}. opera videlicet pro quolibet tenemento lxx. opera. Item tenementi quondam Wardes v. acrarum tenurae weyvati per Ricardum Coyllour lxx. opera. Item tenementi Thomae Southauwe causa ut supra in titulo avenae lxx. opera. Et v. acrarum terrae quondam Galgrim lxx. opera. Item v. acrarum terrae quondam Simonis Spellere lxx. opera. Item v. acrarum terrae quondam Hugonis Baroun lxx. opera. Item ii. acrarum dim. terrae quondam Dorant in manu dominae existentium ut supra xxxiii. opera. Item ii. acrarum dim. terrae weyvatarum per Willelmum Scrape existentium in manu dominae xxxiii. opera[4].

goes. The entry of 1378 continues as follows: Item in allocatione tenementi Crowes quod Rogerus Herberd nuper tenuit in manu dominae et ad firmam i. gallina......in manu dominae ut patet per rotulum curiae et ad firmam ut infra i. gallina hoc anno primo. Item tenementi Spyres eodem modo i. gallina...pro eodem i. gallina. Item tenementi Rogeri Gallard i. gallina. Item liberatae Roberto Creppele ballivo...lx. gallinae pro expensis hospitii dominae. Item in venditione ut infra lxxi. gallinae.

Summa quae supra [clxxvi].   Et aequae.

[1] In roll, mor^a.

[2] 1378. [De quibus in allocation]e redditus pro officio praepositi et messoris x. ova. Item in decasu redditus diversorum terrarum et tenementorum in manu [dominae existentium pro xliii gallinis allocatis supra in defectu ccxv. ova pro qualibet gallina v. ova. Item in venditione [ut infra] vii^{c}iiii^{xx}v. ova.

Summa quae supra.   Et aequae.

[3] 1378. [De quibus in] allocatione operum pro officio praepositi nihil. Item in defectu.

[4] 1378. The entry for this year is continued as follows: Item in allocatione tenementi Crowes quod Rogerus Herberd nuper tenuit in manu dominae ut supra lxx. opera. Item tenementi Splyttes ut supra lxx. opera. Item tenementi Rogeri Gallard ut supra xxxv. opera. Item in consuetudine custumariorum manerii pro fymo extra manerium cariando xliii. opera de consuetudine nihil hoc anno quia non cariatum. In allocatione custumariorum pro arruris secundum quod jungunt inter Purificationem Beatae Mariae et festum Pentecostes pro ix. arruris expendendis in terris dominae arrandis xviii. opera pro qualibet arrura ii. opera de consuetudine. Item in aqua portanda argilla temperanda pro camera senescalli facta in anno praecedente et pro stodio ejusdem camerae ramando non in compoto prae-

Item in consuetudine custumariorum manerii pro fymo extra manerium cariando xliii. opera de consuetudine nihil hoc anno quia non cariandum nec arrandum. Item in allocatione custumariorum pro vi. arruris dim. arrandis secundum quod jungunt inter festum Purificationis Beatae Mariae et festum Pentecostes per xiii. dies Lunae {hoc anno xiii. opera pro qualibet arrura ii. opera de consuetudine} (nihil causa ut supra). Item in splyntes amputandis pro virga molendini et in auxilio pro trostell[1] cariandis ad molendinum et pro molendino sublevando xii. opera. Item in subbosco amputando et pro sepibus faciendis circa manerium ex parte occidentali xx. opera. In stramine spergando aquando et tractando pro coopertura domus ut patet infra xi. opera. Item in aqua portanda et argilla[2] carianda pro dalbura domus manerii de novo aedificatae. Et in auxilio pro dicta domo daubanda cxxxvii. opera. Item in venditione ut infra ccciiii^{xx}x. opera.

Summa quae supra et aequae.

Opera aestivalis. Respondet de cccciiii^{xx}x. operibus de exitu custumariorum manerii per dies integros pretium v. operum ii*d*.

Summa cccciiii^{xx}x. opera.

De quibus in defectu operum[3] diversorum terrarum et tenementorum in manu dominae existentium ut supra videlicet tenementorum Johannis Hors Hippelle, Tedgor, Lestan, Elred et iiii. tenementorum v. acrarum tenurae videlicet Johannis Kynge, Johannis Fornecete, Roberti Jebat et Johannis Wlsy causa ut supra iiii^{xx}x. opera videlicet pro quolibet tenemento x. opera. Item tenementi Wardes et tenementi Thomae Southauwe xx. opera. Et v. acrarum terrae quondam Ricardi Galgrim v. acrarum terrae quondam Simonis Spellere et v. acrarum terrae quon dam Hugonis Baroun xxx. opera pro quolibet eorum x. opera. Et de ii. acris dim terrae quondam Durrant[4] causa ut supra v. opera. Item ii. acris dim. terrae quondam Hugonis Ravon weyvatis per Willelmum Scrape v. opera[5]. In venditione ut infra cccxl. opera.

Summa quae supra. Et aequae.

Arrurae vocatae Medwcerthe. Et de vii. arruris de exitu custumariorum manerii pro eorum pratis pretium arrurae iii*d*. Et de ii. arruris de exitu Hugonis

cedente computata nec allocata pro eo quod dictum opus factum fuit post festum Sancti Michaelis xlvi. opera per tallias inter Willelmum Schuldre messorem anni praecedentis et tenentes dominae. Item in stramine sternendo aquando et tractando pro stabulo et vaccaria facta in compoto praecedente non computata nec allocata eadem causa lx. opera per easdem tallias. Item in batlins colligendis pro rackes ovium dominae vi. opera. Item in broches et ligaminibus colligendis pro domibus vocatis le Heyhous et le Stywardesen et domo deyeriae stabula bovum et pro muro juxta portam manerii xxiiii. opera. Item in splentes colligendis pro eisdem domibus vi. opera. Item in argilla jactanda pro crescura murorum et domorum manerii xxxii. opera. Item in gappes stoppandis circa Gyldryeswode vi. opera. Item in plantes spinarum et fraccinorum traendis pro i. fossato ponendo ex parte australi manerii usque cymiterium xiiii. opera. Item in veteri muro removendo pro novo muro ibidem ponendo cum argilla ad idem cariando xxxii. opera. Item in veteri coopertura traenda de domo vocata le Stywardesen ii. opera. Item in veteribus parietibus ii. camerarum vocatarum Warderop prosternendis viii. opera. Item in stramine sternendo aquando tractando portando pro coopertura domus vocatae le Stywardesen et domus deyeriae lii. opera. Item in larnes fugandis tempore yemalis xii. opera. Item in venditione ut infra. cvi. opera.

Summa quae supra. Et aequae.

[1] Trestles, Halliwell, *Dict. of Archaic Words.*
[2] Clay.   [3] 1378. redditus.
[4] 1378. tenementi Durant.
[5] 1378. The entry continues: [In defectu reddituum] tenementi Crowes et tenement Splyttes in manus dominae ut supra xx. opera pro utroque x. opera. Item ii. acrarum dim. tenementi quod Rogerus Gallard weyvavit v. opera. Item in venditione ut infra cccxv. opera. Summa quae supra. Et aequae. [In margin] clxxv.

ate Hill et Thomae de Fornecete pretium cujuslibet iii*d.* Et de ii. arruris de exitu sokemennorum jungentium xii. equos hoc anno ad seminationem yemalem videlicet de singulis vi. equis i. arrura pretium arrurae iii*d.*

Summa xi.

De quibus in defectu arrurae tenementi Redyng quondam Hugonis ate Hil quia in manu dominae et infra i. arrura. Item in defectu arrurae tenementi Roberti Houlot senioris quia in manu dominae et ad firmam infra i. arrura[1].

Item in venditione ut infra ix. arrurae.

Summa quae supra et aequae.

Arrurae Quadragesimae. Et de ii. arruris Quadragesimae de exitu sokemennorum jungentium xii. bestias ad seminationem Quadragesimae pretium arrurae iii*d. ob.* De i. custumario quae[2] solebat arrare per quamlibet diem Lunae inter festum Purificationis Beatae Mariae et festum Paschae cum tot bestiis quot et jungit nihil quia non jungit hoc anno.

Summa ii. arrurae. Et venduntur ut infra. Et aequae[3].

Arrurae ad ordeum. Et de ii. arruris ad ordeum de exitu sokmennorum jungentium xii. bestias ad seminationem ordei[4], pretium arrurae iiii*d.* De i. custumario quae[2] solebat arrare per v. dies operabiles inter festum Paschae et festum Pentecostes cum tot bestiis quot et jungit nihil hoc anno quia non jungit.

Summa ii.[5] Et venduntur ut infra. Et aequae.

Precariae[6]. Et de ii. precariis ad ordeum de exitu custumariorum de sokmennis jungentibus xii. bestias hoc anno videlicet de singulis vi. bestiis i. precaria, pretium precariae iiii*d.* Et de ii. precariis nullius pretii de exitu liberorum tenentium tamen si faciant illas precarias recapiant de domina pro qualibet precaria ii*d.* de consuetudine.

Summa iiii.[7]

De quibus in venditione ut infra ii. De residuo nihil quia licet non faciant nihil dominae dabunt.

Summa quae supra. Et aequae.

Herciaturae. Et de iii. herciaturis de exitu custumariorum manerii per annum, pretium cujuslibet i*d.* Et computantur in defectu super tenementum Rust vocatum Bert quia in manu dominae et ad firmam Edmundo Lewynge.

Et aequae[8].

Averagia. Et de cccxli. averagiis de exitu custumariorum manerii per annum, pretium cujuslibet i*d. ob.* videlicet faciendo averagia ad equos [vel] ad pedes secundum quod dominae placuerit.

Summa cccxli. averagia.

De quibus in allocatione operum tenementi Willelmi Hernynge jerentis officium praepositi iii. averagia[9].

---

[1] 1378. Entry continues as follows: Item in terris dominae arrandis hoc anno i. arrura. Item in venditione ut infra viii. arrurae.

Summa quae supra. Et aequae.

[2] *Sic.*

[3] 1378. Entry continues as follows: Summa ii. Et expenduntur in terris dominae arrandis hoc anno. Et aequae.

[4] 1378. hoc anno videlicet de singulis vi. bestiis i. arrura.

[5] 1378. Summa ii. Et expenduntur in terris dominae arrandis hoc anno. Et aequae.

[6] 1378. carucarum.

[7] 1378. Summa iiii. Et omnes expenduntur in terris dominae arrandis. Et aequae.

[8] 1378. Entry same as that of 1377.

[9] 1378. De quibus in allocatione operum tenementi Jurdon jerentis officium praepositi iii. averagia. Item pro officio messoris pro tenemento Spir nihil quia dictum tenementum est in manu dominae hoc anno primo et allocantur inferius.

{Item pro officio messoris de Multone iii.} Et pro officio messoris pro tenemento Shuldres iii. averagia[1]. Item in defectu operum diversorum terrarum et
tenementorum in manu dominae existentium et ad firmam ut infra videlicet
tenementi Hors tenementi Lestan tenementi Hippelle et tenementi Bert vocati
Rust xii. averagia pro quolibet tenemento iii. averagia. Item tenementi Tedgor
tenementi Fledede causa ut supra iii. averagia pro quolibet tenemento i. averagium
dim. Item iiii^or. tenementorum v. acrarum tenurae videlicet tenementorum Johannis
Fornecete Johannis Kynge Roberti Jebat et Johannis Ulsi xii. averagia pro quolibet eorum iii. averagia. Item tenementi Elred weyvati per Adam Smythe.
Item tenementi Wardes weyvati per Adam Colliour vi. averagia pro utroque
tenemento iii. averagia. Item tenementi Thomae Southawe ut supra iii. averagia.
Item tenementi Bretoun quia in manu dominae i. averagium. Item tenementi
Mones ii. averagia dim. Item v. acrarum terrae quondam Ricardi Galgrym v.
acrarum terrae quondam Simonis Spellere vi. averagia. Item ii. acrarum dim.
terrae quondam Florance iii. averagia. Item ii. acrarum terrae dim. weyvatarum
per Johannem Statheloc iii. averagia. Item medietatis vii. acrarum terrae quondam
Willelmi Pote i. averagium dim. Item i. cotagii quondam Edward i. averagium.
Item v. acrarum terrae quondam Hugonis Baroun iii. averagia. Item iii. acrarum
dim. terrae de tenemento quondam Geyres quas Elfred nuper tenuit quia in manu
dominae iii. averagia. Item ii. acrarum dim. terrae tenementi quondam Durant
quia in manu dominae i. averagium dim. Item ii. acrarum dim. terrae weyvatarum
per Willelmum Scrape i. averagium[2]. Item v. acrarum terrae in manu dominae
post mortem Rogeri Herberd in manu dominae hoc anno tertio iii. averagia[3].

Item v. acrarum terrae weyvatarum per Johannem Coleman hoc anno tertio
iii. averagia. Item in i. billa senescalli portanda usque Framyngham pro curia
ibidem summonenda i. averagium. Item in i. billa senescalli portanda usque
Lopham pro eodem i. averagium. Item in cibario quaerendo de Norwyco pro
expensis senescalli i. averagium. Item in auxilio pro multonibus provenientibus de
Lopham fugandis usque Framyngham i. averagium. Item in una litera senescalli
portanda usque Jernemuth ad Hugonem Fastolf ii. averagia. Item in venditione
ut infra cclviii. averagia dim.

iii*d.* In venditione super compotum ii. pro[4].

Summa quae supra. Et aequae.

[1] 1378. This entry is omitted.   [2] 1378. Elfred.
[3] 1378. Entry continues: Item v. acrarum terrae tenementi Crowes quod Rogerus
Herberd nuper tenuit in manus dominae iii. averagia. Item v. acrarum terrae weyvatarum
per Johannem Coleman hoc anno iiii°. iii. averagia. Item tenementi Splittes v. acrarum
tenurae in manu dominae ut supra iii. averagia. Item tenementi Spires quod in manus
dominae ut supra iii. averagia. Item tenementi Hulles iii. averagia. Item tenementi quod
Rogerus Gallard weyvavit hoc anno primo iii. averagia. Item in i. billa portanda usque
Lopham pro curia ibidem summonianda i averagium. Item in i. billa portanda usque
Framyngham pro eodem i. averagium. Item in i. billa portanda usque Hocham pro eodem
i. averagium. Item in lx. gallinis de redditu ducendis usque Lopham iii. averagia. |Item
in perdicibus ducendis usque Lopham i. averagium.} In ballivo de Harlestone quaerendo
per ii. vices ad loquendum cum Willelmo Gunnyld ii. averagia. Item in agnis fugandis
usque Lopham ii. averagia. In i. homine laborante usque Bergh per ii. vices pro ballivo
ibidem quaerendo ad loquendum cum Willelmo Gunnyld in negotio dominae ii. averagia.
Item in i. litera domini Walteri Amyas portanda ballivo de Harlestone in negotio dominae
in aestate i. averagium. Item in piscibus salsis quaerendis de Norwyco pro expensis
dominae i. averagium. Item in dictis piscibus ducendis usque Lopham i. averagium. Item
in caponibus et pulcinis ducendis ibidem pro eodem i. averagium. In i. districtione fuganda
de Strystone usque Lopham ii. averagia. Item in i. districtione fuganda de Schotesham
usque Lopham ii. averagia. Item in cibario quaerendo de Norwyco pro
expensis senescalli i. averagium. Item in ii. pullanis fugandis usque Bergh
i. averagium. Item in venditione ut infra ccxxxiii. averagia dim.

cvii. aver-
agia dim.

[4] *Sic* in roll.

Factura brasei. Respondet de factura xxi. qr. iiii. bu. brasei de exitu custu-mariorum manerii pretium quarterii ii*d.*

Summa xxi. qr. iiii. bu.

De quibus in defectu diversorum terrarum et tenementorum in manu dominae existentium ut supra videlicet tenementi Hippele tenementi Tedgor tenementi Elfred tenementi Wardes. Item iiii[or]. tenementorum v. acrarum tenurae videlicet Johannis Fornecete Johannis Kynge Roberti Jebat et Johannis Ulsi causa ut supra factura viii. qr. brasei pro quolibet tenemento i. qr. tenementi Thomae Southawe x. acrarum tenurae ut supra ii. qr. Item tenementi Ricardi Galgrim tenementi Simonis Spellere et tenementi Hugonis Baroun ut supra iii. qr. pro quolibet tenemento i. qr.[1]

Item in venditione ut infra factura viii. qr. iiii. bu.

Summa quae supra. Et aequae.

Opera autumpnalia. Et de M[l]ccxxiiii. operibus autumpnalibus de exitu cus-tumariorum manerii in autumpno pretium operis i*d.*

Summa M[l]ccxxiiii. opera.

De quibus in allocatione operum tenementi gerentis officium praepositi iii. opera. Item pro officio messoris vi. opera[2].

Item in defectu[3] diversorum terrarum et tenementorum in manu dominae existentium ut supra videlicet tenementi Hippelle xxiiii. opera tenementi Lestan xvi. opera tenementi Fleded[e] i. opus et dim. tenementi Hors quia liber[um] xvi. opera tenementi Bert xxiiii. opera. Item iiii[or]. tenementorum v. acrarum tenurae videlicet Johannis Fornecete Johannis Kynge Roberti Jebat et Johannis Ulsi causa ut supra iiii[xx]xvi. opera pro quolibet tenemento xxiiii. opera. Item tenementi Thomae Southawe causa ut supra xxxiiii. opera praeter vi. opera quae faciuntur ex conventione. Item ii. acrarum dim. terrae quondam Florance xvi. opera tenementi weyvati per Matillem Raven quondam Statheloke viii. opera tenementi Bretoun i. opus tenementi Mones x. opera dim. Item medietatis tenementi quondam Willelmi Pote i. opus dim. Item tenementi Ricardi Galgrim xxiiii. opera tenementi Simonis Spellere xxiiii. opera. Item ii. acrarum dim. terrae de i. parcella ii. acrarum dim. terrae de alia parcella quondam Hugonis Baroun xxxii. opera. Item i. acrae terrae quondam Roughey nuper dicti Hugonis iii. opera. Item unius cotagii quondam Edward i. opus. Item iii. acrarum dim. terrae quondam Geyres causa ut supra xi. opera. Item iii. rodarum terrae quon-dam Ricardi Galgrim quia in manu dominae et ad firmam Ricardo Davy cum terris quondam Galgrim iii. opera. Item ii. acrarum dim. terrae quondam Durrant causa ut supra xvi. opera. Item ii. acrarum dim. terrae weyvatarum per Willelmum Scrape xvi. opera. Item ii. acrarum dim. terrae quondam Gosses[4] causa ut supra viii. opera. Item i. acrae dim. terrae quondam Bygges causa ut supra iii. opera dim.[5] Item in parietibus domus feni frangendis et in coopertura ejusdem de-ponenda iiii. opera. In venditione ut infra Dcccxviii. opera dim.

Summa quae supra. Et aequae.

---

[1] 1378. Entry continues: Item tenementi Crowes quod Rogerus Herberd nuper tenuit i. qr. Item tenementi Splittes v. acrarum tenurae ut supra i. qr. Item tenementi quod Rogerus Gallard weyvavit ut supra i. qr. Item in venditione ut infra. v. qr. iiii. bu.

Summa quae supra. Et aequae.

[2] 1378. De quibus in allocatione operum tenementi jerentis officium praepositi iii. opera. Item pro officio messoris nihil causa praedicta.   [3] 1378. operum.

[4] 1378. Gooses.

[5] 1378. Entry continues thus: Item tenementi Crowes quod Rogerus Herberd nuper tenuit causa ut supra xxiiii. opera. Item tenementi Splittes quia in manu dominae ut supra xxiiii. opera. Item tenementi Spires iii. opera. Item tenementi Hulle iii. opera. Item

ii*d. ob.* Et in venditione super compotum ii. opera dim. p[ro].

Cariagia autumpnalia. Et de xliii. cariagiis autumpnalibus de exitu custumariorum manerii in autumpno pretium cariagii i*d.*

Summa xliii.

De quibus in defectu cariagiorum diversorum terrarum et tenementorum in manu dominae ut supra videlicet Fledede dimidium cariagium Roberti Elfred dimidium cariagium tenementi Bretone dimidium cariagium tenementi Matillis Ravene i. cariagium medietatis tenementi Willelmi Pote dimidium cariagium item tenementi Geyres i. cariagium[1].

Item in venditione ut infra xxxix. cariagia.

Summa quae supra et aequae.

Coniculi fesani et perdices. De exitu warrennae ibidem nihil quia nulli capti fuerunt in warrenna dominae ibidem hoc anno[2].

Extrahurae. De extrahura ii. pullanae feminae aetatis iii. annorum provenientium mense Aprilis.

Summa ii. Et remanent ii. pullanae feminae aetatis iii. annorum dim.[3]

tenementi quod Rogerus Gallard weyvavit xvi. opera. Item in fymo ejiciendo de domo manerii in autumpno contra adventus dominae praecepto Willelmi Gunnyld ix. opera dim. Item in stramine sternendo aquando et tractando pro coopertura unius muri juxta portam manerii in autumpno xvi. opera. Item in venditione ut infra vii^c^xxxv. opera dim.

iiii^c^lxxii. opera dim. Summa quae supra. Et aequae.

[1] 1378. Entry continues: Item tenementi Crowes quod Rogerus Herberd weyvavit i. cariagium tenementi Splittes i. cariagium tenementi Spires i. cariagium tenementi Rogeri Hulle i. cariagium. Item tenementi quod Rogerus Gallard weyvavit i. cariagium. Item in venditione ut infra xxxiiii. cariagia.

Summa quae supra. Et aequae.

[2] 1378. De exitu warrennae dominae hoc anno x. perdices.

Summa x. {Et liberantur usque Lopham ut patet in quodam memorando in compoto anni praecedentis.} (quia per dictum memorandum patet quod dicti (*sic*) perdices moriebantur in defectu cariagii).

xx*d.* In venditione super compotum x. perdices pro (*sic*).

[3] 1378. De remanentibus ii. pullanae feminae de extrahura aetatis iii. annorum dim.

Summa ii. Et liberantur Thomae Barfoth ballivo de Berghe ut patet in compoto suo ibidem. Et aequae.

[To the following entry there is nothing to correspond in the earlier account rolls.]

1378. Compotus bidentium.

Hurtardus. De emptione ut infra ad festum Sancti Michaelis in principio anni i. hurtardus per Willelmum Gunnyld.

Summa i. Et computatur in morina inter festum Natalis Domini et festum Circumcisionis Domini. Et aequae.

[*Mult*]*ones.* De emptione ut infra iiii. multones ad festum Sancti Michaelis in principio anni per Willelmum Gunnyld.

Summa iiii. Et remanent iiii. multones unde i. bellewether.

Oves matrices. De emptione ut infra ciiii^xx^vi. oves matrices ad festum Sancti Michaelis in principio anni per Willelmum Gunnyld.

Summa ciiii^xx^vi.

De quibus in morina ante fecundationem et tonsionem iiii. oves. Item in morina post fecundationem et tonsionem vi. oves.

Summa x. Et remanent clxxvi. oves matrices.

Agni. De exitu ovium matricum dominae superius clxiiii. agni et non plures quia xviii. oves matrices non fecaverunt hoc anno.

Summa [*sic*].

De quibus in morina ante separationem xvii. Item in decima xiii. Item liberati usque Stonham pro stauro ibidem ante festum Sancti Michaelis per i. talliam contra Willelmum Gunnyld cxxxiiii. agni.

Summa quae supra. Et aequae.

i. agnus deficit de agnis liberatis [usque S]tonham pro eo quod non oneratur [super] compotum de Stonham.

Lana. De exitu bidentium dominae superius viventium ad tonsionem ciiii^xx^i. vellera.

Summa [*sic*].

De quibus in decima xviii. vellera. Item in venditione ut infra per manus Willelmi

[1]Onus Johannis ate Lound praepositi anni ultimi praecedentis xx*l*. xvii*s*. viii*d*. *ob*. et *di. q*ᵃ. de arreragiis suis ut supra.

Summa patet.

Gunnyld per i. talliam {contra praedictum Willelmum et Johannem ate Lound clxiii. vellera}.

{Summa quae supra.}   Et aequae.

Et remanent clxiii. vellera in manus Willelmi Gunnyld.

Lanuta. De morina bidentium dominae superius ante tonsionem x. pelles.

Summa [*sic*].

De quibus in decima i. {Item in venditione per Willelmum Gunnyld ix. pelles.}

{Summa quae supra.   Et aequae.}

[*Pell*]*ecta nulla.* Et remanent ix. pelles lanutae in manus Willelmi Gunnyld.

[*Pelli*]*culi.* De morina agnorum dominae superius ante separationem xvii.

Summa.

De quibus in decima i. Item in venditione ut infra xvi. pelliculi per ballivum.

Summa quae supra.   Et aequae.

Compotus Johannis Rokel collectoris perquisitorum curiae militum apud Fornecete anno supra dicto.

Arreragia. De arreragiis compoti anni ultimi praecedentis cx*s*. i*d*. unde super Willelmum Brooke ballivum itinerantem de arreragiis suis de anno lᵐᵒ xlix*s*. vi*d*. Item super Willelmum Schuldre collectorem de anno praecedente lx*s*. vii*d*.

Summa cx*s*. i*d*.

In primis respondet de iii*s*. ix*d*. de curia tenta die Lunae proxima ante festum Sanctae Fidis Virginis. Et de viii*s*. iiii*d*. de curia tenta die Lunae in crastino Omnium Sanctorum. Et de vi*s*. vi*d*. de curia tenta die Lunae in festo Sancti Andreae Apostoli. Et de ii*s*. de curia tenta die Lunae in festo Sanctorum Innocentium. Et de xv*d*. de curia tenta die Lunae in festo Conversionis Sancti Pauli. Et de iii*s*. ix*d*. de curia tenta die Lunae in festo Sancti Petri in Cathedra. Et de iiii*s*. viii*d*. de curia tenta die Lunae in festo Sancti Benedicti Abbatis. Et de iii*s*. vii*d*. de curia tenta die Lunae in septimana Paschae. Et de vi*s*. ii*d*. de curia tenta die Lunae proxima ante festum Sancti Dunstani. Et de iii*s*. iiii*d*. de curia tenta die Lunae proxima post festum Sanctae Trinitatis. Et de v*s*. ii*d*. de curia tenta die Lunae proxima post festum Translationis Sancti Thomae Martiris. Et de ii*s*. de curia tenta die Lunae in vigilia Sancti Laurentii. Et de iiii*s*. ix*d*. de curia tenta die Lunae proxima ante festum Nativitatis Beatae Mariae.

lv*s*. iii*d*.

Summa lv*s*. iii*d*.

Firma. Et de vi*d*. de firma i. cotagii in Brakne in manu dominae post mortem Adae Page ratione minoris aetatis haeredis dicti Adae dimissi Johannae quae fuit uxor praedicti Adae ad finem duorum annorum hoc anno primo solvendis ad festum Sancti Petri ad Vincula.

vi*d*.

Summa vi*d*.

[viii*l*.] v*s*. x*d*.

Summa totalis receptae cum arreragiis viii*l*. v*s*. x*d*.

Inde in expensis senescalli per suos adventus pro xi. curiis ibidem tenendis hoc anno ut patet per xi. billas sigillatas xi*s*. vi*d*. *ob*. simul cum expensis suis apud Norwicum in veniendo. Item in expensis ejusdem senescalli ad ii. curias tenendas nihil.

Summa xi*s*. vi*d*. *ob*.

Liberatio denariorum. Computat liberatos domino Henrico de Glastone receptori per i. talliam sigillatam et non scriptam de perquisitis curiae de anno instante de onere {Johannis} (Roberti) Rokel v*s*.

Item liberatos Johanni Lound ballivo manerii de Fornecete de onere ejusdem Roberti per talliam xxii*s*.

Item liberatos Willelmo Gunnyld pro novo aedificio apud Lopham de arreragiis Willelmi Schuldre collectoris anni praecedentis apud Lopham per talliam praedictam lx*s*.

Item liberatos Willelmo Clerke de Kenynghale pro expensis consilii domini ibidem existentis pro quodam breve de audiendo et terminando prosecutionem versus diversos homines per i. talliam xvii*s*.

Summa ciiii*s*.

Summa omnium expensarum et liberationum cxv*s*. v*d*. *ob*. Et debet l*s*. iiii*d*. *ob*.

De quibus allocantur eidem de onere Willelmi Schuldre vii*d*. Et sic debet dominae ulterius xlix*s*. viii*d*. *ob*. Unde super Willelmum Brooke ballivum itinerantem de arreragiis suis de anno lᵐᵒ xlix*s*. vi*d*. Et super Johannem Rokel collectorem perquisitorum curiae ii*d*. *ob*. Memorandum de xxx*s*. de amerciamentis Dominae Margaretae de Norwyco superius in arreragiis nondum allocatis nec levatis.

[1] On the roll a long blank space intervenes between the last entry and this.

Inde liberati Edwardo de Clypesby senescallo curiae pro feodo suo de anno ultimo elapso lxvi*s*. viii*d*.

Item liberati Domino Henrico de Glastone per i. talliam xiiii*l*. x*s*.

Item liberati Willelmo Hernyng praeposito hoc anno per i. talliam iiii*l*.

Item de amerciamento Dominae Margaretae de Norwyco non dum allocato nec levato xxx*s*.

Summa xxiii*l*. vi*s*. viii*d*.

Et sic excedunt xlviii*s*. xi*d*. *q*ᵃ. et *di. qᵃ*.

Compotus Willelmi Schuldir collectoris perquisitorum curiae militum apud Fornecete anno supradicto.

Arreragia. Idem respondet de xlix*s*. vi*d*. de arreragiis Willelmi Brooke ballivi itenerantis de anno ultimo praecedente.

Summa xlix*s*. vi*d*.

Inprimis respondet de xvii*s*. vi*d*. de curia tenta die Jovis proxima ante festum Sancti Lucae Evangelistae. Et de vi*s*. de curia tenta die Lunae proxima ante festum Sancti Edwardi Regis. Et de iii*s*. i*d*. de curia tenta die Mercurii proximo ante festum Sancti Nicholai. Et de ix*s*. x*d*. de curia tenta die Jovis proxima ante festum Conversionis Sancti Pauli. Et de vii*s*. viii*d*. de curia tenta die Lunae proxima ante festum Sancti Mathiae. Et de iii*s*. vi*d*. de curia tenta die Lunae proxima ante festum Annunciationis Beatae Mariae Virginis. Et de v*s*. ix*d*. de curia tenta die Lunae proxima ante festum Sancti Georgii Martiris. Et de iii*s*. iii*d*. de curia tenta die Lunae in septimana Pentecostes. Et de ix*s*. x*d*. de curia tenta die Lunae proxima post festum Sancti Barnabae Apostoli. Et de vi*s*. vii*d*. de curia tenta die Lunae proxima post festum Sancti Benedicti. Et de iiii*s*. iii*d*. de curia tenta die Lunae in festo Sancti Laurentii Martiris. Et de iii*s*. i*d*. de curia tenta die Lunae proxima ante festum Nativitatis Beatae Mariae Virginis.

Summa iiii*l*. iiii*d*.

Summa totalis receptae cum arreragiis vi*l*. ix*s*. x*d*.

Inde in expensis senescalli per suos adventus pro curiis tenendis hoc anno xii*s*. vi*d*. per viii. billas sigillatas.

Item in expensis senescalli pro ii. curiis tenendis iiii*s*. iiii*d*. sine billis per testimonium Willelmi Gunnild. Item in percameno empto pro rotulis curiae viii*d*. et pro rotulis curiae de anno elapso vi*d*. Item in expensis senescalli ad ii. curias tenendas per i. billam xxi*d*.

Summa xix*s*. ix*d*.

{Item computat liberatos Johanni Richer ballivo de Lopham per manum Willelmi Gunnyld pro novo aedificio ibidem faciendo per i. talliam xl*s*.

Summa xl*s*.}

(Quia in compoto suo de onere messoris ut patet in billa huic compoto annexata.)

Summa expensorum xix*s*. ix*d*.

Et debet cx*s*. i*d*. cum xlix*s*. vi*d*. de arreragiis anni ultimi praecedentis.

[Written on a strip of parchment sewn to top of roll.]

Fornecete. Dogget compoti ibidem anno primo.

Arreragia.	xx*l*. xvii*s*. viii*d*. *ob. di. qᵃ*.
Redditus assisae.	xx*l*. xiiii*s*. ix*d*. *qᵃ*.
Firmae terrae.	{xvii*l*. xiii*s*. i*d*.} (xviii*l*. ii*s*. x*d*. *ob*.).
Firmae terrarum dominicalium.	{xiii*l*. xv*s*. v*d*.} (xiiii*l*. vi*s*. ix*d*.).
Redditus mobiles cum operibus venditis.	viii*l*. iiii*s*. v*d*. {*ob*.} (*qᵃ*.).
Officium praepositi.	xl*s*.
Pastura vendita.	xxxviii*s*. {xi*d*.} (ix*d*.)

Subboscum venditum.	vi*s*. iiii*d*.
Bladum venditum.	lxvii*s*. x*d*.
Perquisita curiae.	xxi*l*. xi*s*. vi*d*.
Vendita super compotum.	iiii*s*. vi*d*. *ob*.

xiii*l*. iiii*s*. x*d*.   Summa totalis receptae cum arreragiis {cxi*l*. xv*s*. vi*d*. *di*. *q*ᵃ.}
di. *q*ᵃ.   (cxiii*l*. iiii*s*. x*d*. *di*. *q*ᵃ.)   Probatur.

Decimae solutae.	iii*s*. vi*d*. *q*ᵃ.
Resolutio reddituum et decasus.	l*s*. vii*d*. *q*ᵃ. et *di*. *q*ᵃ.
Custus molendini.	xxviii*s*. v*d*. *ob*.
Novum aedificium.	vi*l*. ii*s*. vii*d*.
Custus domorum et portarum.	xi*s*. xi*d*.
Expensae necessariae.	ix*s*.
Stipendia.	xl*s*.
Expensa senescalli.	iiii*l*. ix*s*. vi*d*. *ob*.
Liberatio denariorum.	{iiii*l*. v*s*. iiii*d*. *ob*. Probatur.}

(lxxviii*l*. v*s*. iiii*d*.)

Memorandum quod i. tallia de li*s*. iiii*d*. deficit

Summa expensarum et liberationum iiiiˣˣ. {xviii*l*. xi*d*. *ob*. *di*. *q*ᵃ.}

(xvi*l*. viii*d*. *ob*. *di*. *q*ᵃ.).

Et debet {xiii*l*. xiiii*s*. vi*d*. *ob*.} (xvii*l*. iiii*s*. i*d*. *ob*.).

Unde super Willelmum Shulder messorem hoc anno vi*l*. x*s*. *ob*. *q*ᵃ.

Cum iiii*l*. de amerciamento Johannis Herlyng resp[ectatis] et super Willelmum Hernynge praepositum vii*l*. iiii*s*. v*d*. *ob*. *q*ᵃ.

Summa totalis receptae cum arreragiis cxiii*l*. iiii*s*. x*d*. *di*. *q*ᵃ.

Summa expensarum et liberationum iiiiˣˣxvi*l*. viii*d*. *di*. *q*ᵃ.

Et debet xvii*l*. iiii*s*. i*d*. *ob*.

De quibus allocati eidem de amerciamento Johannis Herlyng iiii*l*. condonati per Dominam apud Londoniam ut testatur per Dominum W[alterum] Amyas videlicet de onere messoris.

iiiiˣˣxviii*l*. xi*d*. *di*. et *di*. *q*ᵃ.

[Dorse.]

Onus Willelmi Shuldre messoris ibidem anno regni Regis Ricardi primo.

In primis respondet de xxii*s*. de cxxxviii. gallinis venditis pretium capitis ii*d*.

Et de iii*s*. vii*d*. de Dccclx. ovis venditis pro centena v*d*.

Et de x*s*. x*d*. de ccciiiiˣˣx. operibus yemalibus venditis pretium iii. operum i*d*.

Et de xi*s*. iiii*d*. de cccxl. operibus aestivalibus pretium v. operum ii*d*.

Et de ii*s*. iii*d*. de ix. arruris vocatis Medweherth venditis.

Et de vii*d*. de ii. arruris Quadragesimae venditis pretium operis iii*d*. *ob*.

Et de viii*d*. de ii. arruris ad ordeum pretium operis iiii*d*.

Et de viii*d*. de ii. arruris de precariis pretium operis iiii*d*.

Et de xxxii*s*. iii*d*. *ob*. *q*ᵃ. de cclviii. averagiis pretium averagii i*d*. *ob*.

Et de xvii*d*. de factura viii. qr. iiii. bu. brasei pretium quarterii ii*d*.

Et de lxviii*s*. ii*d*. *ob*. de Dcccxviii. operibus autumpnalibus dim. pretium operis i*d*.

Et de vi*s*. viii*d*. de plus in toto de xl. operibus venditis Roberto Herberd pro opere iii*d*.

Et de iii*s*. iii*d*. de xxxix. cariagiis autumpnalibus pretium cariagii i*d*. (ut patet n compoto[1] de anno xlviii.).

Summa vii*l*. xviii*s*. i*d*. *q*ᵃ

---

[1] *compoto* is repeated.

Item v*is.* viii*d.*

Et de x*d.* de agistamento xx. bestiarum euntium in communa de Langemor.

Et de xxi*l.* xi*s.* vi*d.* de v. curiis tentis hoc anno.

Summa xxi*l.* xii*s.* iiii*d.*

Summa totalis receptae xxix*l.* {x*s.* v*d.* *q*ᵃ.} ⟨xvii*s.* i*d.* *q*ᵃ.⟩.

{Inde liberati Johanni Richer ballivo de Lopham per manum Willelmi Gunnyld pro novo aedificio ibidem per talliam xl*s.*} ⟨quia error per cognitionem praedicti Willelmi Shuldre super compotum⟩.

Item liberati Willelmo Hernynge ballivo per i. talliam xxi*l.* iiii*d.* *ob.* cum xl*s.* liberatis Johanni Richer per manus W. Gunnyld prout supra cognovit.

Summa liberationum {xxiiii*l.*} ⟨xxi*l.*⟩ iiii*d.* *ob.*

Et debet {vi*l.*} ⟨viii.⟩ xvi*s.* viii*d.* *ob.* *q*ᵃ. De quibus allocati eidem de amerciamento Johannis Herlyng iiii*l.* ut patet in pleno compoto.

Et sic debet ulterius {lvi*s.* viii*d.* *ob.* *q*ᵃ.} ⟨iiii*l.* xvi*s.* viii*d.* *ob.* *q*ᵃ.⟩.

Postea allocati eidem de quodam amerciamento Willelmi Hore de chacia super Carletonemora ii*s.* in partem lxii*s.* condonati.

{Summa liberationum xxi*l.* iiii*d.* *ob.* Et debet viii*l.* xvi*s.* viii*d.* *ob.* *q*ᵃ. De quibus allocati eidem iiii*l.* de amerciamento Johannis Herlyng ut patet in pleno compoto. Et supra debet ulterius iiii*l.* xvi*s.* viii*d.* *ob.* *q*ᵃ.} ⟨quia error secundum considerationem curiae⟩.

Memorandum quod W. Hernynge praepositus anni instantis oneratur in compoto suo xx*l.* xvii*s.* viii*d.* *ob.* *di.* *q*ᵃ. de arreragiis Johannis Lound praepositi anni praecedentis.

Summa xx*l.* xvii*s.* viii*d.* *ob.* *di.* *q*ᵃ.

De quibus recepti de praedicto J. Lound in denariis per i. talliam iiii*l.*

Item habet allocationem in compoto suo de feodo senescalli soluto per manus ejusdem Johannis Lound lxvi*s.* viii*d.*

Item habet allocationem de denariis liberatis Domino Henrico de Glastone ut patet in pleno compoto xiiii*l.* x*s.*

Summa allocationum xxi*l.* xvi*s.* viii*d.*

Et sic praedictus W. Hernynge debet dominae de dictis iiii*l.* receptis de dicto Johanne Lound praeposito allocationibus allocatis[1] xviii*s.* xi*d.* *q*ᵃ. *di.* *q*ᵃ.

[Written on a piece of coarse paper sewn to top of roll.]

Plese a les auditours ma tres honouree dame de Norffolk allower a la parsone de Fornesete la disme pur le herbage de diverse pasture qui jadis fuist a Roberte Bakoun appele Jermyes qui gist dedeins la paroche de la dite ville lesse as certeins gents par les baillifs ma dite dame cest assavoir a Johan Lopham et a William Anestay en i. parcelle de xv. acres pur iiii*s.* par an. Item a William Shuldre pur xv. acres par an iii*s.* Item a Adam Gallard pur vii. acres par esme ii*s.* ii*d.* Item a Johan Bustard en i. autre parcelle par an xii*d.* Item a mesme celi Johan Bustard en i. autre parcelle xviii*d.*

La somme amonte par an xi*s.* viii*d.* de quele somme la dite parsone demande allowance en droit de Seinte Eglise la disme denier de la pasture susdite qad este aderere environ trois anz et plus puisque il devynt par eschete en la main ma dame chescun an xiiii*d.* pur la disme et que Seinte Eglise ne soit pas desherite en mon temps pur Dieux et pur la savacoun du droit dicelle, etc.

[Endorsed.] Memorandum quod inde allocati sunt xii*d.* *ob.*

[1] all' alloc .

APPENDIX X.

COURT ROLL OF THE MANOR OF FORNCETT, 1400.

Fornessete. Curia prima domini Thomae Mouubray ibidem tenta die Lunae in festo Sanctae Luciae Virginis anno regni Regis Henrici quarti post conquestum secundo[1].

Libere tenentes. Johannes Smythe, Robertus Owlas, Willelmus Bonnewell, Thomas Smythe, Johannes Hert, Thomas Clement, Robertus de Wode, Johannes Boteld, Robertus de Ely, Willelmus Florens, Robertus Baxster, Johannes Skylman, Stephanus Breclys, Willelmus Thuxstone, Johannes Slaxster, Thomas Randolf, Johannes atte Chirche, Galfridus Lomb, **Fidelitas.** Johannes Arnald fecerunt domino fidelitatem. Johannes Aye fecit similiter.

Native tenentes. Willelmus Schuldre, Rogerus Joye, Nicholaus Blake, Rogerus Wadeker, Ricardus Potekyne, Robertus Thaxster, Johannes Lyncolne, Nicholaus Westhale, Thomas Qwytlok, Beatrix Schuldre, Robertus, filius Katerinae Ratche, Johannes Slaywryght, Stephanus Praty, capellanus, Thomas Hynd, Ricardus Keede, Henricus Turnour, Johannes Buke, Robertus Parmonter, Ricardus Soutere, Johannes Dryl, Stephanus Gurle, Robertus Ropere, capellanus, Henricus Rynggere, Walterus Colman, Johannes Drake fecerunt domino fidelitatem.

Nativi domini de sanguine. Robertus Howlot, Walterus Bolytoute, Willelmus Bolytoute, Walterus Bolytoute, junior, Johannes Dosy, Johannes Haugne, Alicia Haugne, Robertus Haugne, Johannes Lound, Willelmus Hyrnyng, Rogerus Hulle, Johannes Howlot, Matthaeus Brakest, Willelmus Brakest, Matthaeus Baxstere, Rogerus Bole, Ricardus Bolytoute, Robertus Dosy, Johannes Pelet, **Fidelitas.** Thomas Fornessete, Rogerus Hulle, Robertus Dosy, junior, fecerunt domino fidelitatem servilem.

Finis vs. Robertus Boole et Agatha uxor ejus in curia examinata sursum reddiderunt in manus domini ii. acras terrae cum uno tofto tenementi Barone et ii. acras terrae cum uno tofto de tenemento Mylys in Fornessete ad opus Willelmi Florens et Emmae uxoris ejus et haeredum suorum. Quibus liberata est inde seisina. Tendendum per virgam ad voluntatem domini per servitia et consuetudines. Salvo jure etc. Et dant domino de fine pro ingressu habendo.

M. iii*d.* De Rogero Hokere pro licentia concordandi cum Roberto de Fornessete de placito debiti.

Praeceptum est distringere Thomam de Brampton, Nicholaum Launde,

[1] Dec. 13, 1400.

Johannem Rees, Willelmum atte Hyl, clericum, Johannem Hickes, capellanum, Johannem Bacoun, capellanum, Johannem Smy hetde Carletone, Willelmum Barker, Adam Celer, Robertum de Eli, Stephanum Reve, Willelmum Gebet, Aliciam Parker (mort'), Emmam Cooke, Agnetem Toke, Simonem Vesq, Robertum Budbeleyn, Robertum Grasyer, Thomam Ingald (mort'), Johannem Uffdale, Thomam atte Moor, Robertum Fayrman, Aliciam Lound, Johannem Sylys, Willelmum filium Johannis Aunfrey, Willelmum Haptone, Alanum Elmyswelle, Johannem Bole, Henricum Baxster, Johannem Torald, Ricardum Cullyng, Walterum Cassaundre, Agnetem Blake (mort'), Sel atte Lane, Ricardum Willyard, Robertum Florens, Olivam Ungot, Galfridum Egelyn, {Agnetem Tooke} ita quod sint ad proximam curiam pro fidelitate domino facienda.

Walterus Bolytoute, Robertus Howlot, (Willelmum Grey), Ricardus Keede, Johannes Skylman, Johannes Lound, Johannes Slaywryghte, Ricardus Potekyn, Johannes Lyncolne, Nicholaus Blak, Robertus Dosy, Adam Gallard, Johannes Dosy, jur'.

Inquisitio ex officio.

Jurat' supradicti praesentant quod Johannes Howlot vendidit Ricardo Quytfote dimidiam acram terrae de tenemento Hucke in Fornessete, qui non venit. Ideo praeceptum est seisire in manus domini. Et medietate temporis respondere domino de exitibus.

Praeceptum est respondere.

Robertus Bramptone sursum reddidit in manus domini unam acram terrae solidatae in Tacolnestone ad opus Andreae Colman et haeredum suorum. Cui liberata est inde seisina. Tenendum per virgam ad voluntatem domini per servitia et consuetudines. Salvo jure etc. Et dat domino de fine etc. Et fecit domino fidelitatem.

Finis iiis.
Fidelitas.

Johannes Lound praesens in curia reddidit sursum in manus domini unam rodam terrae solidatae in Fornessete ad opus Roberti Dosy junioris. Cui liberata est inde seisina. Tenendum sibi et haeredibus suis per virgam ad voluntatem domini per servitia et consuetudines. Salvo jure etc. Et dat de fine etc. Et insuper fecit domino fidelitatem.

Finis viiid.
Fidelitas.

Johannes Lound praesens in curia reddidit sursum in manus domini unam parcellam turbariae continentem in longitudine ix. perticas et in latitudine iiii. perticas de terra solidata ad opus Aliciae filiae Roberti Dosy. Cui liberata est inde seisina. Tenendum sibi et haeredibus suis per virgam ad voluntatem domini per servitia et consuetudines. Salvo jure etc. Et dat de fine pro ingressu.

Finis iiiid.

Item praesentant quod Johannes Howlot vendidit Roberto Dorant et Christianae uxori ejus unam acram et dimidiam terrae nativae de tenemento Huckes in Fornessete qui non venerunt. Ideo praeceptum est seisire in manus domini. Et medietate temporis respondere domino de exitibus.

Praeceptum est liberatur.

Item praesentant quod infra istud manerium est una magna aula quae pejor tempore Margaretae Comitissae Norfolciae per Galfridum personam ecclesiae de Lopham supervisorem praedictae dominae Margaretae ad valentiam xls. Item una domus vocata le Longhous pejor eodem tempore per praedictum Galfridum ad valentiam cs. Item una coquina cum stabula pejor ad valentiam vis. viiid. per praedictum Galfridum. Item una granaria ibidem eodem tempore per praedictum Galfridum ad valentiam xls. Item una aula parva cum una camera dictae aulae enexata pejor eodem tempore per praedictum Galfridum ad valentiam xls. Item una grangia est ibidem quae pejor eodem tempore per praedictum Galfridum ad valentiam xxl. Item una domus juxta portam pejor eodem tempore per praedictum Galfridum ad valentiam xls.

Vastum manerii.

Item praesentant quod Willelmus Stokker persona ecclesiae de Fornessete

M. vi*d.* fecit dampnum in bosco domini apud Bromwode permittendo subboscum suum jacere in germin' ejusdem ad nocumentum. Ideo etc.

Item quod idem Willelmus injuste et sine causa rationabili vexavit Johannem

M. iii*s.* **iiii***d.* Skylman tenentem domini in curia Christianitatis pro rebus tangentibus curiam Regis. Ideo ipse in misericordia.

Praeceptum est retinere in manus domini unam rodam et dimidiam prati et

Praeceptum est. marisci in Fornessete quas Robertus Howlot vendidit Roberto Seriaunt sine licentia. Et medietate temporis respondere domino de exitibus.

Et retinere ii. acras iii. rodas et dimidiam terrae cum parcella unius messuagii de tenemento Rogeri Herberd i. acram terrae nativae de tenemento Baxsteres dimidiam acram terrae soliatae in ii. peciis et i. acram subbosci soliati in Tacolnestone quas Johannes Vyrly vendidit Willelmo Hyrnynge sine licentia. Et medietate temporis respondere domino de exitibus.

Et unum cotagium soliatum in Reveshalle continens in longitudine l. pedes et in latitudine xl. pedes unde Johannes Rougheye obiit seisitus. Et medietate temporis respondere domino de exitibus.

Praeceptum est. Praeceptum est attachiare Robertum Westhale per iiii***or.*** plegios ad respondendum Simoni Say (non pros') de placito debiti.

Respectus. Dies data est prece partium Roberto Butfulleyn querenti et Roberto Howlot defendenti in iii. querelis debiti.

Item praesentant quod Willelmus Stokker persona ecclesiae de Fornessete

M. xii*d.* prosequebatur Ricardum Keede native tenentem domini in curia de Narforth ad grave nocumentum hujus dominii. Ideo ipse in misericordia.

Summa hujus curiae.
xiiii*s.* i*d.*

Afferatores {Willelmus Hyrny[nge].
{Johannes Haug[ne].

APPENDIX XI.

SERIES OF CONVEYANCES RELATING TO A PIECE OF THE DEMESNE OF FORNCETT MANOR.

1422. Dominus concessit Willelmo Broun vi. acras terrae vocatas Heyaldir nuper in firma Johannis Davy cum pertinentiis in Fornsete. Tenendum eidem Willelmo et attornatis suis ad terminum iii. annorum, termino incipiente ad festum Sancti Michaelis Archangeli ultimo praeteritum. Reddendo inde domino per annum iiis. vid. ad terminos usuales. Et testatum est per homagium quod non plus potest dimitti hac vice etc.

1426. Dominus concessit Willelmo Buntyng vi. acras terrae de dominicis domini apud Heyaldir in Forncete nuper in firma dicti Willelmi. Tenendum eidem Willelmo et attornatis suis ad terminum vii. annorum, termino incipiente ad festum Sancti Michaelis Archangeli ultimo praeteritum. Reddendo inde domino per annum iiis. ad terminos usuales.

1437. Domina concessit et ad firmam dimisit Johanni Kyrton vi. acras terrae de dominicis domini apud Heyaldyr nuper in firma Willelmi Buntyng in Forncete. Tenendum eidem Johanni et attornatis suis ad terminum vii. annorum, termino incipiente ad festum Sancti Michaelis Archangeli ultimo praeteritum. Reddendo inde per annum iiis. ad terminos usuales, ut antea consuevit etc.

1451. Dominus concessit et ad firmam dimisit Johanni Kyrton vi. acras terrae de dominicis domini apud Heyaldir nuper in firma dicti Johannis pro firma iiis. in Forneset. Tenendum eidem Johanni et attornatis suis ad terminum xii. annorum, termino incipiente ad festum Sancti Michaelis Archangeli proximum ante datum hujus curiae. Reddendo inde domino per annum iiis. ad terminos usuales ut solvere consuevit etc.

1460. Domina concessit et ad firmam dimisit Johanni Kyrton et Roberto Den vi. acras terrae de dominicis dominae apud Heyghaldre in Forncet nuper in firma dicti Johannis pro firma iiis. Tenendum eisdem Johanni et Roberto et attornatis suis ad terminum xx. annorum, termino incipiente ad festum Sancti Michaelis Archangeli proximum post datum hujus curiae. Reddendo inde dominae per annum iiis. ut solvere consuevit ad terminos usuales manerii etc.

1497. Domina per senescallum suum concessit extra manus suas Stephano Denne de Forncet et Roberto filio suo, sex acras terrae de dominicis manerii insimul jacentes in i. pecia in quodam campo vocato Bromefeld super stadium vocatum Aldcrosse in Forncett, quondam in firma Johannis Kirton ad terminum annorum pro iii*s*. de firma. Quibusquidem Stephano et Roberto liberata est inde seisina. Tenendum eisdem haeredibus et assignatis suis per virgam ad voluntatem domini. Reddendo inde annuatim dominis hujus manerii iii*s*. legalis monetae Angliae nomine novi redditus ad terminos manerii usuales et communem sectam curiae. Et dant dominae de fine pro hac concessione habenda ut in capite etc. Et fecit fidelitatem etc. Finis xx*d*.

1561. Cum ad curiam hic tentam die Lunae proxima ante festum Sanctae Margaretae Virginis anno regni Dominae Reginae nunc Elizabeth primo, praesentatum fuerat per inquisitionem ex officio quod Robertus Denne extra curiam sursum reddidit in manus dominorum per manus Roberti Smith ballivi ac native tenentis hujus manerii in praesentia Briani Outlawe et Launceloti Smith similiter native tenentium vi. acras terrae arrabilis ad opus Launceloti Smith et Katerinae uxoris suae et haeredum suorum prout in curia praedicta plenius patet, modo ad istam curiam venerunt praedicti Launcelotus et Katerina uxor ejus et praesentes in curia petunt admitti ad praedictas vi. acras terrae de dominicis manerii prout insimul jacent in una pecia in quodam campo vocato Bromefeld super stadium vocatum Aldecrosse in Forncett quondam in firma Johannis Kirton tentas per redditum iii*s*. per annum quas praedictus Robertus cepit similcum Stephano Denne patre suo prae se defuncto ex concessione domini ut patet in curia hic tenta die Martis proxima post festum Sancti Hyllarii Episcopi anno r. r. Henrici vii^mi. xii°. secundum formam et effectum sursum redditionis praedicti et admissi sunt inde tenentes. Quibus quidam Launcelotto et Katerinae liberata est inde seisina per virgam. Tenendum illis, haeredibus et assignatis suis ad voluntatem dominorum secundum consuetudinem manerii per servitia et consuetudines etc. Salvo jure etc. Et dant dominis de fine etc. Et praedictus Launcelotus fecit fidelitatem etc.

[In margine.] Finis xiii*s*. iiii*d*. Fidelitas.

1563. Ad hanc curiam venerunt Thomas Denne et Helena uxor ejus et praesentes in curia ipsaque Helena sola per senescallum examinata sursum reddiderunt in manus domini vi. acras terrae de dominicis manerii prout insimul jacent in una pecia [description omitted] quas praedictus Thomas cepit ex sursum redditione Launceloti Smythe et Katerinae uxoris suae ut patet in curia generale hic tenta die Lunae proxima ante festum Sancti Gregorii Episcopi anno regni Dominae Reginae nunc tertio ad opus Edwardi Davye et haeredum suorum. Cui liberata est inde seisina per virgam. Tenendum sibi haeredibus et assignatis suis ad voluntatem domini secundum consuetudinem manerii per servitia et consuetudines, etc. Salvo jure etc. Et dat domino de fine etc. Et fecit fidelitatem etc.

[In marg.] Finis xiii*s*. iiii*d*.

APPENDIX XII.

NUMBER OF CONVEYANCES ANNUALLY.

These numbers are not to be depended upon as complete, since many membranes containing conveyances have been lost from the series, or if preserved are in part illegible. It is believed however that the numbers afford sufficient support for the very general conclusion based upon them. Bracketed numbers are almost certainly incomplete.

	Includes farms	Not including farms
1401	34	30
1402	49	46
1403	41	38
1404	[22	21]
1405	35	30
1406	33	31
1407	[15	15]
1408	38	32
1409	41	38
1410	54	49
1411	59	45
1412	68	52
1423	33	28
1424	22	17
1425	39	35
1426	29	21
1427	[16	11]
1428	20	17
1429	23	20
1430	[5	1]
1431	[21	11]
1432	29	20
1433	21	20
1434	31	26
1435	28	20
1436	19	17
1437	27	18
1438	46	28
1439	26	20
1440	36	29
1441	26	18
1442	38	26
1443	30	21
1444	24	22
1445	[13	9]
1446	29	18
1447	27	20

	Includes farms	Not including farms
1448	9	9
1449	29	26
1450	25	17
1451	19	14
1454	51	39
1455	53	47
1456	25	23
1457	40	36
1458	32	28
1459	25	18
1460	28	23
1461	29	26
1462	[21	15]
1463	32	23
1464	21	18
1465	17	15
1466	20	17
1467	28	23
1468	[8	8]
1469	36	32
1470	35	33
1471	28	26
1472	23	14
1473	[8	8]
1474	43	40
1475	[13	13]
1476	29	25
1477	32	27
1478	28	24
1480	20	17
1481	15	13
1482	13	9
1483	19	18
1484	11	10
1485	14	12
1486	18	15
1487	22	20
1488	21	20

	Includes farms	Not including farms
1489	17	16
1490	15	13
1491	24	18
1492	29	28
1493	21	20
1494	18	17
1495	24	24
1496	[5	5]
1497	33	28
1498	12	9
1499	19	18
1536–7		25
1537–8		19
1538–9		21
1539–40		20
1540–1		19
1541–2		13
1542–3		17
1543–4		24
1544–5		8
1545–6		22
1548–9		15
1549–50		4
1550–1		14
1551–2		23
1553–4		13
1554–5		17
1555–6		11
1556–7		23
1557–8		19
1558–9		34
1559–60		28
1560–1		29
1561–2		17
1562–3		19
1563–4		29
1564–5		22

APPENDIX XIII.

WILLS OF BONDMEN.

Fornsett. Curia ibidem tenta die Martis xi. die mensis Maii anno regni Regis Henrici vii^{mi}. xvi^{mo}.[1]

. . . .

Ad hanc curiam venit Agneta nuper uxor Johannis Haghne nativi Dominae de sanguine qui nuper obiit et tulit testamentum et ultimam voluntatem dicti defuncti ad irrotulandum in haec verba ;

Exhibitio testamenti Johannis Haughene nativi Dominae de sanguine. Haec est ultima voluntas Johannis Haughne de Forncet facta iiii^{to}. die mensis Martii anno Domini millesimo cccc. nonagesimo octavo. In primis commendo animam meam et[2] Deo omnipotenti corpusque meum ad sepeliendum in cimiterio Sanctae Mariae de Forncet praedicta. Item, quod debita mea solvenda. Item, do et lego summo altari ecclesiae praedictae *vid*. Item, ad emendationem praedictae ecclesiae xii*d*. Item, do et lego gildae Sanctae Mariae de Forncet *vid*. Item, gildae Omnium Sanctorum in Tacolneston *vid*. Item, do et lego fratribus Minorum et fratribus Sancti Augustini in Norwico cuilibet i. comb ordei vel xii*d*. Item I wylle that Anneys myn wyffe shall have all myn stuffe within myne hows and with owte with all myne greynez and all myn catell meveable and unmevable to hyr propre use to paye with all myne dettes. Item I geve to the sayde Annys myne crofte of the tenemente Turnour be forne myn gate sowyn with whete and she to haveith as longe as she wille dwelle stylle in Towne etc. Item I geve to the sayde Annys i. halffe acre londe of tenemente Pennynges and lyeth above Mengappe my heymeere and i. acre lyynge in ii. pecys holdyn of the maner of Forncet ; iii. rodes lyynge upon Bergh, i. rod lyynge upon a forlonge clepyde Gyldrys Furlonge to here propyr use to gyve and to selle and aftyr hyre discesse to remayne ageyn to the place yf they wylle beye it fore there money, and also a space to lay in here greynez yerley as longe as she wille abyde terme of lyfe and a shodde lykewyse to sett in here catell at the bernes ende. And all the profight of myn londes that we purpose to sowe with barly into the terme of Mishelmas and oder greynez. Item I be qwethe to Annys myn wyffe myn chambre in the weste ende of myn halle with the chymney and the soler there over terme of here lyff yf she wylle abyde and halff

[1] 1501.   [2] *Sic.*

parte of myne frute gardeyn lykewyse with fre entre and issew at alle tymes lefull. The resydue of all myne goodys I˙beqwethe to Jone myne doughter and aftyr here dysces to remayne to John Wyarde here sone etc.

Et commissa est administratio omnium et singulorum bonorum et catallorum nuper defuncti ad dispositionem praedictae Agnetae in forma juris juratae ad exequendum prout etc. Quae quidem Agneta dat Dominae de fine pro hac administratione habenda ut in capite.

Finis xiid.

Forncet. Curia generalis ibidem tenta die Jovis proxima ante festum Exaltationis Sanctae Crucis anno regni Regis [Henrici] Septimi, vicesimo primo[1].

. . . .

Ad hanc curiam venerunt Johannes Mannynge clericus et Robertus Felmyngham executores Johannis Dosy senioris nativi Dominae de sanguine et tulerunt testamentum et ultimam voluntatem ejusdem Johannis Dosy coram senescallo in plena curia cujus tenor sequitur :

Exhibitio testamenti Johannis Dosy nativi Dominae de sanguine.

In the name of Gode, Amen. I John Dosy the elder of Forncet there beynge in goode memorie and heyle mende the xi. daye of the monethe of Septembre in the yere of oure Lorde Gode millesimo ccccciiii. and in the yere of the regne of Kynge Hary the vii[th]. the xx[ti]. make myne testament and laste wille be the licens of myn Ladye Elizabeth Duches of Norffolk in the manere and forme folowynge. Fyrste, I comende myn soule to Gode Almighty to oure blissed Lady Seynte Marie and to all the seyntes in hevyn my body to ben buried in the cherche yerde of Seynte Marie in Forncet afforsayde be Cristian late my wyve on the sought syde of hyre grave. To the hey auter for my tythez neclengently for getyn and other offences I be qwethe vi*s*. viii*d*. Item, I bequeth to the reparacion of the seyde cherche of Seynte Marie xx*s*. Item to the reparacion of the cherche of Seynte Peter in Forncet affor seyde xx*s*. Item to the reparacion of the cherche of our Blyssed Ladye in Therston vi*s*. viii*d*. Item to the reparacion of the cherche in Tacolneston vi*s*. viii*d*. Item, to the reparacion of the cherche in Hapton iii*s*. iiii*d*. Item, to the reparacion of the cherche of oure Blyssed Ladye in Waketon iii*s*. iiii*d*. Item I beqwethe to the sustentacion of the gylde of oure Blyssed Lady in Forncet aforsayde vi*s*. viii*d*. Item to the sustentacion of the gylde of Seynt Peter in Forncet affore seyde vi*s*. viii*d*. Item, to the iiii[or]. orderes of freyers in the cety of Norwych equaly to ben devyded amonges them xl*s*. Item to the syke men dwellynge with oute the fyve gates in Norwiche vi*s*. viii*d*. that is to sey at eiche gate xx*d*. Item I beqwethe to eiche of myn godsons and goddoughters xii*d*. Item, I bequethe to Emme Botye myn servaunte to be payed as yt maye be borne and taken of myn goodes londes and tenementes xl*s*. Item, I beqweth to John Brandon myn godson v*s*. viii*d*. be syde xii*d*. to gon above in generalte. Item, to the howsez of ankers and ankerassez within the seyd cety to ben evenley devyded amonges them be the discreccion of myn executors xiii*s*. iiii*d*. to praye for me and all my frendes and all trew Christen soulez. Item, I wille have a preste be the space of ii. yeres to synge for me and all my frendes on yere in Seynte Marie Cherche, and a nother yere in Seynte Peters cherche. Item, I bequeth to ieche of myn wyfez chyldren i. cowe. Item, I wille that my meas with all myn londes and tenementes in Forncet Therston or elles where be solde be myn executors to the performans of thys my testament and laste wylle. Item, I wylle that Cecili myn wyffe have to hyre owne use halffe the utensylles and stufte of myn howsold. Item, I wille that

Cop' feci.

----

[1] Sept. 1505.

Cecili my wyffe have to here and here heyres to geve or selle an inclos called Wodewell contineth be estimacion vii. acres in Forncet. The residue of all my goodes and catell not gevyn nor bequeth I putte and gyve in to the handes of myn executors whom I ordeyne and make Master John Mannynge clerke and Robert Felmyngham that theye &c.

Et super hoc commissa est administratio omnium et singulorum bonorum et catallorum dictum testamentum concernentium praefatis Johanni et Roberto executoribus in forma juris juratis ad exequendum prout in forma praedicta. Quiquidem Johannes et Robertus dant Dominae de fine secundum antiquam compositionem inter praedictam Dominam Elizabetham Ducissam et Johannem Dosy pro hujusmodi administratione habenda ut in capite per quamquidem finem Domina de gratia sua speciali acquietat praedictos executores de ulteriori compoto proinde imposterum reddendo per praesens irrotulamentum, etc.

Finis, lxvis. viiid.

Forncett. Curia generalis ibidem tenta die Martis proxima post festum Conversionis Sancti Pauli anno regni Regis Henrici Septimi xxi⁰.[1]

. . . .

Ad hanc curiam venerunt Willelmus Paysshle et Willelmus Hyrnynge executores testamenti et ultimae voluntatis Johannis Hirnynge de Bunwell nativi Dominae de sanguine et ultimae voluntatis[2] ejusdem Johannis Hirnynge coram senescallo in plena curia cujus tenor sequitur :—

Exhibitio testamenti Johannis Hirnynge nativi Dominae de sanguine.

In the name of God, Amen. I, John Hirnynge of Bonwell be the licens of myne ladyes grace of Norffolk make my laste wille and testament in thys wyse the xvi. daye of Octobre the yere of oure Lorde Gode millesimo cccc. and v. Fyrste I be qwethe my soule to almighty Gode and my body to be buried in the cherche yerde of Seynte Mighell of Bonwell. Item, I be qwethe to the hey autere of the same cherche iiis. iiiid. Item I be qwethe to the stepille of Bonwell xiiis. iiiid. Item, I be qwethe to the Gylde of Seynte Michaelis in Bonwell iiis. iiiid. Item I beqwethe to John myn sonne vis. and viiid. Item I beqweth to Annys myn doughter all the stuffe of housold a cowe and a pigge. Item, I beqweth to Margery my belchelde[3] whan she is of lawfull age ii. acres and a rod londe lyynge in Watkers Feld. Item, I be qwethe to the gylde of Seynte Thomas in Wattellesfeld of Wyndham iiis. iiiid. Item, I be qwethe to myne goodson John Yongman vis. viiid. Item I be qwethe to myn goddoughter Richarde Chapmans childe xxd. Item, I wille have don fore me at myn buryynge daye to the valewe of xxs. Item, I wole have [a mass sung] at Scala Cely[4] fore me and anoder fore my weyffe. Item I wille that all my tenementes and londes there to pertenynge to ben solde be myn executorez to full fylle myn wylle and paye myn dettes whome I make and ordeyne William Passhle and William Hyrnynge myne sone and John Crane to be supervisour of this myn laste wille.

Et super hoc commissa est administratio omnium et singulorum bonorum et catallorum dictum testamentum[5] concernentium praefatis executoribus in forma juris juratis ad exequendum prout etc. in forma praedicta. Qui quidem Willelmus et Willelmus dant Dominae de fine pro hujusmodi administratione habenda ut in capite.

Finis xxd.

---

[1] January 27, 1505–6. [2] *sic.* [3] Grandchild.
[4] For an account of the chapel of Scala Cely in the Austin Friars' church in Norwich, see Blomefield, *op. cit.* IV. 90.
[5] MS. *dicti testamenti.*

Fornsett. Prima curia Jacobi Hobart Militis feoffati ad usum Domini Thomae Comitis Surriae ibidem tenta die Iovis xviii^o. die Martii anno regni Regis Henrici vii^{mi}. xxii^{do}.[1]

Ad hanc curiam venit Johannes Crane executor testamenti Ricardi Bolytowte

Exhibitio testamenti Ricardi Bolytowte nativi Domini de sanguine. nativi Domini de sanguine et tulit testamentum et ultimam voluntatem ejusdem Ricardi Bolytowte coram senescallo in plena curia cujus tenor sequitur :—

In the name of God, Amen, etc. The xiiiith. day of Septembre the yere of oure Lord God M^lccccvith. I Richard Bolytowte make my wyll and testment in this wyse. First I bequethe my sowle to almyghty God and all the seyntes in heven and my body to be beryed in the chirche yerde of Seynt Mihell of Bonwell to the which high aulter I bequethe xii*d.* Item, I bequeth to Richard my sone all my house and londes in Bonwell and Carleton. Item, I bequethe to Cecily my wyf a cowe and a pigge and I wull she have hir dewellyng within the northende of the berne terme of hir lyff and an acre of whete and an acre of barley sowyn att my cost and charge and also som mete and wynter mete for hir kowe and pigge yerly founden as longe as she kepith hir a wydowe. Item, I bequethe to iche of my iiii. doughters a kow if it may be borne. Item, I woll that in korne and katell that beleveth be solde to pay John Dawndy c*s.* and other dettes that I owe to diverse persones and I make and ordeyn myn executors John Crane and John Myles etc.

Et super hoc commissa est administratio omnium et singulorum bonorum et catallorum dictum testamentum[2] concernentium praefato Johanni Crane executori in forma juris jurato ad exequendum prout in forma praedicta. Qui quidem Johannes dat Domino de fine pro hujusmodi administratione habenda ut in capite per quam quidem finem Dominus ex gratia sua speciali acquietat praedictos

Finis x*s.* executores de ulteriori compoto inde imposterum reddenda per praesens[3] irrotulamentum.

Ad hanc curiam venerunt Thomas Dosy et Johannes Gallard senior executores testamenti et ultimae voluntatis Johannis Dosy nativi [Domini de]

Exhibitio testamenti Johannis Dosy nativi Domini de sanguine. sanguine et tulerunt testamentum et ultimam voluntatem ipsius coram senescallo in plenam curiam, cujus tenor sequitur :—

In the name of God, Amen. The last day of the monyth of March in the yere of oure [Lord] God a[4] Mcccc. and sexe, I, John Dosy of Forncett, make my will on this wyse. Ferst [I bequethe] my soule to God almyghty and to our Lady Seynt Mary and the holy company of heven [and] my body to be beryed in the chirch yerde of Seynt Petyr of Forncett. Item, I bequethe to the hye aulter of the same town for my tythes neclegently for getyn xii*d.* Item I be quethe to a trentall[5] to be songe for me and all my good frendes sowlys x*s.* Item, I bequethe to the reparacion of the chirche of Seynt Petyr in Forncett xii*d.* Item, I wol that all mov[eable] goodes be sold for to brynge me and my wyffe to the grounde and for to fulfylle my wyll and pay my dettes. Also I will that John my sone have my tenement with all the londe therto longyng and if the seid John my sone dyscese with inne age then I woll that it be sold and disposyd for me and all my good frendys sowles. Also I wull that myn at[torneys] have eche of them an acre of mystlynne[6] of my ferme londe whom I ordeyn and

---

[1] 1506–7.   [2] MS. *dicti testamenti.*   [3] MS. *praesent.*
[4] *Sic.*   [5] Thirty masses for the dead.
[6] Maslin, mixed grain, especially wheat and rye.

make Thomas Dosy my brother and John Gallard the elder for to dispos for [my] sowle and all my good frendes sowlys to the most plesur of almygty God. Item, I bequethe to John my sone a cow and a calfe etc.

Et super hoc commissa est administratio omnium et singulorum bonorum et catallorum dictum testamentum[1] consernentium praefatis Thomae Dosy et Johanni[2] Gallard executoribus in forma juris juratis illud exequendum prout justum est in forma praedicta etc. Qui quidem executores dant Domino de fine pro hujusmodi

Finis vis.
viiid.

administratione habenda ut in capite per quam quidem finem ex gratia sua speciali acquietat praedictos executores de ulteriori compoto inde imposterum reddendo per praesens irrotulamentum.

. . . .

Ad hanc curiam venerunt Anna Hillyng vidua relicta Rogeri Hillyng nuper de Multon defuncti nativi Domini de sanguine et Margareta Hillyng

Exhibitio testamenti et ultimae voluntatis Rogeri Hillyng nativi Domini de sanguine.

filia ejusdem Rogeri ipsaeque Anna et Margareta executores testamenti et ultimae voluntatis praedicti Rogeri et tulerunt testamentum et ultimam voluntatem praedicti Rogeri coram senescallo in plena curia, cujus tenor sequitur :—

In the name of God, Amen, etc. I Roger Hillyng of Multon in my goode mynde beyng the xviii[th]. day of June the yere of our Lord M[l]ccccc. and vi[th]. make my wille and testament in this wyse. First I bequethe my sowle to all myghty Jhesu and my body to be beryed in the chirch yard of Seynt Mighille in Multon aforseyd. Item, I bequethe to the light of our Lord at Estern a cowe the whiche to remayne in my place ever lestyng and I wille that the owners of my tenament pay yerely for the ferme of the seid cowe iii. *lb.* of waxe to the sustentacyon of the seid light and I will that whan the seid cowe is olde febelle that there be bought a nother with mony therof commyng and thus to endure as longe as the worlde leste. Item, I will that Amy my wyf have all my house and londes therto perteynyng terme of hur lyff and aftyr hir decesce I will that Margett my doughter have the seid house and londes holdyng of the maner of Forncett Claveres Thetford excepte i. acre *di.* of lond lyeng in Collesfeld and aftyr my seyd wiffes decesse I wille that Alice my doughter have a tenement with all the londes therto perteynyng holden of the maner of Multon with th forseid i. acre *di.* of londe lyeng in Collesfeld and an acre of lond lyeng in the seid feld holden of the maner of Aslakton and if it fortune ony of my seid dowghters to decesce with oute issue I wille that she on lyve have hir systers parte fyndyng a prest for me and my frendes sowlez be the space of a yere. Item, I bequethe to Amye my wiff all my stuff of houssold corne and catell to fulfille my wille and pay dettes that ben owyng and aftyr my seid wyffes decesce the stuffe of howsold to be departed betwyn my seid dowghters. Item, I will have a preste to synge for my soule a quarter of a yere if it may be borne and I ordeyne and make myn executors Amy my wiffe and Margett my doughter and John Cullyng and Richard Felde over seers of this my laste wille.

Et super hoc commissa est administratio omnium et singulorum bonorum et catallorum dicti Rogeri testamentum concernentium praefatis Annae et Margaretae executricibus in forma juris juratis illud ad exequendum prout in forma praedicta. Quae quidem executrices dant Domino de fine pro hujusmodi administratione habenda ut in capite per quam quidem finem Dominus ex gratia sua speciali

Finis xs.

acquietat praedictas executrices de ulteriori compoto proinde imposterum reddendo per praesens irrotulamentum, etc.

---

[1] MS. *dicti testamenti.*   [2] MS. *Johannis.*

[1] In naym of God, Amen. The vii. day of May the yer of howre Lorde God a Mcccccvixx. I Thomas Hyllyn of Aslacton in conte of Norffowke and the dyocys of Norwyche at the plysans and leve of the nobyll prynce Duke of Norfowke make this my laste wyll and testament in forme felowyn. Forste I be quythe my solle to all myhty Gode and to howr Lady Sancte Mare and to al the sanctes of hevyn, my body to be berret in the cherche yarde of Sancte Mychaell of Aslacton a for sade. Item, I be quythe to the haye halter of the forsade cherche of Aslacton for my tethys neclygent forgottyn and not payt viii*d*. Item, I be quythe to the angor at howre Ladys freers in Norwyche iiii*d*. the wyche I do howe hym of dethe. Also I wyl he have viii*d*. more for the wyche I wyll have a Messe of the Holy Goste and another of howre blyssyde Lady. Item, I wyll have a messe of Schalycely[2] songe at the Austen freers in Norwyche for my solle. Item, I be quythe to the for sade chyrche of Aslacton a cowe blacket dowyt for to be latte by the handes of the chyrche revys then bein to the beste prouefe that can be hade for to fynde a lethe a fore the Sacrament at messe tym fro the begynyn of the gospell onto the weschyn after the howsyn of the Body of Creyste as longe as ever yt ys abyl to be fownde. Item, I be quythe to Robert Chaman a blowe cotte slevet for to pra for my sowlle. Item, I be quythe to them iiii. that schall bere me to the chyrche iiii*d*. Item, I be quythe to the rengers and hym that schall make my grave iiii*d*. Item, I be quythe a stowre cawffe[3] for to be solde for to by as myche meyll for to make pastes as the prysse of the forsade cawe wyll extende also v. buschell of wytte to be grownde with as myche malte as wyll serve therto the wyche schall be done the Sonday after my berryng. Item, I bequythe to mowder of my wyffe thow yerdys and an halfe of blanket for to pra for me. Item, I bequythe to my godmode Tyler halfe a yerde of wyll blanket for to pra for me. Item, I be quythe to Hary Clament my best cape and a blacke cowte for to be gode freynd onto my wyffe. Item, I be quythe and charche that towe pylgramessche the wyche I howe on to Sanct Thomas of Canterberre and the other to the gud rode of Dovercurtte be doyn for me as sone as may be browthe a bowtte. Item, I bequythe to Annes my wyffe my stowffe of howsolde with my catell and goddys unbequythe onto the performans of this my laste [will] and testament and to the bryngyn of my chelder. {Hiis testibus, my gostly fader Sir Hary Watson and Robert Hawlle.} Item, I wyll my bastert lowmys[4] with all the ynstramentys therto lowngyn be solde to the beste pryesse that may be gette for them the mony ther of comyn evynly to be devydyt be twyx thes iii. cherches that ys for to say the cherche of Sanct Mychaell of Aslakton, the cherche of Sanct Mychaell of Mowlton, the cherche of Hawlhalloyn of Mowlton to everyhe on of thes a part evynly to be devydyt and payd savyn of the forsayd pryess I wyll raserve and gyffe to my wyffe iii*s*. Thes wytnesys, my gostly fader Sir Hary Watson, Hary Clament and Robertt Hall.

Forncett. The Inventory of the goodes of Thomas Hillyng late disceased custum man to the maner of Forncett.

xxxiii*s*. iiii*d*.	In primis, v. keen, the price xxxiii*s*. iiii*d*.	
viii*s*.	Item, a whyte mare, the price viii*s*.	
viii*s*. iii*d*.	Item, vi. mother shepe and iii. lambys, the price viii*s*. iii*d*.	

---

[1] The following will and inventory are entered in the Court Book of 1524-31, but they do not form part of the record of any court.
[2] Cf. footnote 4, p. lxxx.   [3] Large calf.
[4] Looms for making "bastard," a kind of "cloth presumably imitating a more expensive material." Beck, *Drapers' Dictionary.*

	xx*d*.	Item, oon brasse potte, the price xx*d*.
		Item, a ketyll of iii. galonez, the price xvi*d*. a brasse panne of oon
	xxii*d*.	galon (vi*d*.).
	xvi*d*.	Item, iii. pewtre dyshes and oon pewtre sawser oon salt, price xvi*d*.
	iiii*d*.	Item, on latyn candelstykes iiii*d*.
		Item, a matras (xx*d*.) a payr of blankettes (xvi*d*.) ii. coverlytes
vii*s*.	iiii*d*.	(iiis.) and ii. payr of shetes (oon payr spent xvi*d*.).
		Item, in whete vii. bus. xvi*d*. (spent v. bus.). In mault vi. bus.
	xxii*d*.	(vi*d*. spent).
vi*s*.		Item, a payr of lowmys with the instrumentes sold for vi*s*.
ii*s*.	i*d*.	Item, iii. pygges and a sowe ii*s*. i*d*.
vi*s*.		Item, his rayment gyven a way in his lyff except a gown (vi*s*.).
	xviii*d*.	Item, in lose wode to the value of xviii*d*.
iiii*li*. xixs. vi*d*.		Summe iiii*li*. xixs. vi*d*.

The Dettes of the said Thomas.

In primis, to John Petygre	iiii*s*. viii*d*.
Item, to Marion Tyler	iii*s*. iiii*d*.
Item, to the parson of Multon All Seyntes	vi*d*.
Item, to Hewse ferme for half yeer and more	vii*s*.
Item, for leture to the parson and for tythe	xiii*d*.
	Summe xvi*s*. vii*d*.

The Legacyes delyvered.

Item, to the Fryer Anker	xii*d*.
Item, att the Fryers Austyn	xvi*d*.
Item; spent att his buryall, 5 bus. whete, v. bushelles of malt and a calf	
and in money to the prest ryngares and clerk	ii*s*.
Item, for a pylgrym' to Dovercourt	xx*d*.
....[1]	viii*d*.
	Summa ultra reprisas lvi*s*. iii*d*.

Finis administrationis bonorum infrascriptorum commissae Agneti Hyllinge
relictae Thomae Hyllyng infranominati   viii*s*.

Nota quod dicta administratio commissa fuit praefatae Agneti ad sustentationem Emmae viii. annorum et Aliciae ii. annorum filiarum eorundem Thomae
et Agnetis.

Forncett. Curia ibidem tenta die Lunae in crastino festi Reliquiarum
anno regni Regis Henrici Octavi vicesimo nono[2].

· · · · · · · · · · · ·

Ad hanc curiam venerunt Johannes Doosy et Johannes Buxston executores
Ostensio testamenti et ultimae voluntatis Thomae Doosy nuper de Forncett
testamenti nativi Domini de sanguine et exhibuerunt curiae hic testamentum
et ultimae et ultimam voluntatem ejusdem Thomae in haec verba :—
voluntatis.
In the name of God, Amen. I Thomas Doosy of Forncett of
good and hoole mynde beyng and of good memory the xxv^th. daye of July in the
yere of our Lorde God M^l.cccccxxxvi^v. make my last wille and testament.

---

[1] The folio is torn away.   [2] Sept. 16, 1537.

First, I bequeth my soule to God Almyghty and to our Lady Seynt Mary and to all the blessid companye in hevyn and my body to be buried in the churche yarde of Seynt Petur in Forncett before the porche doore to the whiche highe aulter I bequeth xii*d*. for my 'tithys necligentlye paide. Item, I giff to the Greye Fryers and the Austyns and to the White Friers in Norwiche to iche place vi*s*. viij*d*. to preye for me and my frendes. Item I wille that Kateryn my wiffe have the chamber with the chymney on the south parte of my place terme of her liff if she kepe her sole and on maried and xl. dayes after her deth for her assignes and the house to be sufficientlie repared by the kepers of the place and free entre and issue at all tymes for her and her assignes. Item, I giffe her a milche cowe. Item, I wille that she have an horsse when she is disposed to goo pilgrymage or markett. Item, I wille that she have a swyne goyng in the same place to their coste and charge. Item, I wille that Kateryn my wiffe have an aker of whete and an aker of barley yerlye terme of her liff and myn assignes to bere the costes of the tilthe and she shall fynde the sede to the londe and shalbe reped and leyde in the house at their coste and charge. Item, I wille that Kateryn my wiff have halffe my stuffe that is to seye beddyng brasse pewter latyn and other small thinges belongyng to howsholde. I will that John my oldest son have my place with all the londe free and bonde and medowes and wodys and all other comoditees in Forncett for to paye to Robert my son xl*s*. and to John Doosy junior myn son xl*s*. and ii. acres of londe lieng in Therston. Item, to George my son xl*s*. Item, to Stevyn my son xl*s*. this money to be paide the seconde yere after my deth xl*s*. and the next yere after that xl*s*. and after the deth [of] my wiffe iiij*li*. to be paide in like manere. Item, I giff to Mary my doughter xiii*s*. iiij*d*. Item, I will that John my eldest son shall fynde Kateryn my wiffe sufficient mete and drynke and necessarye woode for her chamber terme of her liffe and paye to here yerely xiii*s*. iiij*d*. Item, I will that my tabill of cypresse goo never out of my place the terme of eny of my kyn be levyng therin. All my goodes not bequeste I putt them in the disposicion of myn executourz whom I make John Doosy my oldest son and John Buxston and they to have for their labourz betwen them x*s*. to bryng me honestlie to the erthe and see my legattes paide and to doo deedes of charitee that maye be to the pleasure of God and helthe to my soule these witnessez John Spanton skrevener James Glover clerk Thomas Norton frier precher and other.

Et protulerunt etiam curiae hic quoddam warantum excellentis principis Thomae Ducis Norffolciae Domini hujus manerii manu et sigillo ejusdem ducis consignatum et sigillatum et in haec verba declaratum :—Thomas Duke of Norffolk Treasourer of Englonde, to all our officers and servauntes and to all other the kinges liege people to whom the present wrightyng shall come sendith gretyng knowe ye that we the seid Duke have geven and by this our present wrightyng doo giff unto Thomas Doosy of Forncett in the countie of Norffolk our costomman regardaunte to our manere ther full auctoritee and licens to have possede occupie and enjoye all and singler suche londes and tenementes goodes and catalles as at this daye be in the handes and possession of the seid Thomas Doosy or in the handes or possesion of eny other person or persons to his use to giff sell or dispose the same and every parte and parcell therof by his last wille and testament or otherwise at all tymes duryng his liff, and that thexecutourz and assignez of the last will and testament of the seid Thomas Doosy and all other persones what soevere they be shall enjoye have and take all suche londes and tenementes goodes catalles and dettes accordyng to the giffte legacye bequest or sale of them made by the seid Thomas Doosy in his liffe or by his laste wille and testamente withowte lett impedyment vexacion troubill or interuppcion of us our heirez executourz officers or servauntes or eny of them provided alweyes that thexecutourz or administratourz of the goodes and catalles of the seid Thomas Doosy doo prove the wille and testament of the seid Thomas in our courte of Forncett accordyng to the aunceyent usage and custome there payeng suche fyne to us for the same by the vewe and order of our officers of our seid courte as apperteyneth to the ordinarie to have in that behalff. In witnesse wherof we the seid Duke to this our present writyng made at our maner of Kenynghale have sette our seall and signe manuell the x. daye of the moneth of June in the xx^v. yere of the reign of our sovereign lorde kyng Henry the eight.

Et super hoc praefatus Dominus Dux per Robertum Holdiche armigerum supervisorem suum comisit administrationem omnium et singulorum bonorum catallorum et debitorum dicti defuncti ejus testamentum concernentium tempore mortis suae. Necnon executionem ejusdem testamenti praefatis Johanni Doosy et Johanni Buxston executoribus in supradicto testamento nominatis et in forma juris juratis. Et pro hujusmodi administratione habenda iidem executores dant Domino de fine ut in capite, etc.

Finis pro administratione bonorum nativi habenda vs.

Forncett. Curia generalis ibidem tenta die Lunae in crastino Dominicae in Passione Domini anno regni Henrici Octavi Dei gratia Angliae Fraunciae et Hiberniae Regis Fidei Defensoris ac in terra Ecclesiae Anglicanae et Hibernicae Supremi Capitis tricesimo quinto[1].

. . . .

Et eadem Alicia[2] exhibuit curiae hic testamentum et ultimam voluntatem dicti Johannis cujus tenor sequitur in haec[3] verba ut patet :—

Exhibitio testamenti nativi.

In the name of God, Amen. The xx. day of Maye in the xxxiiii^{tie}. yere of the reygn of our Sovereign lorde kyng Henry theight. I John Baxster of Multon All Seyntes beyng in hoole mynde and perfight remembrauns make my testament and last wyll by lycens of my lorde in this wyse. First I bequeth my soule to almightie God and to all the hooly company in heven and my body to be buried in the churcheard of Multon All Seyntes. Item I bequeth to the highe aulter of the same churche for my tythes and offringes neclygently forgotton and not paid xx*d.* Item, to the reparacion of the same churche xx*d.* Item, my mynde and wyll is that my body shalbe brought to the ground honestly with meate and drink. Item, I wyll have fyve Massez of the Five Woundes for me and my frendes. Item, I wyll that Alis my wyff shall have all my house and londes for terme of hur lyff and that the seid Alis shall kepe the seid housez in sufficient reparacion and that the seid Alys shall doo no wast of tymber but for reparacion of the seid housez. Item, my will is that Thomas my son shall have my house with all the londes after my wyffes deceasse on this condicion that the seid Thomas doth paye or cause to be paid to Johan my eldest doughter xl*s.* Item, I wyll the seid Thomas shall paye to Johan my yongest doughter xl*s.* in fourme folowyng that is to seye at the ende and terme of oon hoole yere after my wyffes deceasse then I wyll that the seid Thomas shall paye to Johan my eldest doughter xx*s.* and at thende and terme of the next yere to paye to the seid Johan xx*s.* Item, I wyll at thende and terme of the next yere that the seid Thomas shall paye to Johan my yongest doughter xx*s.* and at thende of the next yere ensueng after that xx*s.* Item, I wyll that if the seid Thomas

---

[1] March 31, 1544.
[2] 'Alicia Baxster vidua nuper uxor Johannis Baxster nuper de Multon.'
[3] MS. *hac.*

dothe refuse and will nott paye my seid doughters then my mynd and will is that my seid doughters shall entre into a closse called Makfase conteyning ii. acres and *di.* to hold to them and to their heirez for ever. Item, I wyll if ony of my seid doughterz fortune to die or depart than I wyll that the other shall have hur parte and if thei die bothe then I wyll that Thomas and Marion have the seid four poundes evynly devyded. Item, I wyll have iii*s.* iiii*d.* geven among poore folke at my buriall daye. Item, I wyll have iii*s.* iiii*d.* dispoosed among poore peple at my mynde daye. Item, I gyve to Nicholas Owle my best dublett of lether and my blake jurken. Item, I gyve to Thomas my son all my part of my harnes that Thomas Cullyng hath in kepyng. All the residue of my goodes I gyve them to Alis my wyff to paye my dettes and to perfourme my will whom I ordeyn and make myne executrix the seid Alis my wyff. Witnes of this my last will Robert Clerke, Robert Broun and Thomas Horne.

Et ulterius exhibuit quoddam inventorium de omnibus bonis et catallis quae fuerunt praedicti Johannis Baxster unacum pretio eorundem quae attingunt ad summam octo librarum quatuor solidorum et quinque denariorum. Et Dominus per Robertum Holdyche armigerum, supervisorem suum, administrationem omnium et singulorum bonorum et debitorum dictum testamentum concernentium

Finis pro administratione bonorum nativi habenda x*s.*

supradictae Aliciae executrici in eodem testamento nominatae in forma juris juratae commisit et committit per praesentes. Et pro hujusmodi administratione habenda praedicta Alicia dat Domino de fine, etc.

Forncett. Curia generalis ibidem tenta die Lunae tertiodecimo die mensis Aprilis anno regni Edwardi Sexti Dei gratia Angliae Fraunciae et Hiberniae Regis Fidei Defensoris ac in terra Ecclesiae Anglicanae et Hibernicae Supremi Capitis, quinto[1].

Ad hanc curiam venit Alicia nuper uxor Willelmi Bolytought nuper de Multon

Exhibitio testamenti nativi.

nativi Dominae de sanguine et exhibuit curiae hic testamentum et ultimam voluntatem ejusdem Willelmi cujus tenor sequitur in Anglicis verbis :—

In the name of God, Amen. The second daye of Marche the thirde yere of the reign of oure Sovereign Lord Kyng Edward the Sixt, I William Bolytowte of Multon beyng hooll of mynde and of perfect remembraunce thankes be to God therfor, under the licens of my Lady Mary hir grace beyng custom man unto her grace to the maner of Forncett do make this my testament and last will in maner and fourme followyng. First, I bequeth my soull to almyghtye God and to Jesu Christ my Redemer by whose passyon and merytes I beleve to have after this wretched and myserable lyfe eternall lyff and joye with hym and his sainctes and my bodye to be buryed where it shall please God and them that shalbe doers for me. Item, I do gyff and bequeth to Alys my wyff my tenement with all the londes therto belongyng for terme of her naturall lyff and after her death to remayne accordyng as herafter shall appere. Item, I do gyff and bequeth to the seid Alys my wyff and to her heires for evere a certeyn pece of lond called Kedenottes conteynyng iiii. acres be it more or lesse. Item, I do gyff to Robert Bolytowte my belchilde iii. half acrez of lond lyeng on the est side of the aforseid lond called Kedenottes and a closse lyeng in Tevitshale conteynyng xv. acres be it more or lesse to hold to hym and to his heires for ever. Item, I will that

---

[1] 1551.

i*f* it shall so happen that my seid belchilde Robert Bolytowte do dey without issue
of his body laufully begotton then the seid closse at Tevitshale and the seid
iii. halff acres aforseid be sold by Robert'Brown of Multon and John Sherman
of Waketon or their assignes to the uttermost price and valewe and the money
therof commyng to be equally devided among the children of Thomas Wright
of Pulham and Amye his wyff and in case John Bolytowte my sonne will purchase
itt to have the preferrement gevyng therfor as an other wyll. Item, I geve and
bequeth to my seid son John and to his heires after my death and my wyfes
my tenement and all my other londes not bequethed uppon this condicion that
he the seid John his heires and assignes shall paye or cause to be paid to my
doughter Amye the wyfe of Thomas Wright or. to her assignes vi*li*. xiii*s*. iiii*d*.
of lawfull Inglysshe money to be payde in tenne yeares begynnyng the first
payment of xiii*s*. iiii*d*. at the feast of all Seyntes next after he doth entre the
aforseid londes and tenement and so then forth every yeare after successyvely
at the aforseid feast of all Seyntes xiii*s*. iiii*d*. till the aforseid som be holly content
and payde and if my seid [son] John his heires executourz or assignes doth refuse
to paye to his seid sister Amye and her assignes the aforseid vi*li*. xiii*s*. iiii*d*. in
maner and fourme as is aforseid that then the aforseid Amye and her heires to
have and enjoye to her and to [her] heires all suche londes as are holden of the
maner of Multon except the three halff acres that is before bequethed to Robert
my'belchylde. Item, I do geve and bequeth to Alys Wright my servaunt a cowe
to be delyvered immediatlye after my death. Item, I will that when soever it
shall please God to call me or my seid wyff Alys to his mercy that my fermour
Nicholas Cullyng shall have uppe the whole yeare in suche londes and goodes
as he doth nowe ferme of me payeng therfore his whole yeare ferme, any thyng
in this my will heretofore rehersed or bequethed to the contrarye notwithstandyng.
Also I will that if it shall so chaunce that I and my seid wyff Alys do depart this
world before the seid Robert Bolytought my belchylde be of laufull age to entre
the londes that I have bequethed hym that is to sey before the age of xxi. yeares
then I will that John Sherman of Waketon and Nicholas Knyght *alias* Kett shall
leate the seid londes to the best pruff to his use and that the woode and tymber
shalbe saved to his use except suche as shall serve for the fensyng of the same.
Item, my mynde and will is that the executourz or admynystratourz of my forseid
wyff Alys shall have free ingate and outgate at my tenement to cary or recary any
thyng or thynges laufull by the space of viii. dayes next after my death. Item,
I do geve and bequeth to my seid wyff Alys all my moveable ·goodes howshold
stuffe and all cattell to her and to her heires and all the rest of my goodes not
bequethed I gyve to the seid Alys my wyff whom I ordayne and make my soole
executrix desyryng for Cristes sake my Lady Mary her grace with all her graces
worshypfull councell belongyng to the aforseid maner of Forncett to se that this
my will may be fulfilled. His testibus, Roberto Brown, ballivo, Johanne Sherman
juniore et Willelmo Button.

Et praedicta Alicia protulit etiam et exhibuit curiae hic inventorium omnium
et singulorum bonorum catallorum et debitorum quae fuerunt praedicti Willelmi
tempore mortis suae per ballivum Dominae et alios tenentes hujus manerii appreciatum ac rotulo hujus curiae annexum, quod attingit ad summam vi*li*. xii*s*. iiii*d*.
Et Domina per senescallum suum concessit et commisit administrationem

Finis pro ad-
ministratione
bonorum
nativi v*s*.

omnium et singulorum bonorum et catallorum et debitorum
praedictorum praefatae executrici in forma juris juratae. Et pro
hujusmodi administratione habenda dat Dominae de fine ut in
capite.

Et similiter venerunt Robertus Brown et Johannes Bolytought executores
testamenti et ultimae voluntatis Aliciae Baxster viduae et protulerunt
curiae hic praedictum testamentum et ultimam voluntatem dictae
Aliciae cujus tenor sequitur in Anglicis verbis :—

Exhibitio
testamenti
nativae.

In the name of God, Amen. The second daye of December in the fourth
yeare of the reign of oure Sovereign Lord Kyng Edwarde the Sixt, I Alys Baxster
wedowe beyng in wholl mynde and perfect remembraunce make my testament and
last will in this wise. First, I bequeth my soule to Almyghtie God and to all the
holy company of heaven, and my bodye to be buryed in the churcheyard of All
Seyntes in Multon. Item, I gyve and bequeth to Jone my yonger daughter
ii. keene and my grey mare colt and my sadill and a bridill. Item, my table
in the hall with the trestilles the fourme and oon chayer. Item, my best gown
and my best cortill, a payer of silver hookes and a sylver pynne. Item, a bedsted
a donge[1] a bolster a payer of sheetes a payer of blankettes and a coveryng. Item,
a table cloth a brasse pott ii. pewter platters. Item, oon salt and oon candelstyke.
Item, a ketill bownd and a fryeng pann. Item, ii. newe bordes. Item, a skeppe
with beynn[2]. Item, a chesepresse. Item, oon booll. Item, my chyst and all my
dyte[3] flax. Item, oon bason, a lewar[4] and oon stonde. Item, iiii. hennys and oon
cok and oon goose. Item, I gyve and bequeth to Robert Brown my godson oon
cowe to be delyvered to his father immedyatly after my deceasse. Item, I gyve
and bequeth to Jone Brown my doughter oon cowe and my medill brasse pott and
oon ketill bound. Item, a payer of sheetes, oon blankett and a pelowe of teake.
Item, oon table cloth, ii. newe bordes and a planke. Item, a bellecandelstyk and
a salt. Item, I gyve to the seid Jone my cart and ii. payer of cart harnesse and
my rownde table and a skeppe with beyn[2]. Item, oon saltyng trough and my
second best gown and all my undyte flax a ley[5] trough and ii. hennys. Item,
I gyve and bequeth to Edmond Brown my sonnylawe my leasse that I have in
Hornynges Closse and a sadle. Item, I gyve and bequeth to Alys Norton my
goddaughter oon cowe to be delyvered immediatlye after my deceasse. Item,
I gyve and bequeth to Maryon Norton my doughter oon ketill of iii. gallons
and a start[6] pan oon payer of sheetes oon blankett and a pillowe of teake. Item,
my frocke and my petycote and my newe smokke and a yard of newe cloth.
Item, ii. newe bordes. Item, I gyve to my seid doughter Marion oon cowe and
ii. hennys. Item, I gyve and bequeth to Thomas Baxster my sonne my mare
and horsfoole and my plough and all my harnesse and xii*s.* that he doth owe
to me. Item, my quernes and my knedyng trough. Item, I gyve to Elizabeth
Baxster my belchilde oon bullok of oon yere old. Item, my mynde and will is
that if Thomas my sonne doth trouble or lett this my last will then I will he shall
have no legett nor no part therof. Item, I gyve and bequeth to Alys Bert my
goddaughter oon bullok of oon yere old. Item, i. ketill of ii. gallons oon newe
pewter disshe and a coffer. Item, my mynde and will is that all my corne in the
berne be geven among poore people. Item, my mynde and will is that iii. keene
iii. store pigges and my hey in the berne be sold by myn executourz to paye
my dettes and other charges. Item, my mynde and will is that all the rest of
moveable goodes not bequethed I gyff them to Jone Browne and Marion Norton
evenlye to be devyded by myne executourz. These witnesse, Thomas Horne,
Robert Clerk, and John Tite.

Et iidem executores protulerunt et exhibuerunt curiae hic inventorium omnium
et singulorum bonorum catallorum et debitorum praedictorum quae fuerunt prae-

---

[1] A mattress.   [2] Hive with bees.   [3] Dight = prepared for use.
[4] Probably same as ' laver,' a basin or water-jug. Cf. Murray, *Eng. Dict.*
[5] Lye.   [6] Handle.

dictae Aliciae tempore mortis suae per ballivum Dominae et alios tenentes hujus manerii appreciatum ac rotulo hujus curiae annexum quod attingit ad summam

[1]. Et Domina per senescallum suum concessit et commisit administrationem omnium et singulorum bonorum catallorum et debitorum praedictorum praefatis executoribus in forma juris juratis. Et pro hujusmodi administratione habenda dant[2] Dominae de fine ut in capite.

Finis pro administratione bonorum nativae xs.

Forncett. Curia Generalis ibidem tenta die Veneris in crastino Annunciationis Beatae Mariae Virginis annis regnorum Philippi et Mariae Dei gratia Regis,et Reginae Angliae Hispaniarum Fraunciae utriusque Ceciliae Jherusalem et Hiberniae, Fidei Defensorum, Archeducum Austriae, Ducum Burgundiae Mediolani et Brabantiae ac Comitum Haspurgi Flandriae et Tirolis tertio et quarto[3].

. . . .

Ad hanc curiam venit Johannes Dowsy senior de Forncett et ostendit quoddam scriptum manumissionis cujus tenor sequitur in haec verba :—

Irrotulacio manumissionis Johannis Doosye senioris Thomae Doosye Johannis Doosye junioris Ricardi Doosye et Rosae Doosye filiorum et filiae dicti Johannis Doosye senioris ac Johannis Doosye Thomasinae Doosye et Katerinae Doosye filii et filiarum dicti Johannis Doosye junioris etc.

Omnibus Christi fidelibus ad quos praesens scriptum pervenerit Thomas Dux Norfolciae Comes Surriae et Mariscallus Angliae, Salutem in Domino sempiternam. Sciatis me eundem Ducem advisamento et unanimi concensu honorabilium virorum Henrici Comitis Arundelliae Senescalli hospitii Dominorum Regis et Reginae nunc et Thomae Eliensis Episcopi ac in consideratione quarumdam summarum pecuniae ad manus meas per quosdam Johannem Dowsy de Forncett in comitatu Norfolciae seniorem patrem ac Thomam Dowsy Johannem Dowsy juniorem Ricardum Dowsy et Rosam Dowsy filios et filiam dicti Johannis Dowsy senioris, Johannem Thomasinam et Katerinam filium et filias dicti Johannis Dowsye junioris quocumque alio cognomine vocantur villanos nativos et nativas meas spectantes ad manerium meum de Forncett in comitatu Norfolciae solutarum manumisisse ac a jugo servitutis dimisisse ac per praesentes manumittere et a jugo servitutis dimittere eosdem Johannem Dowsy patrem ac Thomam Dowsy Johannem Dowsy juniorem Ricardum Dowsy et Rosam Dowsy filios et filiam dicti Johannis Dowsy senioris Johannem Thomasinam et Katerinam Dowsye filium et filias dicti Johannis Dowsy junioris filii et totam sequelam suam tam procreatam quam procreandam ac eosdem per praesentes liberos facere et ab omni jugo servitutis et conditione servili deliberare. Ita videlicet quod nec ego dictus Dux nec haeredes mei nec aliquis alius per me nec haeredes meos seu nomine nostro aliquid juris vel clamii in praedictis Johanne Dowsy patre ac Thoma Dowsy Johanne Dowsy juniore Ricardo Dowsy et Rosa Dowsy filiis et filia dicti Johannis Dowsy patris ac Johanne Thomasina et Katerina filio et filiabus dicti Johannis Dowsy junioris filii sive eorum alicujus nec in sequela et progenie eorum vel alicujus eorum procreatas vel procreandas nec in bonis seu catallis suis seu eorum alicujus ad quascumque partes diverterint deinceps exigere clamare seu vendicare potero seu poterimus nec debemus in futurum. Sed ab omni actione juris et clamii inde penitus sumus exclusi imperpetuum per praesentes. In cujus rei testimonium tam ego dictus Dux quam nos praedicti Comes et Episcopus advisamentum concensum et assensum praedicta affirmantes sigilla nostra praesentibus apposuimus. Datum quinto die Maii annis

---

[1] A space is left in the MS.   [2] MS. *dat.*   [3] March 26, 1557.

regnorum Philippi et Mariae Dei gratia Regis et Reginae Angliae Hispaniarum Fraunciae utriusque Ceciliae Jerusalem et Hiberniae Fidei Defensorum Archeducum Austriae Ducum Burgundiae Mediolani et Brabantiae Comitum Haspurgi Flaundriae et Tirolis secundo et tertio[1].

Forncett. Curia ibidem tenta die Lunae proxima post festum Corporis Christi anno regni Dominae Elizabethae Dei gratia Angliae Fraunciae et Hiberniae Reginae et Fidei Defensoris etc., primo, etc.[2]

.   .   .   .

Cum ad curiam generalem hic tentam die Veneris in crastino Annunciationis Beatae Mariae Virginis annis regnorum Regis et Reginae Philippi et Mariae iii[tio]. et iiii[to]. praesentatum fuerat per inquisitionem ex officio quod Johannes Doosye nuper nativus Dominorum de sanguine extra curiam sursum reddidit in manus Dominorum, per manus Ricardi Baxster adtunc defuncti in praesentia Johannis Jacobb ballivi et Johannis Sherman et aliorum native tenentium hujus manerii, omnia mesuagia sua terras et tenementa nativa et soliata tenta de isto manerio (xvi. acris terrae jacentibus in diversis peciis in campo Sancti Petri de Forncett tantummodo exceptis) ad opus Stephani Buxston et Johannis Cok sub certa condicione sequente, videlicet, quod si idem Johannes Doosye haeredes executores seu administratores sui exonerabunt acquietabunt et indempnes conservent praedictos Stephanum et Johannem et eorum utrumque, haeredes, executores et administratores suos, versus praenobilem principem Thomam Ducem Norffolciae, executores et administratores suos, de et pro solutione summae centum et viginti librarum legalis monetae Angliae ad diversos dies et festa solvendarum, quod tunc praesens sursum redditio vacua erit et nullius effectus, alioquin in omni suo robore permaneat virtute et effectu ad usum praedictorum Stephani Buxston et Johannis Cok et haeredum suorum. Et cum etiam ad ultimam curiam hic tentam praesentatum fuerat per inquisitionem ex officio quod praedictus Johannes Doosye similiter sursum reddidit omnia alia mesuagia terras et tenementa residuum praedictarum xvi. acrarum, ultra xi. acras prius sursum redditas nomine morgagii ad opus Roberti Bootye, ad opus praedictorum Stephani Buxston et Johannis Cok et haeredum suorum, prout in curia praedicta plenius patet : Modo ad istam curiam pro eo quod praesentatum est per homagium quod condicio praedicta ex parte praedicti Johannis Doosye, haeredum et executorum et administratorum suorum, minime fuit perimpleta, et quod praedictus Stephanus Buxston et Johannes Cok filius et haeres praedicti Johannis Cok implacitati sunt ad communem legem ad sectam praedicti Ducis pro non solutione praedictae summae et adjudicati sunt per legem solvere eandem, venerunt iidem Stephanus Buxston et Johannes Cok filius senior et proximus haeres praedicti Johannis Cok et praesentes[3] in curia petunt admitti ad praemissa cum pertinentiis, videlicet, ad[4] .... secundum formam et effectum sursum redditionis sine condicione aliquali. Et admissi sunt inde tenentes. Quibus liberata est inde seisina per virgam tenendam

illis haeredibus et assignatis eorum ad voluntatem Dominorum,

Finis xl*s.* v*d.*
Fidelitas.   secundum consuetudinem manerii per servitia et consuetudines etc.

Salvo jure, etc. Et dant Dominis de fine, etc. Et fecerunt fidelitatem, etc.

---

[1] 1556.   [2] June 12, 1559.   [3] MS. *praesents.*
[4] Here follows a long description of the 66 acres which constituted the property.

APPENDIX XIV.

BILL OF SIR HENRY LEE AGAINST ROBERT BOLITOUT AND
THOMAS LOUND. ANSWER OF THOMAS LOUND.

Excheq. Q. R. Bills, Answers etc. Elizabeth, Norfolk, no. 32.

To the Right Honorable the lorde highe tresorour of Englonde Chauncelor
and barons of the quenes maiesties eschelquer.

Norfolk. Humblie sheweth and on the behalf of our soveraigne Ladie the
quenes maiestie enformeth your honors Sir Henrie lee knight that whereas the
quenes maiestie and her noble progenitors is and longe tyme hath ben seazed
as in the right of her crowne amongest other mannors of and in the mannor
of Forncett in the countie of Norfolk unto the which mannor tyme out of memorie
of man their have ben and yet are divers and sundrie villens and niefes regardaunt,
of whom the quenes maiestie and her most noble progenitors have ben seazed
as of her and their villens and niefes regardaunt to her said mannor of Forncett,
and whereas also by vertue of the quenes maiesties comission sealed with the
seale of her gracies courte of her eschequer directed unto one Thomas Heron
esquier her maiestie hath appoynted the said Thomas Heron to make a survey
vew serch and enquire of all and singuler her maiesties bondemen and niefes
in bloude regardaunte unto any of her maiesties mannors and of all bondemen
and niefes in grosse to her belonginge and of their goodes, cattells, landes,
tenements, and hereditaments aswell by the vew and serche of courte rolles
evidences and writinges as also by the othes of the quenes maiesties tenauntes
or by the examinacion of witnesses uppon their othes or by any other waie or
meanes as shalbe thought expedient by the said Thomas Heron as more at large
doth and maie appere by the said comission. So yt is yf yt maie please your
honors that all thought yt doth most evidentlie and playnelie apere aswell by the
vew and sight of court rolles concerninge the said mannor of Forncett as also
by divers other waies and meanes that Robert Bolytoutt of Forncett afforesaid and
Thomas Lound of Martham in the countie of Norfolk are the quenes maiesties
bondemen regardaunt to her said mannor of Forncett yet they and eyther of them
have and doe refuse to acknowledge and confesse their said bondage to the quenes
majestie and to doe such services to the quenes maiestie as they ought and are
bounde to doe to the utter disinherison of the quenes maiestie her heires and
successors yf some remedie by this honorable courte be not in this behalfe
provided wherefore maie yt please your honors the premisses considered to award
out of this honorable courte the quenes maiesties writte of sub pena to be directed
unto the said Robert Bolitoutt and Thomas Lound comaundinge them and eyther

of them at a certen daie and under a certen payne by your honors to be appoynted to make their personall apparaunce before your honors in the quenes maiesties honorable court of eschequer chamber and then and ther to yelde them selves to such order as your honours shall take therein accordinge to lawe and equitie.

The Answer of Thomas Lounde def[endant] to the bill of complaynte or enformacion of Sir Henry Lee Knyght Complaynante.

The said def[endant] for answer to somoche of the said bill or enformacion as concerneth him the said def[endant] saythe that the def[endant] dothe not knowe whether the Quenes majestie be seized of and in the mannor of Fornecett in the said bill or enformacion mencioned in suche maner and forme as in the said bill or enformacion is supposed or no and further the said def[endant] saithe that yf the Quenes Majestie be seized of and in the said mannor as in the said bill or enformacion is supposed yet he the said def[endant] saythe that he the said def[endant] is free and of free condicion and not a bondman in blodde regardant to the said mannor of Fornecett. With owt that that[1] yt can evydentlye and playnely appere as well by the view and syght of the courte rolles concerninge the said mannor of Fornecett as also by any other wayes and meanes that the said def[endant] is the Quenes maiesties bondman regardant to the said mannor of Fornecett as in the said bill or enformacion is supposed and withowt that there is any cause as the def[endant] thinketh why he showlde or awght to confesse and acknowledge any bondge[1] to the Quenes majestie as villen regardant to the said mannor and withowt that ther is any other matter or thinge in the said bill contayned and towchinge this def[endant] materiall to be answered unto and in this answer not suffycientlye confessed avoyded denyed or traversed is to the knowledge of the def[endant] trewe all which matters the defend[ant] is redye to averre as this honorable courte shall awarde and prayeth to be dismissed.

[1] *Sic.*

INDEX.

INDEX